Developing Applications with Exchange 2000

Developing Applications with Exchange 2000

A Programmer's Reference

Scott Jamison and Alex Gomez
with George Wesolowski

Addison-Wesley

Boston • San Francisco • New York • Toronto • Montreal
London • Munich • Paris • Madrid
Capetown • Sydney • Tokyo • Singapore • Mexico City

The publisher offers discounts on this book when ordered in quantity for special sales. For more information, please contact:

Pearson Education Corporate Sales Division
One Lake Street
Upper Saddle River, NJ 07458
(800) 382-3419
corpsales@pearsontechgroup.com

Visit AW on the Web: www.awl.com/cseng/

Library of Congress Cataloging-in-Publication Data
Jamison, Scott.
Developing applications with Exchange 2000 : a programmer's reference / Scott Jamison and Alex Gomez, with George Wesolowski.
p. cm.
Includes bibliographical references and index.
ISBN 0-201-70379-3
1. Application software—Development. 2. Microsoft Exchange Server (Computer file) I. Gomez, Alex, 1970– II. Wesolowski, George, 1961– III. Title.

QA76.76.D47 J355 2001
005.7'13769—dc21

00–052565

ISBN 0-201-70379-3
Text printed on recycled paper
1 2 3 4 5 6 7 8 9 10—MA—0504030201
First printing, February 2001

Contents

Foreword

It was a very different world when Microsoft Exchange Server was first shipped in March 1996. Microsoft had designed an e-mail system to replace the previous generation of LAN-based post offices. They built Exchange around their proprietary MAPI interface and didn't include very much development capability in the product. Sure, you could create some electronic forms and associate them with public folders, but not many people actually went to the bother. In short, Exchange was used as an e-mail system rather than a development or solutions platform.

Exchange is tremendously successful as an e-mail platform, and Microsoft tried to improve the development platform over the 5.0 and 5.5 releases. Some important things happened in this period. CDO (Collaborative Data Objects) was introduced to make programming easier, and the first version of a workflow system was provided in Exchange Routing Objects. Folder-side events also appeared. Welcome as these advances were, they were bolted onto an architecture constrained by the MAPI legacy. The ongoing success of Lotus Notes, the major competitor for Exchange, underlined the need to do something very different.

Exchange 2000 is different. The basic e-mail engine has been rewritten and moved away from MAPI and X.400 toward SMTP. The directory is gone and replaced by the Windows 2000 Active Directory. Events are pervasive throughout the architecture. But best of all, Microsoft has opened up the doors of Exchange and allowed programmers much better access to standard services and data. The advent of the Web Storage System, support for OLE DB and ADO, and the introduction of WebDAV as a protocol of choice are critical elements of this strategy.

It's good to have a guide when things change. Implementing Windows 2000 and then Exchange 2000 requires a lot of knowledge and good up-front planning, and many books are available to help you tackle this challenge. Going the next step to leverage the power and capability of the Exchange 2000 development platform needs a different set of skills and expertise. Scott and Alex have created a valuable guide to the new development environment. They have explained how critical components such as the namespace and schema underpin the Web Storage System and access to Exchange data, and then taken us into the world of ADO, OLE DB, and Exchange events.

No book will solve all your problems. Good books provide the foundation on which people can build their own skills. The examples found here will allow you to start to work with Exchange interfaces and data structures, understand how they operate, and then go forward to develop the solutions that make a difference in the way that Exchange is used within your company. The challenge is to move from an infrastructure focus, or just keeping the mail flowing, to one that concentrates on building solutions to business problems.

The next couple of years are certainly going to be interesting. When we look back in 2005, it will be fascinating to see just how many companies have used Exchange as a solutions platform and how many still use it just for e-mail.

Tony Redmond
Vice President, Technology
Compaq Global Services

Preface

When Microsoft made the announcement back in early 1999 that they would be including greater development support for Microsoft Exchange Server, we were ecstatic. Microsoft had just released Outlook 2000, the most developer-friendly version of Outlook to date. Microsoft had also enhanced the programmability features of Exchange Server 5.5, enabling workflow and routing features. Outlook 2000, combined with Exchange Server 5.5, was very versatile: You could build a groupware solution in a matter of hours. Moreover, we at Plural were proving that you could also use Outlook and Exchange as components for a large-scale enterprise system. This was the point when we knew Exchange development was here to stay.

We decided that the new features in Exchange 2000 were too compelling to ignore. The book you are about to read is the result of our research.

The Companion Web Site

We have developed a Web page where all code samples, bonus white papers, and presentations are posted. The page contains information in a format that is similar to the book's; you will find a downloadable zip file with folders that match the chapters in the book. In each folder that contains code, you will see a readme file that lists the contents of that chapter. You can find the site at **http://www.plural.com/outlookexchange.asp**.

Another best bet for information on the Web is the Exchange developer site at Microsoft. You'll find articles, downloads, and technical white papers at **http://msdn.microsoft.com/exchange**. The Microsoft Knowledge Base is another excellent resource for known bugs and workarounds for any Microsoft software product. You can access it at **http://search.support.microsoft.com**.

Overview of the Book

You may notice that Chapter 1 contains an overview of the book much as the contents of a preface would contain. We felt that this information was important enough to merit its own chapter. We'd like feedback if you feel otherwise; write to us at **outlookexchange@plural.com**.

Products and Tools You'll Need

To successfully implement some of the examples and code in this book, you'll need to obtain the following products. Most of them are offered for 30-day free trial on Microsoft's Web site (**www.microsoft.com**).

- Microsoft Exchange 2000 Server
- Microsoft Windows 2000 Server (including Internet Information Server 5.0)
- Microsoft Outlook 2000
- Microsoft Visual Basic 6.0

Acknowledgments

This was a difficult book to write. When dealing with brand-new technologies with little documentation, no practical examples, and a buggy help file, one has to rely on proving everything first through research and experimentation and on the knowledge, experience, and native intelligence of several outstanding individuals in the field.

We would first like to thank Rob Erman, who supported this project from day one. Rob's enthusiasm, encouragement, and advice were critical to the success of this book. We'd like to thank Rob for starting something great in Boston.

We would like to thank George Wesolowski for proving, disproving, implementing, and even challenging in practice most of the concepts of developing real-world systems using the new tools offered by both Exchange 2000 and Windows

2000. George's groundbreaking work at Plural stretched the limits of Exchange 2000 as a storage and collaboration platform on one of the first production Internet applications in the world on this platform. He leveraged these experiences by authoring a couple of the chapters in this book. (He's also got the coolest game room this side of the Mississippi.)

We would like to thank Martin Tirion, who has always been on the cutting edge of collaborative application development using Exchange and Outlook. Martin's technical skills are sought for projects all over the world; even Microsoft asks him for advice sometimes. We are very fortunate to have had his input on the manuscripts, as well as his contribution of the ADO Explorer application.

We would like to thank Andy Kawa, another esteemed colleague from Plural, with whom we have both worked on Exchange and Outlook projects. Andy was an early adopter of Exchange 2000, using it for real development efforts. His conscientious review of the manuscripts helped make this a better book.

We would like to thank Chris Kunicki, an exceptional developer and technical evangelist for us at Plural. Chris's expertise in learning and evaluating new technologies shone through in his insightful feedback on the chapters.

We'd also like to thank the rest of the technical review team, including Randell Orner, MCSE, MCP+I, A+, a field service engineer for a medical equipment manufacturer, who has a degree in electronic technology and 13 years of experience in the technology industry.

Several other people contributed to the manuscript from start to finish. Thanks to Michael Slaughter for his patience and his faith in our ability; to Jenie Pak for her dedicated assistance throughout the project life cycle; to Tyrrell Albaugh for her humor and motivation during production; to Stephanie Hiebert for her careful editing and brilliant suggestions that truly made this a better book; and to the rest of the outstanding team at Addison-Wesley.

Last, but certainly not least (especially since she is Scott's lovely wife), we would like to thank Erica Jamison. Erica's precise command of the English language, magnificent writing talent, thorough editing skills, and ability to learn programming brought a fresh perspective to the material in the book.

Scott: Thanks to Erica, the love of my life (especially for not killing me when I started a second book). Also thanks to Seth and Sean for two of the best brothers anyone could ask for, Mike D. for just being cool, GDW for last-minute heroics, and Mom for putting up with me all these years.

Alex: Thanks to God and family both immediate and abroad, especially Mom for being supportive, Pop for being a fighter, J. C. for being responsible, Karen for being inquisitive, and the Gómez and Castillo kinfolk in Costa Rica for your prayers. ¡Que Dios los bendiga! Thanks to everyone who has taught me about the "world we live in and life in general" and to Saints, Panthers, Jumbos, and Terriers.

Part I

Introduction to Exchange 2000

Chapter 1

Introduction to the Book

This is a book about application development using Microsoft Exchange 2000 Server. This book was written because collaboration, knowledge management, and Web accessibility are three of the most sought-after features in a corporate software solution, and one of the key products that address all three of these topics is Microsoft Exchange 2000 Server. Because of this functionality, Exchange 2000 is perhaps one of the most important server products that run on Windows 2000 Server. If you're looking for ways to create Web applications, workflow applications, and e-mail/calendar applications on top of Exchange 2000, you're starting in the right place. This book provides a developer-biased overview of Microsoft's latest version of Exchange and how to develop applications with it, and it provides some insight and "gotchas" regarding the technologies involved. This book is intended to be a tutorial as well as a handy reference.

This book does not cover methodology or process, nor does it provide a one-size-fits-all approach to building applications. A central thrust of the book is a detailed introduction to the development approaches that are available for Exchange 2000. Since Exchange 2000 now supports numerous programming techniques, you'll need to become familiar with all of them before making a decision on a development approach that fits your specific needs. This book will help you do just that.

Topics Covered

Specifically, this book provides an overview of Exchange 2000 Server, the Web Storage System, and the WebDAV Internet protocol. This book also introduces the Exchange OLE DB provider (ExOLEDB), Collaboration Data Objects (CDO) for Exchange 2000, and creating an Outlook 2000 digital dashboard. The following is an introduction to each of the topics that will be discussed in greater detail.

Exchange 2000 Server

Building on the success of Exchange 5.5, Microsoft has updated its messaging server to include new Web-enabled features. In addition to supporting e-mail and collaboration services, Exchange 2000 introduces some new programming models to make use of the Internet and other new technologies, which are introduced in the sections that follow.

The Web Storage System

One of the notable changes to Exchange 2000 is the introduction of the Web Storage System, designed for document management, collaboration, and knowledge management applications. In a nutshell, the Web Storage System is a database technology that you can use to store and share various types of nonrelational data. A good strategy is to have an application that stores relational data in SQL Server and semistructured (nonrelational) data in the Web Storage System. Examples of Web Storage System data include e-mail messages (including attachments), multimedia files, appointments, contacts, and Microsoft Office documents. The Web Storage System is organized much like a traditional file system and is used to store *items* organized within *folders*. "Web Storage System" is somewhat of a marketing spin on the Exchange store's former name—Exchange Information Store. To back this name up, Microsoft has developed some new ways to access the store, including a few Web-based options. The next section will describe each of these programming methods briefly.

Programming with Exchange 2000

Developing applications with Exchange is more complex and more flexible than ever, primarily because of the wide range of application programmer interfaces (APIs) that can now be used. Developers now have the choice of the Messaging API (MAPI), the Outlook object model (or the backward cow: OOM), Collaboration Data Objects (CDO) 1.21, HyperText Transfer Protocol/World Wide Web Distributed Authoring and Versioning (HTTP/WebDAV), CDO 3.0, ActiveX Data Objects

(ADO) 2.5, the Exchange OLE DB provider (ExOLEDB), Active Directory Service Interfaces (ADSI), and the Windows 32-bit (Win32) file system APIs for Exchange development. This book will help guide you through the alphabet soup of choices, with a brief discussion in this chapter and a deeper explanation in later chapters.

Microsoft's selling point here is that Exchange 2000 now supports a wide range of APIs to fit the diverse needs of enterprise developers, solution providers, and independent software vendors. Exchange's integration with other Microsoft server products, such as Windows 2000 Server, Internet Information Server (IIS) 5.0, and SQL Server 2000, provides developers with a dizzying mix of tools to use for building applications. We'll discuss each of the choices in its own chapter; in Chapter 19 we'll help you wade through these choices, providing a comparison to ease API selection.

The following subsections identify the protocols, object libraries, and APIs that we'll cover in this book.

WebDAV

WebDAV, simply put, is an evolving industry standard that extends the HTTP 1.1 protocol to include verbs for reading, writing, and locking files over the Internet. WebDAV stands for World Wide Web Distributed Authoring and Versioning and is described in detail in RFC 2518 (RFC stands for "Request for Comments," which is the way Internet standards are formed). WebDAV, or simply DAV, currently includes three completed features: properties, namespace management, and locking.

DAV is important to Exchange developers because Exchange 2000 contains built-in support for DAV properties and HTTP access. More information on DAV is contained in Chapter 4.

Note: You can find RFC 2518 at **http://www.ietf.org/rfc/rfc2518.txt.**

The Exchange OLE DB Provider and ADO 2.5

In an effort to make good on the promise of a Universal Data Access strategy, Microsoft Exchange 2000 comes with an OLE DB provider. This means that developers now have the option of using ActiveX Data Objects (ADO) 2.5 to access the Web Storage System. This is a distinct advantage for developers who come from a traditional database background; they can leverage their ADO experience. There are benefits and pitfalls to using the Exchange OLE DB provider, as we will see in Part III, Working with ADO and the Exchange OLE DB Provider.

Collaboration Data Objects for Exchange (CDO 3.0)

Exchange 2000 also introduces a major overhaul to its primary programmability component, the Collaboration Data Objects library. Rather than being a MAPI-based library like CDO 1.21, CDO for Exchange (version 3.0) is based on the OLE DB provider. More information on CDO for Exchange (which is currently available only on the server) is found in Part IV.

File System Access

Exchange 2000 comes with the Exchange Installable File System (ExIFS), which mounts itself as standard drive M: when the Exchange information store service starts. This means that you can now access the Web Storage System using the FileSystemObject and Win32 file system APIs. We'll discuss file system access more in Chapter 18.

Microsoft Outlook 2000

Microsoft Outlook, a core application in the Office 2000 suite, is the premier client for Exchange 2000. Outlook provides several benefits over Web-based client access, including offline synchronization, its own object model, and a richer user experience. We'll discuss the use of Outlook in more detail in Chapter 6, where we'll show how to create an Outlook-based digital dashboard using personal Web Parts.

Who Should Read This Book?

This book introduces architects and designers of Web-based collaboration and knowledge management systems to the issues and techniques of developing with Exchange 2000 Server. The book also provides developers with a handy reference to the various APIs and object models involved. For the project manager, this book discusses the potential problems and issues of developing applications with Exchange 2000. Despite its new features, and sometimes because of them, there are numerous things to watch out for in Exchange 2000 Server.

This book is not a developer's guide to Outlook 2000 or CDO 1.21. For a background and reference to those technologies, consult the companion book *Developing Applications Using Outlook 2000, CDO, Exchange and Visual Basic* by Raffaele Piemonte and Scott Jamison (Addison Wesley Longman, 1999).

How This Book Is Organized

This book contains 21 chapters organized into five parts. Part I, Introduction to Exchange 2000, which includes this chapter and Chapters 2 through 4, introduces the new concepts for development with Exchange 2000. Topics include setting up an Exchange 2000 environment; an explanation of schemas, namespaces, and content classes; and WebDAV, the RFC-standard WebDAV specification and its importance to Exchange 2000.

Part II, Exchange Client Access (Chapters 5 and 6), introduces the two primary clients for Exchange 2000: Outlook Web Access and Outlook 2000. This section covers the digital dashboard.

Part III, Working with ADO and the Exchange OLE DB Provider, consists of three chapters (7 through 9). These chapters explain the ADO 2.5 object model, ExOLEDB, and Web Storage System SQL.

Part IV, Collaboration Data Objects (CDO), consists of a whopping seven chapters (10 through 16). This section provides a full explanation of the Collaboration Data Objects libraries, including CDO 1.21, CDO for messaging, CDO for calendaring, CDO for contacts, CDO for workflow, and CDO for Exchange management and ADSI.

Part V, Additional Exchange 2000 Topics, contains three chapters (17 through 19). Topics include the Exchange 2000 Installable File System (ExIFS), a review of the pros and cons of each API, and a quick overview of using XML with Exchange 2000 development.

Part VI, Sample Applications, introduces two applications that you can use to help build your own Web Storage System applications. Chapter 20 provides two useful tools (with source code) that display the ADO, CDO, XML, WebDAV, and MAPI properties for any item in the Web Storage System. Chapter 21 introduces a sample Web application that tracks students and grades.

The Sample Code

All of the sample code used in this book can be found at **http://www.plural.com/outlookexchange.asp**. This site is also where you'll find updates, additional code, and features relating to Exchange and Outlook development.

Chapter 2

Setting Up an Exchange 2000 Environment

This chapter guides you through the process of installing Exchange 2000 Server. Although many Exchange 2000 installations are painless, it is worth having a guide because a wrong choice at any one of the steps can lead to a bad installation.

Exchange 2000 Integration with Windows 2000

Before we begin, here's something you may not be aware of: Exchange 2000 Server requires Windows 2000 Server. You may ask why Exchange 2000 requires a brand-new operating system to run. Although it may be presumptuous to think that Microsoft wrote Windows 2000 just for Exchange 2000, the reason is that Exchange 2000 Server relies heavily on Windows 2000 in several key areas, which we outline in the subsections that follow.

Active Directory

Exchange 2000 uses the Windows 2000 Active Directory to store and share directory information with Windows 2000. Active Directory is the directory service for Windows 2000 Server. It acts as a single source directory for all network objects (users, printers, and computers, for example) in an organization. Active Directory can store and organize information about user accounts such as names, passwords, and phone numbers. The Active Directory schema can also be extended to include custom attributes and object types. Exchange 2000 extends the schema to store configuration and user messaging information. Whereas previous versions of Exchange had their own directory services, Exchange 2000 uses Active Directory in Windows 2000 to provide functionality including the Global Address List (GAL), Address Book Views, and Offline Address Books. All of the directory information created and maintained in Windows 2000 can also be used in Exchange 2000; it is not necessary to maintain separate directories for each.

If your Exchange infrastructure contains both Exchange 2000 and Exchange 5.5 servers, you can use Active Directory Connector (ADC) to replicate directory information between the old 5.5 Exchange directory and Active Directory. ADC is a Windows 2000 service that allows administration of a directory from either Active Directory or the Exchange 5.5 Directory Service.

> **Note:** Although it's possible, it is not recommended that you administer Active Directory objects from the Exchange 5.5 Administrator (or vice versa). This may cause problems in additional ADC synchronization.

Global Catalog

Exchange 2000 uses the Windows 2000 Global Catalog (GC) to store its configuration data. You must have a Global Catalog installed to install Exchange 2000 Server.

Administration through Microsoft Management Console

Exchange 2000 is administered from the Windows 2000 Microsoft Management Console (MMC) rather than the Exchange 5.5 Administrator. As we shall see later, MMC is a common administration console that can be extended through the use of snap-in components.

Integrated Transport Protocols

Windows 2000 Server has integrated support for several standard transport protocols using Internet Information Server (IIS), which is now part of the operating system. Installing Exchange 2000 extends several of these protocol stacks, with additional functionality provided by means of event sinks registered with each protocol. For reference, Exchange 2000 supports the following protocols:

- **HyperText Transfer Protocol (HTTP) and WebDAV (World Wide Web Distributed Authoring and Versioning).** Most people know that HTTP is a standard protocol that allows Web browsers to access data and applications over the Internet. You may not know about the DAV protocol because it is an emerging Internet standard that allows HTTP clients to read and write information over the Web. Exchange 2000 extends DAV so that HTTP\DAV clients can read and write information to the Exchange Web Storage System.

- **Internet Message Access Protocol version 4 (IMAP4).** This protocol enables a client to access e-mail on a server rather than downloading it to the user's computer.
- **Network News Transfer Protocol (NNTP).** This protocol is used over TCP/IP (Transmission Control Protocol/Internet Protocol) networks for accessing newsgroups through an NNTP-compatible client. Exchange 2000 uses NNTP to allow clients to participate in online discussions and access public folders.
- **Post Office Protocol version 3 (POP3).** This Internet protocol allows a client to connect to a mail server, download messages, and then manage those messages on the client side.
- **Simple Mail Transfer Protocol (SMTP).** This Internet e-mail delivery standard is the native protocol that Exchange uses to transfer messages across servers.

Domain Name System

Exchange 2000 requires the Domain Name System (DNS) for name resolution. You must have a DNS server configured to run Exchange 2000.

Windows 2000 Network Infrastructure

Exchange 2000 makes use of the Windows 2000 network infrastructure, allowing your Exchange topology to mirror your Windows 2000 topology.

Setting Up Windows 2000

In order to install Exchange 2000, you have to install Windows 2000 Server. This section will guide you through a typical installation scenario for the purposes of learning to develop on the Exchange 2000 platform. Although this section is no substitute for the documentation that comes with Windows 2000 or your individual computer manufacturer, it will give you some basic insight into the steps involved. Also as a collaborative application developer for several Windows platforms, you may want to dual-boot your computer to have Windows NT 4.0 and

Windows 2000 available on the same machine. It's actually quite trivial. As with anything that you've never done before, it sounds more complicated than it really is. Since most books don't give step-by-step instructions for how to do it, we will.

Note: To install Windows 2000 Server or Windows 2000 Advanced Server on your machine, Microsoft recommends the following minimum system requirements:

- 133MHz or higher-speed Pentium-compatible CPU
- 256MB of RAM (but it has been observed running on 128MB)
- 2GB hard disk with a minimum of 1GB free space

Preparing Your System for an Upgrade or New Installation

Microsoft recommends a few steps prior to upgrading to or installing Windows 2000. First, you should always back up your current files prior to any major install.

Uncompress any DriveSpace or DoubleSpace volumes before upgrading or installing Windows 2000. DriveSpace and DoubleSpace are two disk compression utilities for Windows. Do not upgrade to Windows 2000 on a compressed drive unless the drive was compressed with the NTFS (NT File System) compression feature.

Note: Never install Exchange 2000 Server on a compressed drive of any kind, because performance will be unacceptable.

If you have disk mirroring installed on your target computer, disable it before running **Setup**. In disk mirroring, partitions on two drives store identical information so that one is the mirror of the other. All data written to the partition on the primary disk is also written to the mirror, or secondary, partition. If one disk fails, the system is able to use the data from the other disk. You can reenable disk mirroring after completing the Windows 2000 installation.

If you have an uninterruptible power supply (UPS) connected to your target computer, disconnect the connecting serial cable before running **Setup**. A UPS is a battery-operated power supply connected to a computer to keep the system running during a power failure. Windows 2000 Setup attempts to automatically detect devices connected to serial ports, and UPS equipment can cause problems with the detection process.

Before starting the Windows 2000 Server setup program, be sure to read the applications section of **readme.doc** (in the root directory of the Windows 2000 Server CD-ROM). Look for information regarding applications that need to be disabled or removed before **Setup** is run.

Dual-Boot Setup with Windows NT 4.0

If you are planning to do the dual boot with Windows NT 4.0 that we talked about earlier, we are assuming that you already have NT 4 installed and running properly on your machine. If not, you need to install this before installing Windows 2000. We are also assuming that you have at least two partitions on your machine—a C: drive and a D: drive, for example. In our scenario, we have NT 4 installed on the C: drive, and we are planning to put Windows 2000 on the D: drive. Each operating system needs to be on its own partition.

Be sure to have Windows NT 4.0 Service Pack 4 or later installed on your machine. If you intend to create a dual-boot system with NT 4 and Windows 2000, Windows 2000 will automatically upgrade any NTFS partition it finds on your system to NTFS 5. However, Windows NT 4 requires at least Service Pack 4 to be able to read and write files on an NTFS 5 volume. When you're finished, if you boot your machine in NT 4 you will be able to see the files on the Windows 2000 partition, and if you boot in Windows 2000 you will be able to see the files on the NT 4 partition.

In our test of dual-booting a machine and installing Exchange 2000, the whole process took about four hours. You must also remember that even though you can see files on the other operating system's partition, you can't run programs that are installed on the other partition. The reason is that the program will be looking to the registry of the operating system where it was originally installed. This means that if you want to use a certain software application on both operating systems, you must install it on both. This doesn't mean you have to waste disk space, because you can always install to the same location on both operating systems.

Note: Dual-boot configurations are intended for use only on a development machine to test applications under several platforms; they are not recommended for use in a production environment.

Installation

To install Windows 2000 as a dual-boot server with Windows NT:

1. Log on as Administrator on your NT server.
2. Insert the Windows 2000 CD in the drive. A dialog box will pop up asking "Would you like to upgrade?" Hit **No**.
3. Wait for the setup program to display the Windows 2000 Setup wizard dialog box (Figure 2.1). Choose **Install a new copy of Windows 2000 (Clean Install)** and hit **Next**.

Figure 2.1 The Windows 2000 Setup Wizard

4. Accept the End-User License Agreement (Figure 2.2) by selecting the correct radio button and hit **Next.**
5. You will now be prompted for your 25-character product key (Figure 2.3). Enter it and click **Next.**

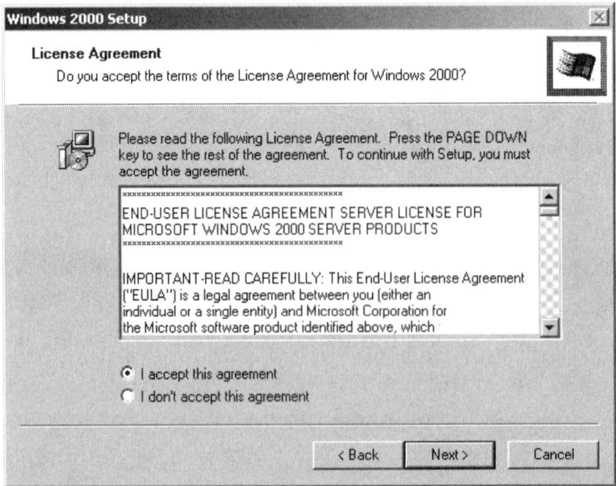

Figure 2.2 Accepting the Windows 2000 license agreement

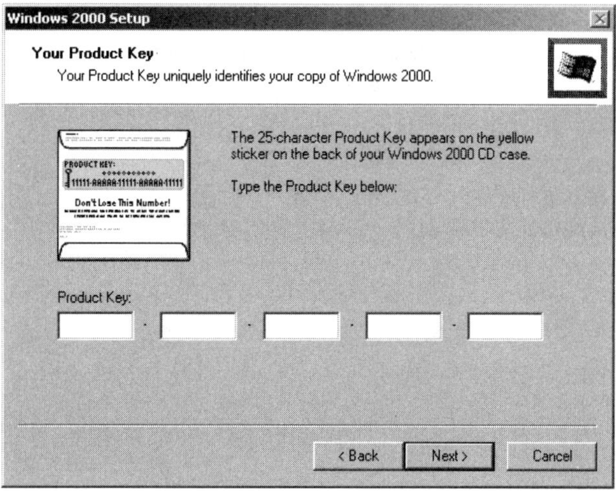

Figure 2.3 Entering your Windows 2000 product key

6. Select **Special Options** from the next dialog box. This next part is key for our dual boot. Click **Advanced Options.** Check **I want to choose the installation partition during setup.** Hit **OK** and click **Next.**
7. You will get an alert saying that the setup program is updating to the Windows 2000 NTFS file system and asking if you wish to continue. Click **Yes.**
8. The next screen (Figure 2.4) gives you the chance to visit the Directory of Applications for Windows 2000 on the Microsoft Web site, at **http://www.microsoft.com/windows/server/deploy/compatible/default.asp**. This is just a listing of compatible and certified applications for Windows 2000. We assume that you'll visit this at your leisure some other time, so for now click **Next.**
9. The setup program will now begin to copy installation files. When it is finished, it will restart the computer.
10. When the computer restarts, you will be prompted to select the operating system. Choose **Windows 2000 Setup.**
11. You will now need to select the drive where you want to install Windows 2000. When we did it, we chose D: and clicked **Enter.** Files will now be copied, and your system will automatically reboot. You will eventually come back to the Windows 2000 Setup wizard, where the setup program will automatically detect and install devices on your computer.

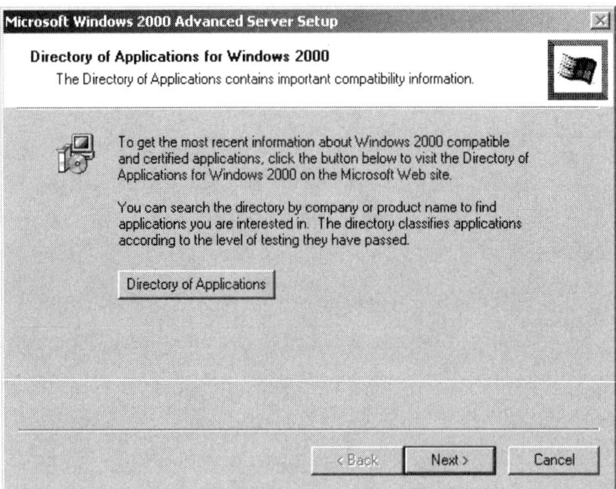

Figure 2.4 Microsoft provides a complete list of applications certified for Windows 2000

12. Now comes the regional-settings part of the setup. If you are happy with the selections for system locale and keyboard layout, hit **Next.**
13. Type in your full name and organization name at the **Personalize Your Software** dialog box and hit **Next.**
14. Choose **Per Server** for the licensing mode. Set the number of connections at 200 and click **Next.**
15. Choose an appropriate computer name and password at the **Computer Name and Administrator Password** dialog box and hit **Next.** Make sure you write them down for reference.
16. At the **Windows 2000 Components** dialog box, choose **Internet Information Services.** Hit **Details** and make sure that **NNTP** and **SMTP** are checked, because they are required for Exchange 2000. Hit **OK.** Accept all of the other default settings by clicking **Next.**
17. At the **Modem Dialing Information** dialog box, select your country/region from the drop-down list, the area code, the number to dial to get an outside line (if necessary), and whether the phone system is tone or pulse dialing. Click **Next.**
18. Verify that the date, time, and time zone settings are correct in the **Date and Time Settings** dialog box and click **Next.**

19. Windows will now install network components. Allow this process to finish; then select **Custom Settings** and click **Next.** Select the network components you need, but leave the defaults (**Client for Microsoft Networks, File and Printer Sharing,** and **Internet Protocol** TCP/IP). Hit **Next.**
20. After the setup program finishes installing components and performing final tasks, the **Completing the Windows 2000 Setup Wizard** dialog box comes up. At this point, remove the Windows 2000 install CD from the drive and click **Finish.** The system will reboot once again and finally prompt you to log in.
21. Log into Windows 2000 using the Administrator login and password you specified earlier and install Microsoft Loopback Adapter. Microsoft Loopback Adapter is a tool for testing in a virtual network environment where a network is not available. It basically emulates a network for you so that you can develop and test applications without a network connection. More importantly, it allows you to code completely untethered on the road or at your kitchen table at home on a laptop. To install it, click the **Start** button, point to **Settings,** click **Control Panel,** and then double-click **Add/Remove Hardware.** The **Add/Remove Hardware Wizard** dialog box will come up; click **Next.** Choose **Add/Troubleshoot a device** (Figure 2.5) and click **Next.**

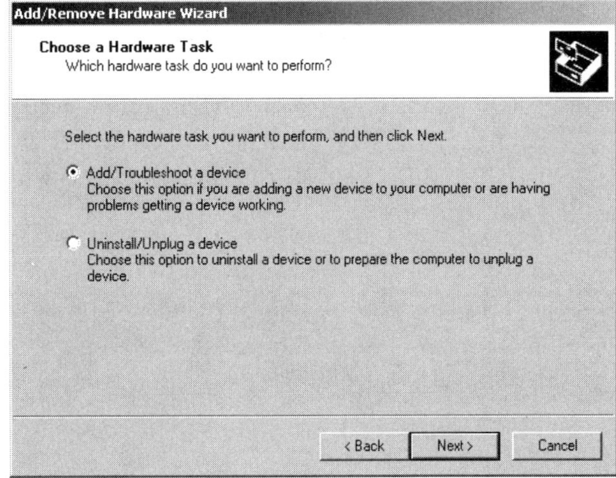

Figure 2.5 For stand-alone machines, your best bet is to install Microsoft Loopback Adapter

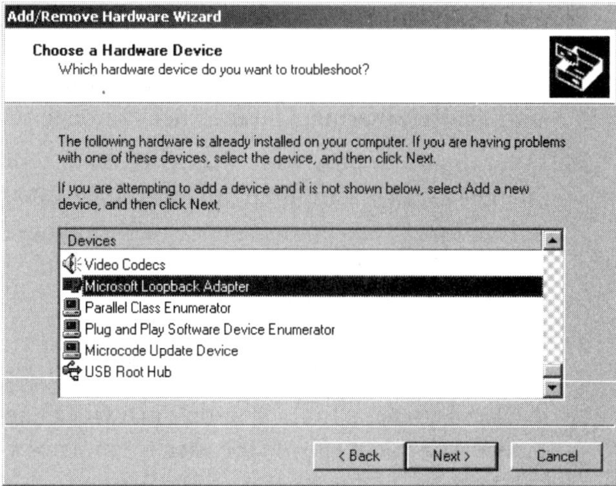

Figure 2.6 Microsoft Loopback Adapter simulates a network adapter

Windows 2000 will now prepare a list of devices. Choose **Microsoft Loopback Adapter** (Figure 2.6) and hit **Next.**

22. After the computer reboots, the **Windows 2000 Configure Your Server** dialog box comes up. If it doesn't, you can get to it by hitting the **Start** button and pointing to **Programs** and then **Administrative Tools.** Click **Configure Your Server.** Select **This is the only server in my network** and click **Next.** You will get a message saying, "If you proceed, Windows will automatically configure this server as a domain controller and set up Active Directory, DHCP and DNS on your network." This is what we're looking for, so click **Next** to accept.

Note: Be careful when selecting DHCP (Dynamic Host Configuration Protocol) because your computer will generate IP addresses for other computers to use. If you are connected to another network, this may cause problems.

23. You will be prompted for a domain name (Figure 2.7). After entering an appropriate domain name, type in the domain name registered on the Internet and click **Next.** In our scenario we chose "local."
24. The final screen summarizes what the setup process is going to do. Hit **Next** and you're done.

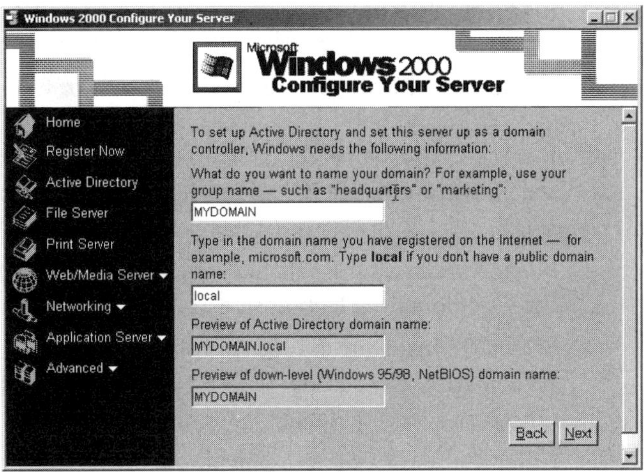

Figure 2.7 Entering a domain name

Note: One of the most controversial features of Office 2000 was the personalized menus, which displayed only recently used menu items and a couple of chevrons to access the complete list. It seemed confusing enough to have to remember where a certain menu command was in the first place without this aid. Unfortunately, this feature also found its way into the Windows 2000 Programs menu. However, the feature is easy to disable by hitting the **Start** button, pointing to **Settings,** and choosing **Taskbar and Start Menu Properties** and unchecking **Use Personalized Menus,** as shown in Figure 2.8. Hit **OK** to apply the change.

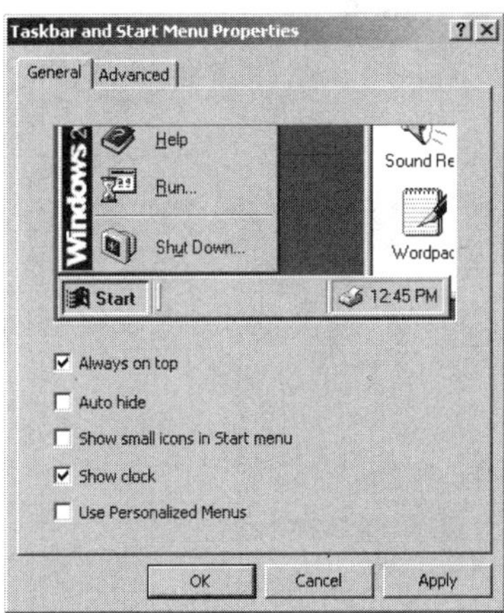

Figure 2.8 Disabling personalized menus

Setting Up Exchange 2000

Now it's time to do the development installation of Exchange 2000 itself.

1. Insert the Exchange 2000 CD in the drive. The Exchange 2000 Setup wizard shown in Figure 2.9 comes up. Click **Exchange Server Setup.**
2. The setup program will remind you to close any running applications. Click **Next**. After accepting the End-User License Agreement, click **Next** to get to the **Component Selection** screen. Select all of the components and click **Next.**
3. Select the installation type from the drop-down list in the **Miscellaneous Information** dialog box. Choose **Create/Join a Microsoft Exchange 2000 Organization** (the default) and click **Next.**
4. Enter the name of the organization you wish to create and click **Next**. We left the default, **First Organization.**
5. Type in the user, domain, and password for the service account and click **Next.**
6. You will then see a component summary similar to that shown in Figure 2.10. Click **Next** to begin installing.
7. The Microsoft Exchange 2000 Installation wizard will bring up a message box (Figure 2.11) informing you that it must extend the Windows 2000 Directory Schema. The schema on the Windows 2000 Active Directory will

Figure 2.9 The Exchange 2000 Server Installation wizard

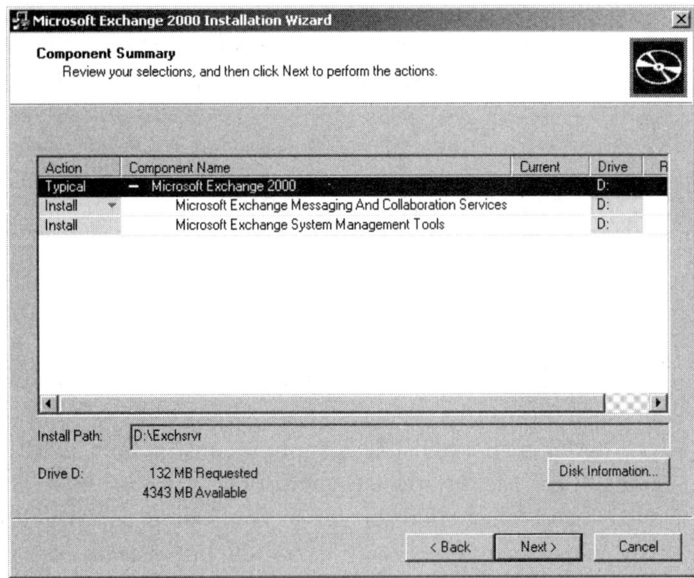

Figure 2.10 Check your Exchange 2000 component summary

be modified to include all Exchange attributes and object classes. To administer these Exchange-specific items, Exchange will extend the Directory Service Administration snap-in to expose the new attributes and classes so that they are both viewable and modifiable in the Microsoft Management Console. Select **OK** to accept.

8. The installation will now begin. When it is completed, click **Finish.**

Installing the Exchange 2000 SDK

Available on the Microsoft Web site is the Exchange 2000 Software Development Kit (SDK), which is chock-full of documentation, sample code, and development

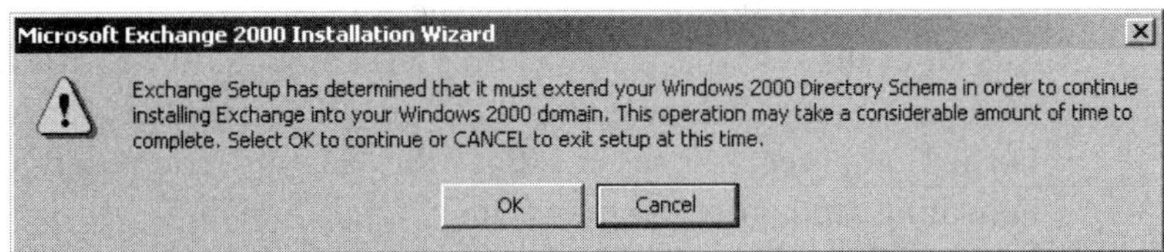

Figure 2.11 The Exchange 2000 installation process extends the Active Directory Schema

tools. It is highly recommended that you install the SDK because it provides a wealth of reference and example materials. The SDK (sometimes referred to as the Web Storage System SDK) can be found at **http://msdn.microsoft.com/exchange**.

The Microsoft Management Console

Now that you have Exchange 2000 installed, you will need to set up some test users, mailboxes, and public folders to test your applications. In Exchange 5.5, the Exchange Administrator program was used to configure most of Exchange's folders and settings. In Exchange 2000, we use Microsoft Management Console (MMC) to perform these tasks.

MMC is an extensible, common console framework for management applications. It is a user interface framework that you use to administer both the operating system and other Microsoft server applications, such as IIS. MMC does not provide any management functionality by itself, but instead acts as a host for snap-ins. Snap-ins are management components that can be integrated into MMC in much the same way as COM (Component Object Model) add-ins are integrated into Outlook 2000. They allow a system administrator to extend and customize the console. Multiple snap-ins can be combined to build a custom management tool. MMC contains snap-ins, such as the Exchange System Manager snap-in, that control a specific set of functions within the operating system or, in this case, an application.

Customizing the MMC

On the Windows 2000 **Start** menu, click **Run**, type "mmc," and then hit the **OK** button to get an empty MMC. Remember that the empty console has no management functionality until you add some snap-ins.

Click **Console**. On the **Console** menu, choose **Add/Remove Snap-in...** to get the dialog box shown in Figure 2.12. The **Add/Remove Snap-in** dialog box lets you enable extensions, configure snap-ins, and specify where they should be inserted. For this exercise, we'll just leave **Console Root**, the default in the **Snap-ins added to:** drop-down list.

Hit the **Add** button to display the **Add Standalone Snap-in** dialog box, which lists all of the snap-ins installed on your computer. From the list of snap-ins, double-click **Computer Management** to open the Computer Management wizard. Click **Local Computer** and select **Allow the selected computer to be changed when launching from the command line**. Click **Finish** to return to the **Add/Remove Snap-ins** dialog box and click **Close**. Click the **Extensions** tab (Figure 2.13). Selecting **Add all extensions** means that all locally installed extensions on the computer

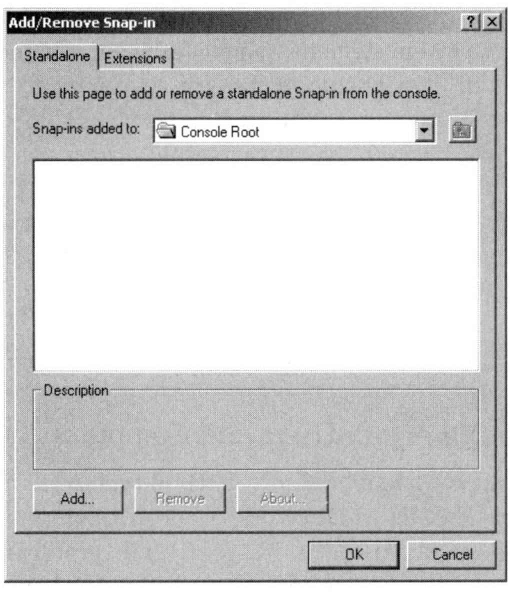

Figure 2.12 MMC allows you to customize your snap-in list

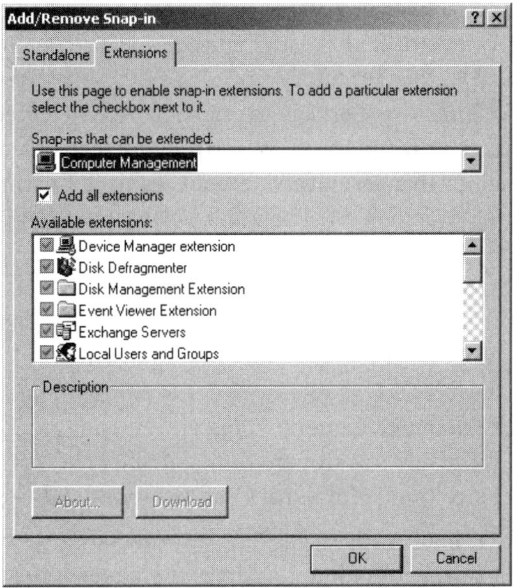

Figure 2.13 The **Extensions** tab allows you to add all local MMC extensions

are used. Click **OK** to close the dialog box. The **Console Root** now has a snap-in, **Computer Management**, rooted at the console root folder.

From the **Console** menu, select **Options** to bring up the MMC options. This allows you to rename the custom MMC as something a bit more meaningful than "Console 1" and prevents users from further customizing your console. For example, changing the console mode by selecting **User mode-limited access, single window** from the drop-down list will prevent a user from adding new snap-ins to the console file or rearranging windows.

You can save the console file by selecting **Save As...** from the **Console** menu. It will be saved as a ".msc" file, which you can distribute to anyone who needs to configure a Windows 2000 computer with these tools.

Active Directory Users and Computers

Having now had a brief introduction on how to modify an MMC, you should realize that the Active Directory Users and Computers tool and the System Manager tool in the Microsoft Exchange program group are really just customized consoles with specialized snap-ins for managing Exchange 2000 servers. In fact, you will find the Users and Computers ".msc" file and the Exchange System Manager ".msc" file in the **Exchsrvr\BIN** directory.

The Active Directory Users and Computers (ADUAC) MMC is used to manage most of the administration of Exchange 2000 recipients. Exchange 2000 recipients (and recipients from previous versions of Exchange if you have set up Active Directory Connector and created connection agreements) are located in the **Users** container of Active Directory under the domain name by default. Windows 2000 uses Active Directory Service to manage Active Directory objects such as Exchange recipients. A recipient is an Active Directory object that is mail enabled or mailbox enabled, or that can receive e-mail. Table 2.1 compares some recipient objects from previous versions of Exchange with the corresponding Exchange 2000 Active Directory objects.

Right-clicking on a user in the **ADUAC** console and choosing **Properties** will bring up a multitab dialog box. The Exchange extensions to the regular Windows 2000 **ADUAC** console include the following tabs:

- **Exchange General.** This option configures basic e-mail attributes, including mailbox storage limits, delivery restrictions, delivery options, mailbox size limits, forwarding address, and delivery.
- **E-mail Addresses.** This option configures multiple e-mail addresses of any type and includes address templates for the most common types.
- **Exchange Features.** This option allows an administrator to enable and disable Exchange features for mailbox-enabled users, such as voice messaging and instant messaging.

Table 2.1 Exchange 5.5 versus Exchange 2000 Active Directory Objects

Exchange 5.5 Object	Exchange 2000 Active Directory Object	Comments
Mailbox	Mailbox-enabled user	When a user is mailbox enabled, he or she has an e-mail address and a corresponding mailbox on an Exchange server.
Custom recipient	Mail-enabled user and contact	When a user or contact is mail enabled, he or she has an e-mail address used by Exchange to properly route e-mail. A mail-enabled contact is an object with a Windows 2000 authentication account but no Exchange 2000 mailbox.
Distribution list	Mail-enabled group	E-mail sent to the mail-enabled group is routed to the e-mail address of each group member.

- **Exchange Advanced.** This option configures advanced e-mail attributes, including protocol settings, Exchange custom attributes, and the Internet Locator Service. The **Exchange Advanced** tab displays only in the **Advanced Features** view. From ADUAC, click **Advanced Features** from the **View** menu to get the **Advanced** tab.

Let's now look at how to perform some simple tasks needed to test collaborative applications.

Adding a New Mailbox-Enabled User

A mailbox-enabled recipient has one Exchange mailbox associated with it, as well as an e-mail address, and can therefore send and receive e-mail. Using the ADUAC, you can create a new Windows 2000 user object and make it mailbox enabled in one step.

1. In the **ADUAC** console, navigate to the node that will contain the new user. Right-click the node, click **New**, and then click **User**. In the **New Object—User** dialog box, fill in the user's information in the **First Name**, **Initials**, **Last Name**, and **User Logon Name** boxes and click **Next**.
2. Type a password for the new user in the **Password** box and confirm it by typing it again in the **Confirm Password** box. Select the appropriate password options and hit **Next**.

3. Verify that **Create an Exchange Mailbox** is selected. Verify that the information in the **Alias** box and in the **Server** and **Mailbox Store** drop-down lists is correct and hit **Next.**
4. Verify that the information in the final view is correct and hit **Finish.**

Adding a New Mail-Enabled User

A mail-enabled user has at least one e-mail address defined but no Exchange mailbox. Such a user can receive messages at a specified address but can't store them on the Exchange Server. To add a new mail-enabled user, follow steps 1 and 2 in the exercise of the previous section (Adding a New Mailbox-Enabled User). Then continue with the following steps:

1. Unselect **Create an Exchange Mailbox.** The **Alias**, **Server**, and **Mailbox Store** selections will be grayed out.
2. Verify that the information in the final view is correct and hit **Finish.**
3. In the **Details** pane, right-click the newly created user and click **Exchange Tasks....** In the **Exchange Tasks Wizard** dialog box click **Next.** Choose **Establish e-mail addresses** from the **Available Tasks** drop-down list and click **Next.**
4. Verify the alias and click **Modify** in the dialog box. In the **New E-mail Address** dialog box, select the address type and hit **OK.** You'll likely choose **SMTP Address.**
5. In the **Internet Address Properties** dialog box, enter the address and hit **OK.** Hit **Next**, verify that the information in the final dialog box is correct, and hit **Finish.**

Adding a New Mail-Enabled Contact

A Windows 2000 contact is an Active Directory Object that represents a user who does not have a Windows log-on account or a mailbox. For example, a contact could represent a user outside of your organization. It is equivalent to a custom recipient in previous versions of Exchange.

1. In the **ADUAC** console, navigate to the node that will contain the new contact. Right-click the node, click **New**, and then click **Contact.** In the **New Object—Contact** dialog box, enter the contact information and click **Next.**
2. Verify the alias, make sure that **Create an Exchange e-mail address** is selected, and click **Modify.** In the **New E-mail Address** dialog box, select the address type and hit **OK.** For our purposes we chose **SMTP Address.**

3. In the **Internet Address Properties** dialog box, enter the address and hit **OK**. Hit **Next**, verify that the information in the final dialog box is correct, and hit **Finish**.

Adding a New Mail-Enabled Group

A group is a collection of users, groups, and contacts roughly equivalent to a distribution list in previous versions of Exchange. There are two types of groups: distribution groups and security groups. Distribution groups are used only for e-mail; security groups are used to grant access to resources. As we have seen, only users can be mailbox enabled, so we will use the **ADUAC** console to create a new mail-enabled group.

1. In the **ADUAC** console, navigate to the node that will contain the new mail-enabled group. Right-click the node, click **New**, and then click **Group**. In the **New Object—Group** dialog box, fill in the **Group Name**, **Group Scope**, and **Group Type** fields and hit **Next**.
2. Verify that **Create an Exchange e-mail address** is selected and that the alias is correct, and hit **Next**.
3. Verify the information for the group and hit **Finish**.

Exchange System Manager and Public Folders

The Exchange 2000 System Manager is a framework for containing all Exchange snap-ins in a Microsoft Management Console. On the **Start** menu, choose **Programs**, **Microsoft Exchange**, and then **System Manager** to start a **System Manager** console similar to the one shown in Figure 2.14. Although this console can be used to manage most aspects of an Exchange server, we will focus on public folder management. A public folder stores messages or information that can be shared with designated Exchange users. An administrator can create public folders through the System Manager, or a user can create them through Microsoft Outlook. There is a catch in creating them through Outlook, however.

In Exchange 2000 we have the concept of a top-level hierarchy (TLH). This is a folder hierarchy tree in the Exchange information store. Creating your own TLHs is useful for managing several custom applications in a single Exchange organization. Using Exchange System Manager, you can see that under the **Folders** object we have the lone default top-level hierarchy called **Public Folders**. Using Outlook, this is the only TLH you can access. New top-level hierarchies are designed to be accessible by applications and are not visible to MAPI clients such as Outlook. If you want the public folder hierarchy to be visible to MAPI clients, you must create the folders under the **Public Folders** hierarchy. If you are creating new folders only

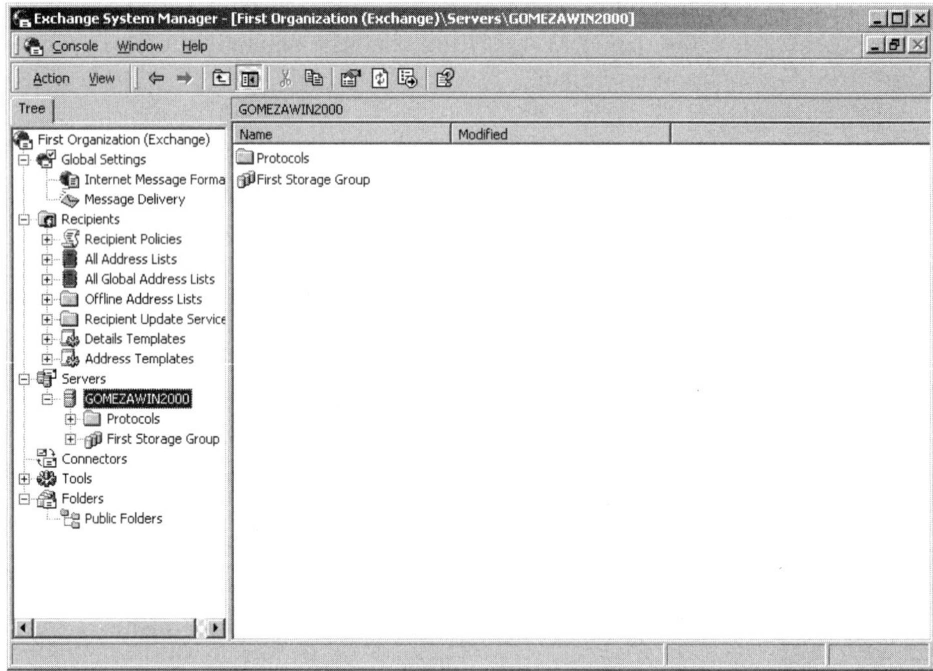

Figure 2.14 The Exchange 2000 System Manager is where you administer Exchange 2000

under **Public Folders**, then you don't need a new TLH. Otherwise you need **System Manager** to create a new TLH.

Configuring a New Public Folder Hierarchy

The first step is to create a new top-level root. Each top-level root exists on the same level as **Public Folders** and uses its own database to store folder structure and contents.

1. Start up the Exchange System Manager, right-click **Folders**, point to **New**, and then click **Public Folder Tree**.
2. Type in a name for the new public folder tree and hit **OK**.
3. Each public folder hierarchy uses its own store in the information store. We now need to create a store for the public folder tree and connect the folder to it. In the Exchange System Manager, expand the server to which you want to add a public folder store. Right-click on a specific storage group, point to **New**, and then click **Public Store**. Type in a name for the new database.

4. Click the **Browse** button and then select the public folder hierarchy you just created. Click **OK** to save your settings. You will now get a message box asking you for confirmation to mount the brand-new store. Hit **Yes**.
5. Now you have to connect to the public folder store. In Exchange System Manager, navigate to the **Folders** object in the console tree. Right-click on the public folder hierarchy and click **Connect To...**. Select the available public store that you just created from the list and click **OK**.
6. Now you can set permissions for the public folder hierarchy. Right-click on the folder hierarchy again and select **Properties**. Click the **Security** tab to reveal the security options. To modify an existing user, click the user name. To assign a specific permission, select **Allow** or **Deny** next to that permission. To grant additional users access, click **Add**, select a user, and then click **Add** again. Use the check boxes to control user access to folder contents. Similarly, to remove users, select a user and then click **Remove**.

Configuring a New Public Folder

For our purposes, creating a new simple public folder under an existing TLH (**Public Folders**, for example) is generally enough. To do this, start up **System Manager** as described earlier and navigate to the **Folders** object.

1. Right-click on the root of the folder hierarchy, point to **New**, and then click **Public Folder**.
2. You can now set individual permissions on the folder as explained in step 6 in the previous section.

Exchange 2000 Services

To monitor services in Windows 2000, select **Programs** in the **Start** menu, then select **Administrative Tools**, and finally click **Services**. The **Services** management console comes up (Figure 2.15).

Double-click on one of the services to get more detail (Figure 2.16). Click the **Dependencies** tab (Figure 2.17) to see the services on which the selected service depends and the services that depend on the selected service. Exchange 2000 relies on Windows 2000 services for access to system resources, so this is definitely a place to look when troubleshooting Exchange problems.

Now you can monitor key Exchange services in the Exchange System Manager itself. In the console tree, right-click on an Exchange server and choose **Properties**. Click the **Monitoring** tab. Click **Default Microsoft Exchange Services** and then hit

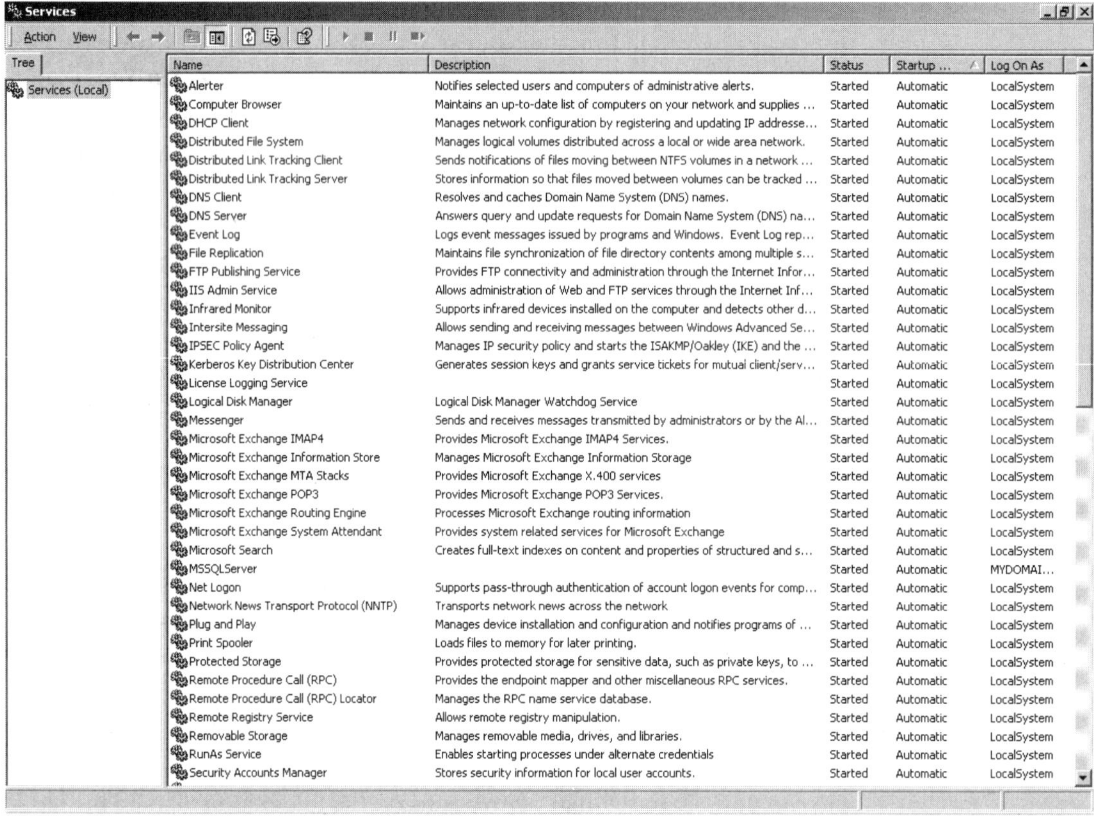

Figure 2.15 The **Services** MMC enables you to view the Windows 2000 services

the **Detail** button. Here is where you can add or remove services that you would like to monitor. The following is a list of Exchange 2000 Server services:

- Microsoft Exchange Chat (MSExchangeChat)
- Microsoft Exchange Conferencing (MSExchangeConf)
- Microsoft Exchange Event (MSExchangeES)
- Microsoft Exchange Information Store (MSExchangeIS)
- Microsoft Exchange Internet Message Access Protocol (IMAP4Svc)
- Microsoft Exchange Message Transfer Agent (MSExchangeMTA)
- Microsoft Exchange Post Office Protocol version 3 (POP3Svc)
- Microsoft Exchange Routing Engine (RESvc)
- Microsoft Exchange Site Replication (MSExchangeSRS)
- Microsoft Exchange System Attendant (MSExchangeSA)

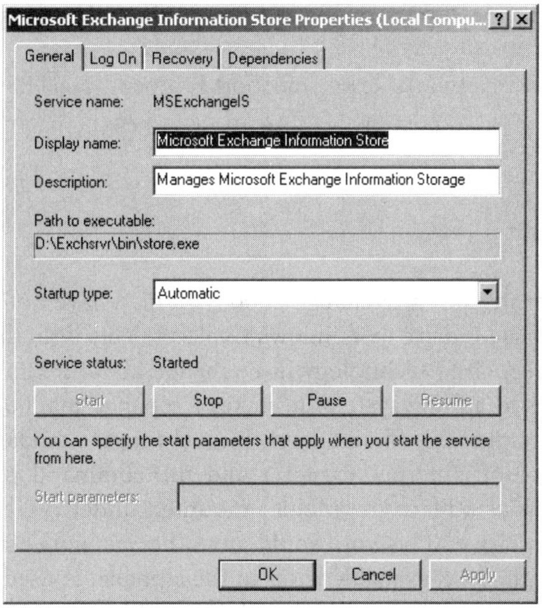

Figure 2.16 Double-clicking on a service enables you to view detailed information

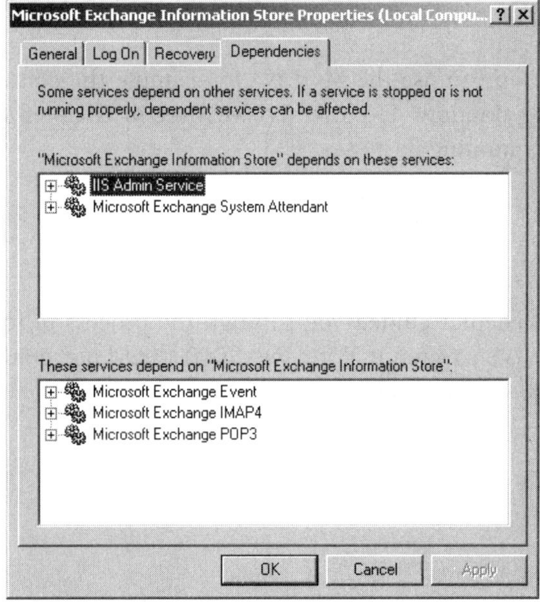

Figure 2.17 The **Dependencies** tab enables you to view dependent services

Exchange 2000 Server also relies on the following services:

- Network News Transport Protocol (NNTPSvc)
- Simple Mail Transport Protocol (SMTPSvc)

The M: Drive

After installing Exchange 2000, you may have noticed the appearance of the mysterious M: drive in Windows Explorer. This is all thanks to the new Installable File System (IFS) technology in Exchange 2000. IFS is a storage technology that functions as a filing system. It makes Exchange mailboxes and public folders available as traditional folders and files through standard Win32 processes, such as Microsoft Internet Explorer and the command prompt. Each information store exists as a file system folder mounted under drive M: of the host server. You can share drive M: as you would any other network drive. If the letter M is already in use, the next available letter in the alphabet is used. The default names for the first public and private stores are **Public Folders** and **MBX**, respectively.

Note: The M: drive does not appear until the Microsoft Exchange Information Store service has completely started.

You can use the M: drive to examine the contents of the Web Storage System using Windows Explorer. As we'll see in Chapter 18, you can also use the IFS for programming purposes.

Summary

This chapter guided you through the process of installing Exchange 2000 Server. We also covered a Windows 2000 dual-boot configuration and customizing the MMC. The next chapter will cover schemas and namespaces.

Chapter 3

Schemas, Namespaces, and Content Classes

To organize a set of data properly, one must understand how the data are structured. In a relational database, in which data are organized into tables, rows, and columns, normally a schema is defined beforehand. This schema defines what fields exist in which table, identifying the name, data type, and default values for each field.

This chapter provides an overview of how Exchange 2000 Server and the Web Storage System allow developers to organize information. We'll cover three main topics that are important to the rest of the book:

1. Schemas
2. Namespaces
3. Content classes

About URIs, URLs, and URNs

Before we get into schemas, namespaces, and content classes, let's define the differences between a Uniform Resource Identifier and a Uniform Resource Locator.

A URI (Uniform Resource Identifier) is an address string referring to an object, typically one that resides on the Internet. Two types of URIs are the URL and the URN (which will be explained in a moment). The URI is specified in RFCs 1630 and 1808.

> **Note:** RFC stands for "Request for Comments." This is the way Internet standards recommendations are submitted and approved. The number is a reference to the particular document that describes the standard. You can view all of the RFC documents at **http://www.ietf.org**.

A URL (Uniform Resource Locator) is a standardized string used to specify a resource on the Internet, such as an HTML document or a disk file. The format of a URL is "protocol://server/path/resource". For an HTML document, this could be "http://server/path/filename.htm"; for a disk file, "file://server/sharename/path/filename.ext". The terms "URI" and "URL" are often used interchangeably.

A URN (Uniform Resource Name) is a standardized string used to specify a property or resource. The format of a URN normally follows a convention whereby entities provide uniqueness by using a registered domain name in the URN. For example, "http://schemas.microsoft.com/exchange/propertyname."

> **Note:** The URLs in this chapter do not refer to actual Web sites. Company DNS names are merely a convenient way to get a unique, human-readable qualifier.

Schemas

A relational database schema defines the tables and columns (fields) that exist in a database, including the field name, its type, whether it can be null, and maybe even a default value. In eXtensible Markup Language (XML), a schema defines the elements that can appear within the XML document and the attributes that can be associated with an element. The schema also defines the structure of the document, such as describing which elements are children of others, the sequence in which the child elements can appear, and the number of child elements. Just as in a database, the schema also defines whether an element is empty or can include text, as well as default values for attributes. In the Web Storage System world, a schema is very similar—with a handful of differences.

Schemas and the Web Storage System

The operating rules of the Web Storage System schema are different from those of a typical relational database schema. In the Web Storage System, the schema is not used for maintaining relational database integrity or primary key constraints. Instead, the schema is simply used primarily as a mechanism for discovery of content class and property definitions by applications. In fact, there's no requirement to use a schema (try that with your SQL Server database!). You can simply add properties to an item using ADO's **Append** method, specifying only a name and data type. However, these properties are lost if you delete the item. Whether or not you define a schema, a set of core properties exists for every item.

> **Note:** Although the Web Storage System seems like an ideal place to keep all of your information, you'll want to keep your relational database around for applications that require relational integrity. The Web Storage System is good for document management and workflow—places that don't require strong relational constraints. In fact, a typical Web application will use both a relational store such as SQL Server 2000 and a semistructured store such as Exchange 2000 Server.

Schemas for default Exchange types are stored in the root folder of the information store. For custom Exchange 2000 applications, schemas are stored in a **schema** folder, just under the application folder. For example, a custom application in **MyAppFolder** could have a custom schema in the **schema** folder as follows:

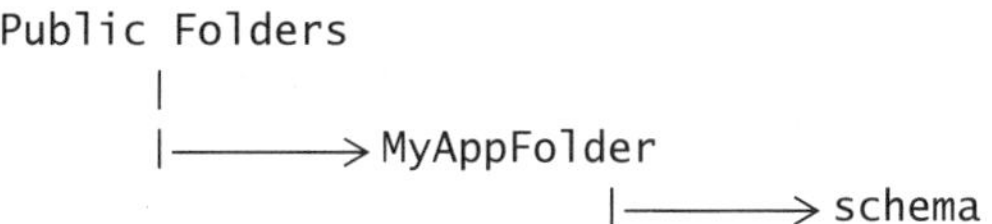

We'll cover the use of schemas in applications in more detail in Chapter 5.

Namespaces

Let's say you've defined a property named "ID" that you've assigned to one of your items. Normally, one property would have that name—no problem. However, let's say you've extended another schema to create your property set. A field named "ID" may already be defined, causing confusion over which field you desire. One way to alleviate this problem is to use namespaces, which provide context for your property (to whom does this property belong?). Another way to say this is that namespaces provide scope and uniqueness.

Default Web Storage System Namespaces

The Web Storage System schema includes several default namespaces for accessing data, including namespaces for messaging, calendaring, and contacts. Table 3.1 briefly describes the default Web Storage System namespaces.

Table 3.1 Default Web Storage System Namespaces

Namespace	Description
DAV:	Properties defined for the DAV (Distributed Authoring and Versioning) protocol.
http://schemas.microsoft.com/exchange/	Properties specific to Microsoft Exchange 2000 Server and Web Storage System.
http://schemas.microsoft.com/exchange/events/	Properties used to create items that bind to event sinks.
urn:schemas:microsoft-com:datatypes:	Definitions for data types used during the creation of schema items.
urn:schemas:microsoft-com:exch-data:	Definitions for Exchange-specific data types used for Web Storage System properties.
urn:schemas:microsoft-com:xml-data:	Definitions for defining XML namespaces that incorporate dynamic data typing and binding.
urn:schemas:microsoft-com:office:office	Properties specific to Microsoft Office files.
urn:schemas:calendar:	Properties used for calendaring. Several properties are also available on CDO calendar objects: **Appointment**, **CalendarMessage**, **CalendarPart**, **Exception**, **RecurrencePattern**, and **Addressee**.
urn:schemas:contacts:	Properties for managing contacts. Several properties are also available on the CDO **Person** object.
urn:schemas:httpmail:	Fields used to create and process the body of a message. For fields in the header of a message, use the mail header namespace.
urn:schemas:mailheader:	Standard mail header properties for messages. Several properties are also available on the CDO **Message** object.

Namespace Rules

Since namespaces typically must travel over HTTP, there are rules regarding how to identify the namespace and the name portions of a fully qualified property name. The first rule is the property/namespace delimiter; these are the valid separator values:

- Slash (/)
- Colon (:)

Table 3.2 Examples of Namespaces, Property Names, and Fully Qualified Names

Namespace	Name	Fully Qualified Property Name
DAV:	propname	DAV:propname
urn:schemas-microsoft-com:	propname	urn:schemas-microsoft-com:propname
http://microsoft.com/schema	propname	http://microsoft.com/schema#propname
http://exchange.microsoft.com/schema/	propname	http://exchange.microsoft.com/schema/propname

- Semicolon (;)
- Pound sign (#)
- Question mark (?)

The namespace name is everything to the left of the delimiter, plus the separator character itself. The only exception to this rule is the pound sign (#): Namespaces that use this delimiter do not include the separator character as part of the name. Everything to the right of the delimiter is the property name. Table 3.2 shows some examples of how a fully qualified property name is broken down.

Custom Namespace Guidelines

When creating a name for a custom property, you should use a namespace to provide scope and uniqueness for the name. The Exchange 2000 SDK provides a guideline for creating namespaces when adding custom properties: Use your registered InterNIC domain name to construct a namespace for your custom properties. If your organization does not have a registered domain name, you can still generate a namespace that will render your property names unique. One way to guarantee a unique name is to generate a GUID (globally unique identifier) and use it in the namespace. This approach does guarantee unique namespaces, but the results are cumbersome (e.g., "3f0a69e0-7f56-11d2-b536-00aa00bbb6e6") and hard to read.

Content Classes

Content classes are data classes that describe sets of Web Storage System item properties. A content class defines types of content in terms of the expected properties that are stored with an item. The content class does not explicitly define a property stored with an item but rather provides the means for applications to ascertain the purpose of particular Web Storage System items and the properties that are likely to be available. The parallel concept in MAPI/Microsoft Outlook is a message class. For more information on Outlook message classes, see "About Outlook Message Classes."

About Outlook Message Classes

All Outlook items contain a special property called **MessageClass.** This property determines the type of the message and identifies the form that is used to present it. When an item is selected, Outlook uses the message class to determine the appropriate form to use and expose its properties. Specifically, message classes are character strings that specify the class and subclasses for an item, delimited by periods. Each class name represents a level of subclassing. To see how a message class works, take a look at the message class for a standard e-mail message:

```
IPM.Note
|    |
class subclass
```

The first class specified here is IPM, which stands for "interpersonal message." All messages that are created and read by human users use the IPM superclass. The Note subclass inherits some of the properties from the IPM message class. You can customize a standard mail form in Outlook and assign your own subclass name. For example, you could add a field called "ManagerName" and then publish the form using the message class **IPM.Note.MyForm.** This form would allow you to create custom items that can store information in a workgroup application. Message classes for the standard Outlook item types are shown in the following table:

Item Type	**Message Class**	**Purpose**
Appointment	IPM.Appointment	Scheduling meetings and appointments.
Contact	IPM.Contact	Storing names and other contact information.
Distribution List	IPM.DistList	Storing distribution lists.
Journal	IPM.Activity	Tracking calls and other items.
Mail	IPM.Note	Storing standard e-mail messages.
Post	IPM.Post	Generic items saved to public folders.
Task	IPM.Task	Storing lists of tasks to complete and reminder items.

Why Use Content Classes?

Content classes are useful because they allow an application to determine actions that may be necessary to take on an item. For example, an application may use the content class to instantiate a specific object to display or update an item. Content classes are also useful for selecting a corresponding form or icon for the item.

Putting Content Classes to Work

All Exchange folders and items have content class values that denote their intended purpose. Figure 3.1 shows the folders in a typical Exchange mailbox and the content class that goes along with each folder. A folder, in terms of the underlying Exchange class hierarchy, is an item that is a collection of other items. Exchange applications can use content class values to determine how to process the data an item contains. As you will see in later chapters, you'll want to check the content class of an item (by examining the **DAV:contentclass** field) using an ADO **Record** object before you instantiate any CDO objects.

Here's a sample Web application that runs through Exchange folders and displays the content class of each folder it encounters:

```
<HTML>
<TITLE>
Exchange 2000 Mailbox Folders and Content Classes
```

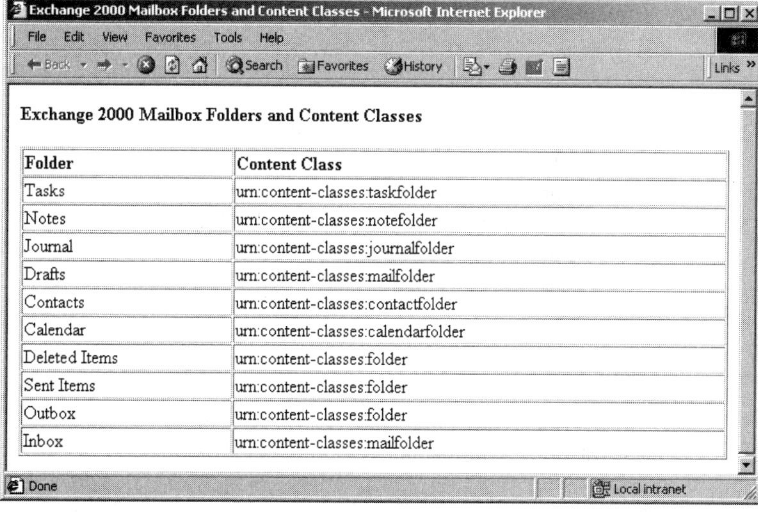

Figure 3.1 A Web page that displays the content class of typical mailbox folders

```
</TITLE>
<HEAD>
<B>
Exchange 2000 Mailbox Folders and Content Classes
</B>
</HEAD>
<p>
<BODY>
<%

Dim objRec 'as ADODB.Record
Dim objRS 'as ADODB.Recordset
Dim sMailBoxURL 'as String

Set objRec = CreateObject("ADODB.Record")
Set objRS = CreateObject("ADODB.Recordset")

sMailBoxURL = "file://./backofficestorage/EXCHDOM.local/MBX/
                        administrator"

objRec.Open sMailboxURL

Set objRS = objRec.GetChildren

%>

<TABLE border=1 cellPadding=1 cellSpacing=1 width="100%">
<TR>
<TD><B>Folder</B></TD>
<TD><B>Content Class</B></TD>
</TR>

<%
objRS.MoveFirst
Do Until objRS.EOF
   Response.Write "<TR><TD>"
   Response.Write objRS.Fields("DAV:displayname") & "</TD><TD>"
   Response.Write objRS.Fields("DAV:contentclass") & "</TD></TR>"
   objRS.MoveNext
Loop

objRec.Close

Set objRS = Nothing
Set objRec = Nothing

%>
```

```
</TABLE>
</P>
</BODY>
</HTML>
</TABLE>
</HTML>
```

Content Class Definitions

Content class definitions typically exist in a designated **schema** folder. This is a folder named "schema" that resides directly under the application folder. For example, a public folder application that resides in **public folders/myapplication** would have a schema folder at **public folders/myapplication/schema.**

Content Class Hierarchies

Web Storage System content classes support single and multiple inheritance from other content classes. The Web Storage System provides the **urn:content-class:item** content class as a "base" class. This content class contains default properties, defined in the schema folder located in the default store. The following illustration shows the hierarchy of the classes for the dsn (delivery status notification), calendar folder, and contact item types. Notice how all content classes are derived from the item content class:

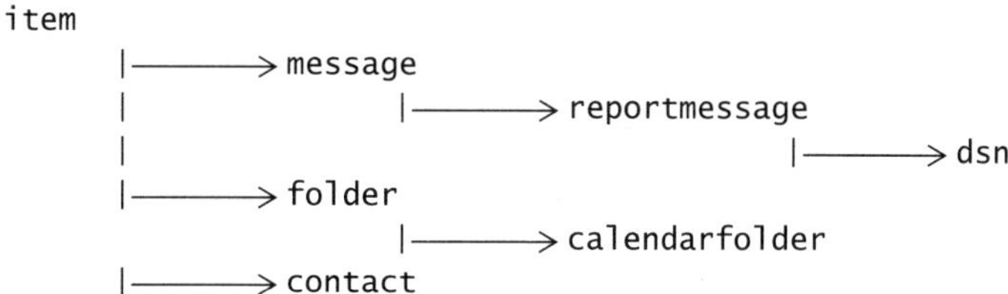

Table 3.3 lists the content classes in the Web Storage System.

Mapping Content Classes to Outlook Message Classes

If you're migrating Outlook applications to Exchange 2000 Web applications, you may find it useful to understand the relationship between content classes and Outlook message classes. Table 3.4 shows how the two map to each other.

Table 3.3 Web Storage System Content Classes

Content Class	Description	Extends	Programmatic ID
urn:content-classes:appointment	Defines a set of properties for appointment items.	urn:content-classes:item	CDO.Appointment
urn:content-classes:calendarfolder	Defines a set of properties for a calendar folder.	urn:content-classes:folder	CDO.Folder
urn:content-classes:calendarmessage	Defines a set of properties for message items that contain meeting requests.	urn:content-classes:message	CDO.CalendarMessage
urn:content-classes:contactfolder	Defines a set of properties for a contacts folder.	urn:content-classes:folder	CDO.Folder
urn:content-classes:contentclassdef	Defines a set of properties for an item that defines a content class for the Web Storage System schema.	urn:schemas-microsoft-com:xml-data#ElementType	CDO.Item
urn:content-classes:document	Defines a set of properties for Office document items.	urn:content-classes:item	CDO.Item
urn:content-classes:dsn	Defines a set of properties for an item that is a delivery status notification (DSN) message.	urn:content-classes:reportmessage	CDO.Message
urn:content-classes:folder	Defines a set of properties for a folder.	urn:content-classes:item	CDO.Folder
urn:content-classes:freebusy	Defines a set of properties for an item that contains information about whether a user's calendar is free or busy.	urn:content-classes:item	CDO.Item
urn:content-classes:item	Defines a set of base properties for an item.	urn:content-classes:object	CDO.Item
urn:content-classes:journalfolder	Defines a set of properties for a journal folder.	urn:content-classes:folder	CDO.Folder
urn:content-classes:mailfolder	Defines a set of properties for a mail folder (e.g., **Inbox**).	urn:content-classes:folder	CDO.Folder
urn:content-classes:dsn	Defines a set of properties for an item that is a mail delivery notification (MDN) message.	urn:content-classes:reportmessage	CDO.Message
urn:content-classes:message	Defines a set of properties for message items.	urn:content-classes:item	CDO.Message
urn:content-classes:notesfolder	Defines a set of properties for note folders.	urn:content-classes:folder	CDO.Folder

Table 3.3 Web Storage System Content Classes (*continued*)

Content Class	Description	Extends	Programmatic ID
urn:content-classes:object	Defines the base object.	(none)	CDO.Item
urn:content-classes:person	Defines a set of properties for contact items.	urn:content-classes:item	CDO.Person
urn:content-classes:propertydef	Defines a set of properties for an item that defines a property for the Web Storage System schema.	urn:schemas-microsoft-com:xml-data#ElementType	CDO.Item
urn:content-classes:recallmessage	Defines a set of properties for a recall message.	urn:content-classes:message	CDO.Message
urn:content-classes:recallreport	Defines a set of properties for a recall report message item.	urn:content-classes:reportmessage	CDO.Message
urn:content-classes:taskfolder	Defines a set of properties for a task folder.	urn:content-classes:folder	CDO.Folder
urn:schemas-microsoft-com:xml-data	Defines a set of properties for schema definition items.	urn:content-classes:item	CDO.Item

Table 3.4 Outlook Message Classes and Their Content Class Equivalents

Outlook Object	Outlook Message Class	Web Storage System Content Class
Calendar folder	IPF.Calendar	urn:content-classes:calendarfolder
Calendar item	IPM.Appointment	urn:content-classes:appointment
Contacts folder	IPF.Contact	urn:content-classes:contactfolder
Contact item	IPM.Contact	urn:content-classes:person
Inbox folder (or any e-mail folder)	IPF.Note	urn:content-classes:mailfolder
Inbox item (or any e-mail item)	IPM.Note	urn:content-classes:message
Journal folder	IPF.Journal	urn:content-classes:journalfolder
Journal item	IPM.Activity	urn:content-classes:item (journal items are not supported other than as items)
Tasks folder	IPF.Task	urn:content-classes:taskfolder
Task item	IPM.Task	urn:content-classes:item (tasks are not supported other than as items)

Automatic Property Promotion

One of the interesting features of the Web Storage System is that many of the Microsoft Office properties, such as **Author** and **Title**, are turned into Web Storage System properties when the document is saved. Exchange does this with a built-in event sink that "promotes" a specific set of properties in the Office document. The Web Storage System then contains a set of properties that relate to the document properties.

> **Warning:** Property promotion is a one-way action. Properties are not demoted back to the Office document. This means that newly created custom properties on documents already stored in the Web Storage System are not pushed back down to the client.

Office documents have a content class of **urn:content-classes:document**. Promoted Office properties have a namespace of **urn:schemas-microsoft-com:office:office#*propertyname*.**

Summary

Understanding how Exchange organizes data is an important consideration when you're developing applications on the Web Storage System. *Schemas* define the elements, attributes, and structure of Web Storage System items. *Namespaces* provide scope and uniqueness for an attribute name. *Content classes* define the purpose of a particular Web Storage System item and help indicate which properties are likely to be available. These terms will be used throughout the remainder of the text, so it's important that we have a general understanding of each.

Chapter 4

WebDAV: An Overview

This chapter introduces one of the protocols that Exchange 2000 natively supports: WebDAV. We'll provide an overview of the WebDAV Internet protocol, with specific applications to Exchange Server. Although the WebDAV protocol is not specific to Exchange 2000, it will probably be new for many developers.

Traditionally, the Web has been a great place for one-way document access, most commonly for reading pages of documents from Web servers. Over time, however, the Web community has realized that the ability to write to a Web server in a standard way has benefits. One example of a (nonstandard) way of writing to a Web server is Microsoft's FrontPage extensions. FrontPage extensions were designed to allow Web authors to write, rename, copy, and manage files and directories on a Web server using a standard HTTP connection. This protocol eliminated the need for a file-share mapping or FTP session to the remote computer.

In response to the need for an industry standard for remote authoring over HTTP, the WebDAV standard was created. WebDAV, which stands for World Wide Web Distributed Authoring and Versioning, is roughly equivalent to Microsoft's FrontPage Server Extensions (which is proprietary to Microsoft). Since WebDAV is sometimes simply referred to as DAV, you'll see both terms used here.

Note: Microsoft sometimes refers to WebDAV as simply "the Web Protocol."

WebDAV: The Basics

WebDAV, simply put, is an evolving Internet standard that extends the HTTP 1.1 protocol to include verbs for reading, writing, and locking files. The DAV specification is described in RFC 2518 and includes primarily three completed features:

1. **Properties.** DAV supports an extensible property set for metadata by using XML. These properties can be retrieved, set, and deleted by use of the DAV protocol.
2. **Namespace management.** DAV supports local copy, move, and rename operations. DAV also supports the concept of collections (such as a file directory or Exchange folder). This is a distinct advantage over straight HTTP, in which copying a file meant downloading it and then reuploading it.
3. **Locking.** DAV supports locking, which prevents two authors from overwriting each other's changes.

Additional features are in the works, including support for advanced collections, versioning, and access control lists.

WebDAV Client Support

Some client applications already support WebDAV. For example, Windows 2000 supports Web Folders, which is a way to map a drive to a DAV-enabled Internet address. Web Folders allows you to use a DAV server as you would a regular drive. Microsoft Office 2000 also supports DAV by allowing you to enter a Web address in the **Open** and **Save As** dialog boxes.

Microsoft Web Folders

Shortcuts to Web servers are known as Web folders (sometimes referred to as HTTP folders). The shortcuts are created automatically in **My Network Places** whenever you open resources on a Web server, provided that you have read and write access to the server. You can also use the Add Network Place wizard to create shortcuts to Web servers and other computers. Web Folders provides an easy way to view files and folders on DAV-enabled Web servers. You can manage files and folders on a Web server using Windows Explorer (Figure 4.1).

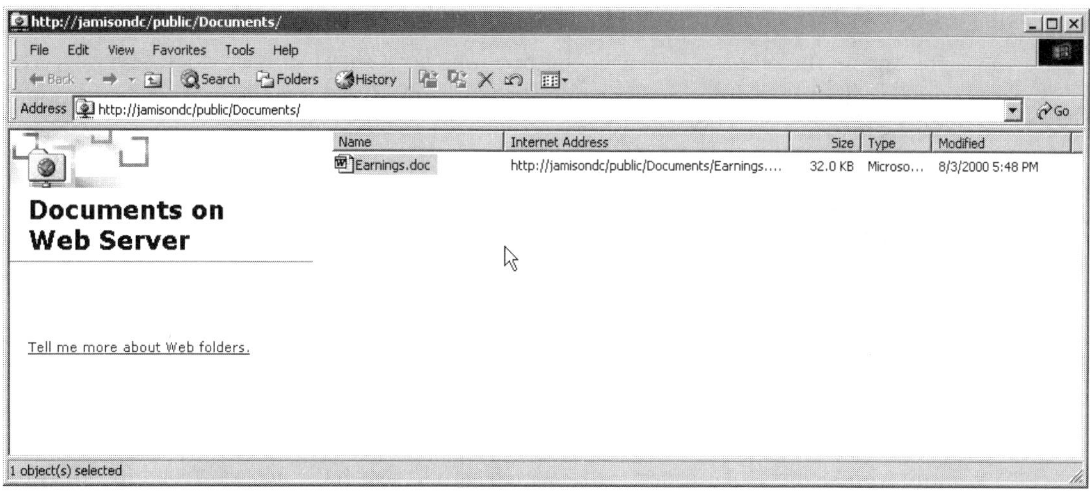

Figure 4.1 Web Folders allows you to use a WebDAV store just like a local folder on your hard drive

Setting Up a Web Folder

Before you can manage files and folders on a Web server, the Web server must support Web Folders. To do so, the server requires either the Web Extender Client (WEC) protocol and FrontPage extensions or the WebDAV protocol and IIS. Exchange 2000 and IIS 5.0 together are an example of a DAV-enabled file server (specifically, it's called DAVfs). You must also have read and write access to the Web server. To create a Web folder in Windows 2000, simply do the following:

1. Double-click **My Network Places** on the desktop to open it.
2. Double-click **Add Network Place.** Enter the Internet address of a Web server to which you can save files (e.g., "http://MyServer/WebDAVDocs").
3. Enter a name for the shortcut (e.g., "MyDAVFolder").
4. Click **Finish**.

How WebDAV Works

Since WebDAV is simply an extension of the HTTP 1.1 protocol, it's really nothing more than a bunch of new verbs that enable a new set of actions. Let's explore them here.

DAV Verbs

To enable the features listed in the previous section, DAV has added several verbs (also called methods or commands) to the HTTP 1.1 protocol. These additional verbs instruct the DAV-compliant Web server to perform actions such as creating a folder, deleting an item, or inspecting a property set. Table 4.1 lists some of the verbs that can be used with DAV and HTTP 1.1.

We'll put the new DAV methods to work later in this chapter in a sample application that uses the Microsoft XML Parser (MSXML) component. First, however, let's discuss how DAV uses XML.

DAV and XML

One of the advantages of using WebDAV to access information on a Web server is the standard set of properties to which you'll also have access. In addition to its standard information (the data), every file and directory has additional information associated with it (the metadata). Files typically have attributes such as name, size, and modification date. Standard HTTP lets some of this information be defined through headers; one of the most common is the HTTP **Content-Type** header, which is used to associate a MIME type with the data in the body of the HTTP request or response. **Content-Type** headers let clients see what kind of data is coming down the pipe (e.g., "application/word" is the **Content-Type** header for a Microsoft Word document). To allow a virtually unlimited number of file and directory properties, DAV makes use of XML to let clients make property queries.

All resources (including collections) have properties. Properties consist of a name and a value. Names are described by use of an XML element (e.g., "<displayname/>"); values are described by use of an XML tree (e.g., "<displayname>My Document</displayname>").

Live versus Dead Properties

Because properties are represented as an XML text string, and because XML documents can be pulled down onto the client machine, we must distinguish between "live" and "dead" properties. A live property is one that resides on the server (in the Exchange 2000 Web Storage System database) and is always current and accurate. A dead property resides on the client and may not be current and accurate. The property may need to be refreshed.

Namespaces: Are Those My Properties?

As we saw in Chapter 3, namespaces are an important aspect of development because we need to make sure all references to our properties are unambiguous. DAV is no exception: The namespace for DAV properties is "DAV." The complete

Table 4.1 DAV/HTTP 1.1 Verbs

Verb Name	Description	Introduced by DAV?
COPY	Copies a resource or collection specified in the URL.	Yes. **COPY** simplifies server-side resource or collection copying.
DELETE	Deletes the resource or collection specified in the URL.	No. **DELETE** is part of the HTTP 1.0 specification, but it has been updated for collections.
GET	Retrieves a URL from the server. A **GET** request for a specific URL—say, **/default.htm**—retrieves the **default.htm** file.	No. **GET** works on all kinds of Web servers, regardless of DAV support.
LOCK	Locks a resource or collection specified in the URL.	Yes. **LOCK** provides a way to set a shared or exclusive lock on a server-side resource or collection.
MKCOL	Creates a collection resource at the indicated URL on the server. This method is typically used to create subfolders.	Yes. **MKCOL** must be used for adding collections (e.g., a folder).
MOVE	Moves a resource or collection specified in the URL.	Yes. **MOVE** simplifies server-side resource or collection moving.
OPTIONS	Returns a list of all supported HTTP methods. Useful to test server support for DAV.	No. **OPTIONS** works on all kinds of Web servers, but you will get different results on servers with DAV support.
PROPFIND	Retrieves property values at the specified URL.	Yes. **PROPFIND** provides a way to retrieve document properties on a Web server.
PROPPATCH	Sets or deletes properties at the specified URL.	Yes. **PROPPATCH** provides a way to set or delete properties on a Web server.
PUT	Creates a resource at the indicated URL on the server. The server takes the body of the request, creates the file specified in the URL, and copies the received data to the newly created file.	No. **PUT** works on all kinds of Web servers, but DAV servers still use it for writing files.
UNLOCK	Unlocks a resource or collection specified in the URL.	Yes. **UNLOCK** provides a way to remove a shared or exclusive lock on a server-side resource or collection.

DAV property set is listed in Table 4.2. The colon separates the namespace from the property name.

> **Note:** For complete coverage and updates to the WebDAV standard, visit **http://www.webdav.org**.

Table 4.2 DAV Properties Supported by Exchange 2000

Property Name	Description	Read-Only?
DAV:abstract	Brief text for this item.	
DAV:autoversion	Specifies whether the resource is versioned automatically.	✓
DAV:checkintime	A time stamp set by the server indicating when a resource was checked in.	✓
DAV:childautoversioning	Specifies whether automatic versioning is set for folder items, including any subfolders.	✓
DAV:childcount	The number of objects, including subfolders, in a folder.	✓
DAV:childversioning	Specifies whether versioning is set for items and subfolders in a folder.	✓
DAV:comment	A free-text comment on the item.	
DAV:contentclass	The content class of the item. For more on content classes, see Chapter 3.	
DAV:creationdate	Date and time (Greenwich Mean Time, GMT) that the item was created.	✓
DAV:defaultdocument	The name of the default item in a folder; the name of the default document in a structured document.	
DAV:displayname	The common name of the item (e.g., the subject of a message or the **FileAs** value for a contact).	✓
DAV:getcontentlanguage	The default language header for content within this item.	✓
DAV:getcontentlength	The size of the item in bytes.	✓
DAV:getcontenttype	The content type of the item (such as "image/gif" or "text/plain").	✓
DAV:getetag	The entity tag associated with a cached entry.	✓
DAV:getlastmodified	Date and time (GMT) that the item was last updated.	✓
DAV:haschildren	Indicates whether the item has child objects (applies only to collection items).	✓
DAV:hassubs	Indicates whether the folder item has subfolders (applies only to folders).	✓
DAV:href	The URL of the item.	✓
DAV:id	A unique ID of the item.	✓
DAV:iscollection	Indicates whether this item is a collection type (such as a folder or structured document).	✓

Table 4.2 DAV Properties Supported by Exchange 2000 (*continued*)

Property Name	Description	Read-Only?
DAV:isfolder	Indicates whether this item is a folder.	✓
DAV:ishidden	Indicates whether this item is designated as hidden (you must specify this when the item is first created).	
DAV:isreadonly	Indicates whether this item is read-only.	
DAV:isroot	Indicates whether this item is a root folder.	
DAV:isstructureddocument	Indicates whether this item is a structured document.	✓
DAV:isversioned	Indicates whether this item is being versioned.	✓
DAV:lastaccessed	Date and time (GMT) that the item was last accessed.	✓
DAV:lockdiscovery	The list of all current locks on an item.	✓
DAV:mergedfrom	The resource from which this item was merged.	
DAV:nosubs	Indicates whether subfolders can be created in this folder.	✓
DAV:objectcount	The number of items in a folder that are not folders, including hidden objects.	✓
DAV:parentname	The name of this item's parent.	✓
DAV:resourcetype	The type of this item: either "<collection/>" (the item is a collection) or empty (the item is not a collection).	✓
DAV:revisioncomment	A comment for a particular revision of the document.	
DAV:revisionid	The ID for this version of the document (usually a version number).	✓
DAV:revisionlabel	A label for a particular version of the document.	✓
DAV:revisionuri	Reserved for future use.	✓
DAV:searchrequest	The original query used to build the search folder being inspected.	✓
DAV:searchtype	The type of the search.	✓
DAV:supportedlock	Lock conditions for this item, formatted in XML.	✓
DAV:uid	A unique identifier for this item.	✓
DAV:uri	The item's URI—same as **DAV:href.**	✓
DAV:visiblecount	The number of visible nonfolder items in a folder.	✓
DAV:vresourceid	A unique ID for the versions of this item. All versions of an item that is under revision control have the same identifier (set by the Web Storage System service).	✓

DAV Support in IIS 5.0

Several Microsoft products have already implemented the DAV standard. Windows 2000, and IIS 5.0 in particular, has implemented support for DAV, which supports writing to IIS folders using the DAV standard. Clients such as Microsoft Office 2000 and Internet Explorer 5.0 also support DAV. Exchange 2000 supports accessing content in either public or private folders through the DAV standard.

You can use DAV in Exchange 2000 by simply creating a folder under the public folders root. Give the folder a name (e.g., "WebDAVDocs") and be sure to specify read/write access to a specific user or group.

Let's take a look at client support to this new folder. For the following example, a file named **MyDocFile.doc** has been copied into the new folder. From a client computer, open Word 2000. From the menu bar, select **File** and then **Open** and specify "http://ExchServerName/public/WebDAVDocs/MyDocFile.doc" in the filename text box (Figure 4.2). You can edit the document and save it directly to the Exchange store using WebDAV.

Creating a DAV-Enabled Application

There are several client-based COM components that you can use to develop applications using the DAV protocol. The next section will cover two of the most com-

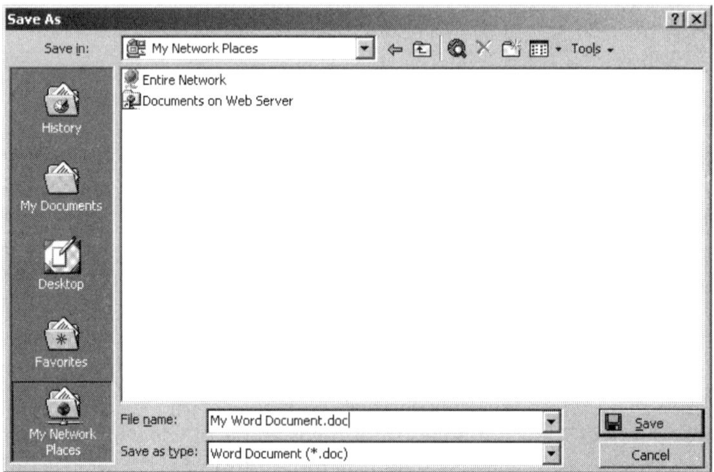

Figure 4.2 Microsoft Word provides ways to access a Web folder using the standard **Save As** dialog box

mon components: the Microsoft XMLHTTP component and the MDAIPP OLE DB provider. (In Chapter 7 we'll cover the Exchange OLE DB provider as a way to access WebDAV properties.)

MSXML COM Component

After setting up DAV, you'll want to know how you might use it in applications. One way to send DAV requests programmatically to a server is through the MSXML component, which ships with Internet Explorer 5.0. You can use the MSXML component to create and send HTTP requests and parse XML data. Using HTTP and XML, you can format pure DAV verbs and related headers, sending raw commands to the DAV server. In turn, your client must be able to understand and interpret response headers. Let's create a sample application that does just that.

To begin creating the sample client, open Visual Basic and create a new Standard EXE project. Since the application will be using Microsoft's XMLHTTP component, you'll want to select **Microsoft XML, version 2.0** from the **References** menu dialog box (Figure 4.3).

The main form contains a text box where the user can enter a URL, such as "http://server/exchange/jamisons". There are also some command buttons—one for each DAV method that we implement. We'll implement five of the DAV methods here: **OPTIONS**, **MKCOL**, **DELETE**, **PROPFIND**, and **PROPPATCH**. Another text box on the form displays the results of the request (Figure 4.4).

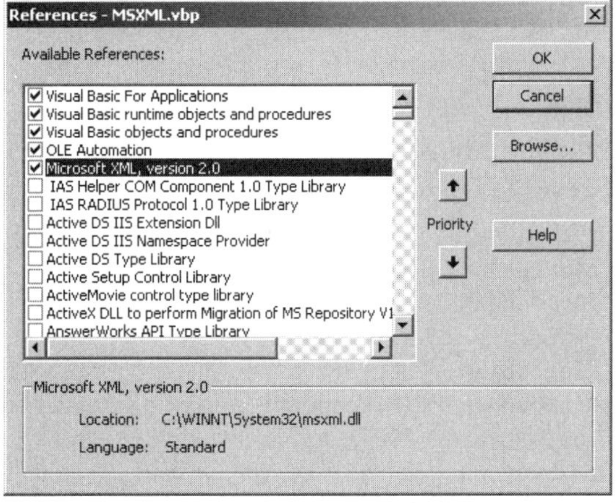

Figure 4.3 Selecting the Microsoft XML version 2.0 library

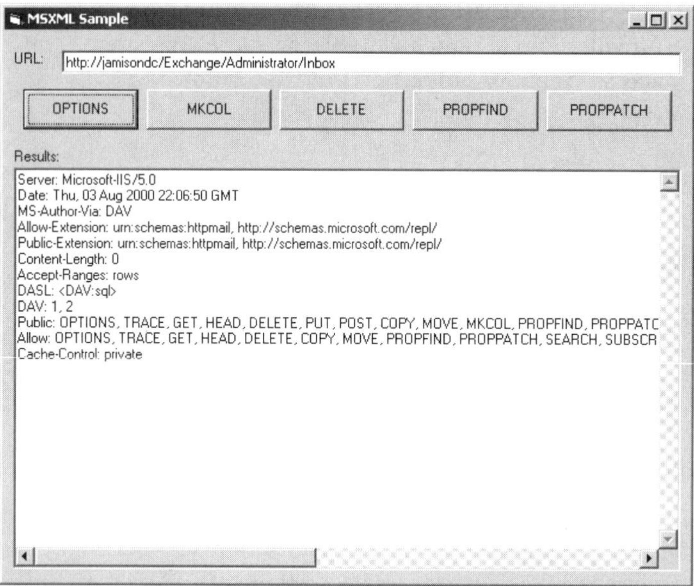

Figure 4.4 A sample VB application that implements WebDAV verbs using the MSXML component

> **Warning:** Do not use the MSXML version 2.0 component for middle-tier, high-volume applications. This component library should be used for client applications only. If you need to perform server-side safe HTTP calls, make sure you use the MSXML version 3.0 component.

OPTIONS

The first button we'll add is the **OPTIONS** button, which will send a request to the DAV server to see what methods it supports:

```
Private Sub cmdOptions_Click()
  Dim objXML As XMLHTTPRequest
  ' Create XMLHTTP object
  Set objXML = CreateObject("Microsoft.XMLHTTP")
  ' Open an HTTP connection to the server using the entered URL
  objXML.open "OPTIONS", txtURL, False
  ' Send our request to the server
  objXML.send
  txtResponse.Text = objXML.getAllResponseHeaders
```

```
  Set objXML = Nothing
End Sub
```

After the **OPTIONS** request is executed, here's what a response from the Exchange 2000 Server should look like:

```
Server: Microsoft-IIS/5.0
Date: Sun, 05 Mar 2000 21:46:16 GMT
WWW-Authenticate: Negotiate
ZjBkoAMCAReiXQRb4qdB3AJyolJh4xWf5sYkqiWz9QOR3VQ6UWDTIHU0VXMWwj0pxp
MS-Author-Via: DAV
Allow-Extension: urn:schemas:httpmail, http://schemas.microsoft.com/
                                                            repl/
Public-Extension: urn:schemas:httpmail, http://schemas.microsoft.com/
                                                            repl/
Content-Length: 0
Accept-Ranges: rows
DASL: <DAV:sql>
DAV: 1, 2
Public: OPTIONS, TRACE, GET, HEAD, DELETE, PUT, POST, COPY, MOVE, MKCOL,
PROPFIND, PROPPATCH, LOCK, UNLOCK, SEARCH, SUBSCRIBE, UNSUBSCRIBE,
POLL, BDELETE, BCOPY, BMOVE, BPROPPATCH, BPROPFIND
Allow: OPTIONS, TRACE, GET, HEAD, DELETE, COPY, MOVE, PROPFIND,
PROPPATCH, SEARCH, SUBSCRIBE, UNSUBSCRIBE, POLL, BDELETE, BCOPY, BMOVE,
BPROPPATCH, BPROPFIND, MKCOL, LOCK, UNLOCK
Cache-Control: private
```

Because the Web server replied with verbs like **PROPFIND** and **PROPPATCH**, we know we're dealing with a server that supports WebDAV.

MKCOL

Next we'll add the code for the **MKCOL** button, which requests that a new folder be created on the DAV server. Here's the MSXML code to request a new folder:

```
Private Sub cmdMKCOL_Click()
  Dim objXML As XMLHTTPRequest
  ' Create XMLHTTP object
  Set objXML = CreateObject("Microsoft.XMLHTTP")
  ' Open an HTTP connection to the server using the entered URL
  objXML.open "MKCOL", txtURL, False
  ' Send our request to the server
  objXML.send
  txtResponse.Text = objXML.getAllResponseHeaders
  Set objXML = Nothing
End Sub
```

After the **MKCOL** request is executed, a new subfolder will be created as specified in the URL. Here's what a response from the Exchange 2000 Server should look like:

```
Server: Microsoft-IIS/5.0
Date: Sun, 05 Mar 2000 21:51:22 GMT
WWW-Authenticate: Negotiate
AMCAQWhAwIBD6JmMGSgAwIBF6JdBFvzyoT83oYIBLjCCASqgAwo
MS-Exchange-Permanent-URL: http://servername/Exchange/username/
    -FlatUrlSpace-/36338d18e8d9116da32be353a2632cf3-2b1c/
Location: http://servername/Exchange/username/Folder/NewSubFolder/
    Content-Length: 0
ResourceTag:
<rt:36398d18e8d4844da398d18e8d4844da32be353a2632cf3000000002e04>
```

DELETE

We can add the code for the **DELETE** button in a similar fashion. This code will delete the resource specified in the URL:

```
Private Sub cmdDELETE_Click()
  Dim objXML As XMLHTTPRequest
  ' Create XMLHTTP object
  Set objXML = CreateObject("Microsoft.XMLHTTP")
  ' Open an HTTP connection to the server using the entered URL
  objXML.open "DELETE", txtURL, False
  ' Send our request to the server
  objXML.send
  txtResponse.Text = objXML.getAllResponseHeaders
  Set objXML = Nothing
End Sub
```

After the **DELETE** request is executed, the resource will be deleted. Here's what a response from the Exchange 2000 Server might look like:

```
Server: Microsoft-IIS/5.0
Date: Sun, 05 Mar 2000 22:06:30 GMT
WWW-Authenticate: Negotiate
Content-Length: 0
ResourceTag: <rtd:36398d18e3a2632cf30000000014a8>
```

PROPFIND

To access properties in the Web Storage System, we use the **PROPFIND** method. This method is a little trickier than the ones we have implemented up to now because we have to send along an XML request string that specifies the types of properties we are looking for. We're also setting the request header with a new DAV header: **Depth**. This new header instructs that the search be one level or many levels (recursive):

```
Private Sub cmdPropfind_Click()
  Dim objXML As XMLHTTPRequest
  Dim strRequest As String
  Dim domResponseDoc As DOMDocument

  ' Create XMLHTTP object
  Set objXML = CreateObject("Microsoft.XMLHTTP")

  ' Open an HTTP connection to the server using the entered URL
  objXML.open "PROPFIND", txtURL, False

  ' Build request string
  strRequest = "<?xml version='1.0'?>"
  strRequest = strRequest & "<d:propfind xmlns:d='DAV:'>"
  strRequest = strRequest & "<d:prop><d:displayname/></d:prop></
               d:propfind>"

  ' Set the request header to be "text/xml"
  objXML.setRequestHeader "Content-type:", "text/xml"
  objXML.setRequestHeader "Depth", "1"

  ' Send our request to the server
  objXML.send (strRequest)

  Set domResponseDoc = objXML.responseXML

  ' Parse out elements

  Dim objNodeList
  Dim objNode
  Dim i As Long
  Dim sOutput As String

  Set objNodeList = domResponseDoc.getElementsByTagName("*")
  For i = 0 To (objNodeList.length - 1)
      Set objNode = objNodeList.nextNode
      sOutput = sOutput & objNode.namespaceURI & vbCrLf
                & objNode.nodeName & vbCrLf & objNode.Text & vbCrLf
  Next
  txtResponse.Text = sOutput
  Set objXML = Nothing
End Sub
```

After sending the **PROPFIND** request to the server, we get back a response that contains the values we requested. Here's a subset of the response:

```
DAV:
a:status
HTTP/1.1 200 OK
urn:schemas-microsoft-com:office:office
d:Comments
Plan for an Analysis effort.  This may need to be paired with other
process elements such as GUI Prototype, Environmental Analysis.
urn:schemas-microsoft-com:office:office
d:LastAuthor
DAV:
a:contentclass
urn:content-classes:document
urn:schemas-microsoft-com:office:office
d:Author
Scott Jamison
DAV:
a:revisionid
+LmxqSYd/kaXQAAAABi9Q
urn:schemas-microsoft-com:office:office
d:Security
0
urn:schemas-microsoft-com:office:office
d:Title
MyDocument
```

PROPPATCH

To create, update, or delete properties on the items in the Web Storage System, we can use DAV's **PROPPATCH** method. We send an XML request string that specifies the namespace and property we wish to modify:

```
Private Sub cmdPROPPATCH_Click()
  Dim objXML As XMLHTTPRequest
  Dim strRequest As String
  Dim domResponseDoc As DOMDocument

  ' Create XMLHTTP object
  Set objXML = CreateObject("Microsoft.XMLHTTP")

  ' Open an HTTP connection to the server using the entered URL
  objXML.open "PROPPATCH", txtURL, False

  ' Build request string
  strRequest = "<?xml version='1.0'?>"
```

```
    strRequest = strRequest & "<d:propertyupdate xmlns:d='DAV:'
                 xmlns:o='urn:schemas-microsoft-com:office:office'>"
    strRequest = strRequest & "<d:set>"
    strRequest = strRequest & "<d:prop>"
    strRequest = strRequest & "<o:Author>Scott Jamison</o:Author>"
    strRequest = strRequest & "</d:prop>"
    strRequest = strRequest & "</d:set>"
    strRequest = strRequest & "</d:propertyupdate>"

    ' Send our request to the server
    objXML.send (strRequest)

    txtResponse.Text = objXML.getAllResponseHeaders
    Set objXML = Nothing
End Sub
```

If the property update is successful, we'll get a response back from the server that looks something like this:

```
Server: Microsoft-IIS/5.0
Date: Sat, 11 Mar 2000 22:20:43 GMT
Connection: close
Content-Type: text/html
Content-Length: 3212
```

Now that we have the raw DAV/HTTP 1.1 verbs down, let's shift gears and see how we can use Microsoft's Universal Data Access strategy to access our DAV server. The next section shows how to create a sample client that uses ADO 2.5 and the Microsoft OLE DB Provider for Internet Publishing to access a DAV server.

MSDAIPP and ADO

Developers can use the Microsoft OLE DB Provider for Internet Publishing (MSDAIPP) in their own applications simply by using ADO 2.5 and by specifying MSDAIPP as the OLE DB provider. Doing this lets client-side applications read and write information in a DAV-compliant data store, such as IIS 5.0 or the Web Storage System.

Note: MSDAIPP is not officially supported by Microsoft for calls into the Web Storage System. For client-side requests to Exchange 2000 using ADO, you'll need to use Office 10 or Tahoe.

It's easy to make use of the WebDAV protocol by using MSDAIPP. First make sure the provider is installed on your client machine. Version 1.0 of the provider is included in a typical installation of Internet Explorer 5.0. (Office 2000 installs MSDAIPP as part of Internet Explorer, so if the user chooses not to install Internet Explorer 5.0, the provider is not installed.) Version 1.5 of the provider is installed by default in Windows 2000.

In this section you will create a sample client application that accesses the contents of a remote WebDAV-enabled store using the Microsoft OLE DB Provider for Internet Publishing. Examples of DAV-enabled stores include IIS 5.0, Exchange 2000 Web Storage System, and even Personal Web Server with FrontPage extensions (which actually uses WEC, the Web Extender Client, rather than DAV).

To begin creating the sample DAV client, open Visual Basic and create a new Standard EXE project. Because the application will be using Microsoft's ActiveX Data Objects (ADO), you'll want to select **Microsoft ActiveX Data Objects 2.5 Library** from the **References** menu dialog box.

On the main form, you provide two main areas with which the user can interact. The first is a URL that points to the folder you want to browse. Add a command button to invoke the retrieval process. The second area lists the current URL (helpful when the user drills into a folder), the contents of the current folder, and some DAV properties of the selected item.

Into the Code

Begin your code by declaring a couple of ADO objects that you'll use everywhere. They are created in the subroutine **Form_Load**:

```
Option Explicit
Private gobjADORec As ADODB.Record
Private gobjADORS As ADODB.Recordset

Private Sub Form_Load()
    ' Create global (really form-level) objects
    Set gobjADORec = New ADODB.Record
    Set gobjADORS = New ADODB.Recordset
End Sub
```

Next program the **Go** button, which takes the URL entered by the user and retrieves the contents of the folder. This code begins by issuing an **Open** call method using the ADO **Record** object. Note that you don't have to create a **Connection** object, nor specify a specific provider. Here's why: The **Record** object, which is new in ADO 2.5, lets you open a record directly (without retrieving a **Recordset** object first). This object automatically creates a connection to your data source. You don't have to specify a provider because the "http://" syntax is the default syntax for MSDAIPP. The OLE DB engine parses the syntax and automatically loads the correct provider.

After the **Record** is open, use the **GetChildren** call method to reveal the contents of the folder. Assume that if the **dav:isfolder** property is True, it's a folder (since documents can actually be DAV collections). Then add the item's display name to the list box:

```
Private Sub cmdGo_Click()
    Dim sItemInfo As String
    Dim sItemType As String

    ' Update the current URL
    lblCurrentURL.Caption = txtURL.Text

    ' Open the record using the URL
    gobjADORec.Open txtURL.Text
    ' Get the contents of this folder (subfolders and files)
    Set gobjADORS = gobjADORec.GetChildren
    Do While Not (gobjADORS.EOF)
        If gobjADORS.Fields.Item("DAV:isfolder") Then
            sItemType = "(Folder)"
        Else
            sItemType = "(File)"
        End If
        sItemInfo = gobjADORS.Fields.Item("DAV:displayname") _
            & " " & sItemType
        lstContents.AddItem sItemInfo
        gobjADORS.MoveNext
    Loop

    ' Enable buttons
    cmdAddFolder.Enabled = True
End Sub
```

Now that you have the contents of the folder listed, program the click event to show the DAV properties that are returned for that item (Figure 4.5).

Note that the code filters out the non-DAV properties by checking for the "DAV:" namespace:

```
Private Sub lstContents_Click()
    Dim objRec As ADODB.Record
    Dim objRS As ADODB.Recordset
    Dim objField As ADODB.Field

    Set objRec = New ADODB.Record
    Set objRS = New ADODB.Recordset
```

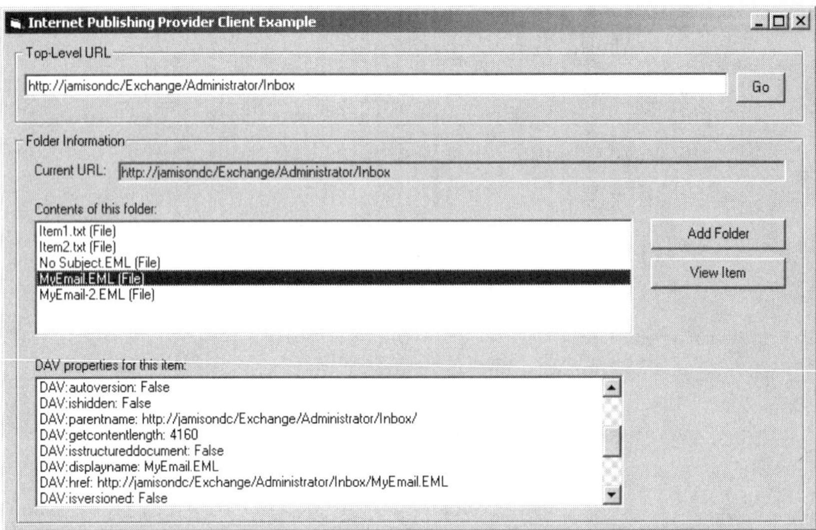

Figure 4.5 Our sample MSDAIPP application allows us to explore properties of a remote WebDAV store

```
' Get information by moving cursor to selected element
gobjADORS.MoveFirst
gobjADORS.Move lstContents.ListIndex
lstDetails.Clear
objRec.Open gobjADORS

If objRec.Fields("DAV:iscollection") Then
    ' We have a folder
    cmdViewItem.Enabled = False
Else
    ' We have a file
    cmdViewItem.Enabled = True
End If

' Show properties for DAV namespace
For Each objField In objRec.Fields
    If Left$(objField.Name, 4) = "DAV:" Then
       lstDetails.AddItem objField.Name & ": " & objField.Value
    End If
Next

objRec.Close
```

```
        Set objField = Nothing
        Set objRS = Nothing
        Set objRec = Nothing
    End Sub
```

To add the ability to "drill into" a folder, you can program the double-click event for the list box. Here, we're simply getting the contents of the selected folder and repopulating the box with the subfolders and items:

```
    Private Sub lstContents_DblClick()
        Dim objRec As ADODB.Record
        Dim objRS As ADODB.Recordset
        Dim objField As ADODB.Field

        Set objRec = New ADODB.Record
        Set objRS = New ADODB.Recordset

        ' Move cursor to selected element
        gobjADORS.MoveFirst
        gobjADORS.Move lstContents.ListIndex

        objRec.Open gobjADORS

        If objRec.Fields("DAV:iscollection") Then
            ' We have a folder, so continue
        Else
            ' We have a file, so exit (files don't have children)
            Set objRS = Nothing
            Set objRec = Nothing
            Exit Sub
        End If

        lstDetails.Clear
        lstContents.Clear

        ' Update the current URL
        lblCurrentURL.Caption = lblCurrentURL.Caption & "/"
                                & objRec.Fields("DAV:displayname").Value

        ' Drill into selected folder
        Set objRS = objRec.GetChildren
        Do While Not (objRS.EOF)
           lstContents.AddItem objRS.Fields.Item("DAV:displayname").Value
           objRS.MoveNext
        Loop
```

```
    Set gobjADORS = objRS
    objRec.Close

    Set objField = Nothing
    Set objRS = Nothing
    Set objRec = Nothing
End Sub
```

To add some more functionality to your sample application, add a button to let you add a new folder. First prompt for a folder name; then construct the full URL using the existing path. Next issue a **Rec.Open** command, specifying that you want to create a collection. Finally, refresh the contents of the list box so that you see the new folder:

```
Private Sub cmdAddFolder_Click()
    Dim sFolderName As String
    Dim sNewURL As String
    Dim sItemInfo As String
    Dim sItemType As String

    ' First free up the existing record object
    gobjADORec.Close

    ' Prompt for the new folder name
    sFolderName = InputBox("Enter folder name")

    ' Create the full path for the new folder
    sNewURL = lblCurrentURL.Caption & "/" & sFolderName

    ' Open the record using the URL (this creates the folder)
    gobjADORec.Open sNewURL, , adModeReadWrite, adCreateCollection _
        + adCreateOverwrite

    ' Free up the record object so we can use it to refresh the list
    gobjADORec.Close

    ' Open the record using the URL
    gobjADORec.Open lblCurrentURL.Caption
    ' Refresh the contents
    lstContents.Clear
    Set gobjADORS = gobjADORec.GetChildren
    Do While Not (gobjADORS.EOF)
        ' Determine the type of the object (file or folder)
        If gobjADORS.Fields.Item("DAV:iscollection") Then
            sItemType = "(Folder)"
```

```
            Else
                sItemType = "(File)"
            End If
            sItemInfo = gobjADORS.Fields.Item("DAV:displayname") _
              & " " & sItemType
            lstContents.AddItem sItemInfo
            gobjADORS.MoveNext
        Loop
    End Sub
```

The last bit of functionality you add is to view the contents of a selected file. For now, support text files by checking the **Content-Type** header for "text/plain." You use ADO's **Stream** object to stream the contents to a local text variable. Figure 4.6 shows the contents of our file:

```
    Private Sub cmdViewItem_Click()
        Dim objRec As ADODB.Record
        Dim objRS As ADODB.Recordset
        Dim objField As ADODB.Field
        Dim objStream As ADODB.Stream
        Dim txtFile As String
        Dim txtTemp As String

        ' Create ADO objects
        Set objRec = New ADODB.Record
```

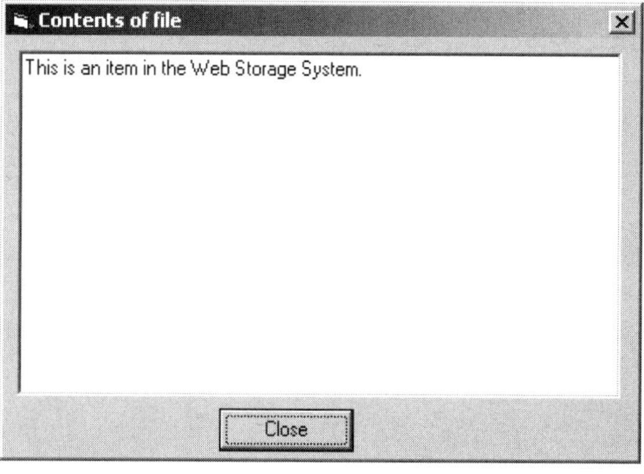

Figure 4.6 Using ADO 2.5 and the **Stream** object, we can view the contents of a WebDAV store item

```
        Set objRS = New ADODB.Recordset
        Set objStream = New ADODB.Stream

        ' Position cursor on selected element
        gobjADORS.MoveFirst
        gobjADORS.Move lstContents.ListIndex
        lstDetails.Clear
        objRec.Open gobjADORS

        ' Make sure it's a text file, then stream contents
        If objRec.Fields.Item("DAV:getcontenttype") = "text/plain" Then
            With objStream
               .Open objRec, adModeRead, adOpenStreamFromRecord
               .Charset = "ascii"
               .Type = adTypeText
               txtFile = .ReadText(adReadAll)
            End With
        End If

        ' Release record, since we have its contents
        objRec.Close

        Set objField = Nothing
        Set objRS = Nothing
        Set objRec = Nothing
        Set objStream = Nothing

        ' Show contents of file in a new window
        Load frmViewFile
        frmViewFile.txtContents.Text = txtFile
        frmViewFile.Show vbModal
    End Sub
```

This application lets you create remote DAV folders, explore folder contents, and view text files. You can add DAV functionality to any application because the MSDAIPP is a standard library.

Summary

WebDAV (or simply DAV) is the emerging standard for reading and writing over the Web. Windows 2000 and IIS 5.0 have implemented a simple version of DAV: DAVfs. MSXML is a component that provides HTTP access to a remote DAV server. The Microsoft OLE DB Provider for Internet Publishing (MSDAIPP) provides access using standard ADO. Exchange 2000 and the Web Storage System support multiple programming models, including WebDAV.

Part II

Exchange Client Access

Chapter 5

Outlook Web Access and Web Forms

This chapter looks at the major enhancements made to Outlook Web Access for Exchange 2000. It discusses the architectural and functional differences with the Exchange 5.5 predecessor and gives a brief introduction to Web Storage System forms, which act as custom Web pages for displaying and adding data to the Web Storage System.

Outlook Web Access

Outlook Web Access (OWA) is an HTTP virtual server that is installed and configured with the installation of Exchange 2000. It is the Exchange component that allows roaming users to access e-mail, personal calendars, group scheduling, public folders, and any custom collaborative applications on a remote Exchange server through a Web browser.

Although Microsoft Outlook 2000 is the most feature-rich and functional Exchange Server client, the real beauty of OWA is that it is a stateless client. A stateless client leaves no footprint on the PC. With Outlook, you have to install the entire application locally and configure a MAPI profile on the machine to access the Exchange server. With OWA, the local machine does not need to hold any user data, so users can move between PCs without worrying about creating a user profile each time.

Nevertheless, when the first version of OWA was introduced as part of Exchange Server 5.0, its feature set was so far behind that of Outlook that Outlook power users were easily frustrated. Although OWA 2000 doesn't give you all of the functionality of Outlook 2000, it does begin to narrow the gap and it is a complete makeover from the "better than nothing" approach of its predecessor. Simply look at the difference in the Exchange 5.5 OWA desktop depicted in Figure 5.1 and the near Outlook experience of the Exchange 2000 OWA desktop in Figure 5.2.

OWA Features and Limitations

Before going into the cool new features of OWA 2000, let us first say that the phrase "best viewed with Microsoft Internet Explorer 5.0 (or above)" is no joke when it comes to OWA 2000. Although OWA supports any browser that is fully compliant with the HTML 3.2 standard (including Netscape Navigator 4.0 or later

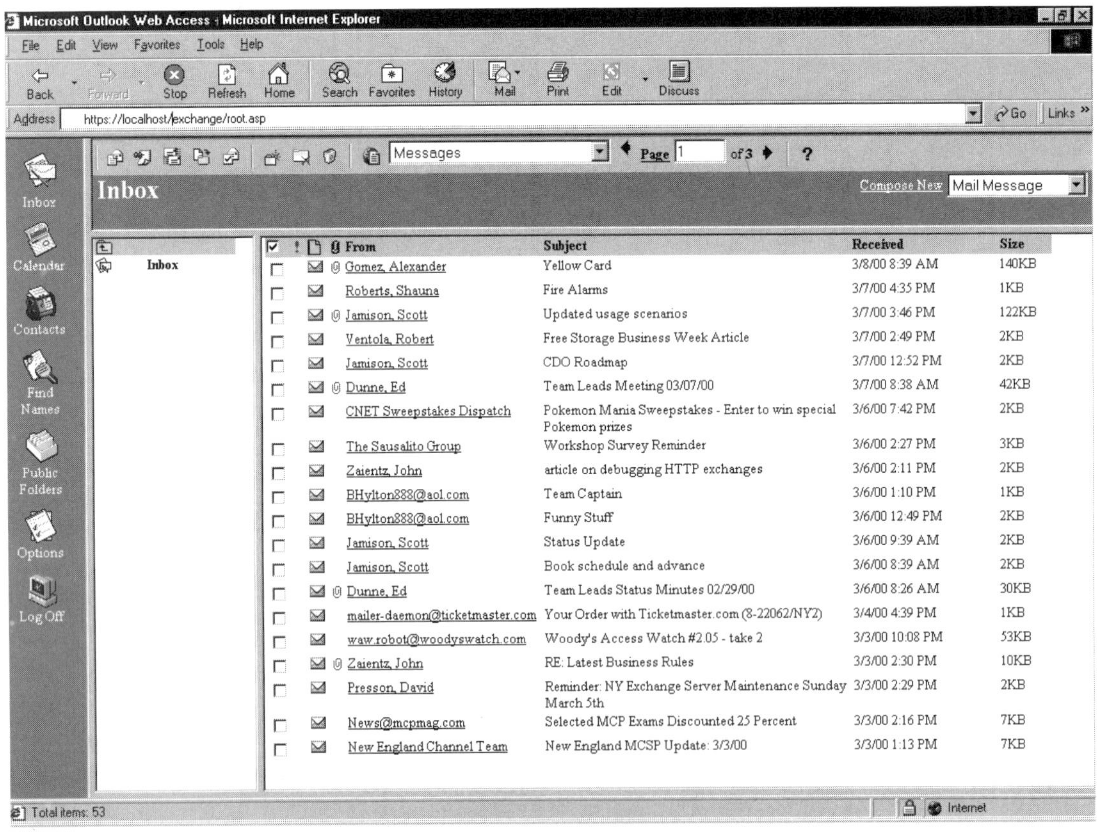

Figure 5.1 OWA for Exchange 5.5

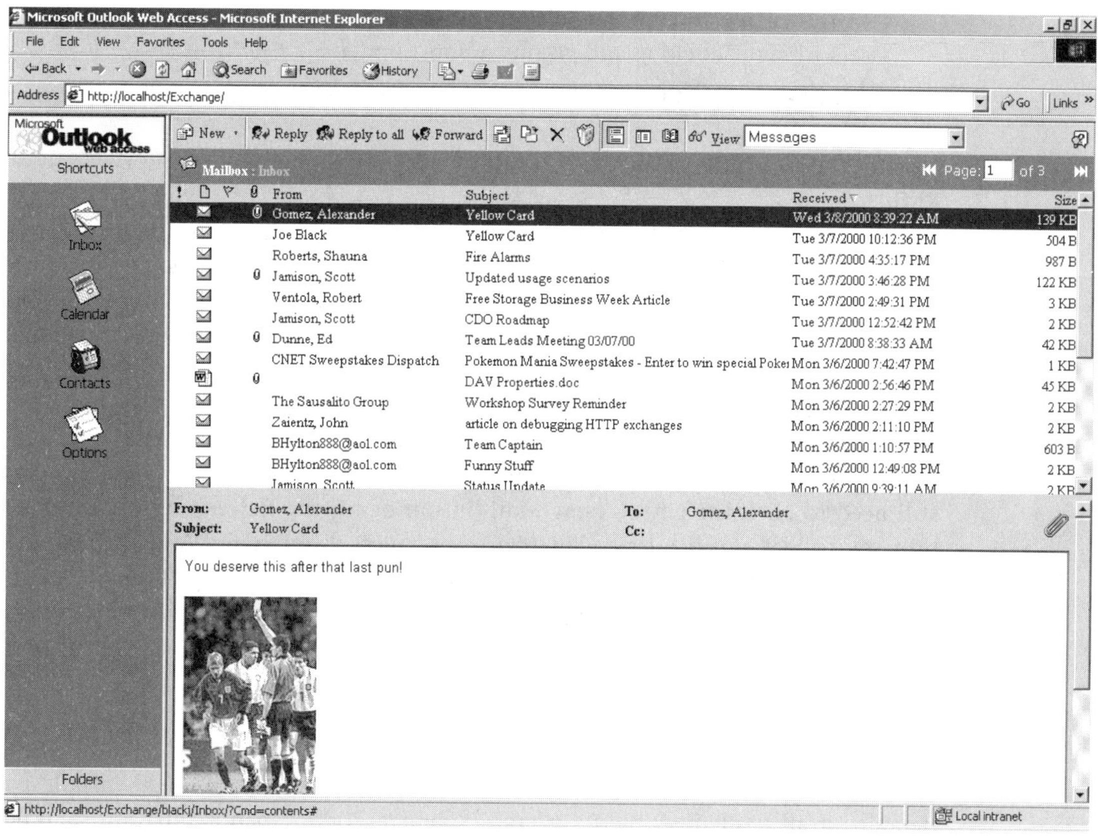

Figure 5.2 OWA for Exchange 2000

and Microsoft Internet Explorer 4.0 or later), several features work only with Internet Explorer 5—for example:

- Support for complex Outlook views, such as **View by Conversation Topic** for mail folders, a **Monthly** view for the **Calendar** folder, and the **Address Card** view for the **Contacts** folder
- Drag-and-drop capability, which lets you do such things as moving items between folders or resizing calendar appointments
- Context-sensitive toolbars depending on the folder you're in, such as **Inbox**, **Calendar**, and **Contacts**
- The preview pane for looking at the contents of a mail message without having to open it

- A folder tree control that allows you to open, create, rename, or delete folders by right-clicking and getting a pop-up menu
- Hot-key support (**<Ctrl><Enter>** to send a message, for example)

Most of the lost functionality is a result of a browser's not supporting DHTML or XML.

Of course, not all of the improvements in OWA 2000 are dependent on Internet Explorer 5. OWA now supports embedded items such as messages, appointments, meeting requests, contacts, and posts. It supports public folders that contain contacts and calendar items. It enables you to add audio and video clips directly inside a message and send it.

OWA forces updates to the browser when it knows that a new item has been added to a certain view—a new appointment in your calendar, for example. Unfortunately, it still can't determine whether new mail has arrived in your inbox, so you still need to click the **Check New Mail** button or hit the **Refresh** button on your browser to get notifications. You can't set rules through OWA, although the Exchange server will honor any rules that you set through an Outlook client. Table 5.1 summarizes the availability of certain key features in the Outlook client, the OWA 2000 client, and the OWA 5.5 client.

OWA Installation

OWA was an optional component in Exchange 5.5, but OWA 2000 installs by default on all Exchange 2000 servers. Exchange 2000 depends on IIS to handle incoming requests for all Internet protocols (including HTTP, POP3, and IMAP4). Luckily, IIS 5.0 is part of the Windows 2000 operating system. When you install Exchange 2000, it registers as an Internet Server API (ISAPI) application with IIS, and the setup program creates four virtual directories exclusive to OWA 2000:

1. **/Exchweb** stores graphics and other OWA 2000 ancillary files.
2. **/Exadmin** is used by the Exchange administration tool to administer public folders.
3. **/Exchange** stores the mailbox root.
4. **/public** contains the default public folder tree.

Figure 5.3 shows these virtual directories (along with all of the other ones in the same system) in the **Internet Information Services** management console. This tool is accessible in the Administrative Tools program group as Internet Services Manager.

Table 5.1 Outlook versus OWA 2000/5.5: Comparison of Key Features

Feature	Outlook 2000	OWA 2000	OWA 5.5
E-mail	Yes	Yes	Yes
Calendaring	Yes	Yes	Yes
Contacts	Yes	Yes	Yes
Tasks	Yes	No	No
Rich text	Yes	Yes	Yes
HTML	Yes	Yes	Yes
Drag-and-drop editing	Yes	Yes (Internet Explorer 5 only)	No
Shortcut menus (obtained by right-clicking)	Yes	Yes (Internet Explorer 5 only)	No
Offline use	Yes	No	No
Journal	Yes	No	No
Printing templates	Yes	No	No
Outlook rules	Yes	No	No
OLE	Yes	No	No
Timed delivery	Yes	No	No
Expiration	Yes	No	No
Spelling checker	Yes	No	No
Reminders	Yes	No	No
Notes	Yes	No	No
Complex Outlook views	Yes	Yes (Internet Explorer 5 only)	No
Context-sensitive toolbars	Yes	Yes (Internet Explorer 5 only)	No
Copying between public and private folders	Yes	No	No
Telephony options	Yes	No	No
Direct editing in the **Calendar** view	Yes	No	No
Access to personal folder files (PSTs, for "Personal Stores")	Yes	No	No
Message recall	Yes	No	No
Recovery of deleted items	Yes	No	No
Maintaining distribution lists	Yes	No	No
Modifying permissions on public folders	Yes	No	No
Setting the out-of-office assistant	Yes	Yes	No

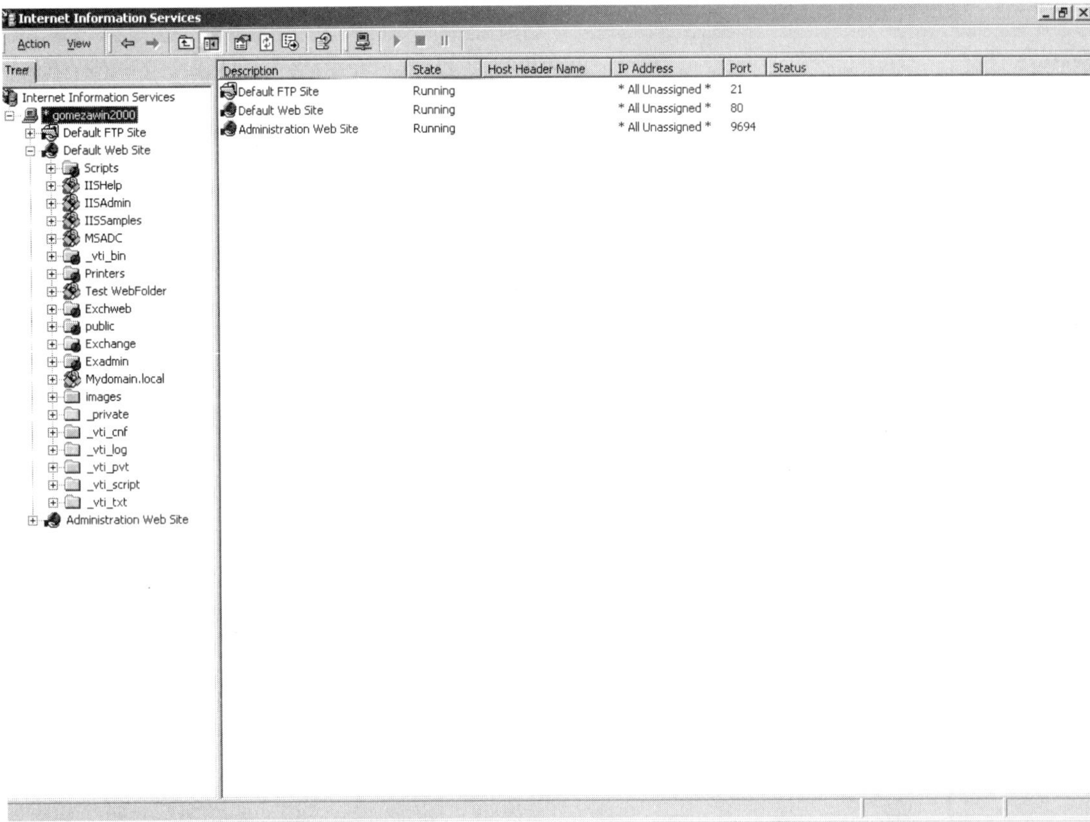

Figure 5.3 OWA virtual directories in the IIS console

> **Note:** If you are having trouble getting OWA to work on your Exchange 2000 Server, open IIS and check the status of the Exchange virtual directories. If the directories appear with a stop sign icon to the left, they are not available. What you usually need to do is right-click on the directory and choose **Properties**. On the **Virtual Directory** tab, hit the **Browse** button to the left of the local path and reselect the physical directory on the machine. This should turn the stop sign into the friendlier "globe on folder" motif shown in the virtual directories in Figure 5.3, which indicates that the virtual directory is ready for use.

OWA Architecture

The original OWA architecture was based on frames, Active Server Pages (ASP), Collaborative Data Objects (CDO), and MAPI. The ASP pages contained VBScript code that referenced CDO objects to manipulate such items as mailboxes, folders, and calendars. The application ran under Microsoft Internet Information Server (IIS) and communicated with Exchange through MAPI because this was the only way to access the Exchange server data. OWA interpreted the incoming HTTP requests, translated them into MAPI functions, and then sent the results back to the browser as standard HTML. Interestingly, OWA 5.5 was the only product in the Microsoft suite for which the end users had access to the source code. The vast majority of the code was in ASP pages, which could be edited in Microsoft FrontPage, for example.

Given the architecture of OWA 5.5, scalability was the biggest problem. The interpretive nature of the ASP code, coupled with the huge amount of work that OWA performed to pass requests back and forth between the Exchange server and the browser, limited scalability. The maximum number of concurrent connections that OWA 5.5 could support was under 800 no matter how powerful the server was in terms of CPU and available memory.

Let's move on to the basic architecture for OWA 2000. Among the radical changes are the following: Most of the crucial code (such as the code that renders output for browser display) is compiled into DLLs, yielding a significant performance increase. OWA no longer uses MAPI to communicate with the mailbox store, and ASP pages are not used for client access. Instead, the Exchange 2000 Information Store is now Web enabled through the new Microsoft Web Storage System, which allows a URL to access every item in the information store. OWA 2000 relies on DHTML, XML, and HTTP-DAV protocols in Internet Explorer 5 to handle the page rendering.

Accessing the Exchange Server

The basic URL to connect to OWA is in the form **http://<servername>/exchange**; for example, if you can run OWA directly from your development machine, you could use **http://localhost/exchange**. IIS interprets incoming HTTP requests from browsers and scans the URL to determine which application needs to be called to handle the request. The OWA URL causes IIS to conduct a log-on sequence, if necessary, to identify which mailbox to connect the user to. We say "if necessary" because Internet Explorer 5's default behavior is to use your cached Windows credentials for authentication, so you'll see the screen only if these credentials have expired or you're attempting to connect to an Exchange server in a domain different from the one you are currently logged into.

The code for the Exchange Server ISAPI resides in **davex.dll**, which can connect to mailboxes or public folders in the Information Store. While OWA 5.5 uses MAPI for these connections, OWA 2000 uses EXIPC (Epoxy), a new high-speed interprocess link to connect IIS to an HTTP stub within the Information Store. The stub then links to **exoledb.dll**, which in turn processes the requests for mailbox, folder, or item data.

> **Note:** For more information on the transport components used in Exchange 2000 Server, see Knowledge Base article Q260995, which can be found at **http://support.microsoft.com/support/kb/articles/q260/9/95.asp**.

As mentioned earlier, you can address most of the OWA functions and components by defining a specific URL. You can open specific folders by entering the name of the folder after the mailbox name. For example, **http://localhost/Exchange/gomeza/calendar/** opens our calendar, **http://localhost/Exchange/gomeza/contacts** opens our contacts folder, and so on. But that's not all. You can combine actions and command verbs in your URL using the following syntax:

```
http://server_name/virtual_root/folder/?option= Modifier
```

or

```
http://server_name/virtual_root/folder/item_name?Option=&Modifier
```

Table 5.2 lists some of the more common options.

So using the URL syntax, we could create a new message in our inbox with the URL

```
http://localhost/exchange/gomeza/?Cmd=new
```

A more daring example would be the following URL, which displays our calendar in monthly view starting March 1, 2000, as shown in Figure 5.4:

```
http://localhost/Exchange/gomeza/calendar/?View=Monthly&Date=20000301
```

Basic Administration

Because OWA 2000 installs by default with Exchange 2000 and is automatically configured to be up and running when you reboot your machine, there may be times when you want to disable it. For example, you may want to perform routine maintenance on the server. OWA 2000 is administered through the Exchange System Manager console in the Microsoft Exchange program group under System

Table 5.2 Common OWA URL Options and Actions

Option/Action	Description
Option	
Page=x	Displays the navigation bar.
View=x	Uses the Outlook view named x.
Sort=x	Sorts by column x.
Date=yyyymmdd	Displays the date in **Calendar.**
Cmd=action	Performs the stated action.
Actions	
Navbar	Displays the navigation bar.
Contents	Displays the contents of a folder.
New	Creates a new default item in a folder.
New&Type=x	Specifies the type of item to create.
Options	Sets options.
Open	Opens a message or appointment for reading.
Edit	Opens a message or appointment for editing.
Reply, ReplyAll, Forward	Perform message operations.
Accept, Decline, Tentative	Perform appointment operations.

Manager. This tool allows you to start, stop, or pause an HTTP virtual server. When the virtual server is paused, it continues to support existing client connections but refuses new client session requests.

To start, pause, or stop a virtual server, open Exchange System Manager and navigate to HTTP. Right-click **Exchange Virtual Server** (Figure 5.5) and choose **Start**, **Stop**, or **Pause** as appropriate.

You can also enable and disable OWA on a user basis through the **Active Directory Users and Computers** console (also found in the Microsoft Exchange program group). First click **Advanced Features** on the **View** menu. Navigate to users in the console tree. In the **Details** pane, right-click on a user and select **Properties.** Click the **Exchange Advanced** tab and then **Protocol Settings.** Click **HTTP** and then hit the **Settings** button. Check or uncheck the **Enable for mailbox** check box (see Figure 5.6) to enable OWA or disable it, respectively, for the user.

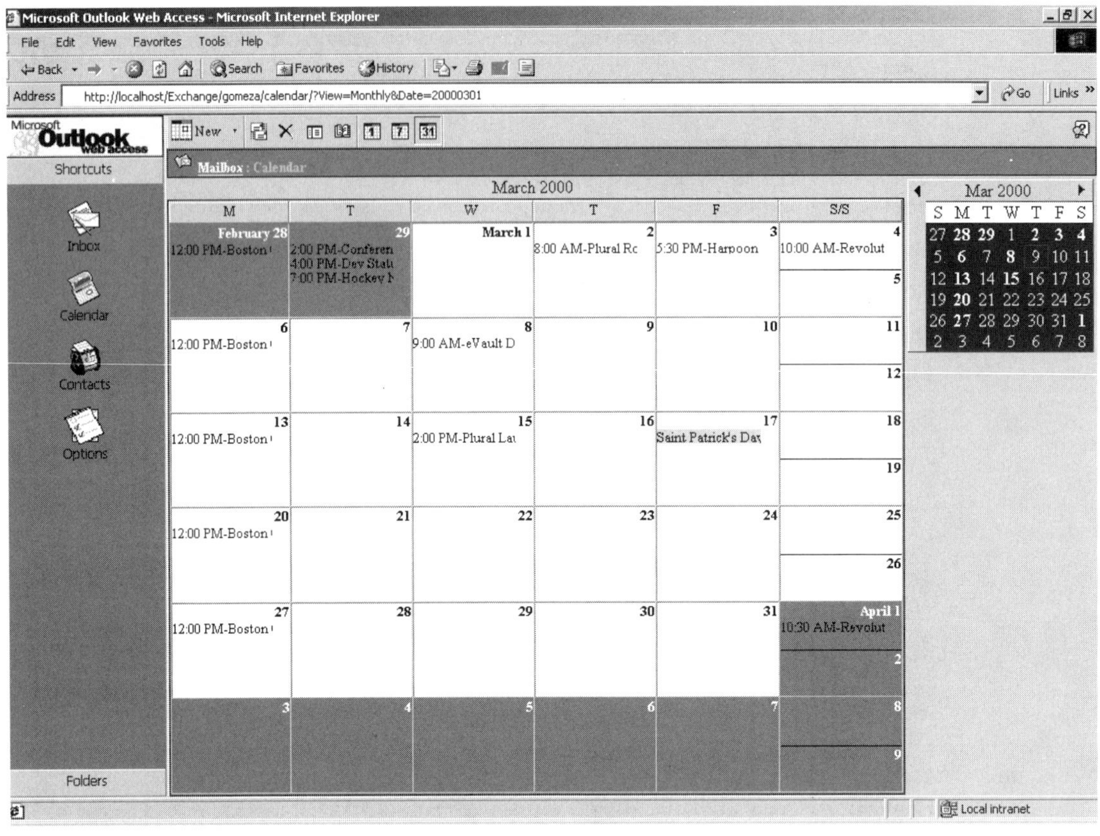

Figure 5.4 Outlook Web Access 2000 monthly calendar view

Web Storage System

Exchange 2000 stores both messaging and file information in what's known as the Web Storage System. The Web Storage System is a storage platform that provides a single repository for managing multiple types of unstructured information within one infrastructure. It combines the features and functionality of the file system, the Web, and a collaborative server (such as Exchange 2000) through a single, URL-addressable location for storing, accessing, and managing information, as well as building and running applications. The Web Storage System is based on the technology that drives the Exchange Server Information Store.

One of the key features in a Web Storage System is that the schema is extensible. To ensure that new properties defined in the schema are globally unique, they are

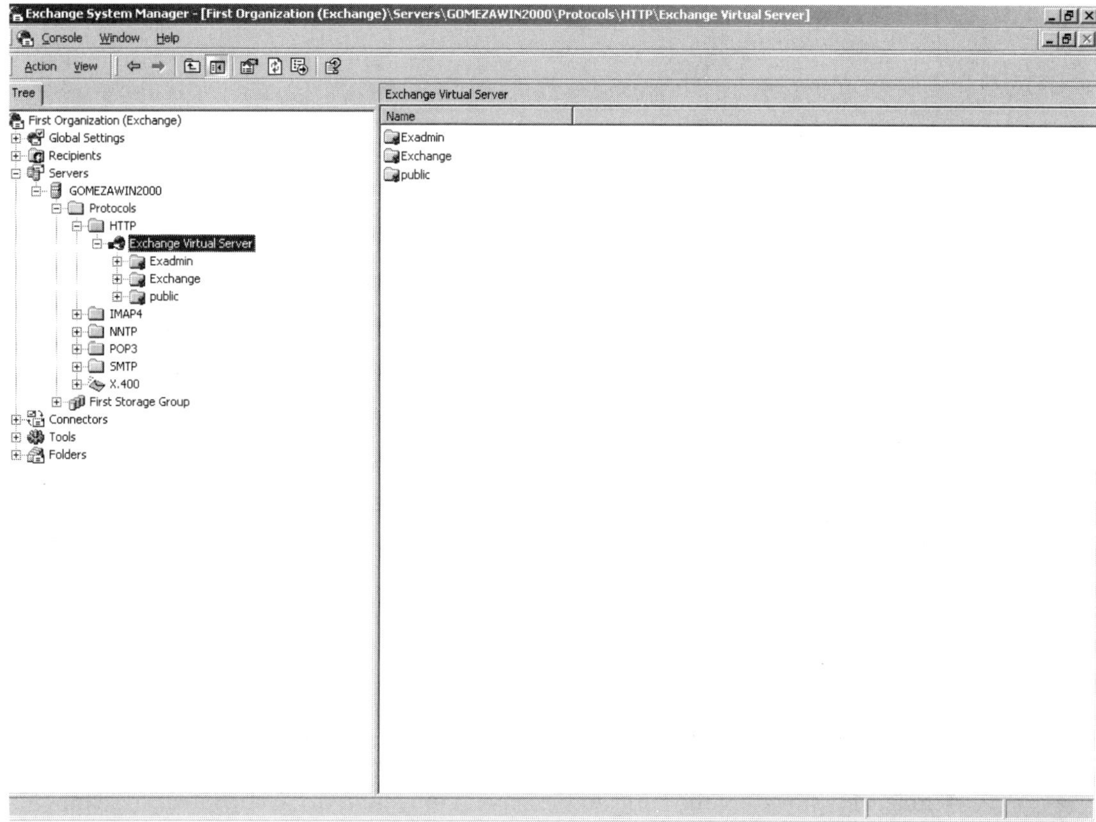

Figure 5.5 Selecting **Exchange Virtual Server** in the **Exchange System Manager** console

identified by both a name and a namespace. For example, default namespaces are defined for Microsoft Office documents, Exchange objects, and CDO **Person** and calendaring objects.

Content classes loosely define types of content in the Web Storage System. Content classes do not define the actual properties stored in the item. They do define the set of properties returned by **SELECT** * commands on folders that have the particular class as the expected content class, as we'll see in our discussion on Web Storage System SQL (WSS SQL) in Chapter 7.

Web Storage System Forms

Essentially, a Web Storage System application can be developed by use of the same set of tools as traditional database applications because it is a database. It can even be

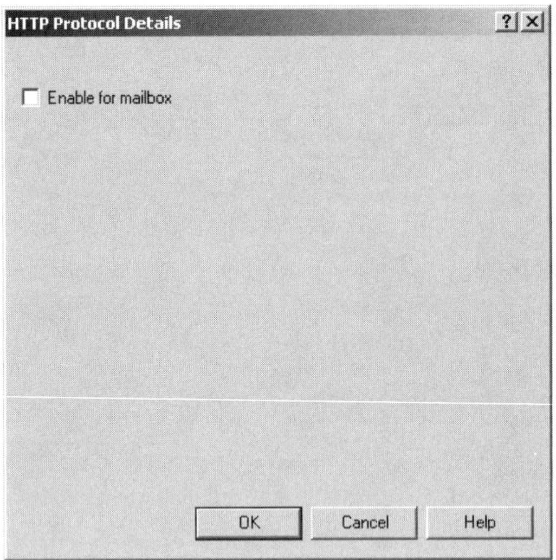

Figure 5.6 Disabling OWA on a per user basis

queried with a SQL-like syntax (WSS SQL). With a few adjustments, you can have data-bound forms that dynamically display Web Storage System data. The Web Storage System is also a great environment for running a Web site using ASP and HTML files. If you are using Microsoft Visual InterDev or FrontPage, you can create a Web project by providing the name of the server containing the Web Storage System.

Which brings us to Web Storage System forms. You can think of a Web Storage System form as being similar to a Microsoft Outlook form, except that Web Storage System forms can be accessed by any Web browser supporting HTML 3.2 or later. Just as Outlook uses forms to display Exchange items, OWA 2000 uses Web Storage System forms to allow users to access their Exchange mailboxes, public folders, and other options through a Web browser. The predefined forms and views that OWA uses are actually in a compiled resource file and are not editable. However, developers can still create their own customized Web Storage System forms.

Web Storage System forms are actually Web pages that are registered in the Web Storage System. The registration is a single record in an application schema folder in the Exchange store, which tells Exchange when to use the form. A Web Storage System form can be registered as the default view for a folder, or it can be registered to be displayed in response to a command such as open or edit. Specifically, a Web Storage System form is stored in a folder created for that form and forms of that type. As with any other item in the Web Storage System, a form has a content class property denoting its purpose. As you add fields to a form, they are added to the schema, and if you create another form in the same folder, you have immediate access to the entire schema created with previous forms in that folder.

When you access a document or folder from a Web form, the Web Storage System will use a template to tell it how to render the data and perform any actions. A registry in the Web Storage System accesses these templates, which reside in a unique namespace that is based on the form's content class.

Web Storage System forms work as follows: When an HTTP request comes in, the request is transferred to IIS. The form registry checks for a form registration as previously described. This registration provides a set of form-specific attributes, such as content class, user action, language, browser type, and item state. The form registry uses this information to choose which form to display. If a Web Storage System form has been registered, it is selected; otherwise one of the predefined OWA forms is selected. The form-rendering engine then fills out the form and sends it back to the user's browser.

Registering a Web Storage System Form

A custom Web Storage System form must be properly registered in the Web Storage System before your Exchange users can access it. What exactly does registering a form mean? As alluded to earlier, there is a Web Storage System Form Registry to store the form registration itself. A form registration is a set of form-specific properties stored as a single record (a form definition) in an application schema folder in the Exchange store. Table 5.3 lists the properties in a form definition.

Another key part of registering a form is setting the Schema Collection Reference (SCR). Objects in the Exchange Web Storage System define the locations of their schemas through the SCR. The SCR is the URL to begin searching for schema information; it is also the **urn:schemas-microsoft-com:exch-data:schema-collection-ref** property on a folder.

Registering a Web Storage System Form as the Default Form

Now let's put everything together and see how to register a Web Storage System Form as a default form. When you open a public folder in OWA, a list of the contents of that folder will be displayed. If a Web Storage System form has been registered as the default form, you will see that form in place of the usual list of items. To register your form, follow these steps:

1. Create the form in your favorite Web page editor (Microsoft FrontPage, for example).
2. Log in to the Exchange server as a user with rights to write to the intended directory.
3. Set the **Schema Collection Reference**.
4. Register the form with a content class of **urn:content-classes:document**.
5. Register the name "DAV:defaultdocument."

Table 5.3 Form Definition Properties

Property Name	Description
urn:schemas-microsoft-com:office:forms#binding	Used to determine where the binding of data to the form takes place. There are three case-insensitive possible values: "Webclient," "client," and "server." A client binding specifies that the client can interpret dynamic HTML, whereas a server binding specifies that the client cannot.
urn:schemas-microsoft-com:office:forms#browser	Case-insensitive string indicating the type of browser (Internet Explorer, for example). An asterisk (*) indicates a wild card.
urn:schemas-microsoft-com:office:forms#cmd	Case-insensitive string denoting the "action" or behavior being performed on an object. This is the first parameter after the command (?Cmd= of the URL returned from IIS roughly corresponding to the ISAPI **QUERY_STRING**). The **QUERY_STRING** is delimited by ampersands (&) that represent modifiers of the action. In the case of "server" binding, the entire URL is passed to the related ISAPI extension, to parse and handle the URL, including **QUERY_STRING**, appropriately.
urn:schemas-microsoft-com:office:forms#contentclass	Case-insensitive string specifying the content class for which the form is registered. It is associated with a set of schemas and a set of forms. Example: **urn:content-classes:message**.
urn:schemas:microsoft-com:office:forms#contentstate	Case-insensitive property that is used to match forms against the **http://schemas.microsoft.com/exchange/contentstate** URL that can be set on any item.
urn:schemas-microsoft-com:office:forms#executeparameters	Parameters to pass to the form-rendering engine specified by the **executeurl** property. *Must* be URL escaped.
urn:schemas-microsoft-com:office:forms#executeurl	The URL to execute to render a form.
urn:schemas-microsoft-com:office:forms#formurl	The URL of the form or template to handle and render, via the binding method.
urn:schemas-microsoft-com:office:forms#language	Automatically provided as part of the HTTP request headers, this is the language of the form. This attribute corresponds to a case-insensitive ISO value that represents language and/or country in the **Accept-Language** HTTP header.
urn:schemas-microsoft-com:office:forms#majorver	Browser major version.
urn:schemas-microsoft-com:office:forms#messagestate	The state of the item. Case-insensitive values include normal, submitted, read, unread, and importance level.
urn:schemas-microsoft-com:office:forms#minorver	Browser minor version.

Table 5.3 Form Definition Properties (*continued*)

Property Name	Description
urn:schemas-microsoft-com:office:forms#platform	Case-insensitive string specifying the platform of the browser to match against for forms registrations.
urn:schemas-microsoft-com:office:forms#registration	Item in store representing a form registration. This is not URL escaped.
urn:schemas-microsoft-com:office:forms#request	Case-insensitive string specifying whether the form uses **GET** or **POST** requests. There are two possible values: "GET" and "POST." **GET** asks for information; **POST** writes information.

The following is a bare-bones Active Server Page that registers **WebStoreOrder.htm** in a public folder:

```
<HTML>
<HEAD>
<%@ LANGUAGE = "VBScript" %>
<%
Const adModeReadWrite       = 3
Const adFailIfNotExists     = -1
Const adCreateNonCollection = 0
Dim strURL
' This is assuming your server is local host and you have a public
    folder named
' TheWebStore under the default Public Folder hierarchy:
strURL = "file://./backofficestorage/localhost/public folders/
                 TheWebStore/"
Dim Rec
Set Rec = CreateObject("ADODB.Record")
response.write strURL
Rec.Open strURL,,adModeReadWrite, adFailIfNotExists
response.write "<P>"
Dim Flds
Set Flds = Rec.Fields

' Set the SCR and the default document
Flds("urn:schemas-microsoft-com:exch-data:schema-collection-ref")
    = strURL & "MyNewSchema/"
' Specify the Web Storage System form:
Flds("DAV:defaultdocument") = "WebStoreOrder.htm"
Flds.Update
Response.write(Err.number) & "<P>"
response.write"<H3>SUCCESS</H3>"
Rec.Close
%>
</HEAD>
<BODY>
```

```
</BODY>
</HTML>
```

FrontPage Extensions for Web Storage Forms

Luckily, there is now a tool available to help speed up the development of Web Storage System forms using FrontPage 2000.

Installation

Go to the Microsoft Exchange developer Web site (**http://msdn.microsoft.com/exchange/default.asp**) and download the FrontPage Extensions for Web Storage System forms. Once you have finished the download, double-click **MSFPWSS.exe** to unzip the **FrontPage_Client.MSI** file into a directory. Double-click on this file and follow the prompts to install the product.

The next time you open FrontPage 2000, you will have an additional menu of options specifically for Web Storage System (WSS) forms (see Figure 5.7).

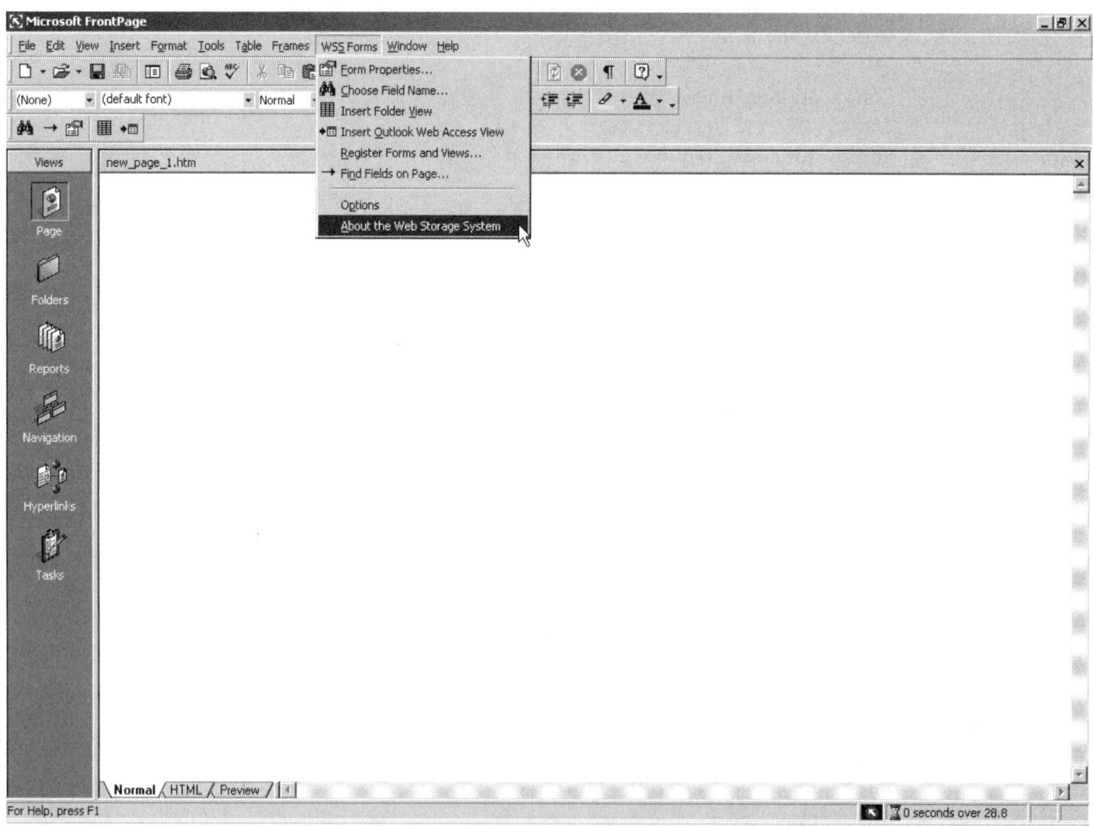

Figure 5.7 FrontPage 2000 extensions for Web Storage System forms

> **Note:** At press time, this tool was still in beta testing, but this integrated, easy-to-use tool gives a good indication of how Microsoft is trying to make Web Storage System forms more accessible.

Summary

OWA for Exchange 2000 represents a complete rewrite of this application for rendering Exchange items on any Web browser. Its new architecture allows it to be more scalable and perform better, and it narrows the functional gap with Outlook 2000. Web Storage System forms are a new tool for storing and displaying data in the Web Storage System. All indications are that these forms will become easier to develop with the emergence of new tools.

Chapter 6

Outlook 2000 and Digital Dashboards

In this chapter we discuss the concept of the digital dashboard and the mechanisms that allow it to integrate with Outlook 2000. We preview Microsoft's new Digital Dashboard Resource Kit and the notion of Web Parts. We focus on personal Web Parts, which provide all of the rich features of the Outlook 2000 client inside a digital dashboard by means of the Outlook View Control. Finally we give an exhaustive review of the properties and methods of the Outlook View Control, complete with coding examples.

The Digital Dashboard

Outlook 2000 lets users manage personal day-to-day information such as e-mail, schedules, tasks, and contact data. Outlook also offers significant programming functionality through its object model (Figure 6.1).

What if you combined Outlook's information management features with its programmability model to provide access to disparate corporate data, news, traffic reports, sports scores, and stock quotes from the Web within Outlook itself? What if you could combine information stored in an Exchange public folder with information from a corporate intranet or extranet without leaving the familiar environs of Outlook? Integrating the personal information in Outlook 2000 with key corporate and external information is what a digital dashboard is all about.

A digital dashboard is a customized Office 2000–based solution that brings together information from a variety of sources into a single, integrated view on a

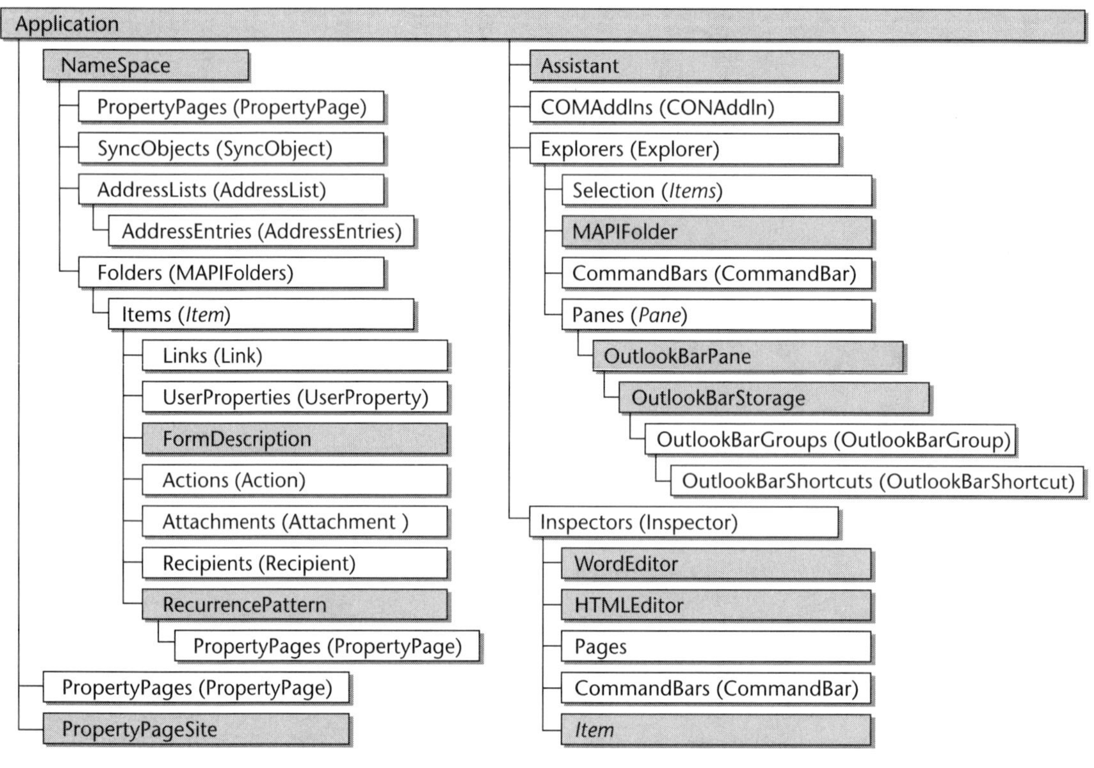

Figure 6.1 The Outlook 2000 object model

user's desktop. Figure 6.2 shows a sample digital dashboard. A user can be looking at the items in his or her inbox on an Exchange server, the results of a query run against a SQL Server database, and a pivot table in Excel without ever being aware of the source of the information and without ever having to learn different user interfaces. The digital dashboard is a tool to centralize, categorize, and filter essential information, but the example in Figure 6.2 shows just some of its possibilities. Let's take a closer look at the underlying technologies.

Folder Home Pages

As you may have noticed, parts of the digital dashboard in Figure 6.2 resemble the Outlook Today home page, which was the digital dashboard's predecessor. The Outlook Today page was first introduced in Outlook 98 as an HTML page providing a consolidated view of a user's inbox, daily appointments, and tasks. While it was technically *possible* to customize, customization was not trivial, and you could have an Outlook Today page only associated with the Outlook Today folder.

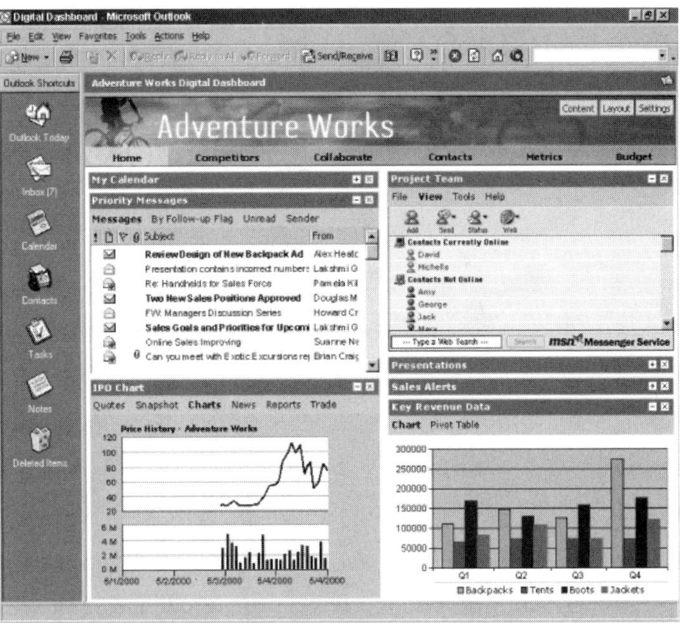

Figure 6.2 A digital dashboard

The key technical concept enabling a digital dashboard within Outlook 2000 is the ability to associate any public or private Outlook folder with an HTML home page. By doing this, you replace the default folder view in the Outlook explorer window with a Web page. This feature lets you develop a Web portal, hosted within Outlook, using standard HTML. To associate a Web page with an Outlook folder, right-click on a folder and select **Properties.** Under the **Home Page** tab, type in a Web address in the **Address** text box (e.g., "www.plural.com") and select **Show home page by default for this folder,** as shown in Figure 6.3.

When you click on this folder, the specified Web page appears in the main Outlook pane, rather than the traditional Outlook view of items. Behind the scenes, Outlook hosts an instance of Internet Explorer within the Outlook view pane that allows you to use HTML, DHTML, and COM components in your dashboards.

Digital Dashboard Resource Kit 2.01

In July 2000, Microsoft released the latest version of its digital dashboard development toolkit, Digital Dashboard Resource Kit (DDRK) (Figure 6.4). The DDRK

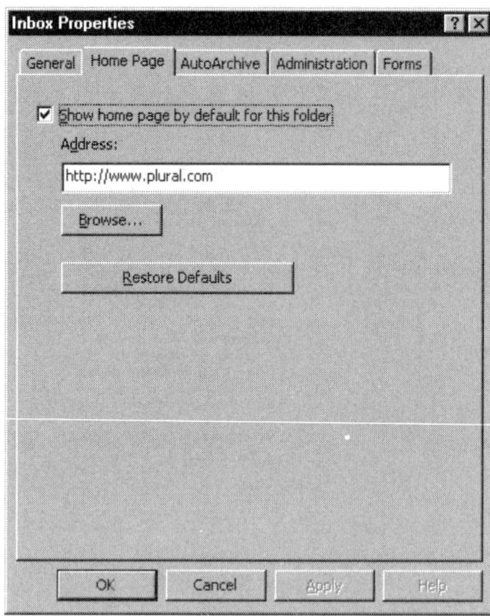

Figure 6.3 Configuring a home page in Outlook 2000

replaces the successful Digital Dashboard Starter Kit (from April 1999) and the Team Folders Wizard even before that. It introduces the concept of Web Parts, which are reusable components containing XML, HTML, and scripting language code that have their own properties and methods for controlling particular functions of the digital dashboard.

Note: Digital Dashboard Resource Kit 2.01 and updates can be downloaded from **http://www.microsoft.com/business/digitaldashboard/**.

The DDRK contains sample digital dashboards for the Windows 2000 File System and SQL Server 7, demonstrating the platform versatility of Web Parts. It also contains documentation on digital dashboard concepts and a primer on digital dashboard development.

Note: The DDRK also promises a sample digital dashboard devoted exclusively to the Exchange 2000 platform. At press time, the sample had not been released, but be sure to check the link referenced earlier for DDRK updates.

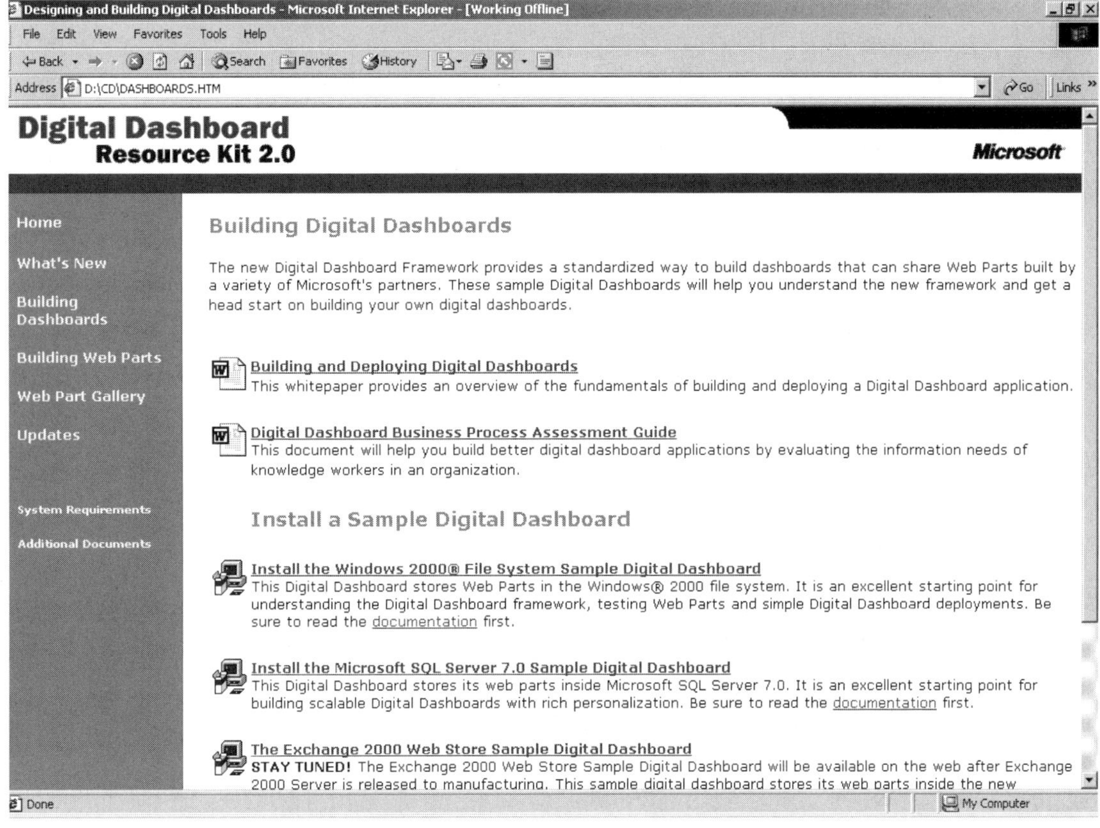

Figure 6.4 Digital Dashboard Resource Kit

A major section in the DDRK called the Web Part Gallery showcases prebuilt Microsoft and third-party Web Parts that developers can include in their digital dashboards. Interestingly, the two Microsoft offerings under personal Web Parts feature a technology that has been around since the first digital dashboard: the Outlook View Control. Although the documentation in the DDRK is good, scarcely any of it deals with the properties and methods of the Outlook View Control, which is a robust component for client-side digital dashboards.

Outlook View Control

The Outlook View Control is a COM component that exposes key features of the Outlook 2000 visual interface. It gives an Outlook folder home page the ability to display the contents of an Outlook folder, to control folder views, open the Outlook Address Book, and create, open, print, and delete folder contents. The key thing to remember about the Outlook View Control is that it does not in any way replace Outlook 2000 on your machine; you still need Outlook 2000 installed on any clients running your application. For the control to display any information, a copy of Outlook 2000 needs to be running in memory. The control attempts to start Outlook if there's no running instance following the way you have Outlook configured to start up on your machine. For example, if you have Outlook set up to always use your default profile, the control starts Outlook in the background and shuts down once you close the page hosting the control. If, on the other hand, you have Outlook set up to prompt you for a profile, Outlook will do so before the control becomes live.

Note: You might get an "Invalid Page Fault in Outllib.dll" or an "Access violation in Outllib.dll" error when using the Outlook View Control. The reason is that there is a conflict with the Outlook View Control and a custom Microsoft Exchange Client extension. An Exchange Client extension was the precursor to the Outlook 2000 COM add-in. It was a C++ component that extended the functionality of Outlook. You will have to disable any custom Exchange Client extensions through the Add-in Manager in Outlook 2000 to get the Outlook View Control to work correctly. See article Q244398 in the Microsoft Knowledge Base (**http://support.microsoft.com/support/kb/articles/q244/3/98.asp**) for more information.

When you place the Outlook View Control on an HTML page, the following code is generated by default:

```
<OBJECT classid=ClsID:
0006F063-0000-0000-C000-000000000046
id=ViewCtlFolder
width="100%"
height="430">
<param name="View" value>
<param name="Folder" value="\\Mailbox - Gomez, Alexander\Inbox">
<param name="Namespace" value="MAPI">
<param name="Restriction" value>
<param name="DeferUpdate" value="0">
</OBJECT>
```

The HTML **<OBJECT>** tags are needed for the Web page to link to the control. The **ClsID** parameter specifies the globally unique identifier (GUID) used to map information about a component class. COM uses the information mapped by the **ClsID** to locate and create an instance of the object associated with the **ClsID**.

You can set the value of any of the Outlook View Control's Properties by using **<PARAM>** tags. Simply set the name attribute to the name of the property you want and the value attribute to the value you want to assign to that property. For example, if we changed the value of view in the code snippet above to

```
<param name="View" value="Unread Messages">
```

we would see only the unread messages in our inbox, since that is the view that would be applied. The value of the folder property in the code example is pointing to our inbox.

Properties of the Outlook View Control

We will now delve into the properties and methods of the Outlook View Control, providing examples and warnings. Our examples will focus on how to use the control from within a digital dashboard—namely, from within an HTML page. Remember that the Outlook View Control is a typical ActiveX control, which means that you can use it from any COM-compliant language, such as Visual Basic. To use the control in Visual Basic, select **Components** in the **Project** menu and select **outlctlx 1.0 Type Library**. You now have such niceties as IntelliSense and a built-in object browser in the Visual Basic development environment. However, most of the functionality of the Outlook View Control is contingent on the control being hosted in an Outlook folder home page and not in a separate program.

As we talked about in the previous section, we can set the properties of the control by using a **<PARAM>** tag of the form

```
<param name="property name" value="property value">
```

Now what if we want to read the return value of a property or execute a method of the control for that matter? The **<PARAM>** tag has no facility for getting a return value, so we have to write code in a scripting language (such as JavaScript or VBScript) and insert it into the Web page to manipulate the control's object model. We are going to use VBScript for our examples and assume that the reader has a basic understanding of the language.

> **Note:** For more information on Microsoft Visual Basic Scripting Edition (VBScript), including code samples, documentation, and help files, see Microsoft's scripting Web site: **http://msdn.microsoft.com/scripting/**.

We use **<SCRIPT>** tags in a Web page to delineate any script code. The **LANGUAGE** parameter allows us to specify whether it is VBScript or JScript. Once we have an Outlook View Control on the folder home page, we can use its **id** property to refer to it in our VBScript code. So using our earlier example, we can write some code to bring up a message box and show us the name of the folder that the control is displaying with the following code:

```
<SCRIPT LANGUAGE=VBScript>
MsgBox ViewCtlFolder.Folder
</SCRIPT>
```

The ActiveFolder Property

The **ActiveFolder** property is a read-only property that returns the folder displayed in the control as an Outlook MAPI folder object. The control must be hosted in an Outlook folder home page or else this property returns Nothing. Once we have a reference to the folder, we can use any of its properties and methods from the Outlook object model. For example, the code that follows displays the path of the folder displayed by the control, retrieves the active folder from the control, and displays the folder's name, entry ID, and item count. This code assumes that we have an Outlook View Control on the home page named **ViewCtlFolder.**

```
<SCRIPT LANGUAGE=VBScript>
MsgBox ViewCtlFolder.Folder
Dim objFolder
Set objFolder = ViewCtlFolder.ActiveFolder
MsgBox objFolder.Name
MsgBox objFolder.EntryID
MsgBox objFolder.Items.Count
</SCRIPT>
```

The DeferUpdate Property

The **DeferUpdate** property controls whether property changes affect the control display. If it is set to True, this property prevents changes to control properties from being displayed in the control. When set to False, it allows the control to update to reflect current property settings. For example, in the code that follows we set the value of **DeferUpdate** to –1 (i.e., True) in the **<PARAM>** tags when we initialize the Outlook View Control. What this means is that when we view the folder home page in Outlook, the control will not be populated with any of the messages in our inbox. Later in the VBScript section of the page we check the value of the property, and if it is True we inform the user and set it to False. The control is now dynamically updated with all of the messages. Any new messages, changes, deletions, and such in the inbox would automatically be shown on this page as well.

> **Note:** When setting a Boolean property within a **<PARAM>** tag, you must use –1 for True and 0 for False. When setting this property in VBScript code in the Web page, you are allowed to use the familiar True and False values.

```
<OBJECT classid=ClsID:
0006F063-0000-0000-C000-000000000046
id=ViewCtlFolder
width="100%"
height="430">
<param name="View" value>
<param name="Folder" value="\\Mailbox - Gomez, Alexander\Inbox">
<param name="Namespace" value="MAPI">
<param name="Restriction" value>
<param name="DeferUpdate" value="-1">
</OBJECT>
<SCRIPT LANGUAGE=VBScript>
If ViewCtlFolder.DeferUpdate Then
    MsgBox "Loading the Outlook View Control..."
    ViewCtlFolder.DeferUpdate = False
End If
</SCRIPT>
```

The Folder Property

The **Folder** property returns or sets the full path of the folder displayed by the control. Despite the warning in the documentation that says that the name of the folder's root message store is returned only if the folder is not in the user's personal mailbox, every time we tried it we got the full path. Some examples of full folder path values that the property expects and returns are

- **\\Mailbox - Alex Gomez\Calendar** for our calendar file
- **\\Public Folders\All Public Folders\MyTeamFolder\My Team Project\Administration** for a public folder we created on our Exchange 2000 server
- **\\MMA Demo\Inbox** for a folder we created in a ".pst" file

If neither the control's **Namespace** property nor **Folder** properties are set and the control is contained in an Outlook folder home page, the control displays whatever the current folder is. If the control's **Namespace** property is set to "MAPI" but the **Folder** property is not set, the control just displays the user's inbox. So, for example, the following code displays the user's inbox (even though the **View** setting suggests that a calendar folder should be displayed):

```
<OBJECT classid=ClsID:
0006F063-0000-0000-C000-000000000046
id=ViewCtlFolder
width="100%"
height="430">
<param name="View" value="Day/Week/Month">
<param name="Namespace" value="MAPI">
<param name="Restriction" value>
<param name="DeferUpdate" value="-1">
</OBJECT>
```

The Namespace Property

The **Namespace** property returns or sets the namespace for the control. The namespace represents the abstract root object for any data source, although MAPI is the only one supported by the control. Again we should mention the tight integration between the **Namespace** property and the **Folder** property. If neither the control's **Namespace** property nor **Folder** property is set and the control is contained in an Outlook folder home page, the control displays whatever the current folder is. If the control's **Namespace** property is set to "MAPI" but the **Folder** property is not set, the control just displays the user's inbox. To set the property in an Outlook folder home page, use the following **<PARAM>** tag:

```
<param name="Namespace" value="MAPI">
```

The OutlookApplication Property

The **OutlookApplication** property is a read-only property that returns the Outlook **Application** object. The control must be hosted in an Outlook folder home page or else this property returns Nothing. Once we have a reference to the **Application** object, we can use any of its properties and methods from the Outlook object model. For example, the following code gets an instance of the Outlook 2000 **Application** object and uses it to send a message:

```
<SCRIPT LANGUAGE=VBScript>
Dim objOLApp
Dim objMailItem
Set objOLApp = ViewCtlFolder.OutlookApplication
Set objMailItem = objOLApp.CreateItem(olMailItem)
objMailItem.Subject = "This is a new message."
```

```
objMailItem.Body = "This is just a test."
objMailItem.Recipients.Add("Alex Gomez")
objMailItem.Send
</SCRIPT>
```

If you try running the same code in Microsoft FrontPage 2000, you will get an "Object required" error because the control is not hosted in an Outlook folder home page.

The Restriction Property

The **Restriction** property is used to apply a filter to the items in the control. The filter is a string with one or more filter clauses joined by the logical operators AND, NOT, and OR. A filter clause is an expression that evaluates to True or False. The syntax is similar to that used in the **Restrict** or **Find** methods in the Outlook 2000 object model. The property names are delimited by square brackets, and the comparison operators allowed within the filter expression are >, <, >=, <=, =, and <>. Comparisons are not case sensitive and do not include subject prefixes added when a message was replied to or forwarded. The Restriction property also does not persist if either the view or the current folder changes.

However, there is a serious limitation to the **Restriction** property, as outlined in article Q249166 in the Microsoft Knowledge Base (see **http://support.microsoft.com/support/kb/articles/q249/1/66.asp**). The **Restriction** property works correctly only if you use table or card views. In a table view, items are in a grid of rows and columns such as a **Simple List** view in a tasks folder. In a card view, items appear as individual cards such as the **Address Cards** view in a contacts folder. For example, the following code displays only our esteemed colleague Andrew Kawa's contact in the control:

```
<OBJECT classid=ClsID:0006F063-0000-0000-C000-000000000046
    id=ViewCtlFolder width="100%" height="430">
    <param name="View" value="Address Cards">
    <param name="Folder" value="\\Mailbox - Gomez, Alexander\Contacts">
    <param name="Namespace" value="MAPI">
    <param name="Restriction" value="[FileAs]= 'Kawa, Andrew'">
    <param name="DeferUpdate" value="0"></OBJECT>
```

And the next block of code displays only the one task item from our **Tasks** folder:

```
<OBJECT classid=ClsID:0006F063-0000-0000-C000-000000000046
    id=ViewCtlFolder width="100%" height="430">
    <param name="View" value="Simple List">
    <param name="Folder" value="\\Mailbox - Gomez, Alexander\Tasks">
    <param name="Namespace" value="MAPI">
```

```
<param name="Restriction" value="[Subject] = 'Chapter Due: XML'">
<param name="DeferUpdate" value="0"></OBJECT>
```

However, the code that follows incorrectly shows all appointments for January instead of just the one hockey game we were interested in. This example illustrates the need to be careful when using **Restriction** values:

```
<OBJECT classid=ClsID:0006F063-0000-0000-C000-000000000046
    id=ViewCtlFolder width="100%" height="430">
    <param name="View" value="Day/Week/Month">
    <param name="Folder" value="\\Mailbox - Gomez, Alexander\Calendar">
    <param name="Namespace" value="MAPI">
    <param name="Restriction" value="[Subject] = 'BU vs UNH'">
    <param name="DeferUpdate" value="0"></OBJECT>
```

You can also simply retrieve the value of the **Restriction** property at any given time. For example, back in our task example, the following code would display a message box reading "[Subject] = 'Chapter Due: XML'":

```
<SCRIPT LANGUAGE=VBScript>
MsgBox ViewCtlFolder.Restriction
</SCRIPT>
```

An empty string is returned if the **Restriction** property is not set.

The View Property

The **View** property returns or sets the Outlook view to use in the control. The view names are case sensitive, and if the **View** parameter value does not exactly match the name of a view available for the current folder, the view in the control does not change. For example, the following code shows only the yearly events set up in our Outlook calendar:

```
<OBJECT classid=ClsID:0006F063-0000-0000-C000-000000000046
    id=ViewCtlFolder width="100%" height="430">
    <param name="View" value="Annual Events">
    <param name="Folder" value="\\Mailbox - Gomez, Alexander\Calendar">
    <param name="Namespace" value="MAPI">
    <param name="Restriction" value>
    <param name="DeferUpdate" value="0"></OBJECT>
```

If we change the value of **View** to a view that does not exist in this folder, the request to change the view is ignored. A summary of the Outlook View Control properties is shown in Table 6.1.

Table 6.1 Properties of the Outlook View Control

Property Name	Description	Type	Access Level
ActiveFolder	Returns the Outlook MAPI Folder object of the folder displayed in the control.	Object	Read-only
DeferUpdate	If set to True, prevents changes to control properties from being displayed in the control.	Boolean	Read/write
Folder	Returns or sets the folder displayed by the control.	String	Read/write
Namespace	Returns or sets the namespace property of the control. Supports only MAPI.	String	Read/write
OutlookApplication	Returns an Outlook Application object.	Object	Read-only
Restriction	Applies a filter to the items displayed in the control.	String	Read/write
View	Returns or sets the Outlook view to use in the control.	String	Read/write

Methods of the Outlook View Control

The AddressBook Method

The **AddressBook** method displays the Outlook **Address Book** dialog box (as shown in Figure 6.5), which allows the user to edit and search on e-mail addresses in the system. The code to call it is quite simple:

```
<SCRIPT LANGUAGE=VBScript>
ViewCtlFolder.AddressBook
</SCRIPT>
```

The AddToPFFavorites Method

The **AddToPFFavorites** method adds the current public folder to the user's Exchange Server public folders **Favorites** folder. Unfortunately, this method consistently generates the error message "Object doesn't support this property or method" (Figure 6.6).

The AdvancedFind Method

The **AdvancedFind** method brings up the **Advanced Find** dialog box (Figure 6.7) when the control is hosted in an Outlook folder home page. The **Advanced Find**

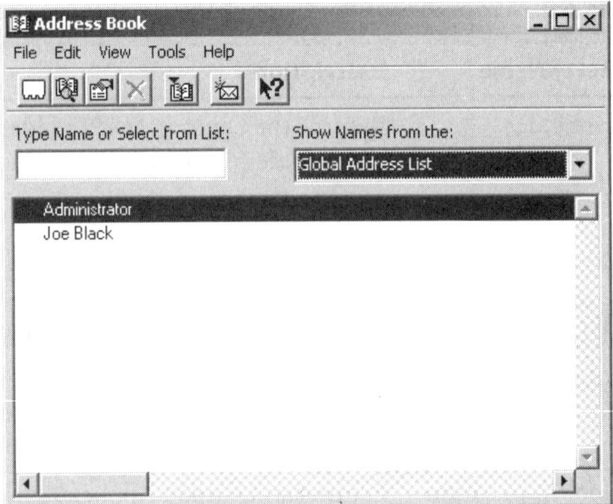

Figure 6.5 The **Address Book** dialog box

dialog box allows the user to search for specific Outlook items on the basis of some pretty robust search criteria, including categories associated with the item, the source of the item, the values of custom or standard Outlook fields in the item, the item's size, and strings in the body of the item. The code to call it is straightforward:

```
<SCRIPT LANGUAGE=VBScript>
ViewCtlFolder.AdvancedFind
</SCRIPT>
```

The Categories Method

The **Categories** method displays the Outlook **Categories** dialog box (Figure 6.8) for the currently selected item or items in the control. The user can select categories for the selected items or modify the master category list. A category is a key-

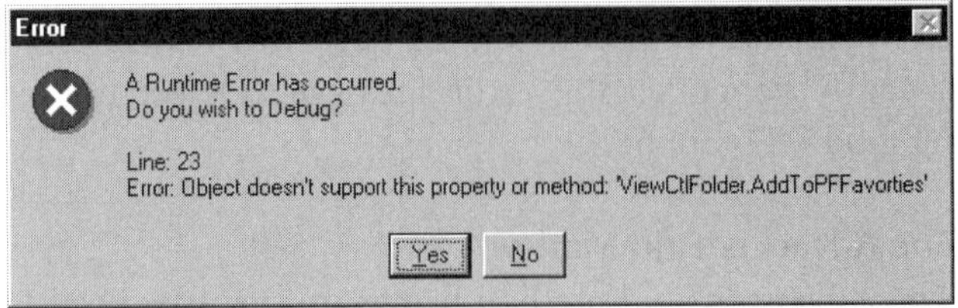

Figure 6.6 The **AddToPFFavorites** error

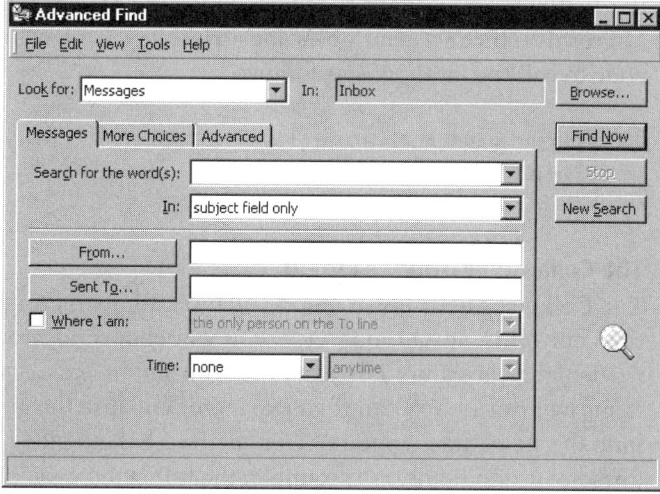

Figure 6.7 The **Advanced Find** dialog box

word or phrase that helps you keep track of Outlook items so that you can easily sort, filter, or group them. It is probably most useful for keeping track of items that are related but stored in different folders. The master category list installed with Outlook 2000 and any additional custom categories you add are stored locally on

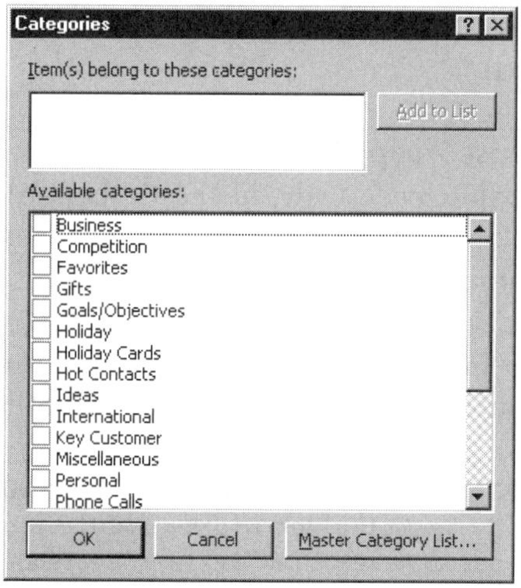

Figure 6.8 The **Categories** dialog box

the Outlook 2000 client machine under the **HKEY_CURRENT_USER\Software\Microsoft\Office\9.0\Outlook\Categories** key under the **MasterList** value. The code to call the method is as follows:

```
<SCRIPT LANGUAGE=VBScript>
ViewCtlFolder.Categories
</SCRIPT>
```

The CollapseAllGroups Method

The **CollapseAllGroups** method collapses all open groups in the view displayed in the control. In an Outlook view you can choose to group items on the basis of a particular field value. For example, you might have a view that shows you mail items by priority. You can then expand or collapse the group headings to display or hide the items they contain. This method has no effect if the view in the control does not group items. For example, the following code displays the contents of our inbox grouped by sender (note the setting of the **View** property). The VBScript code calls the **CollapseAllGroups** method to close the groupings:

```
<OBJECT classid=ClsID:0006F063-0000-0000-C000-000000000046
    id=ViewCtlFolder width="100%" height="430">
    <param name="View" value="By Sender">
    <param name="Folder" value="\\Mailbox - Gomez, Alexander\Inbox">
    <param name="Namespace" value="MAPI">
    <param name="Restriction" value>
    <param name="DeferUpdate" value="0"></OBJECT>
    </td></tr></table>
<SCRIPT LANGUAGE=VBScript>
ViewCtlFolder.CollapseAllGroups
</SCRIPT>
```

The CollapseGroup Method

The only difference between the **CollapseAllGroups** method and the **CollapseGroup** method is that **CollapseGroup** collapses only the group currently selected in the control. If the view in the control does not group items, or if an item in the view is selected rather than a group heading, the method has no effect. For example, if our inbox has the **By Sender** view turned on and **Jamison, Scott** is selected (as in Figure 6.9), the following code will collapse only that group:

```
<OBJECT classid=ClsID:0006F063-0000-0000-C000-000000000046
    id=ViewCtlFolder width="100%" height="430">
    <param name="View" value="By Sender">
    <param name="Folder" value="\\Mailbox - Gomez, Alexander\Inbox">
    <param name="Namespace" value="MAPI">
```

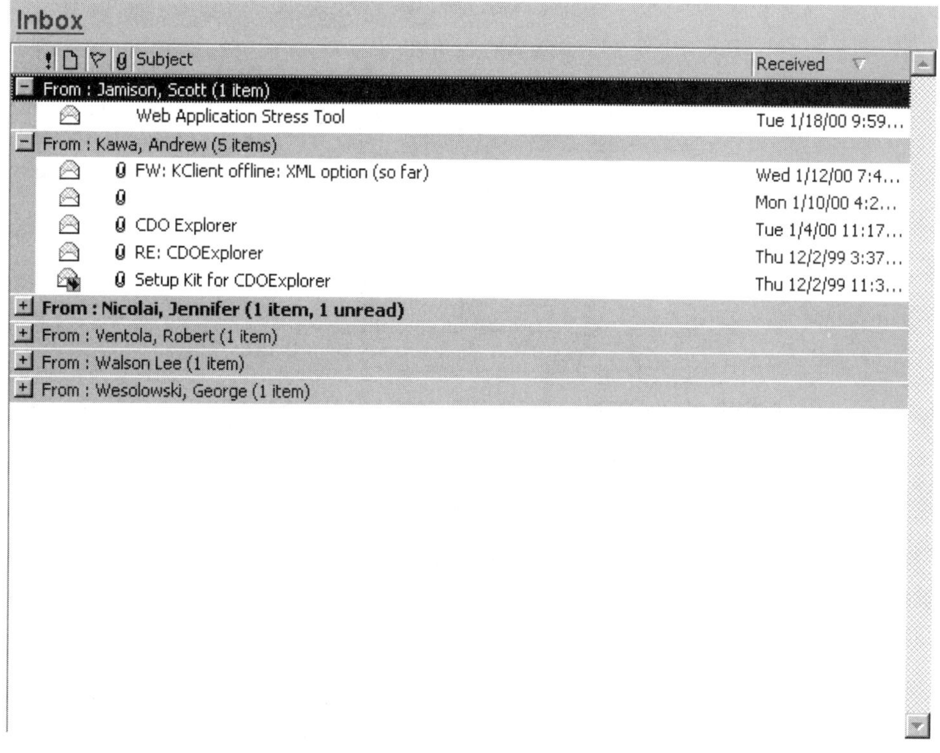

Figure 6.9 CollapseGroup in Outlook 2000

```
        <param name="Restriction" value>
        <param name="DeferUpdate" value="0"></OBJECT>
        </td></tr></table>
    <SCRIPT LANGUAGE=VBScript>
    ViewCtlFolder.CollapseGroup
    </SCRIPT>
```

The CustomizeView Method

The **CustomizeView** method displays the Outlook **View Summary** dialog box (Figure 6.10), which allows the user to customize the current view in the control. This is the same as choosing **Customize Current View...** from the **View** menu in Outlook.

```
<SCRIPT LANGUAGE=VBScript>
ViewCtlFolder.CustomizeView
</SCRIPT>
```

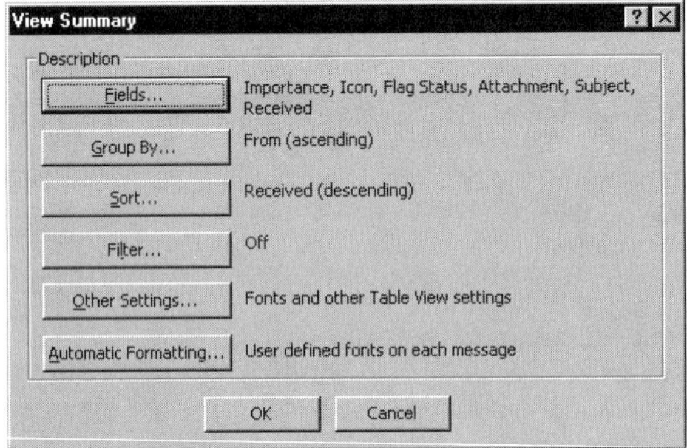

Figure 6.10 The **View Summary** dialog box

The Delete Method

The **Delete** method deletes the groups or items currently selected in the control, after prompting the user for confirmation. If one or more groups are selected, the groups and all of the items in the groups are deleted.

Of course, the way Outlook works is that all items end up going from the folder where the control is pointing to the **Deleted Items** folder when the **Delete** method is executed. There is a setting that empties the **Deleted Items** folder when you exit Outlook (see Figure 6.11). If you don't have this setting turned on, the items removed from your private mailbox stay in the **Deleted Items** folder indefinitely. This begs the question of what happens if you execute the **Delete** method in the **Deleted Items** folder itself, as shown in the following code:

```
<OBJECT classid=ClsID:0006F063-0000-0000-C000-000000000046
    id=ViewCtlFolder width="100%" height="430">
    <param name="Folder" value="\\Mailbox - Gomez, Alexander\
                                Deleted Items">
    <param name="Namespace" value="MAPI">
    <param name="Restriction" value>
    <param name="DeferUpdate" value="0"></OBJECT>
    </td></tr></table>
<SCRIPT LANGUAGE=VBScript>
ViewCtlFolder.Delete
</SCRIPT>
```

If you have selected the setting to warn before permanently deleting items, you will be prompted for confirmation. If you consent, the item or items will be permanently deleted.

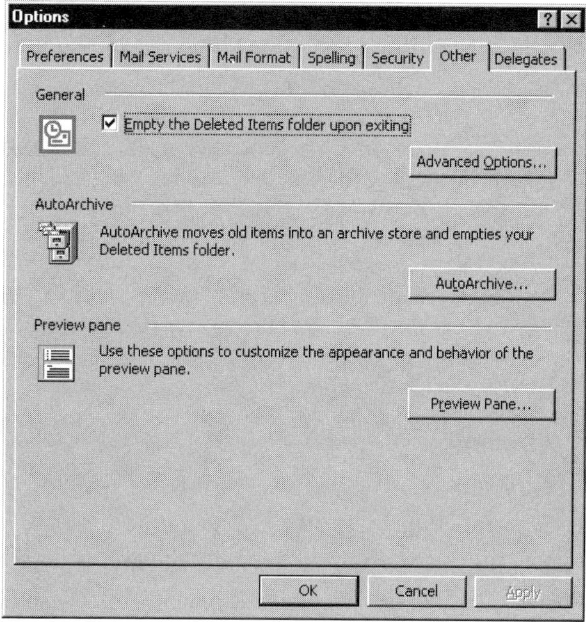

Figure 6.11 The **Options** dialog box

The ExpandAllGroups Method

The **ExpandAllGroups** method expands all of the groups displayed in the control. This has the same effect as choosing **Expand/Collapse Groups** and then **Expand All** from the Outlook **View** menu. For example, the following code expands all of the group headings to show the messages underneath:

```
<OBJECT classid=ClsID:0006F063-0000-0000-C000-000000000046
    id=ViewCtlFolder width="100%" height="430">
    <param name="View" value="By Sender">
    <param name="Folder" value="\\Mailbox - Gomez, Alexander\Inbox">
    <param name="Namespace" value="MAPI">
    <param name="Restriction" value>
    <param name="DeferUpdate" value="0"></OBJECT>
    </td></tr></table>
<SCRIPT LANGUAGE=VBScript>
ViewCtlFolder.ExpandAllGroups
</SCRIPT>
```

If the view displayed in the control does not group items, the method has no effect, as in the following code, which shows the items in our inbox using the regular **Messages** view:

```
<OBJECT classid=ClsID:0006F063-0000-0000-C000-000000000046
    id=ViewCtlFolder width="100%" height="430">
    <param name="View" value="Messages">
    <param name="Folder" value="\\Mailbox - Gomez, Alexander\Inbox">
    <param name="Namespace" value="MAPI">
    <param name="Restriction" value>
    <param name="DeferUpdate" value="0"></OBJECT>
    </td></tr></table>
<SCRIPT LANGUAGE=VBScript>
ViewCtlFolder.ExpandAllGroups
</SCRIPT>
```

The ExpandGroup Method

The **ExpandGroup** method expands the currently selected group or groups in the control. This has the same effect as choosing **Expand/Collapse Groups** and then **Expand Group** from the Outlook **View** menu. For example, the following code expands the first group in our inbox:

```
<OBJECT classid=ClsID:0006F063-0000-0000-C000-000000000046
    id=ViewCtlFolder width="100%" height="430">
    <param name="View" value="By Sender">
    <param name="Folder" value="\\Mailbox - Gomez, Alexander\Inbox">
    <param name="Namespace" value="MAPI">
    <param name="Restriction" value>
    <param name="DeferUpdate" value="0"></OBJECT>
    </td></tr></table>
<SCRIPT LANGUAGE=VBScript>
ViewCtlFolder.ExpandGroup
</SCRIPT>
```

If the view in the control does not group items or if an item is selected, the method has no effect.

The FlagItem Method

The **FlagItem** method brings up the Outlook **Flag for Follow Up** dialog box for the selected item in the control (Figure 6.12). This box allows you to flag an Outlook message or contact to remind you to take some sort of follow-up action. It even allows you to schedule reminders on the date and time that the follow-up action is

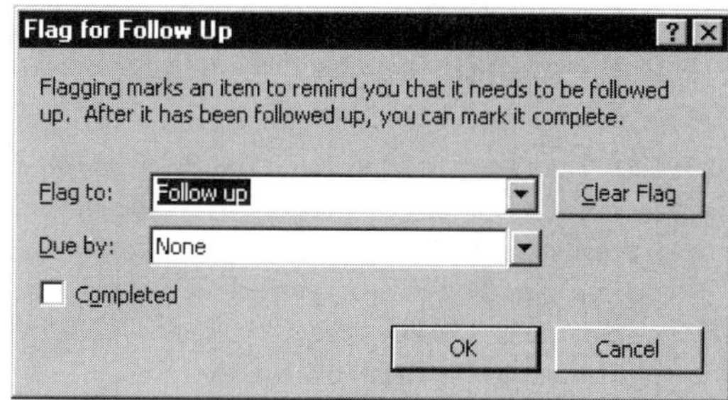

Figure 6.12 The **Flag for Follow Up** dialog box

due. If more than one item is selected in the control, the dialog box applies only to the last item selected. This has the same effect as selecting **Flag for Follow Up...** from the **Actions** menu in Outlook. The following code calls the dialog box for the first item in our inbox:

```
<OBJECT classid=ClsID:0006F063-0000-0000-C000-000000000046
    id=ViewCtlFolder width="100%" height="430">
    <param name="View" value="Messages">
    <param name="Folder" value="\\Mailbox - Gomez, Alexander\Inbox">
    <param name="Namespace" value="MAPI">
    <param name="Restriction" value>
    <param name="DeferUpdate" value="0"></OBJECT>
    </td></tr></table>
<SCRIPT LANGUAGE=VBScript>
ViewCtlFolder.FlagItem
</SCRIPT>
```

The ForceUpdate Method

The **ForceUpdate** method refreshes the view control, applying any property changes made since the **DeferUpdate** property was last set to True. As you may recall, the **DeferUpdate** property controls whether property changes affect the control display. If **DeferUpdate** is set to True, any changes to the control's properties are prevented from being displayed in the control. The **ForceUpdate** method acts as an override to the **DeferUpdate** property. For example, in the following code we set up the Outlook View Control to initially display our inbox. Notice that we first set the **DeferUpdate** property to 0 (False) so that the control will display the inbox. In the VBScript section, we set **DeferUpdate** to True. We then set up the same control to display our calendar, but the control doesn't change until the user responds to the prompt and the **DeferUpdate** method is executed:

```
<OBJECT classid=ClsID:0006F063-0000-0000-C000-000000000046
    id=ViewCtlFolder width="100%" height="430">
    <param name="View" value="Messages">
    <param name="Folder" value="\\Mailbox - Gomez, Alexander\Inbox">
    <param name="Namespace" value="MAPI">
    <param name="Restriction" value>
    <param name="DeferUpdate" value="0"></OBJECT>
    </td></tr></table>
<SCRIPT LANGUAGE=VBScript>
MsgBox "Here's your Inbox."
ViewCtlFolder.DeferUpdate=True
ViewCtlFolder.View="Day/Week/Month"
ViewCtlFolder.Folder="\\Mailbox - Gomez, Alexander\Calendar"
If MsgBox ("Do you want to update the control now?", vbYesNo
           + vbQuestion, "Outlook View Control Demo") = vbYes Then
           ViewCtlFolder.ForceUpdate
End If
</SCRIPT>
```

The Forward Method

The **Forward** method executes a forward on the item or items selected in the control. This sets up an e-mail message for you to forward to another user. If you forward a regular Outlook mail message, you will see the text of the original message in the body of the forwarded e-mail along with any attachments in the original message. If you try to forward an Outlook contact, task, appointment, or note, you will see the original Outlook contact, task, appointment, or note as an attachment to the forwarded message.

For example, the following code displays the items in our task folder using an Outlook View Control. A VBScript subroutine called **cmdMethod_Click** calls the **Forward** method on any selected items. In addition, a button on the form called **cmdMethod** can be pressed when the items to be forwarded have been selected. The **cmdMethod_Click** subroutine is called when the button is clicked because the click event of the button has been bound to the subroutine. Figure 6.13 shows the results of executing the **Forward** method on a selected task in the Outlook View Control.

```
<OBJECT classid=ClsID:0006F063-0000-0000-C000-000000000046
    id=ViewCtlFolder width="100%" height="430">
    <param name="View" value="Simple List">
    <param name="Folder" value="\\Mailbox - Gomez, Alexander\Tasks">
    <param name="Namespace" value="MAPI">
```

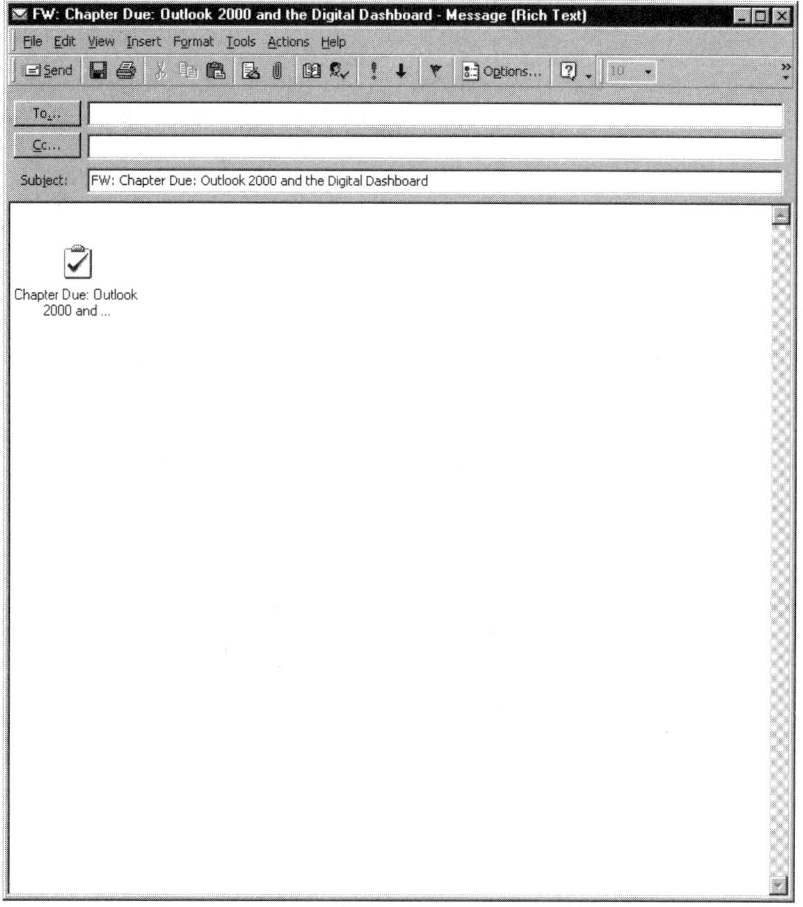

Figure 6.13 Forwarding a task in Outlook 2000

```
    <param name="Restriction" value>
    <param name="DeferUpdate" value="0"></OBJECT>
    </td></tr></table>
<SCRIPT LANGUAGE=VBScript>
Sub cmdMethod_Click
    If MsgBox ("Do you want to forward the selected item(s) in your task
               list?", vbYesNo + vbQuestion, "Outlook View Control
               Demo") = vbYes Then ViewCtlFolder.Forward
    End If
End Sub
</SCRIPT>
```

```
<form method="POST" action="--WEBBOT-SELF--">
    <!--webbot bot="SaveResults" U-File="fpweb:///_private/
        form_results.txt"
    S-Format="TEXT/CSV" S-Label-Fields="TRUE" -->
    <p><input type="button" value="Forward" name="cmdMethod"
        onclick=cmdMethod_Click>
    <input type="submit" value="Submit" name="B1">
    <input type="reset" value="Reset" name="B2"></p>
</form>
```

The GoToToday Method

The **GoToToday** Method sets the day displayed in the control to the current day. This method works only for **Timeline** and **Day/Week/Month** views. The code that follows displays the items in our calendar folder. A VBScript subroutine called **cmdMethod_Click** calls the **GoToToday** method. In addition, there is a button on the form called **cmdMethod**. The **cmdMethod_Click** subroutine is called when the button is clicked because the click event of the button has been bound to the subroutine.

```
<OBJECT classid=ClsID:0006F063-0000-0000-C000-000000000046
    id=ViewCtlFolder width="100%" height="430">
    <param name="View" value="Day/Week/Month">
    <param name="Folder" value="\\Mailbox - Gomez, Alexander\Calendar">
    <param name="Namespace" value="MAPI">
    <param name="Restriction" value>
    <param name="DeferUpdate" value="0"></OBJECT>
    </td></tr></table>
<SCRIPT LANGUAGE=VBScript>
Sub cmdMethod_Click
    If MsgBox ("Do you want to change the view to the current day?",
               vbYesNo + vbQuestion, "Outlook View Control Demo") =
               vbYes Then ViewCtlFolder.GoToToday
    End If
End Sub
</SCRIPT>
<form method="POST" action="--WEBBOT-SELF--">
    <!--webbot bot="SaveResults" U-File="fpweb:///_private/
        form_results.txt"
    S-Format="TEXT/CSV" S-Label-Fields="TRUE" -->
    <p><input type="button" value="Go To Today" name="cmdMethod"
        onclick=cmdMethod_Click>
    <input type="submit" value="Submit" name="B1">
    <input type="reset" value="Reset" name="B2"></p>
</form>
```

The GroupBy Method

The **GroupBy** method displays the Outlook **Group By** dialog box (Figure 6.14), which allows the user to group items in the current view displayed in the control.

Note that this method is valid only for table-type views. The following code displays our inbox and calls the **GroupBy** method when the user hits the button:

```
<OBJECT classid=ClsID:0006F063-0000-0000-C000-000000000046
    id=ViewCtlFolder width="100%" height="430">
    <param name="View" value="Messages">
    <param name="Folder" value="\\Mailbox - Gomez, Alexander\Inbox">
    <param name="Namespace" value="MAPI">
    <param name="Restriction" value>
    <param name="DeferUpdate" value="0"></OBJECT>
    </td></tr></table>
<SCRIPT LANGUAGE=VBScript>
Sub cmdMethod_Click
    If MsgBox ("Do you want to see the Group By dialog box?", vbYesNo
             + vbQuestion, "Outlook View Control Demo") = vbYes Then
             ViewCtlFolder.GroupBy
    End If
End Sub
</SCRIPT>
<form method="POST" action="--WEBBOT-SELF--">
    <!--webbot bot="SaveResults" U-File="fpweb:///_private/
        form_results.txt"
    S-Format="TEXT/CSV" S-Label-Fields="TRUE" -->
    <p><input type="button" value="Group By" name="cmdMethod"
        onclick=cmdMethod_Click>
    <input type="submit" value="Submit" name="B1">
    <input type="reset" value="Reset" name="B2"></p>
</form>
```

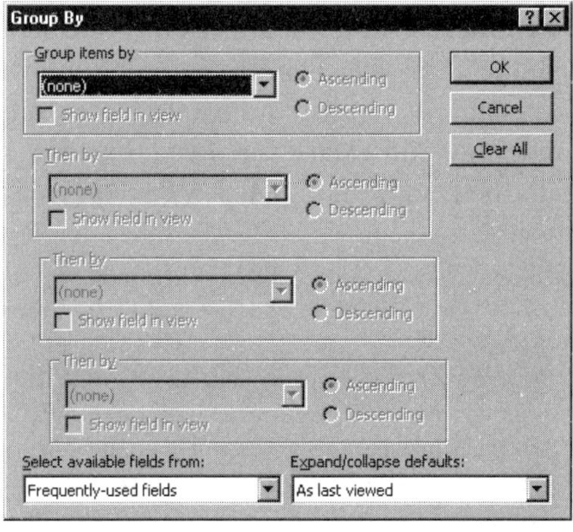

Figure 6.14 The **Group By** dialog box

The MarkAllAsRead Method

The **MarkAllAsRead** method marks as read all of the items in the folder displayed in the control. The user is prompted for confirmation before any change is made. The following code marks all of the items in our inbox as read when the appropriate button is clicked:

```
<OBJECT classid=ClsID:0006F063-0000-0000-C000-000000000046
    id=ViewCtlFolder width="100%" height="430">
    <param name="View" value="Messages">
    <param name="Folder" value="\\Mailbox - Gomez, Alexander\Inbox">
    <param name="Namespace" value="MAPI">
    <param name="Restriction" value>
    <param name="DeferUpdate" value="0"></OBJECT>
    </td></tr></table>
<SCRIPT LANGUAGE=VBScript>
Sub cmdMethod_Click
ViewCtlFolder.MarkAllAsRead
End Sub
</SCRIPT>
<form method="POST" action="--WEBBOT-SELF--">
    <!--webbot bot="SaveResults" U-File="fpweb:///_private/
        form_results.txt"
    S-Format="TEXT/CSV" S-Label-Fields="TRUE" -->
    <p><input type="button" value="Mark All As Read" name="cmdMethod"
        onclick=cmdMethod_Click>
    <input type="submit" value="Submit" name="B1">
    <input type="reset" value="Reset" name="B2"></p>
</form>
```

The MarkAsRead Method

The **MarkAsRead** method marks as read the selected items in the folder displayed in the control. The user is prompted for confirmation before any change is made. The code that follows displays the items in our inbox. We can then select a few items and press the **Mark As Read** button, which executes the **MarkAsRead** method in the **cmdMethod_Click VBScript** subroutine:

```
<OBJECT classid=ClsID:0006F063-0000-0000-C000-000000000046
    id=ViewCtlFolder width="100%" height="430">
    <param name="View" value="Messages">
    <param name="Folder" value="\\Mailbox - Gomez, Alexander\Inbox">
    <param name="Namespace" value="MAPI">
    <param name="Restriction" value>
    <param name="DeferUpdate" value="0"></OBJECT>
    </td></tr></table>
```

```
<SCRIPT LANGUAGE=VBScript>
Sub cmdMethod_Click
ViewCtlFolder.MarkAsRead
End Sub
</SCRIPT>
<form method="POST" action="--WEBBOT-SELF--">
    <!--webbot bot="SaveResults" U-File="fpweb:///_private/
        form_results.txt"
    S-Format="TEXT/CSV" S-Label-Fields="TRUE" -->
    <p><input type="button" value="Mark As Read" name="cmdMethod"
        onclick=cmdMethod_Click>
    <input type="submit" value="Submit" name="B1">
    <input type="reset" value="Reset" name="B2"></p>
</form>
```

The MarkAsUnread Method

The **MarkAsUnread** method marks as unread the selected items in the folder displayed in the control. The user is prompted for confirmation before any change is made. The code that follows displays the items in our inbox. We can then select a few of them and press the **Mark As Unread** button, which executes the **MarkAsUnread** method in the **cmdMethod_Click VBScript** subroutine:

```
<OBJECT classid=ClsID:0006F063-0000-0000-C000-000000000046
    id=ViewCtlFolder width="100%" height="430">
    <param name="View" value="Messages">
    <param name="Folder" value="\\Mailbox - Gomez, Alexander\Inbox">
    <param name="Namespace" value="MAPI">
    <param name="Restriction" value>
    <param name="DeferUpdate" value="0"></OBJECT>
    </td></tr></table>
<SCRIPT LANGUAGE=VBScript>
Sub cmdMethod_Click
ViewCtlFolder.MarkAsUnread
End Sub
</SCRIPT>
<form method="POST" action="--WEBBOT-SELF--">
    <!--webbot bot="SaveResults" U-File="fpweb:///_private/
        form_results.txt"
    S-Format="TEXT/CSV" S-Label-Fields="TRUE" -->
    <p><input type="button" value="Mark As Unread" name="cmdMethod"
        onclick=cmdMethod_Click>
    <input type="submit" value="Submit" name="B1">
    <input type="reset" value="Reset" name="B2"></p>
</form>
```

The MoveItem Method

The **MoveItem** method displays the Outlook **Move Items** dialog box (Figure 6.15), which allows the user to select a folder into which the selected items in the control will be moved. The following code allows us to select items in our inbox and move them to a designated folder:

```
<OBJECT classid=ClsID:0006F063-0000-0000-C000-000000000046
    id=ViewCtlFolder width="100%" height="430">
    <param name="View" value="Messages">
    <param name="Folder" value="\\Mailbox - Gomez, Alexander\Inbox">
    <param name="Namespace" value="MAPI">
    <param name="Restriction" value>
    <param name="DeferUpdate" value="0"></OBJECT>
    </td></tr></table>
<SCRIPT LANGUAGE=VBScript>
Sub cmdMethod_Click
ViewCtlFolder.MoveItem
End Sub
</SCRIPT>
<form method="POST" action="--WEBBOT-SELF--">
    <!--webbot bot="SaveResults" U-File="fpweb:///_private/
        form_results.txt"
    S-Format="TEXT/CSV" S-Label-Fields="TRUE" -->
    <p><input type="button" value="Move" name="cmdMethod"
        onclick=cmdMethod_Click>
    <input type="submit" value="Submit" name="B1">
    <input type="reset" value="Reset" name="B2"></p>
</form>
```

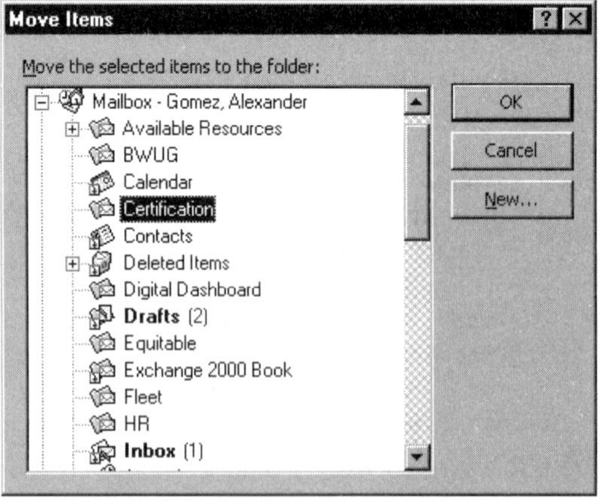

Figure 6.15 The **Move Items** dialog box

The NewAppointment Method

The **NewAppointment** method creates and displays a new Outlook **Appointment** item. If the control is displaying a folder capable of holding calendar items, the new appointment will be saved in the folder displayed in the control. Otherwise the appointment is saved to the user's default calendar folder. In Outlook, folders can display items of only the particular type specified when the folder is created. The following code displays our default calendar folder and provides a button that allows the user to create a new **Appointment** item at will:

```
<OBJECT classid=ClsID:0006F063-0000-0000-C000-000000000046
    id=ViewCtlFolder width="100%" height="430">
    <param name="View" value="Day/Week/Month">
    <param name="Folder" value="\\Mailbox - Gomez, Alexander\Calendar">
    <param name="Namespace" value="MAPI">
    <param name="Restriction" value>
    <param name="DeferUpdate" value="0"></OBJECT>
    </td></tr></table>
<SCRIPT LANGUAGE=VBScript>
Sub cmdMethod_Click
ViewCtlFolder.NewAppointment
End Sub
</SCRIPT>
<form method="POST" action="--WEBBOT-SELF--">
    <!--webbot bot="SaveResults" U-File="fpweb:///_private/
        form_results.txt"
    S-Format="TEXT/CSV" S-Label-Fields="TRUE" -->
    <p><input type="button" value="New Appointment" name="cmdMethod"
        onclick=cmdMethod_Click>
    <input type="submit" value="Submit" name="B1">
    <input type="reset" value="Reset" name="B2"></p>
</form>
```

The NewContact Method

The **NewContact** method creates and displays a new Outlook contact. If the control is displaying a folder capable of holding contact items, the new contact will be saved in the folder displayed in the control. Otherwise, it is saved to the user's default contacts folder. The following code displays our default contacts folder in the control and provides a button that allows the user to create a new contact there:

```
<OBJECT classid=ClsID:0006F063-0000-0000-C000-000000000046
    id=ViewCtlFolder width="100%" height="430">
    <param name="View" value="Address Cards">
    <param name="Folder" value="\\Mailbox - Gomez, Alexander\Contacts">
    <param name="Namespace" value="MAPI">
```

```
    <param name="Restriction" value>
    <param name="DeferUpdate" value="0"></OBJECT>
    </td></tr></table>
<SCRIPT LANGUAGE=VBScript>
Sub cmdMethod_Click
ViewCtlFolder.NewContact
End Sub
</SCRIPT>
<form method="POST" action="--WEBBOT-SELF--">
    <!--webbot bot="SaveResults" U-File="fpweb:///_private/
        form_results.txt"
    S-Format="TEXT/CSV" S-Label-Fields="TRUE" -->
    <p><input type="button" value="New Contact" name="cmdMethod"
        onclick=cmdMethod_Click>
    <input type="submit" value="Submit" name="B1">
    <input type="reset" value="Reset" name="B2"></p>
</form>
```

The NewDefaultItem Method

The **NewDefaultItem** method creates and displays a new Outlook item. The item type is the default item type for the folder displayed in the control. This means that if you execute the method on the **Tasks** folder, you will create an Outlook **Task** item. If you execute the method on the **Contacts** folder, you will create an Outlook **Contact** item and so on. The code that follows displays the **Notes** folder in the Outlook View Control. Therefore, when the user hits the **New Item** button and executes the **NewDefaultItem** method, we can create a new Outlook **Note**.

```
<OBJECT classid=ClsID:0006F063-0000-0000-C000-000000000046
    id=ViewCtlFolder width="100%" height="430">
    <param name="View" value="Notes List">
    <param name="Folder" value="\\Mailbox - Gomez, Alexander\Notes">
    <param name="Namespace" value="MAPI">
    <param name="Restriction" value>
    <param name="DeferUpdate" value="0"></OBJECT>
    </td></tr></table>
<SCRIPT LANGUAGE=VBScript>
Sub cmdMethod_Click
ViewCtlFolder.NewDefaultItem
End Sub
</SCRIPT>
<form method="POST" action="--WEBBOT-SELF--">
    <!--webbot bot="SaveResults" U-File="fpweb:///_private/
        form_results.txt"
    S-Format="TEXT/CSV" S-Label-Fields="TRUE" -->
    <p><input type="button" value="New Item" name="cmdMethod"
        onclick=cmdMethod_Click>
```

```
    <input type="submit" value="Submit" name="B1">
    <input type="reset" value="Reset" name="B2"></p>
</form>
```

The NewDistributionList Method

The **NewDistributionList** method creates and displays a new personal distribution list. A personal distribution list is a collection of contacts that provides an easy way to send an e-mail message to a group of people. For example, in Figure 6.16 we have a distribution list of college hockey fans. If the control is displaying a folder capable of holding Outlook contacts, the new distribution list is saved to the folder displayed in the control. Otherwise, it is saved in the default contacts folder. The following code displays our default contacts folder and provides a button that creates a new distribution list by calling the **NewDistributionList** method:

```
<OBJECT classid=ClsID:0006F063-0000-0000-C000-000000000046
    id=ViewCtlFolder width="100%" height="430">
    <param name="View" value="Address Cards">
    <param name="Folder" value="\\Mailbox - Gomez, Alexander\Contacts">
```

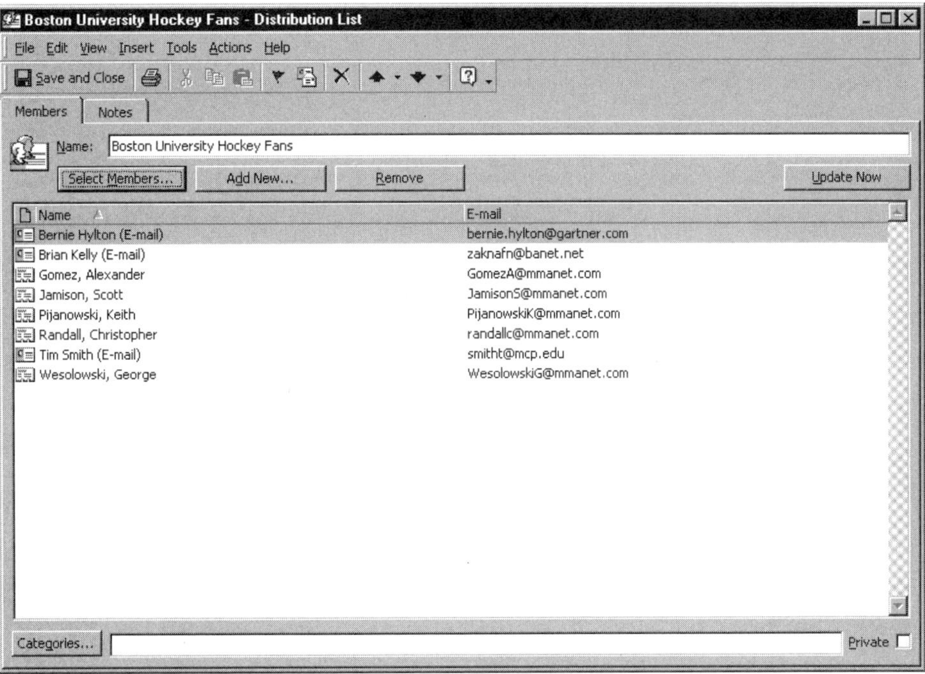

Figure 6.16 A distribution list in Outlook 2000

```
    <param name="Namespace" value="MAPI">
    <param name="Restriction" value>
    <param name="DeferUpdate" value="0"></OBJECT>
    </td></tr></table>
<SCRIPT LANGUAGE=VBScript>
Sub cmdMethod_Click
ViewCtlFolder.NewDistributionList
End Sub
</SCRIPT>
<form method="POST" action="--WEBBOT-SELF--">
    <!--webbot bot="SaveResults" U-File="fpweb:///_private/
        form_results.txt"
    S-Format="TEXT/CSV" S-Label-Fields="TRUE" -->
    <p><input type="button" value="New Distribution List" name="
        cmdMethod" onclick=cmdMethod_Click>
    <input type="submit" value="Submit" name="B1">
    <input type="reset" value="Reset" name="B2"></p>
</form>
```

The NewForm Method

The **NewForm** method displays the Outlook **Choose Form** dialog box (Figure 6.17), which allows the user to create a new Outlook item by selecting a form from a forms library. The form can be any of the standard Outlook forms or a custom form. If the folder displayed in the control can't contain an item based on the form you've selected, the new item is saved in that type's default Outlook folder. For

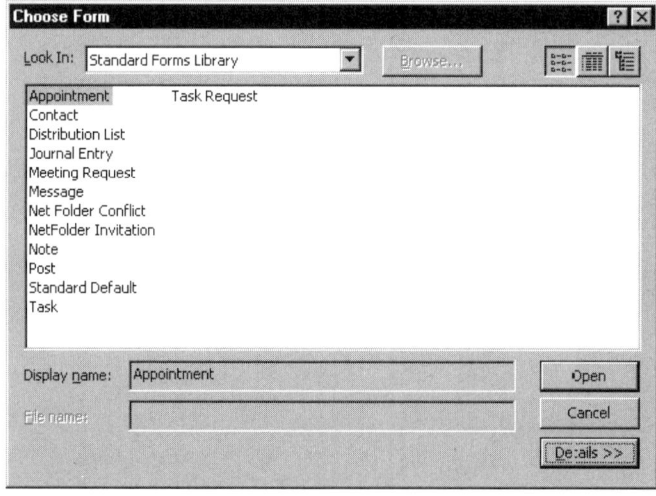

Figure 6.17 The **Choose Form** dialog box

example, if the control is displaying a contacts folder and the user selects the Outlook **Task** form, that new item will be saved in the user's default **Tasks** folder. The following code provides a button that executes the **NewForm** method and brings up the **Choose Form** dialog box:

```
<SCRIPT LANGUAGE=VBScript>
Sub cmdMethod_Click
ViewCtlFolder.NewForm
End Sub
</SCRIPT>
<form method="POST" action="--WEBBOT-SELF--">
    <!--webbot bot="SaveResults" U-File="fpweb:///_private/
        form_results.txt"
    S-Format="TEXT/CSV" S-Label-Fields="TRUE" -->
    <p><input type="button" value="New Form" name="cmdMethod"
        onclick=cmdMethod_Click>
    <input type="submit" value="Submit" name="B1">
    <input type="reset" value="Reset" name="B2"></p>
</form>
```

The NewJournalEntry Method

The **NewJournalEntry** method creates and displays a new journal entry. If the control is displaying a journal folder, the new journal entry is saved to the folder displayed in the control. Otherwise, the journal entry is saved to the user's default journal folder. The following code provides a button on an Outlook folder home page to execute the **NewJournalEntry** method:

```
<SCRIPT LANGUAGE=VBScript>
Sub cmdMethod_Click
ViewCtlFolder.NewJournalEntry
End Sub
</SCRIPT>
<form method="POST" action="--WEBBOT-SELF--">
    <!--webbot bot="SaveResults" U-File="fpweb:///_private/
        form_results.txt"
    S-Format="TEXT/CSV" S-Label-Fields="TRUE" -->
    <p><input type="button" value="New Journal Entry" name="cmdMethod"
        onclick=cmdMethod_Click>
    <input type="submit" value="Submit" name="B1">
    <input type="reset" value="Reset" name="B2"></p>
</form>
```

The NewMeetingRequest Method

The **NewMeetingRequest** method creates and displays a new meeting request. If the control is displaying a **Calendar** folder, the corresponding appointment is saved to the folder displayed in the control when the meeting request is sent. Otherwise, the appointment is saved to the user's default **Calendar** folder. Responses to the meeting request are tallied only if the appointment is saved to the user's default **Calendar** folder. The following code calls the **NewMeetingRequest** method when the user presses the appropriate button on an Outlook folder home page:

```
<SCRIPT LANGUAGE=VBScript>
Sub cmdMethod_Click
ViewCtlFolder.NewMeetingRequest
End Sub
</SCRIPT>
<form method="POST" action="--WEBBOT-SELF--">
    <!--webbot bot="SaveResults" U-File="fpweb:///_private/
        form_results.txt"
    S-Format="TEXT/CSV" S-Label-Fields="TRUE" -->
    <p><input type="button" value="New Meeting Request" name="
        cmdMethod" onclick=cmdMethod_Click>
    <input type="submit" value="Submit" name="B1">
    <input type="reset" value="Reset" name="B2"></p>
</form>
```

The NewMessage Method

The **NewMessage** method creates and displays a new e-mail message. The following code executes the **NewMessage** method when the user hits the **New Message** button:

```
<OBJECT classid=ClsID:0006F063-0000-0000-C000-000000000046
    id=ViewCtlFolder width="100%" height="430">
    <param name="View" value="Messages">
    <param name="Folder" value="\\Mailbox - Gomez, Alexander\Inbox">
    <param name="Namespace" value="MAPI">
    <param name="Restriction" value>
    <param name="DeferUpdate" value="0"></OBJECT>
    </td></tr></table>
<SCRIPT LANGUAGE=VBScript>
Sub cmdMethod_Click
ViewCtlFolder.NewMessage
End Sub
</SCRIPT>
<form method="POST" action="--WEBBOT-SELF--">
    <!--webbot bot="SaveResults" U-File="fpweb:///_private/
        form_results.txt"
    S-Format="TEXT/CSV" S-Label-Fields="TRUE" -->
    <p><input type="button" value="New Message" name="cmdMethod"
        onclick=cmdMethod_Click>
```

```
    <input type="submit" value="Submit" name="B1">
    <input type="reset" value="Reset" name="B2"></p>
</form>
```

The NewNote Method

The **NewNote** method creates and displays a new **Note** item. Notes are the electronic equivalent of paper sticky notes, which you can use to jot down questions, ideas, reminders—in short, anything you would write on notepaper. You can leave notes open on the screen while you work, and when you change a note the changes are saved automatically.

If the control is displaying a **Notes** folder, the new note is saved to the folder displayed in the control. Otherwise, the note is saved to the user's default **Notes** folder. The following code displays our default notes folder in the control. If the user hits the **New Note** button, the **NewNote** method is executed:

```
<OBJECT classid=ClsID:0006F063-0000-0000-C000-000000000046
    id=ViewCtlFolder width="100%" height="430">
    <param name="View" value="Notes List">
    <param name="Folder" value="\\Mailbox - Gomez, Alexander\Notes">
    <param name="Namespace" value="MAPI">
    <param name="Restriction" value>
    <param name="DeferUpdate" value="0"></OBJECT>
    </td></tr></table>
<SCRIPT LANGUAGE=VBScript>
Sub cmdMethod_Click
ViewCtlFolder.NewNote
End Sub
</SCRIPT>
<form method="POST" action="--WEBBOT-SELF--">
    <!--webbot bot="SaveResults" U-File="fpweb:///_private/
        form_results.txt"
    S-Format="TEXT/CSV" S-Label-Fields="TRUE" -->
    <p><input type="button" value="New Note" name="cmdMethod"
        onclick=cmdMethod_Click>
    <input type="submit" value="Submit" name="B1">
    <input type="reset" value="Reset" name="B2"></p>
</form>
```

The NewOfficeDocument Method

The **NewOfficeDocument** method creates and displays a new Microsoft Office document. This method first prompts the user to select the type of Office document to create (as shown in Figure 6.18): a Microsoft Excel worksheet or chart, a Microsoft Word document, or a Microsoft PowerPoint presentation. It then asks the user whether the document is to be sent as a mail message or posted to the folder displayed in the control. If you choose to post the document to the folder displayed in the control, you get the standard Word, Excel, or PowerPoint interface with a **Post** button to post the item when finished. If you choose to send the document as a mail message, you get a custom Outlook form with two tabs. In the **Message** tab you can choose the message's recipients. In the **Document** tab you can edit the document in the appropriate Office user interface. The following code executes the **NewOfficeDocument** method at the touch of a button:

```
<OBJECT classid=ClsID:0006F063-0000-0000-C000-000000000046
    id=ViewCtlFolder width="100%" height="430">
    <param name="View" value="Messages">
    <param name="Folder" value="\\Mailbox - Gomez, Alexander\Inbox">
    <param name="Namespace" value="MAPI">
    <param name="Restriction" value>
    <param name="DeferUpdate" value="0"></OBJECT>
    </td></tr></table>
<SCRIPT LANGUAGE=VBScript>
Sub cmdMethod_Click
ViewCtlFolder.NewOfficeDocument
End Sub
</SCRIPT>
<form method="POST" action="--WEBBOT-SELF--">
    <!--webbot bot="SaveResults" U-File="fpweb:///_private/
        form_results.txt"
```

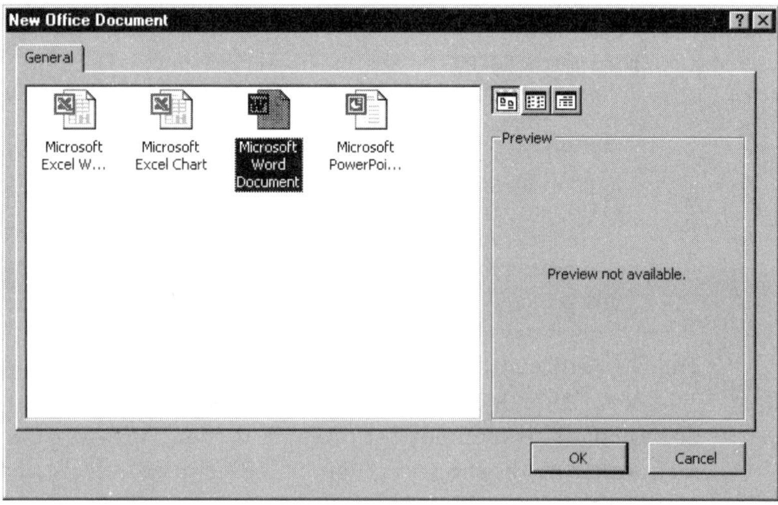

Figure 6.18 Choosing your Office document type in Outlook 2000

```
    S-Format="TEXT/CSV" S-Label-Fields="TRUE" -->
    <p><input type="button" value="New Office Document" name="
        cmdMethod" onclick=cmdMethod_Click>
    <input type="submit" value="Submit" name="B1">
    <input type="reset" value="Reset" name="B2"></p>
</form>
```

The NewPost Method

The **NewPost** method creates and displays a new **Post** item. A **Post** item is a standard Outlook item used to carry on discussions with other users, usually in a public folder. When the user posts the message, it is posted to the folder displayed in the control. This method has no effect if the folder displayed in the control does not support messages. For example, the code that follows displays our inbox in the control. When the user clicks the **New Post** button, a blank post form comes up and the post is saved to our inbox:

```
<OBJECT classid=ClsID:0006F063-0000-0000-C000-000000000046
    id=ViewCtlFolder width="100%" height="430">
    <param name="View" value="Messages">
    <param name="Folder" value="\\Mailbox - Gomez, Alexander\Inbox">
    <param name="Namespace" value="MAPI">
    <param name="Restriction" value>
    <param name="DeferUpdate" value="0"></OBJECT>
    </td></tr></table>
<SCRIPT LANGUAGE=VBScript>
Sub cmdMethod_Click
ViewCtlFolder.NewPost
End Sub
</SCRIPT>
<form method="POST" action="--WEBBOT-SELF--">
    <!--webbot bot="SaveResults" U-File="fpweb:///_private/
        form_results.txt"
    S-Format="TEXT/CSV" S-Label-Fields="TRUE" -->
    <p><input type="button" value="New Post" name="cmdMethod"
        onclick=cmdMethod_Click>
    <input type="submit" value="Submit" name="B1">
    <input type="reset" value="Reset" name="B2"></p>
</form>
```

If the control were displaying our **Tasks** folder, for example, pressing the **New Post** button would have no effect. The post form wouldn't even come up.

The NewTask Method

The **NewTask** method creates and displays a new task. A task is a personal or work-related errand you want to track through completion in Outlook. A task can occur once or repeatedly (a recurring task). A recurring task can repeat at regular intervals, or it can repeat on the basis of the date you mark the task complete.

If the control is displaying a **Tasks** folder, the new task is saved to the folder displayed in the control. Otherwise, the task is saved to the user's default **Tasks** folder. The following code displays our **Tasks** folder and provides a button that executes the **NewTask** method:

```
<OBJECT classid=ClsID:0006F063-0000-0000-C000-000000000046
    id=ViewCtlFolder width="100%" height="430">
    <param name="View" value="Simple List">
    <param name="Folder" value="\\Mailbox - Gomez, Alexander\Tasks">
    <param name="Namespace" value="MAPI">
    <param name="Restriction" value>
    <param name="DeferUpdate" value="0"></OBJECT>
    </td></tr></table>
<SCRIPT LANGUAGE=VBScript>
Sub cmdMethod_Click
ViewCtlFolder.NewTask
End Sub
</SCRIPT>
<form method="POST" action="--WEBBOT-SELF--">
    <!--webbot bot="SaveResults" U-File="fpweb:///_private/
        form_results.txt"
    S-Format="TEXT/CSV" S-Label-Fields="TRUE" -->
    <p><input type="button" value="New Task" name="cmdMethod"
        onclick=cmdMethod_Click>
    <input type="submit" value="Submit" name="B1">
    <input type="reset" value="Reset" name="B2"></p>
</form>
```

The NewTaskRequest Method

The **NewTaskRequest** method creates and displays a new **Task Request** item. A task request is a request sent in an e-mail message asking the recipient of the message to complete the task from the sender. If the recipient of the message accepts the task, the task is added to the recipient's task list and the recipient becomes the new owner of the task. If the recipient declines the task, he or she has the opportunity to give a reason why and the task is returned to the sender. If the recipient assigns the task to someone else, he or she can choose to keep an updated copy in his or her task list and receive status reports, but ownership is transferred to the person to whom the recipient assigned the task. The following code provides a button to execute the **NewTaskRequest** method and assumes that on the Web page we have an Outlook View Control named **ViewCtlFolder**:

```
<SCRIPT LANGUAGE=VBScript>
Sub cmdMethod_Click
```

```
ViewCtlFolder.NewTaskRequest
End Sub
</SCRIPT>
<form method="POST" action="--WEBBOT-SELF--">
    <!--webbot bot="SaveResults" U-File="fpweb:///_private/
        form_results.txt"
    S-Format="TEXT/CSV" S-Label-Fields="TRUE" -->
    <p><input type="button" value="New Task Request" name="cmdMethod"
        onclick=cmdMethod_Click>
    <input type="submit" value="Submit" name="B1">
    <input type="reset" value="Reset" name="B2"></p>
</form>
```

The Open Method

The **Open** method opens the items currently selected in the control. Although it probably goes without saying, note that the method has no effect if no items are selected in the control. No errors are generated. The following code once again assumes that on the Web page there is an Outlook View Control named **ViewCtlFolder** and provides a button that executes the **Open** method:

```
<SCRIPT LANGUAGE=VBScript>
Sub cmdMethod_Click
ViewCtlFolder.Open
End Sub
</SCRIPT>
<form method="POST" action="--WEBBOT-SELF--">
    <!--webbot bot="SaveResults" U-File="fpweb:///_private/
        form_results.txt"
    S-Format="TEXT/CSV" S-Label-Fields="TRUE" -->
    <p><input type="button" value="Open" name="cmdMethod"
        onclick=cmdMethod_Click>
    <input type="submit" value="Submit" name="B1">
    <input type="reset" value="Reset" name="B2"></p>
</form>
```

The OpenSharedDefaultFolder Method

The **OpenSharedDefaultFolder** method displays a specified user's default folder in the control. The method takes two required arguments. The first is a string containing the name of the owner of the folder. The string must contain a display name or alias that Outlook can resolve to a valid recipient. The second argument is of type Long, specifying the type of folder to display. The folder type can be one of the following **OlDefaultFolders** constants: **olFolderCalendar** (9), **olFolderContacts** (10), **olFolderDeletedItems** (3), **olFolderDrafts** (16), **olFolderInbox** (6), **olFolderJournal** (11), **olFolderNotes** (12), **olFolderOutbox** (4), **olFolderSentMail** (5), or **olFolderTasks** (13). The code that follows executes the **OpenSharedDefaultFolder** method at the click of a button, showing the default task folder for a user named Joe Black on our Exchange server. Remember that in VBScript we must define any constants we want to use, so here the folder type constants are defined before being used in the subroutine:

```
<SCRIPT LANGUAGE=VBScript>
' The Outlook Default Folder Constants:
Const olFolderCalendar = 9
Const olFolderContacts = 10
Const olFolderDeletedItems = 3
Const olFolderDrafts = 16
Const olFolderInbox = 6
Const olFolderJournal = 11
Const olFolderNotes = 12
Const olFolderOutbox = 4
Const olFolderSentMail = 5
Const olFolderTasks = 13
Sub cmdMethod_Click
Dim sOwner
sOwner = "Joe Black"
ViewCtlFolder.OpenSharedDefaultFolder sOwner, olFolderTasks
End Sub
</SCRIPT>
```

The PrintItem Method

The **PrintItem** method prints the items currently selected in the control. If a group is selected, the items in the group are selected and printed. The **Print** dialog box (Figure 6.19) is displayed to allow the user to specify how the items are to be printed. As customary, the following code provides a button that executes the **PrintItem** method:

```
<SCRIPT LANGUAGE=VBScript>
Sub cmdMethod_Click
ViewCtlFolder.PrintItem
End Sub
</SCRIPT>
<form method="POST" action="--WEBBOT-SELF--">
    <!--webbot bot="SaveResults" U-File="fpweb:///_private/
        form_results.txt"
    S-Format="TEXT/CSV" S-Label-Fields="TRUE" -->
    <p><input type="button" value="Print Item" name="cmdMethod"
        onclick=cmdMethod_Click>
    <input type="submit" value="Submit" name="B1">
    <input type="reset" value="Reset" name="B2"></p>
</form>
```

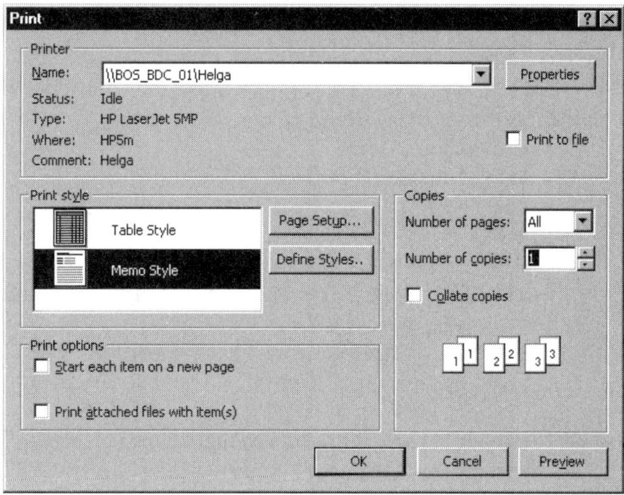

Figure 6.19 The **Print** dialog box

The Reply Method

The **Reply** method executes the reply action for the item or items selected in the control. The following code allows you to respond to messages you select in an Outlook View Control named **ViewCtlFolder** by pressing the **Reply** button on the Web page:

```
<SCRIPT LANGUAGE=VBScript>
Sub cmdMethod_Click
ViewCtlFolder.Reply
End Sub
</SCRIPT>
<form method="POST" action="--WEBBOT-SELF--">
    <!--webbot bot="SaveResults" U-File="fpweb:///_private/
        form_results.txt"
    S-Format="TEXT/CSV" S-Label-Fields="TRUE" -->
    <p><input type="button" value="Reply" name="cmdMethod"
        onclick=cmdMethod_Click>
    <input type="submit" value="Submit" name="B1">
    <input type="reset" value="Reset" name="B2"></p>
</form>
```

The ReplyAll Method

The **ReplyAll** method executes the reply all action for the item or items selected in the control. The following code allows you to respond to messages you select in an

Outlook View Control named **ViewCtlFolder** by pressing the **Reply All** button on the Web page:

```
<SCRIPT LANGUAGE=VBScript>
Sub cmdMethod_Click
ViewCtlFolder.ReplyAll
End Sub
</SCRIPT>
<form method="POST" action="--WEBBOT-SELF--">
    <!--webbot bot="SaveResults" U-File="fpweb:///_private/
        form_results.txt"
    S-Format="TEXT/CSV" S-Label-Fields="TRUE" -->
    <p><input type="button" value="Reply All" name="cmdMethod"
        onclick=cmdMethod_Click>
    <input type="submit" value="Submit" name="B1">
    <input type="reset" value="Reset" name="B2"></p>
</form>
```

The ReplyInFolder Method

The **ReplyInFolder** method creates a post item for each message currently selected in the control. The post item contains the text of the message to which it is replying and has the same conversation topic. The following code creates posts in our inbox folder when the user presses the appropriate button:

```
<OBJECT classid=ClsID:0006F063-0000-0000-C000-000000000046
    id=ViewCtlFolder width="100%" height="430">
    <param name="View" value="Messages">
    <param name="Folder" value="\\Mailbox - Gomez, Alexander\Inbox">
    <param name="Namespace" value="MAPI">
    <param name="Restriction" value>
    <param name="DeferUpdate" value="0"></OBJECT>
    </td></tr></table>
<SCRIPT LANGUAGE=VBScript>
Sub cmdMethod_Click
ViewCtlFolder.ReplyInFolder
End Sub
</SCRIPT>
<form method="POST" action="--WEBBOT-SELF--">
    <p><input type="button" value="Reply In Folder" name="cmdMethod"
        onclick=cmdMethod_Click>
    <input type="submit" value="Submit" name="B1">
    <input type="reset" value="Reset" name="B2"></p>
</form>
```

The SaveAs Method

The **SaveAs** method saves the items selected in the control as a file. The **Save As** dialog box is displayed to allow the user to select the location and format of the resulting file. If more than one item is selected, the items are concatenated and saved as a text file; otherwise, the user is allowed to choose from several file formats, including Rich Text Format, Outlook Template, and Message Format. If you save the Outlook item as a plain text file, no attachments will be saved. The following code executes the **SaveAs** method on the selected items in our inbox when the user hits the **Save As...** button:

```
<OBJECT classid=ClsID:0006F063-0000-0000-C000-000000000046
    id=ViewCtlFolder width="100%" height="430">
    <param name="View" value="Messages">
    <param name="Folder" value="\\Mailbox - Gomez, Alexander\Inbox">
    <param name="Namespace" value="MAPI">
    <param name="Restriction" value>
    <param name="DeferUpdate" value="0"></OBJECT>
    </td></tr></table>
<SCRIPT LANGUAGE=VBScript>
Sub cmdMethod_Click
ViewCtlFolder.SaveAs
End Sub
</SCRIPT>
<form method="POST" action="--WEBBOT-SELF--">
    <p><input type="button" value="Save As..." name="cmdMethod"
        onclick=cmdMethod_Click>
    <input type="submit" value="Submit" name="B1">
    <input type="reset" value="Reset" name="B2"></p>
</form>
```

The SendAndReceive Method

The **SendAndReceive** method sends messages in the **Outbox** folder and checks for new messages. In most cases, messages are received automatically and appear in the **Inbox**. However, you might be working offline and decide that you now want to temporarily connect to your Exchange server, check for new messages, and deliver messages you want sent to others. This is precisely what this method does. In fact, it is exactly the same functionality as selecting **Send/Receive** from the **Tools** menu in Outlook. The following code executes the **SendAndReceive** method at the touch of a button, assuming you have an Outlook View Control named **ViewCtlFolder** in your Outlook folder home page:

```
<SCRIPT LANGUAGE=VBScript>
Sub cmdMethod_Click
```

```
ViewCtlFolder.SendAndReceive
End Sub
</SCRIPT>
<form method="POST" action="--WEBBOT-SELF--">
    <p><input type="button" value="Send/Receive" name="cmdMethod"
        onclick=cmdMethod_Click>
    <input type="submit" value="Submit" name="B1">
    <input type="reset" value="Reset" name="B2"></p>
</form>
```

The ShowFields Method

The **ShowFields** method displays the Outlook **Show Fields** dialog box (Figure 6.20), which allows the user to select the fields to be displayed in the current view of the control. Adding and removing fields from the current view updates the control, as well as the default view in the folder that the control is displaying. Again, the following code assumes an Outlook View Control named **ViewCtlFolder** on the Outlook folder home page:

```
<SCRIPT LANGUAGE=VBScript>
Sub cmdMethod_Click
ViewCtlFolder.ShowFields
End Sub
</SCRIPT>
<form method="POST" action="--WEBBOT-SELF--">
    <p><input type="button" value="Show Fields" name="cmdMethod"
        onclick=cmdMethod_Click>
    <input type="submit" value="Submit" name="B1">
    <input type="reset" value="Reset" name="B2"></p>
</form>
```

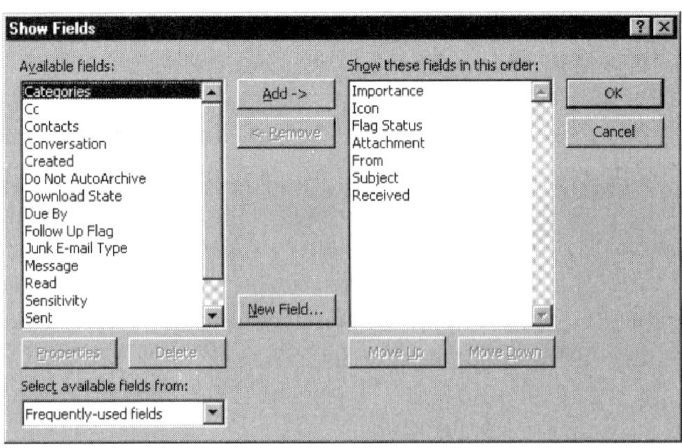

Figure 6.20 The **Show Fields** dialog box

The Sort Method

The **Sort** method displays the Outlook **Sort** dialog box (Figure 6.21), which allows the user to sort the contents of the control using multiple criteria. The following code allows the user to sort the folder displayed by the **ViewCtlFolder** Outlook View Control:

```
<SCRIPT LANGUAGE=VBScript>
Sub cmdMethod_Click
ViewCtlFolder.Sort
End Sub
</SCRIPT>
<form method="POST" action="--WEBBOT-SELF--">
    S-Format="TEXT/CSV" S-Label-Fields="TRUE" -->
    <p><input type="button" value="Sort" name="cmdMethod"
        onclick=cmdMethod_Click>
    <input type="submit" value="Submit" name="B1">
    <input type="reset" value="Reset" name="B2"></p>
</form>
```

The SynchFolder Method

The **SynchFolder** method synchronizes the folder displayed in the control for offline use. Outlook lets you keep copies of your Exchange Server folders locally on your computer as offline folders. Outlook can automatically update the contents of an offline folder and its corresponding server folder so that they're identical. While synchronization can take place automatically in the background, you can also manually synchronize the folders and then continue to work offline. The

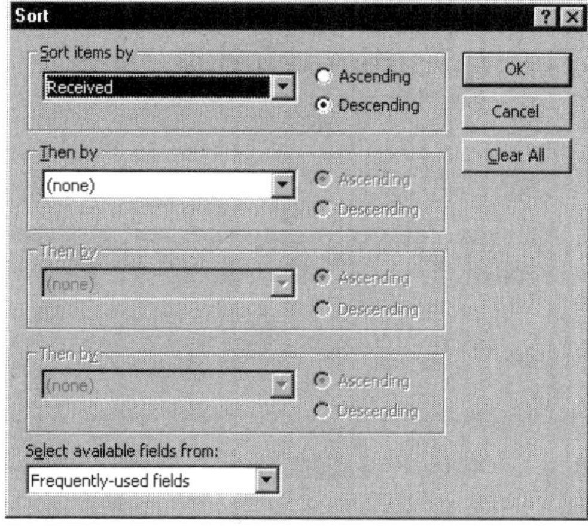

Figure 6.21 The **Sort** dialog box

SynchFolder method has the same functionality as selecting **Synchronize** from the **Tools** menu and then choosing **This Folder**. When Outlook synchronizes your folder, it copies the changes made to the other folder and then disconnects. Any item that's deleted from either the offline folder or the corresponding server folder is deleted from both. The following code synchronizes our inbox when the user presses the **Synchronize** button:

```
<OBJECT classid=ClsID:0006F063-0000-0000-C000-000000000046
    id=ViewCtlFolder width="100%" height="430">
    <param name="View" value="Messages">
    <param name="Folder" value="\\Mailbox - Gomez, Alexander\Inbox">
    <param name="Namespace" value="MAPI">
    <param name="Restriction" value>
    <param name="DeferUpdate" value="0"></OBJECT>
    </td></tr></table>
<SCRIPT LANGUAGE=VBScript>
Sub cmdMethod_Click
ViewCtlFolder.SynchFolder
End Sub
</SCRIPT>
<form method="POST" action="--WEBBOT-SELF--">
    <p><input type="button" value="Synchronize" name="cmdMethod"
        onclick=cmdMethod_Click>
    <input type="submit" value="Submit" name="B1">
    <input type="reset" value="Reset" name="B2"></p>
</form>
```

Methods of the Outlook View Control are summarized in Table 6.2.

Choosing a Different Outlook Today Page

As you may have noticed, when you right-click **Outlook Today – [Mailbox]** and access **Properties**, you do not have permission to change the folder's home page address. You can get around this by manually editing the registry. Start the Registry Editor (**regedit.exe**) and find or create the following subkey:

```
HKEY_CURRENT_USER\Software\Microsoft\Office\9.0\Outlook\Today.
```

If there is no URL value under this key, go into the **Edit** menu, point to **New**, click **String Value**, and type "URL" as the new value name. Double-click the URL value. In the **Value** data box, type the path to your Web page. If you ever need to go back to the default Outlook Today page, just get rid of the URL value.

Table 6.2 Methods of the Outlook View Control

Method Name	**Description**
AddressBook	Displays the Outlook **Address Book** dialog box.
AddToPFFavorites	Adds the current public folder to the user's Microsoft Exchange Server public folders **Favorites** folder.
AdvancedFind	Displays the Outlook **Advanced Find** dialog box.
Categories	Displays the Outlook **Categories** dialog box for the selected items in the control.
CollapseAllGroups	Closes all groups displayed in the control.
CollapseGroup	Closes the group currently selected in the control.
CustomizeView	Displays the Outlook **View Summary** dialog box.
Delete	Deletes the group or items currently selected in the control after prompting the user for confirmation.
ExpandAllGroups	Expands all the groups displayed in the control.
ExpandGroup	Expands the group currently selected in the control.
FlagItem	Displays the Outlook **Flag for Follow Up** dialog box for the selected item.
ForceUpdate	Refreshes the view in the control, applying any property changes since the last time that the **DeferUpdate** property was set to True.
Forward	Executes the forward action for the item or items selected in the control.
GoToToday	Sets the day displayed in the control to the current day if the control is displaying either a **Timeline** or a **Day/Week/Month** view.
GroupBy	Displays the Outlook **Group By** dialog box.
MarkAllAsRead	Marks as read all of the items in the folder displayed in the control.
MarkAsRead	Marks as read the selected items in the control.
MarkAsUnread	Marks as unread the selected items in the control.
MoveItem	Displays the Outlook **Move Items** dialog box for the selected items in the control.
NewAppointment	Creates and displays a new appointment.
NewContact	Creates and displays a new contact.
NewDefaultItem	Creates and displays the default item type for the folder displayed in the control.
NewDistributionList	Creates and displays a new distribution list.

Continued on next page.

Table 6.2 Methods of the Outlook View Control *(continued)*

Method Name	Description
NewForm	Displays the Outlook **Choose Form** dialog box.
NewJournalEntry	Creates and displays a new journal entry.
NewMeetingRequest	Creates and displays a new meeting request.
NewMessage	Creates and displays a new e-mail message.
NewNote	Creates and displays a new note item.
NewOfficeDocument	Creates and displays a new Microsoft Office document.
NewPost	Creates and displays a new post item.
NewTask	Creates and displays a new task.
NewTaskRequest	Creates and displays a new task request.
Open	Opens the item or items currently selected in the control.
OpenSharedDefaultFolder	Displays a specified user's default folder in the control.
PrintItem	Prints the items currently selected in the control.
Reply	Executes the reply action for the item or items selected in the control.
ReplyAll	Executes the reply all action for the item or items selected in the control.
ReplyInFolder	Creates a post item for each message currently selected in the control.
SaveAs	Saves the item selected in the control as a file.
SendAndReceive	Sends messages in the **Outbox** folder and checks for new messages.
ShowFields	Displays the Outlook **Show Fields** dialog box.
Sort	Displays the Outlook **Sort** dialog box.
SynchFolder	Synchronizes the folder displayed in the control for offline use.

Summary

The digital dashboard is a knowledge management concept that has grown over the last few years. It is by no means an instant solution for all of an organization's needs. As you have seen, there is still a fair amount of coding involved to achieve a digital dashboard solution that has any substance. However, there seems to be a steady supply of tools available and under development to help application programmers. It's clear that the digital dashboard has mastered the Outlook client, and Microsoft is now setting its sights on other platforms for the digital dashboard, such as SQL Server and the Windows 2000 File System. Check the book Web site (**http://www.plural.com/outlookexchange.asp**) for updates as the digital dashboard phenomenon evolves.

Part III

Working with ADO and the Exchange OLE DB Provider

Chapter 7

Accessing the Web Storage System Using ADO and ExOLEDB

Microsoft's Universal Data Access (UDA) strategy is finally starting to come to fruition with the advent of the Exchange 2000 Web Storage System. This release of Exchange supports ADO 2.5 with a native OLE DB provider. A developer can use the familiar ADO object model to deal with Exchange data and even write SQL queries against it. In this chapter we'll see exactly how this can be done and look at the underlying technologies that make this type of data access possible.

The ADO/OLE DB Conspiracy

By now, most programmers working with the Microsoft development tool set have heard of Microsoft's Universal Data Access (UDA) strategy. The basic tenet is that regardless of the type of repository that houses your data, you should be able to get to it using just one application programming interface (API)—namely, ActiveX Data Objects (ADO). Sure, some component is going to have to know the low-level details of where the data lives, but that component (known as an OLE DB provider) hides all of these details from the ADO programmer. He or she just uses the ADO object model to programmatically manipulate data from a disparate bunch of data stores. Microsoft Data Access Components (MDAC) ties it all together by packaging ADO with the necessary OLE DB providers.

Figure 7.1 shows the big picture that we have described here. Consider the real-world scenario in which your company has corporate data stored in several heterogeneous data sources. You need to write an application that has access to all of the data.

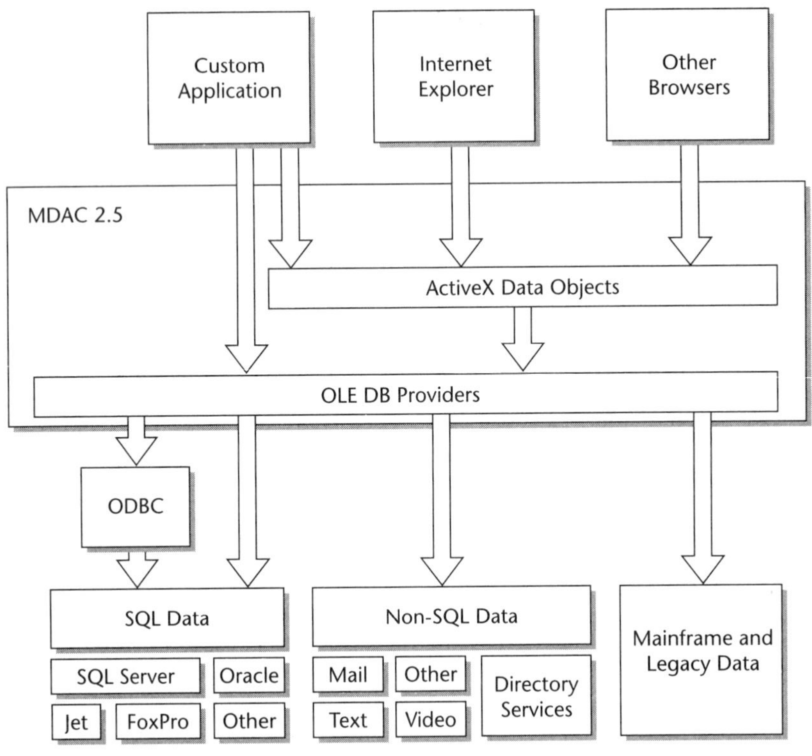

Figure 7.1 Universal Data Access

The same application needs to be available from any Web browser. With ADO, your application can have one consistent programming interface to access all of the data. As long as the data store supplies an OLE DB provider that conforms to Microsoft's standard, a developer can use ADO to access the underlying data.

As the diagram in Figure 7.1 clearly suggests, you can bypass ADO and directly code against the interfaces provided natively by the OLE DB providers. Well, you could. However, the code is not trivial, and you are limited to C++ as a language choice.

■ What Does ADO 2.5 Have to Do with Exchange 2000?

Thus we arrive at ADO 2.5, the latest release of the ActiveX Data Objects library. Even if you were already familiar with the preceding whirlwind explanation of ADO and OLE DB, you might still be wondering how ADO works with Exchange data. Figure 7.2 shows the ADO 2.5 object model.

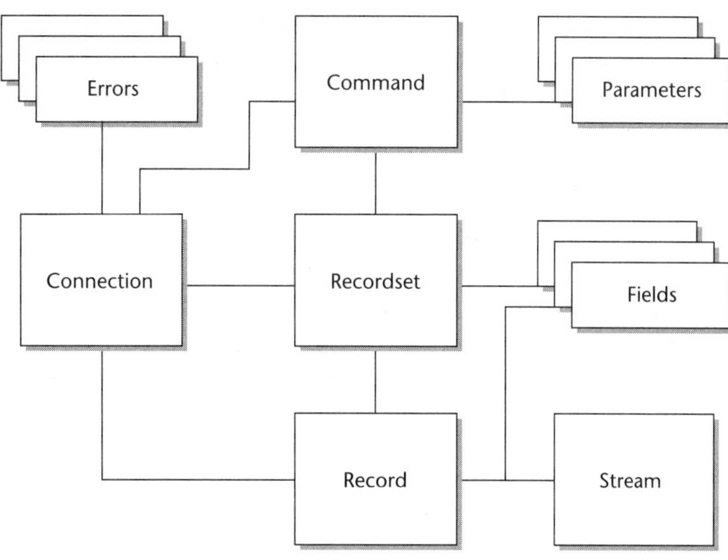

Figure 7.2 The ADO 2.5 object model

You are probably accustomed to using ADO to access relational databases such as Microsoft SQL Server. You know all about **Recordset** objects and writing SQL queries against tables in a database. You can leverage all of that programming experience when using ADO 2.5 to manipulate what we call semistructured data, such as that produced by Exchange. In fact, most of the enhancements to ADO 2.5 have been implemented for the purpose of working with hierarchical data stores such as a file system or a mail store. Table 7.1 summarizes how the major objects in ADO 2.5 can be used with Exchange 2000.

Table 7.1 The Use of ADO 2.5 Objects in Exchange 2000

ADO 2.5 Object	Exchange 2000 Use
Record	Opens or creates an item or folder using a URL.
Recordset	Returns a collection of items in a folder or folder hierarchy. Also allows you to navigate a folder hierarchy.
Fields	Accesses the properties of an Exchange item.
Connection	Opens a connection to a folder, although this is not always required.
Stream	Accesses resources as streaming bits of data (i.e., open attachments in e-mail).

The Role of the Web Storage System

Another piece of the puzzle that makes this whole technology work is the Web Storage System. The Web Storage System is a database technology just introduced with the Windows 2000 operating system that you can use to store, share, and manage many types of data. For example, you can store e-mail messages, Web content, multimedia files, and Office documents all together in the Web Storage System.

The Web Storage System is organized as a hierarchy of folders much like a traditional file system, in which each folder can contain any number of items, including other folders.

With Exchange 5.5 and earlier releases, all Exchange data were squirreled away in a proprietary database that a user could manipulate really only from within Exchange itself or from an Exchange client (such as Microsoft Outlook), or programmatically through the Collaboration Data Objects (CDO) 1.21 API. With Exchange 2000, all Exchange data is now stored in either the Web Storage System or the Active Directory. For purposes of this chapter, all we have to know about the Windows 2000 Active Directory is that it contains information about users, groups, organizations, and services in an enterprise, including which users have Exchange mailboxes on the system and what their e-mail addresses are. What is really interesting to us is how Exchange 2000 uses the Web Storage System. As Figure 7.3 shows, Exchange 2000 data saved in the Web Storage System appears in your standard Windows Explorer just like anything else saved on your file system.

When you install Exchange 2000 on a server, a virtual drive (usually the M: drive) is created. Each Exchange store exists as a file system folder mounted under the M: drive on the host server. The Windows Explorer and standard Win32 file system APIs can now access the Exchange data through the Exchange Installable File System (ExIFS) technology. If you look at the folder list on the left-hand side of the Explorer window in Figure 7.3, you will see the aforementioned M: drive, and underneath that a folder with the sample name of a domain set up on a Windows 2000/Exchange 2000 laptop (**GOMEZAMOBILE.LOCAL**). Below that is a special folder called **MBX**, which is where Exchange 2000 stores all of the user mailboxes. In this case a mailbox has been created for the user's Administrator account and beneath the **Administrator** folder are all of the standard folders in Outlook 2000—namely, **Calendar**, **Contacts**, **Deleted Items**, **Drafts**, **Inbox**, **Journal**, **Notes**, **Outbox**, **Sent Items**, and **Tasks**. The right-hand pane shows three e-mail messages in the Administrator's inbox. Notice that they all have a **.eml** file extension, which indicates the Internet E-Mail Message file type. All of the standard Outlook message types have this **.eml** extension, including **Contacts**, **Appointment Items**, and **Tasks**.

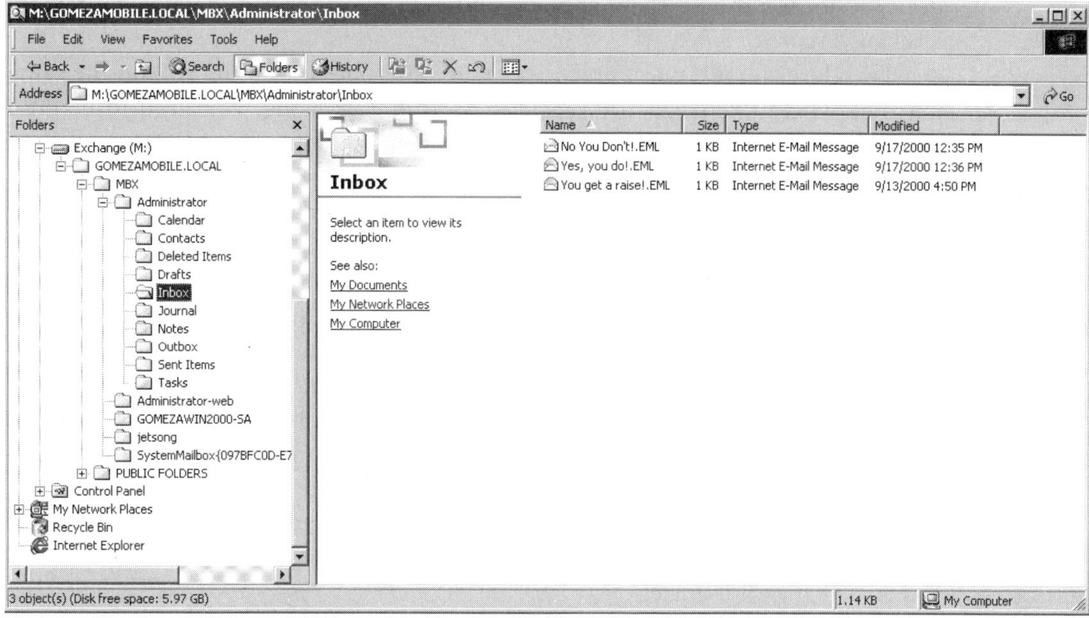

Figure 7.3 Exchange 2000 data in the Web Storage System

Note: For a much more in-depth discussion of the M: drive and the Exchange Installable File System, see Chapter 18.

All of this is important because every item in the Web Storage System can be identified by a standard URL. We'll look at the syntax for these URLs later in this chapter when we get into some code.

The Exchange OLE DB Provider

The final key to accessing Exchange data through ADO 2.5 is the Exchange OLE DB provider (ExOLEDB). **Exoledb.dll** is installed with the Exchange 2000 Server and is used to access Web Storage System items on a local server. This is really important. The Exchange OLE DB provider is a server-side component, meaning that currently it can be used only to access public folder and mailbox stores that reside locally on the server. ExOLEDB is designed for use in COM+ components, ASP pages, and Web Storage System event sinks that run on the server. It is not designed for use from a client application for accessing back-end data on a remote Exchange server.

Therefore, all of the examples here will work only if they are run on the same machine where Exchange 2000 resides. So to follow along, you need to be on a machine running Windows 2000 and Exchange 2000 and have a COM-compliant development language such as Microsoft Visual Basic or Visual Basic Scripting edition handy. We'll be using VB 6, but with a few modifications the sample code will work in VBScript. MDAC 2.5, which contains ADO 2.5, comes with Windows 2000, so you're all set there. Finally we recommended that you obtain the Exchange 2000 Software Development Kit (SDK) from the Exchange Server developer center (**http://msdn.microsoft.com/exchange/**). It is chock-full of documentation and sample code on all of the technologies described in this book.

To start, create a new Standard EXE project in Visual Basic 6.0 and set a reference to the Microsoft ActiveX Data Objects 2.5 library (from the **Project** menu in the VB integrated development environment), as shown in Figure 7.4. While you're at it, set a reference to the Microsoft CDO for Exchange 2000 library as well. This is part of the standard Exchange 2000 installation and defines some Exchange-specific constants, which we'll use later.

Opening an ADO Connection to Exchange

The first thing we need to do is tell ADO that we want to deal with the Exchange OLE DB provider (and not another OLE DB provider, such as the SQL Server OLE

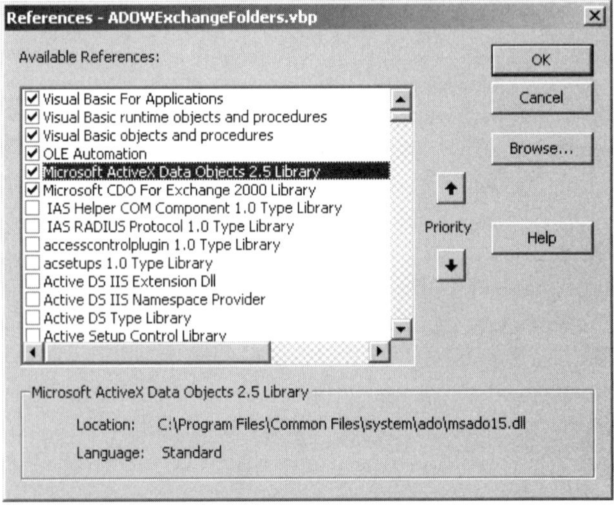

Figure 7.4 For reference, the ADO 2.5 library

DB provider). If you want to create an ADO **Connection** object, you must set the **Provider** property to "ExOLEDB.DataSource." The Visual Basic code that follows opens the Administrator's inbox on the machine represented in Figure 7.3. We declare a global constant in our project that we'll use whenever we have to reference the Exchange OLE DB provider. We declare a standard ADO **Connection** object and, for illustrative purposes only, a string variable in which we hard-code the complete URL path of the inbox. Just by setting the **Provider** property of the **Connection** object and using the **Open** method with the URL as an argument, we now have a reference to the **Inbox** folder:

```
Option Explicit
Global Const gblsExchangeProvider As String = "ExOLEDB.DataSource"
    Dim objConn As ADODB.Connection
    Dim sURL As String
    ' Reference a folder on my Exchange server:
    sURL = "http://gomezawin2000.gomezamobile.local/exchange/
                   Administrator/Inbox"
    ' Connect to the local Exchange server:
    Set objConn = New ADODB.Connection
    objConn.Provider = gblsExchangeProvider
    objConn.Open sURL
```

As you may recall, we don't need to explicitly open a connection to Exchange. We could have just passed a URL to the **Open** method of an ADO **Record** object like so:

```
Dim objRec As ADODB.Record
Set objRec As New ADODB.Record
objRec.Open sSomeFileURL
```

However, there are advantages to explicitly opening a **Connection** object. You can use transactions in your code to bundle together a bunch of ADO operations as a single unit of work. You can access the **Errors** collection to see if your ADO code is working error free. Most importantly, you can write SQL **SELECT** queries against Exchange items in the Web Storage System, as we'll see later in this chapter.

Now that we know how to open a connection, creating Exchange items is not much more difficult.

Creating a Folder

The first thing we might want to do is create a folder. Let's create a form in our VB project called **frmMain**. Let's add to that two text boxes called **txtConnect** and **txtNewFolder**, respectively. Drop in a button on the form called **cmdNewFolder**.

You should type in the name of the folder structure that you want to connect to in **txtConnect**. In the example of Figure 7.3, **http://gomezawin2000.gomezamobile.local/public/** connects to the **Public Folders** hierarchy on the Exchange server. You should type in the full URL path to the folder that you want to create in **txtNewFolder**. In our example, **http://gomezawin2000.gomezamobile.local/public/NewFolder** will create a new public folder on the Exchange server named **NewFolder**. All that said, the following VB code does the trick:

```
Option Explicit
Global Const gblsExchangeProvider = "ExOLEDB.DataSource"
Private Sub cmdNewFolder_Click()
    Dim objReturnRecord As ADODB.Record
    Dim objConn As ADODB.Connection
    Dim sConnect As String

    Set objConn = New ADODB.Connection

    ' Get the existing folder structure to connect:
    ' Should be something like http://gomezawin2000.gomezamobile.local/
                                     public/
    sConnect = frmMain.txtConnect.Text

    ' Connect to the local Exchange server:
    objConn.Provider = gblsExchangeProvider
    objConn.Open sConnect

    Set objReturnRecord = CreateFolder(frmMain.txtNewFolder.Text,
                                       objConn)

End Sub
Public Function CreateFolder(ByVal sURL As String, _
                             ByVal objConn As ADODB.Connection) As
                             ADODB.Record
' The sURL argument is an HTTP URL to the new public folder we want to
    create.
' For example, let's pass in
' "http://gomezawin2000.gomeza.local/public/NewFolder" as sURL.
' The objConn as an ADO Connection to your Exchange server.
' The function returns the new folder as an ADO Record.
    Dim objRec As ADODB.Record
    Dim sContentClass As String
    ' Let Exchange know you want to create a folder:
    sContentClass = "urn:content-classes:folder"

    ' Try to create the folder:
    Set objRec = New ADODB.Record
    objRec.Open sURL, objConn, adModeReadWrite, adCreateCollection
```

```
    objRec.Fields("DAV:contentclass") = sContentClass
    objRec.Fields.Update

    ' Set the return value:
    Set CreateFolder = objRec

    ' Clean up:
    objRec.Close
    Set objRec = Nothing

End Function
```

A lot is going on here. The key in creating the folder was twofold: Use the **Open** method of the ADO **Record** object and feed it the correct URL. Let's first take a closer look at the syntax for referring to folders as URLs, and then we'll tackle the **Open** method.

File URLs

In case you haven't heard already (tongue planted firmly in cheek), every item in Exchange 2000 is accessible via a URL. All programming tasks in Exchange are also URL based. When dealing with the Exchange OLE DB provider, you can use either "file://" or "http://" URLs. Let's look at the ground rules for each.

Your file URL can take two forms, depending on what you want to access. Use this one when you want to access a private mailbox:

```
file://./backofficestorage/<domain-name>/MBX/<user-alias>/<path>
```

Use this one when you want to access a public folder tree:

```
file://./backofficestoreage/<domain-name>/<public-folder-tree-name>/
     <path>
```

In both forms:

- **domain-name** refers to the fully qualified domain in which the store resides (e.g., "mydomain.local" or "somedomain.plural.com").
- **public-folder-tree-name** refers to the public folder tree in which the item resides. Several values can be used here. "Public Folders" is the default folder tree name for the backward-compatible MAPI public folder hierarchy that you see under **All Public Folders** in Outlook. Elsewhere in the book we talk about top-level hierarchies (TLHs), which are new public folder

trees that you can create. If you create a TLH, you can use its name here. You can also use the string "MBX" to refer to the private mailbox store.

- **user-alias** refers to a user's Exchange mailbox alias (i.e., "gomeza" in our example).
- **path** is the folder path to the item, consisting of folder names separated by "/", just like any other folder path.

Some examples will help illustrate. For example, Table 7.2 shows how to access the standard default mailbox folders using file URLs.

Similarly, if we wanted to access a brand-new TLH called **The Web Storage System** that we had created on our local Exchange 2000 server, we could use the following URL:

```
file://./backofficestorage/mydomain.local/The%20Web%20Storage%20System/
```

If we created a new public folder called **Exchange Book Talk** under the default Exchange public store, we could use the URL

```
file://./backofficestorage/Public%20Folders/Exchange%20Book%20Talk
```

> **Note:** When using the "file://" URL namespace to refer to Exchange items, you do not need to explicitly specify the Exchange OLE DB provider. To avoid confusion, however, you should always explicitly open a connection and set the provider as shown earlier in the chapter.

Table 7.2 Default Mailbox Folder File URLs

Folder	URL
Calendar	file://./backofficestorage/<domain-name>/MBX/<user-alias>/Calendar
Contacts	file://./backofficestorage/<domain-name>/MBX/<user-alias>/Contacts
Drafts	file://./backofficestorage/<domain-name>/MBX/<user-alias>/Drafts
Inbox	file://./backofficestorage/<domain-name>/MBX/<user-alias>/Inbox
Journal	file://./backofficestorage/<domain-name>/MBX/<user-alias>/Journal
Notes	file://./backofficestorage/<domain-name>/MBX/<user-alias>/Notes
Outbox	file://./backofficestorage/<domain-name>/MBX/<user-alias>/Outbox
Sent Items	file://./backofficestorage/<domain-name>/MBX/<user-alias>/Sent%20Items
Tasks	file://./backofficestorage/<domain-name>/MBX/<user-alias>/Tasks

HTTP URLs

With Internet Information Server 5.0 (IIS) being part of the Windows 2000 operating system, we are also allowed to use HTTP URLs to reference Exchange items using the following form:

```
http://<server-name>/<virtual-directory>/<virtual-path>
```

where

- **server-name** refers to the local Exchange 2000 server name. In our example the machine name is "GOMEZAWIN2000." We can also use "localhost" for the server name. Remember that the Exchange OLE DB provider was designed only for accessing items on the local Exchange server.
- **virtual-directory** is the Exchange HTTP virtual server virtual directory mapped to the public folder or private mailbox store. If you go into the **Internet Services Manager** MMC in the Administrative Tools program group in Windows 2000, you can see all of the virtual directories for your Exchange server. The name of the virtual directory does not have to coincide with the name of the public folder on the Exchange server. Basically, as long as the virtual directory is mapped to a valid public folder here, your user can type in "http://localhost/Raspberries" in a Web browser to get to a public folder on the Exchange server under **Public Folders/Iced Tea Flavors/My Favorites/**. See Chapter 5 for more on how IIS works with Outlook Web Access. We also have two default virtual directories that Exchange uses:
  1. **exchange.** All private mailboxes in any store are available through this virtual directory.
  2. **public.** This virtual directory is mapped to the top public folder in the default public folder tree. The default public folder name is "Public Folders."
- **virtual-path** is the rest of the path to the item. Let's look at some examples. Table 7.3 shows how to access the standard default mailbox folders using HTTP URLs.

Similarly, if we wanted to access a brand-new TLH called **The Web Storage System** that we had created on our local Exchange 2000 server, we could use the following URL:

```
http://localhost/The%20Web%20Storage%20System
```

Table 7.3 Default Mailbox Folder HTTP URLs

Folder	URL
Calendar	http://<server-name>/exchange/<user-alias>/Calendar
Contacts	http://<server-name>/exchange/<user-alias>/Contacts
Drafts	http://<server-name>/exchange/<user-alias>/Drafts
Inbox	http://<server-name>/exchange/<user-alias>/Inbox
Journal	http://<server-name>/exchange/<user-alias>/Journal
Notes	http://<server-name>/exchange/<user-alias>/Notes
Outbox	http://<server-name>/exchange/<user-alias>/Outbox
Sent Items	http://<server-name>/exchange/<user-alias>/Sent%20Items
Tasks	http://<server-name>/exchange/<user-alias>/Tasks

If we had created a new public folder called **Exchange Book Talk** under the default Exchange public store, we could use the URL

```
http://localhost/public/Exchange%20Book%20Talk
```

Programmatically Getting a User's HTTP Mailbox Folder URLs

Returning to our sample VB project, go to the **Project** menu in the VB integrated development environment and click **Components...**. In the **Controls** tab select **Microsoft Forms 2.0 Object Library.** Drop a Forms 2.0 list box on **frmMain** and call it **lstMailboxURLs.** This is the gray list box shown in Figure 7.5. This is part of the standard Microsoft Office installation. If you don't have Office on your computer, then you can use a regular VB list box and modify the sample code accordingly. It just seems easier to work with this list box in demo code. Create a button on **frmMain** and call it **cmdGetMailboxURLs.**

In the click event of your **cmdGetMailboxURLs** button, insert the following code:

```
Private Sub cmdGetMailboxURLs_Click()
    Dim vaURLs As Variant
    Dim nCounter As Integer
    Dim sText As String
    ' These 2 objects allow us to dynamically figure out the computer
      name and
```

Figure 7.5 The Microsoft Forms 2.0 object library list box

```
' the domain name, respectively, as in the call to
' GetStdWellKnownMailboxURLs:
Dim objInfo As New ActiveDS.ADSystemInfo
Dim objInfoNT As ActiveDS.WinNTSystemInfo

' The URL should be something like:
' http://gomezawin2000.gomezamobile.local/exchange/Administrator
vaURLs = GetStdWellKnownMailboxURLs("http://" & _
         LCase(objInfoNT.ComputerName) & "." & _
         objInfo.domaindnsname & "/exchange/" & objInfoNT.UserName)

' Display it:
frmMain.lstMailboxURLs.Clear
For nCounter = LBound(vaURLs) To UBound(vaURLs)
               frmMain.lstMailboxURLs.AddItem vaURLs(nCounter)
Next
```

```
    Set objInfo = Nothing
    Set objInfoNT = Nothing
End Sub
```

When using functions such as the ones we have seen in the sample code, we often need to pass a fully qualified URL. When writing production applications, it is rarely feasible to hard-code such things as server names and domains. Using the following technique, we can dynamically determine the local machine name and domain. We can do this thanks to two standard ADSI interfaces for Windows 2000 that you get automatically on any Windows 2000 system. The **ADSystemInfo** and **WinNTSystemInfo** objects give us all sorts of useful information about our environment (like the name of our computer). All we have to do is declare them. We use them to build our "http://" URL to the Administrator's mailbox, which we pass to **GetStdWellKnownMailboxURLs**.

Note: To use **ADSystemInfo** and **WinNTSystemInfo** in your VB project, set a reference to the "Active DS Type Library" (found in **C:\WINNT\System32\activeds.tlb**). To use them in VBScript code, use **CreateObject** like so:

```
Set objInfo = CreateObject("ADSystemInfo")
Set objInfoNT = CreateObject("WinNTSystemInfo")
```

For more information, see the ADSI Platform SDK on the Microsoft Developer Network (**http://msdn.microsoft.com/library/default.asp**).

The preceding discussion showed how to reference default mailbox folder files. Now we will write some code to programmatically get all default mailbox folder URLs for a given user. This approach avoids having to hard-code the paths in your application. We will once again use our Administrator user's mailbox. The following VB function will return an array of the default mailbox URLs for a given mailbox:

```
Public Function GetStdWellKnownMailboxURLs(sMailboxFolderURL As String)
    As Variant
    Dim objRec As ADODB.Record
    Dim objConn As ADODB.Connection
    Dim objFields As ADODB.Fields

    Set objRec = New ADODB.Record
    Set objConn = New ADODB.Connection

    ' Connect to the local Exchange server:
```

```
    ' We previously declared: _
    ' Global Const gblsExchangeProvider = "ExOLEDB.DataSource"
    objConn.Provider = gblsExchangeProvider
    objConn.Open sMailboxFolderURL

    objRec.Open sMailboxFolderURL

    Set objFields = objRec.Fields

    ' Return the Mailbox URLs as an array:
    GetStdWellKnownMailboxURLs = Array( _
        "Calendar: ", objFields(cdoCalendarFolderURL), _
        "Contacts: ", objFields(cdoContactFolderURL), _
        "DeletedIt:", objFields(cdoDeletedItems), _
        "Inbox: ", objFields(cdoInbox), _
        "Journal: ", objFields(cdoJournal), _
        "MsgRoot: ", objFields(cdoMsgFolderRoot), _
        "Notes: ", objFields(cdoNotes), _
        "Outbox: ", objFields(cdoOutbox), _
        "SendMsg: ", objFields(cdoSendMsg), _
        "SendItems: ", objFields(cdoSentItems), _
        "Tasks: ", objFields(cdoTasks))
    ' Clean up:
    objRec.Close
    objConn.Close
    Set objRec = Nothing
    Set objConn = Nothing
End Function
```

This code returns a variant array (which we display in our form by doing simple **AddItem** calls) containing the following strings:

```
http://gomezawin2000.GomezaMobile.local/exchange/Administrator/Calendar
http://gomezawin2000.GomezaMobile.local/exchange/Administrator/Contacts
http://gomezawin2000.GomezaMobile.local/exchange/Administrator/
       Deleted%20Items
http://gomezawin2000.GomezaMobile.local/exchange/Administrator/Inbox
http://gomezawin2000.GomezaMobile.local/exchange/Administrator/Journal
http://gomezawin2000.GomezaMobile.local/exchange/Administrator
http://gomezawin2000.GomezaMobile.local/exchange/Administrator/Notes
http://gomezawin2000.GomezaMobile.local/exchange/Administrator/Outbox
http://gomezawin2000.GomezaMobile.local/exchange/Administrator/ _
       %23%23DavMailSubmissionURI%23%23
http://gomezawin2000.GomezaMobile.local/exchange/Administrator/
       Sent%20Items
http://gomezawin2000.GomezaMobile.local/exchange/Administrator/Tasks
```

Table 7.4 Mailbox Folder URL Constants

cdoHTTPMail Constant	Value	Mailbox Folder Name
cdoCalendarFolderURL	urn:schemas:httpmail:calendar	Calendar
cdoContactFolderURL	urn:schemas:httpmail:contacts	Contacts
cdoDeletedItems	urn:schemas:httpmail:deleteditems	Deleted Items
cdoInbox	urn:schemas:httpmail:inbox	Inbox
cdoJournal	urn:schemas:httpmail:journal	Journal
cdoNotes	urn:schemas:httpmail:notes	Notes
cdoOutbox	urn:schemas:httpmail:outbox	Outbox
cdoSentItems	urn:schemas:httpmail:sentitems	Sent Items
cdoTasks	urn:schemas:httpmail:tasks	Tasks
cdoSendMsg	urn:schemas:httpmail:sendmsg	Exchange Mail Submission URI
cdoMsgFolderRoot	urn:schemas:httpmail:msgfolderroot	Mailbox root URL

The CDO HTTP mail constants we used in the code for this example (e.g., **cdoCalendarFolderURL**, **cdoContactFolderURL**, **cdoDeletedItems**) were defined courtesy of the Microsoft CDO for Exchange 2000 library to which we set a reference earlier. We will look specifically at CDO for Exchange 2000 in other chapters; Table 7.4 summarizes the value of these constants (in case you need to use this code in VBScript, for example).

As we shall see in much greater detail later in the book, the connection between ADO and CDO comes down to this: We use ADO to get the data and CDO to interpret it.

The Open Method of the ADO 2.5 Record Object

Let's return to our initial example of creating a folder using the **Open** method of the **Record** object from earlier in the chapter:

```
objRec.Open sURL, objConn, adModeReadWrite, adCreateCollection
```

The **Open** method is used to bind to and open data from an item specified by a valid URL. The signature for the **Open** method is as follows:

```
Open (ByVal SourceURL as String,
     [ByVal ActiveConnection as Object],
     [ByVal Mode as ConnectModeEnum],
     [ByVal CreateOptions as RecordCreateOptionsEnum],
     [ByVal Options as RecordOpenOptionsEnum],
     [ByVal UserName as String],
     [ByVal Password as String])
```

where

- **SourceURL** specifies the URL of the existing item to open.
- **ActiveConnection** (optional) is a reference to an ADO **Connection** object specifying the connection to use when opening the URL. A new **Connection** object (session) is implicitly created if none is specified.
- **Mode** (optional) is a reference to the ADO-defined **ConnectModeEnum.** The default value is always **adModeRead** (1), which means that at least read access is requested when an item is opened. You can add the values as appropriate for your application needs. The possible values are shown in Table 7.5.
- **CreateOptions** (optional) is a reference to the ADO-defined **RecordCreateOptionsEnum.** For our purposes, **adCreateCollection** creates a folder item (a collection of other items), and **adCreateNonCollection** creates a file (noncollection). The possible values are shown in Table 7.6.

Table 7.5 ConnectModeEnum Values

Name	**Value**
adModeRead	1
adModeReadWrite	3
adModeRecursive	4194304 (&H400000)
adModeShareDenyNone	16 (&H10)
adModeShareDenyRead	4
adModeShareDenyWrite	8
adModeShareExclusive	12 (&H0C)
adModeUnknown	0
adModeWrite	2

Table 7.6 RecordCreateOptionsEnum Values

Name	Value
adCreateCollection	8192 (&H2000)
adCreateNonCollection	0
adCreateOverwrite	67108864 (&H4000000)
adCreateStructDoc	–2147483648 (&H80000000)
adFailIfNotExists	–1 (&HFFFFFFFF)
adOpenIfExists	33554432 (&H2000000)

- **Options** (optional) is a reference to the ADO-defined **RecordOpenOptionsEnum**. The possible values are shown in Table 7.7.
- **UserName** (optional) is normally used to pass a user name if needed for authentication; however, this value is not supported in the ExOLEDB provider
- **Password** (optional) is normally used to pass a password if needed for authentication; however, this value is not supported in the ExOLEDB provider.

The **Open** method is crucial because it allows us to bind to any existing item in the Web Storage System or even create new ones. For example, the following code creates a simple CDO item at the requested URL (assuming that **sURL** holds a valid URL and **objConn** represents a valid connection to the Exchange server):

```
Dim objRec As New ADODB.Recordset
objRec.Open sURL, objConn, adModeReadWrite, adCreateNonCollection
objRec.Fields("DAV:contentclass") = "urn:content-classes:item"
objRec.Fields("urn:schemas:mailheader:content-type") = "text/plain"
objRec.Fields.Update
```

Table 7.7 RecordOpenOptionsEnum Values

Name	Value
adDelayFetchFields	32768 (&H8000)
adDelayFetchStream	16384 (&H4000)
adOpenAsync	4096 (&H1000)
adOpenRecordUnspecified	–1 (&HFFFFFFFF)
adOpenSource	8388608 (&H800000)

The same code with a minor change will try to bind to an existing item:

```
Dim objRec As New ADODB.Recordset
objRec.Open sURL, objConn, adModeReadWrite
```

Rather than indiscriminately getting one item, we can combine the **Open** statement with a form of SQL to query folders for a "result set" that can be returned as a standard ADO **Recordset**.

Using Web Storage System SQL to Get a List of Folders

Web Storage System SQL (WSS SQL) is a SQL dialect that you can use to query items in the Web Storage System. It can't quite do everything that, say, T-SQL can do for SQL Server (see Web Storage System SQL in the Exchange 2000 SDK for a complete language reference), but its familiar syntax will ease programmers into the transition from querying a standard relational database to querying semistructured data.

A common task is to traverse a list of folders within a folder. In Exchange 2000, you do this by writing a WSS SQL query. In the example that follows, we want to retrieve all of the folders under our Exchange server's **Public Folders.** In our case, we want to retrieve everything under **http://gomezawin2000.gomezamobile.local/public.** Note that this is the MAPI client public store installed with Exchange 2000. This is the **Public Folders** hierarchy that users see when opening Outlook 2000. Since this folder hierarchy is there for backward compatibility with Exchange 5.5, we still have to write extra code to retrieve the contents of folders underneath the top-level folders. This means that the scope of our SQL query is limited to "shallow traversal," as the following code shows:

```
SELECT "DAV:displayname", "DAV:contentclass", "DAV:href"
    FROM SCOPE('shallow traversal of
        "http://gomezawin2000.gomezamobile.local/public"')
    WHERE "DAV:ishidden" = False
    AND "DAV:isfolder" = True
```

If we were querying another TLH or even a private store, we could specify "deep traversal" in the scope. With deep traversal, the specified folder is searched, and any subfolders found underneath are recursively searched.

In addition, we want to limit the **DAV:isfolder** property to True and the **DAV:ishidden** property to False in the **WHERE** clause. Otherwise we'll get all of the "hidden" MAPI values along with the folders. The sample Visual Basic code follows. It requires that you establish a valid ADO connection to your Exchange server and pass it in along with the folder hierarchy you wish to query. The function returns an ADO **Recordset** object to the calling routine:

```
Public Function GetFolderList(ByVal sURL As String, _
                              ByVal objConn As ADODB.Connection) As
                              ADODB.Recordset

    ' sURL should be a valid URL
       like http://gomezawin2000.gomezamobile.local/public
    ' The objConn is a valid connection to the above folder path.
    Dim objADORS As ADODB.Recordset
    Dim sSQL As String

    Set objADORS = New ADODB.Recordset

    sSQL = "select ""DAV:displayname"", ""DAV:contentclass"",
           ""DAV:href"" from"
    sSQL = sSQL & " scope('shallow traversal of """ & sURL & """')"
    sSQL = sSQL & " where ""DAV:ishidden"" = False and ""DAV:isfolder""
          = True"

    objADORS.Open sSQL, objConn
    Set GetFolderList = objADORS
End Function
```

The code that calls this routine will now have a standard ADO **Recordset** with each folder represented as a **Record**. Your code can now loop through the **Recordset**.

We know that was a lot of new information to digest, but it will all start to make sense as you learn how to write your own queries. Let's take a closer look at the special dialect of SQL that we need to speak in order to master manipulating Exchange items.

Web Storage System SQL

At first glance, SQL queries for retrieving Exchange items may seem a bit syntactically "off"—like the difference between American English and the Queen's English—but the more you study the syntax, the more familiar it will become. The Web Storage System provides a means to define schema information for the items it contains. It can provide this information to other applications, such as the WSS SQL query processor.

You can use WSS SQL to locate specific items or create views of data. You *cannot* use WSS SQL to update data in the Web Storage System. As we'll see, there is no support for such SQL staples as **SET**, **UPDATE**, **CREATE**, and so on. When using WSS SQL, ADO returns the search results as **Recordset** objects.

The Microsoft Indexing Service is the search engine for WSS SQL. If you open up the **Services** MMC, it is the Microsoft Search (MSSearch) service. This search engine operates using a system account that enables it to read all stores, including private mailboxes. However, the **Recordset** objects returned from a WSS SQL query are evaluated against the access control lists (ACLs) of the item or folder searched and the security identifier (SID) of the user making the query. Any item to which the user does not have access is removed before the search result is returned.

The SELECT Statement

The starting point for any query is a well-formed **SELECT** statement. The **SELECT** statement returns the values of properties in a particular folder or folders within a store. It has the following general syntax:

```
SELECT <list of properties separated by commas or *>
FROM SCOPE (shallow traversal of <some folder URL>
            deep traversal of <some folder URL>)
WHERE <some search condition>
ORDER BY <list of properties separated by commas>
```

To select specific properties, you need to enclose each property name in quotation marks and separate each property name with commas:

```
SELECT "DAV:href", "DAV:displayname", "urn:schemas:contacts:fileas"
```

SELECT * and ADO's GetChildren Method

SELECT * is also valid syntax in a WSS SQL query. A **SELECT** * query returns *all* of the properties defined by the expected content class of the specified folder. However, just because you can do something doesn't mean you should. Although using **SELECT** * might be interesting when playing with WSS SQL to identify every value you can return, you should *never* use it in production code. It is both extremely time-consuming and unnecessarily broad, and it even makes the Exchange server perform unnecessary processing to get the **Stream** objects.

Another argument against using **SELECT** * is that unless you define your custom properties in a schema, you will not get them using the **SELECT** * query. As we'll see later, adding your own custom properties to an item is as easy as adding them to the item's **Fields** collection. However, since they are not defined specifically in the item's schema, **SELECT** * doesn't know anything about them. If you do specify the custom properties in the **SELECT** statement, they will be retrieved.

While we're on the subject, you may have noticed the **GetChildren** method of the ADO **Record** object. Its purpose is to return a **Recordset** whose rows represent the files and subdirectories in the directory represented by the **Record.** For example, let's assume that we have a valid ADO **Record** called **objRec.** If **objRec.RecordType** = **adCollectionRecord**, meaning that the record consists of a collection of records, we can use the code

```
Dim objRecordset As ADODB.Recordset
Set objRecordset = objRec.GetChildren
```

to get a **Recordset** consisting of all of the records in the collection. Unfortunately, this is the computational equivalent of the **SELECT *** query and should be avoided in production code.

Query Scope

Another component of a well-formed WSS SQL query is its scope. Instead of querying a table in a database, in WSS SQL you issue a query on a folder scope. A folder scope consists of two parts: a folder specified by a URL and a depth. We are already familiar with building URLs; the scope part is even simpler. A scope of deep traversal on a folder means that the folder and all of its subfolders will be searched. A scope of shallow traversal means that only the specified folder will be searched.

As we mentioned earlier, the **Public Folders** TLH, which is the MAPI client public folder store, is limited to shallow traversal (as are also, you may remember, such Exchange clients as Outlook 2000's **All Public Folders**). It is simply not implemented like the other public stores in the Web Storage System. Veteran collaborative application programmers will remember that they had to write some recursive code to get at all of the folders in the MAPI store. In Exchange 2000, this is still true for the **Public Folders** TLH *only.* Any other public folder store or private folder store allows deep traversals. For example, the following code finds all child folders contained in the particular folder. The query is limited to all visible folders contained in the specified folder; subfolders are not searched:

```
SELECT "DAV:href", "DAV:displayname"
FROM SCOPE ('shallow traversal of _
"file://./backofficestorage/GomezaMobile.local/MBX/Administrator/
        Contacts"')
WHERE "DAV:isfolder" = True and "DAV:ishidden" = False
```

On the other hand, this next query will include any and all subfolders:

```
SELECT "DAV:href", "DAV:displayname"
FROM SCOPE ('deep traversal of _
"file://./backofficestorage/GomezaMobile.local/MBX/Administrator/
        Contacts"')
WHERE "DAV:isfolder" = True and "DAV:ishidden" = False
```

Note: Lest you believe that WSS SQL accepts only file URLs, let's set the record straight. You can use either file or HTTP URLs in WSS SQL. Therefore, the following query is equivalent to the one given in the text:

```
SELECT "DAV:href", "DAV:displayname"
FROM SCOPE ('deep traversal of  _
"http://GOMEZAWIN2000.GomezaMobile.Local/exchange/Administrator/
        Contacts"')
WHERE "DAV:isfolder" = True and "DAV:ishidden" = False
```

In our previous examples we used the full URL path. The **SCOPE** operator can also accept relative URL paths because WSS SQL queries are executed on the basis of the context of an ADO connection. For example, let's pretend that you already have a connection open to the Administrator's root mailbox folder:

```
file://./backofficestorage/GomezaMobile.local/MBX/Administrator
```

The following query gets everything (including subfolders) under the Administrator's **Contacts** folder:

```
SELECT "DAV:href", "DAV:displayname"
FROM SCOPE ('deep traversal of "/Contacts"')
WHERE "DAV:isfolder" = True and "DAV:ishidden" = False
```

Note: This relative URL syntax works only with file URLs. If you are writing WSS SQL queries using HTTP URL syntax, you must specify the entire path.

SCOPE Shorthand

A couple of syntax shortcuts are possible when you're working with **SCOPE**. Use of the **SCOPE** keyword in a **SELECT** statement is optional. If you do not use the **SCOPE** keyword (as in the query that follows), the search depth defaults to shallow:

```
SELECT "DAV:href" from
"file://./backofficestorage/GomezaMobile.local/MBX/Administrator/
        Contacts"
WHERE "DAV:isfolder" = True and "DAV:ishidden" = False
```

Note: Not using the **SCOPE** keyword but still specifying the scope (as in the malformed query that follows) is a simple syntax error:

```
SELECT "DAV:href", "DAV:displayname"
FROM 'shallow traversal of _
"file://./backofficestorage/GomezaMobile.local/MBX/Administrator/
        Contacts"'
WHERE "DAV:isfolder" = True and "DAV:ishidden" = False
```

If you do use the SCOPE keyword but fail to specify shallow or deep traversal, the SELECT statement defaults to deep traversal, as in this query:

```
SELECT "DAV:href", "DAV:displayname"
FROM SCOPE _
('"file://./backofficestorage/GomezaMobile.local/MBX/Administrator/
        Contacts"')
WHERE "DAV:isfolder" = True and "DAV:ishidden" = False
```

Then there is the sin of omission when dealing with the public folder tree designed for MAPI clients. As we have mentioned several times, a deep traversal on that tree results in an error. As you probably would expect, a query that defaults to a deep traversal (as in the preceding syntax) also generates an error.

Note: When you do not use the **SCOPE** keyword, you can simply surround the URL with double quotation marks. However, when you do use the **SCOPE** keyword, not only must you use double quotation marks around the URL, but you must also surround the entire clause with single quotation marks. This syntax must be followed to the letter. More on this later.

You can specify more than one folder in your SCOPE clause as long as you separate each one with commas, as in the following example:

```
SELECT "DAV:href", "DAV:displayname"
FROM SCOPE ('shallow traversal of _
"file://./backofficestorage/GomezaMobile.local/MBX/Administrator/
        Contacts"', _
'shallow traversal of  _
"file://./backofficestorage/GomezaMobile.local/MBX/Administrator/
        Inbox"')
WHERE "DAV:isfolder" = True and "DAV:ishidden" = False
```

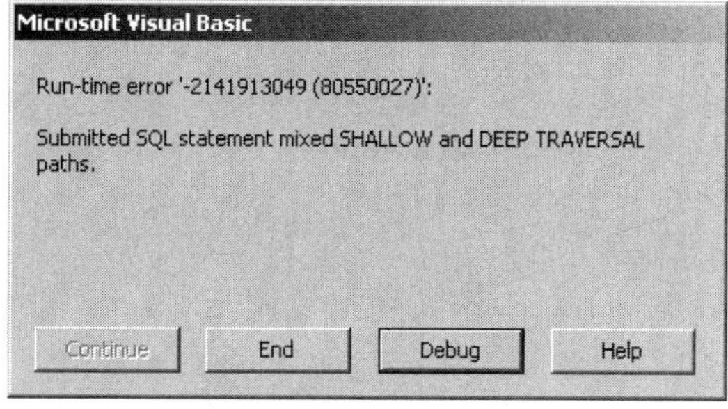

Figure 7.6 Error resulting from mixing shallow and deep traversals in a single **SELECT** statement

SCOPE Errors

When you search more than one folder, you must specify the same depth for each folder. You cannot mix and match deep and shallow searches in the same **SELECT** statement. If you do, you get the error shown in Figure 7.6.

While we're on the subject of things that can go wrong when you're working with **SCOPE**, remember how security works. If you try to execute a query against a folder to which you do not have access, you will get the error message "URL is outside of scope" (see Figure 7.7). The query uses the connection that you specify to do its work. So, for example, if you open a connection to a user's private mailbox and then run a query against a public folder store, you will get the same "URL is outside of scope" error.

If you decide to do something wrong, such as specifying deep traversal of the MAPI public folder store, you will get the error message "Specified resource was out-of-scope" (see Figure 7.8).

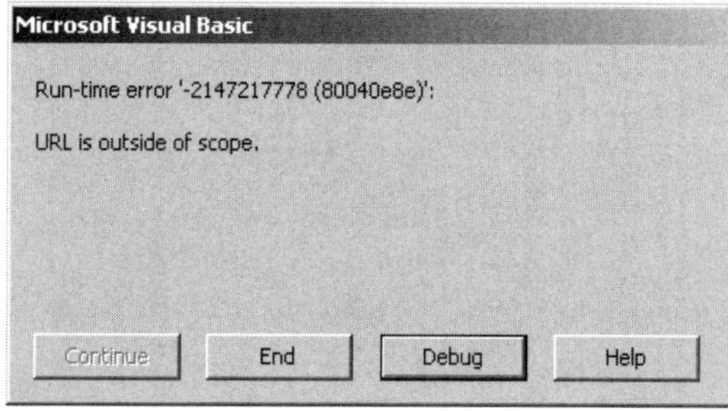

Figure 7.7 Error resulting from querying against a folder that the connection can't access

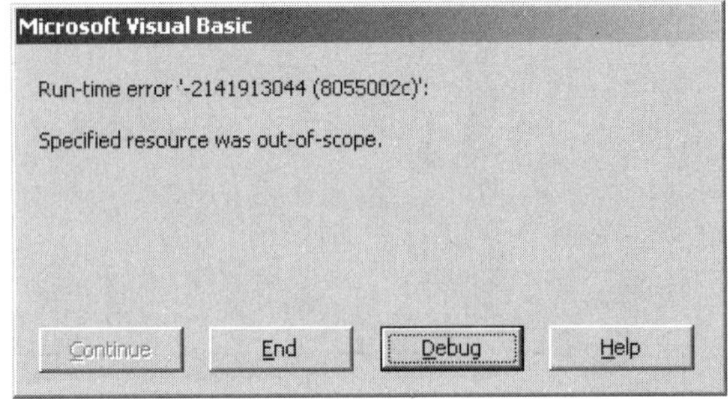

Figure 7.8 Error resulting from specifying deep traversal on a MAPI public folder store

A generic catchall error message for any syntax error in WSS SQL is "Submitted SQL statement was incomplete" (see Figure 7.9). As you may suspect, this is the most common error.

The WHERE Clause

We now come to the most diverse part of the **SELECT** statement: the **WHERE** clause. It is diverse because **WHERE** clauses can contain any number of logical conditions chained together by AND and OR keywords. What's more, the **WHERE** clause can have predicates (**GROUP BY**, **LIKE**, **ORDER BY**, and so on).

The Web Storage System uses tokens as values for search conditions in a WHERE clause. Tokens are surrounded by single quotation marks. They are the lit-

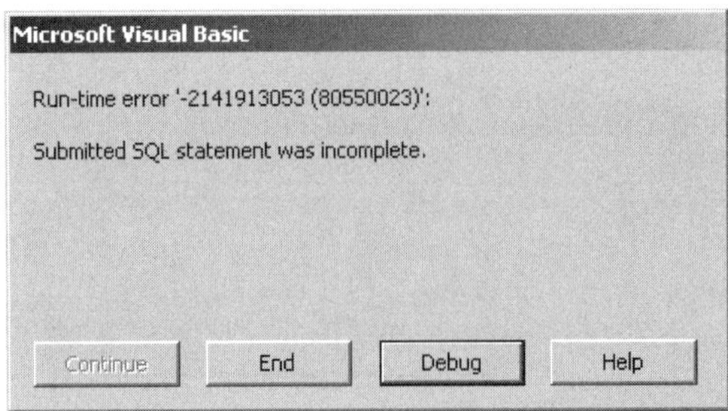

Figure 7.9 General WSS SQL syntax error

eral values on which you want to search. For example, the following query returns all contacts in the Administrator's **Contacts** folder that work in Massachusetts:

```
SELECT "DAV:href", "urn:schemas:contacts:fileas",
    "urn:schemas:contacts:email1"
FROM "file://./backofficestorage/GomezaMobile.local/MBX/Administrator/
            Contacts"
WHERE ("urn:schemas:contacts:st" = 'MA')
```

Note that field names used in the **WHERE** clause are surrounded by double quotation marks, just as field names used in the **SELECT** clause are. So far, you would expect to specify a literal in SQL by using single quotation marks anyway. Now here's the catch. A token can contain only alphabetical characters unless it is surrounded by double quotation marks. For example, how would one get all contacts who were also vice presidents? Would the following code work?

```
SELECT "DAV:href", "urn:schemas:contacts:fileas",
    "urn:schemas:contacts:email1"
FROM "file://./backofficestorage/GomezaMobile.local/MBX/Administrator/
            Contacts"
WHERE ("urn:schemas:contacts:title" = 'Vice President')
```

As it turns out, this code would not work. Since the token contains a space, we need to surround it in double quotation marks first and then tack on the single quotation marks. The following query is syntactically correct and returns the desired results:

```
SELECT "DAV:href", "urn:schemas:contacts:fileas",
    "urn:schemas:contacts:email1"
FROM "file://./backofficestorage/GomezaMobile.local/MBX/Administrator/
            Contacts"
WHERE ("urn:schemas:contacts:title" = '"Vice President"')
```

As we have seen in prior examples, a couple of values can go in the **WHERE** clause that do not need single or double quotation marks. These are the Boolean True and False values, as in the following query:

```
SELECT "DAV:href", "DAV:displayname"
FROM SCOPE ('shallow traversal of _
"file://./backofficestorage/GomezaMobile.local/MBX/Administrator/
        Contacts"', _
'shallow traversal of  _
"file://./backofficestorage/GomezaMobile.local/MBX/Administrator/
        Inbox"')
WHERE "DAV:isfolder" = True and "DAV:ishidden" = False
```

Specifying a Date Range in a WHERE Clause

When you're specifying date values in the **WHERE** clause, the single quotation marks around the date value are all you need. For example, the following query is syntactically correct if you're asking for contacts in the Administrator's **Contacts** folder that were created on that person's birthday:

```
SELECT "DAV:href", "urn:schemas:contacts:fileas",
    "urn:schemas:contacts:email1"
FROM "file://./backofficestorage/GomezaMobile.local/MBX/Administrator/
             Contacts"
WHERE "DAV:creationdate" = '2000-07-28'
```

However (there always seems to be a however), dates are not stored in items in this format. They also contain the hour, minute, second, and millisecond of creation. So a more plausible **WHERE** clause would be the following:

```
WHERE "DAV:creationdate" = '2000-07-28 11:39:39.275'
```

However (again), you most likely will not know the exact fraction of a second when a particular item was created. A more practical way to guarantee that you get all contacts in the Administrator's **Contacts** folder that were created on that person's birthday would use the following code:

```
SELECT "DAV:href", "urn:schemas:contacts:fileas",
    "urn:schemas:contacts:email1"
FROM "file://./backofficestorage/GomezaMobile.local/MBX/Administrator/
             Contacts"
WHERE "DAV:creationdate" > '2000-07-27' AND "DAV:creationdate"
    < '2000-07-29'
```

In this case we are looking for everything greater than the day before and less than the day after.

Embedded WSS SQL

As you may have gathered, WSS SQL suffers from the same problems that plague any embedded SQL code and have discouraged its use. The parsing and overcompensating for the quotation marks that are part of the syntax can become really cumbersome. To make sure that everything looks good to the query parser (in virtually every circumstance), we come up with some string beauties in our VB code, as in the following example, which gets everything from the currently logged-on user's **Contacts** folder:

```
Dim objMailbox As CDO.IMailbox
Dim objPerson As New CDO.Person
Dim sSQL As String

' Get the currently logged-on user:
' UserName should be something like:
' CN=Administrator,CN=Users,DC=GomezaMobile,DC=local
objPerson.DataSource.Open "LDAP://" & objInfo.UserName

' Get his or her mailbox:
Set objMailbox = objPerson

sSQL = "select ""DAV:href"", " & _
               """urn:schemas:contacts:fileas"", " & _
               """urn:schemas:contacts:email1""" & _
               " from "
sSQL = sSQL & """" & objMailbox.Contacts & """"
```

Here's what seems to be another interesting WSS SQL anomaly. Let's assume in the following VB code snippet that **EX_DISPLAYNAME** and **EX_ISFOLDER** are previously defined constants containing the schema field names and that **RootURL** is a valid URL that was passed into the hypothetical function as an argument. This is valid embedded WSS SQL syntax:

```
sRootSQL = "SELECT " & """" & EX_DISPLAYNAME & """ " & _
           "FROM scope('shallow traversal of """ & RootURL & """') " & _
           "WHERE (" & """" & EX_ISFOLDER & """ = True) " & _
           "ORDER BY " & """" & EX_DISPLAYNAME & """"
```

No doubt some of the more experienced SQL/ADO programmers in the reading audience are cringing. Isn't this one of the reasons we have stored procedures and parameterized queries in SQL databases—to get rid of ugly embedded code in programs and help maintainability? Yes it is, but consider the fact that WSS SQL is in its infancy and embedded is all we have right now. So when developing production code, just be careful, use your best judgment, and test, test, test.

> **Note:** You may have noticed from the plethora of WSS SQL query examples that the keywords in the language are *not* case sensitive. "SELECT" is as good as "select."

Another feature that makes the **WHERE** clause versatile is the fact that you can add what are called predicates to it. The next few sections discuss these in more detail.

The CAST Function

The **CAST** function is similar to cast functions in other languages in that it explicitly converts a field to another data type. In WSS SQL, you use **CAST** to attribute a data type to a property in the returned **Recordset** object. The Web Storage System recognizes all data types in the Exchange 2000 schema installed with the product. **CAST** is used mainly for working with custom properties because the Web Storage System might not know what their types are. Using **CAST** in a WSS SQL query is entirely optional. If you don't use it, your custom properties are evaluated as string values. Boolean properties don't need to be cast.

The basic syntax of the **CAST** function is as follows:

```
CAST ("<some value>" AS "<some datatype>")
```

"<Some value>" can be the name of a property or a literal string (both need to be surrounded by double quotation marks). Here's the catch: The **CAST** function supports only XML data types. Therefore "<some datatype>" needs to be replaced with one of the values from Table 7.8 (surrounded by double quotation marks, of course).

Some examples will help illustrate all of this. This first one casts a custom date property to a data time before comparing it:

```
WHERE CAST("custom:mydateprop" AS "datetime") > "2001-12-01T10:00"
```

The next example casts the string "0" as an integer to compare it with another integer:

```
WHERE "custom:count" > CAST("0" AS "int")
```

UUID properties are recognized with or without the braces, as in the next two examples:

```
WHERE CAST ("myguid" AS "uuid")
    = "F04DA480-65B9-11d1-A29F-00AA00C14882"
WHERE CAST ("myguid" AS "uuid")
    = "{F04DA480-65B9-11d1-A29F-00AA00C14882}"
```

All Microsoft Exchange 2000 binary properties are base 64 encoded by default because this is a format that can be sent in XML:

```
WHERE CAST ("custom:mybinaryprop" AS "bin.base64") > "a98k231KJg823kj"
```

Table 7.8 XML Property Data Types Supported by **CAST**

XML Type	**Description**
bin.base64	Binary data (base 64 encoded)
bin.hex	Hex data
Boolean	In an XML string, this value is 1 for True and 0 for False.
char	Character data
date	Just the date
dateTime	Date and time
dateTime.tz	Full date and time stamp, including time zone
fixed.14.4	Fixed floating-point number
float	Floating-point number
i2	2-byte integer (Smallint)
i4	4-byte integer
i8	8-byte integer
int	4-byte integer
number	General numeric data
r4	4-byte floating-point number (Float)
r8	8-byte floating-point number (Real)
string	2-byte character string (Unicode)
time	Time stamp
time.tz	Time stamp, including time zone
ui1	Tinyint
ui2	Numeric (5, 0)
ui4	Numeric (10, 0)
ui8	Numeric (19, 0)
uri	A valid Uniform Resource Identifier
uuid	GUID in string format

If you want to encode using hex, you must cast the property *and* the value against which you are comparing it:

```
WHERE CAST ("custom:mybinaryprop" AS "bin.hex") = _
CAST("08AF183B82" AS "bin.hex")
```

Enabling Full-Text Indexing

The next four predicates deal with character and pattern matching in WSS SQL. First we'll introduce each one, and then we'll explain how to use them in WSS SQL queries. Most of these predicates work only if full-text indexing is applied to the store being searched. To implement full-text indexing (Figure 7.10), open the Exchange System Manager, expand **Servers**, and then expand your Exchange server and right-click on the store to be indexed.

You will be prompted for where to put the catalog. After you create the index, right-click on the store and choose **Properties.** You will see a new **Full-Text Indexing** tab similar to the one in Figure 7.11, where you can regulate how often the index is updated and when it should be rebuilt.

> **Note:** In order to use the index in your queries, you *must* check off **This index is currently available for searching by clients.**

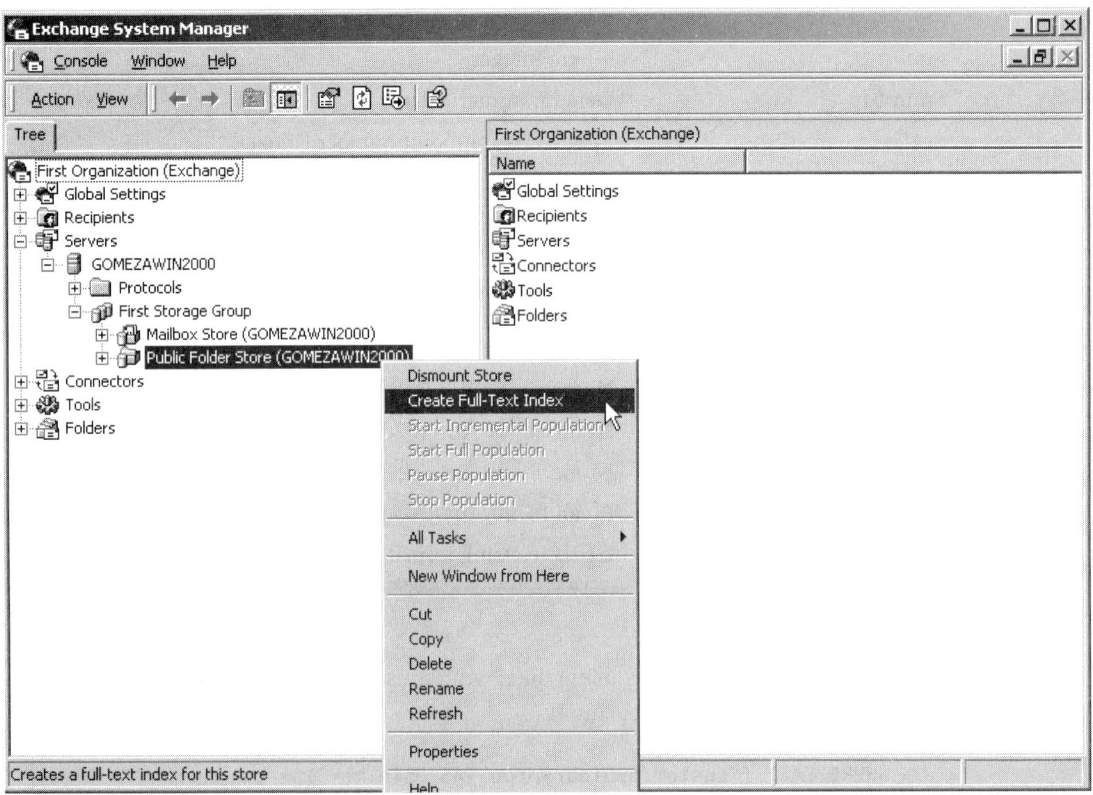

Figure 7.10 Implementing full-text indexing using the Exchange System Manager

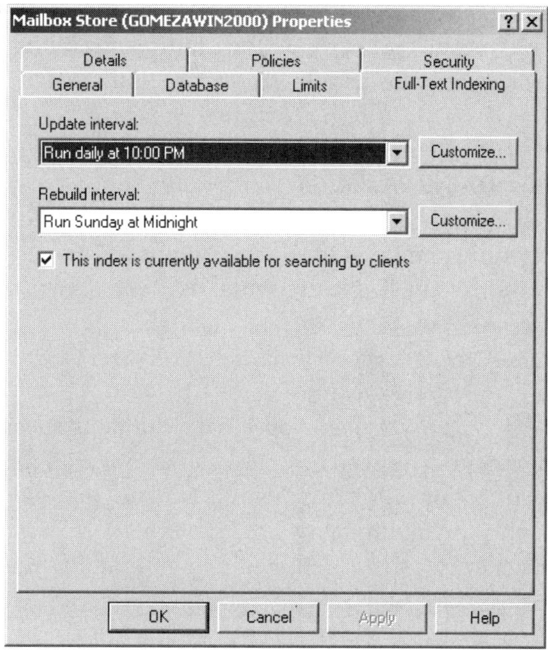

Figure 7.11 Full-text indexing maintenance using the Exchange System Manager

Even after doing this, you will get the error depicted in Figure 7.12 because the index has been enabled but not actually created.

To build the index, right-click on the store in the Exchange System Manager and select **Start Full Population.** You will be warned that it might take a long time depending on the size of your store. However, this option will build the complete index right away. You can check on the progress of the index by expanding the

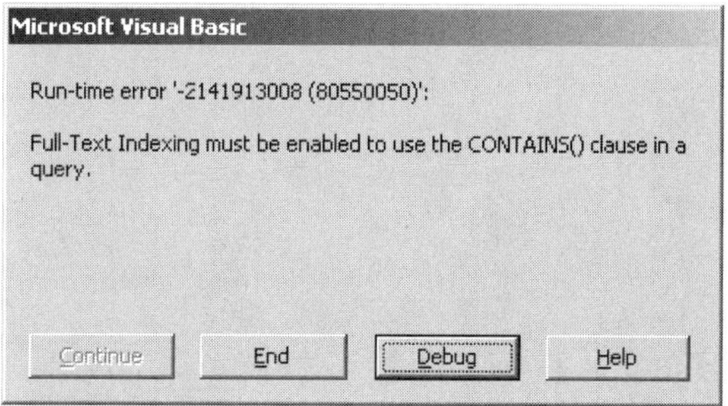

Figure 7.12 A full-text index must be built before it can be used

store in Exchange System Manager, clicking **Full-Text Indexing**, and inspecting the "last build time" property, as shown in Figure 7.13.

For more information, search on "Full-Text Indexing" in the Exchange 2000 SDK.

The CONTAINS Predicate

The **CONTAINS** predicate allows you to search for a specific word or phrase in a predetermined order. Only whole words are matched, so you cannot use wild-card expressions here. The basic syntax is

```
CONTAINS ("<property name>", '<search specification>')
```

The property name is optional. If none is specified, then only the message or document body is searched. You can also use an asterisk (*) to include all properties marked for full-text indexing. The property name must be a string surrounded by double quotation marks, such as **urn:schemas:mailheader:to**. The asterisk does not have to be surrounded by the quotation marks.

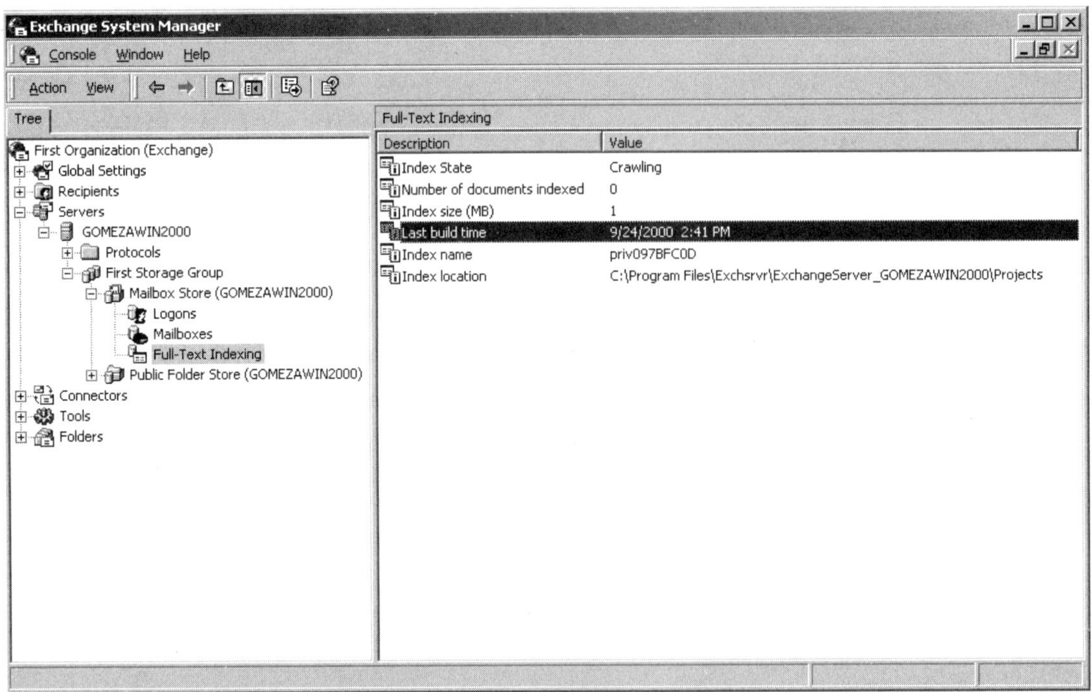

Figure 7.13 Checking on the Exchange System Manager's progress

The search specification is the string to search for, surrounded by single quotation marks and following the same rules as discussed earlier for tokens in a **WHERE** clause. You can use the AND and OR keywords and the **FORMSOF** predicate (discussed in the next subsection). The NOT operator is allowed only if it follows the AND keyword.

> **Note:** The search specification parameter of the **CONTAINS** predicate is case sensitive, and the property must match exactly. For example, in the clause that follows, only contacts that work at Sanford And Son will be returned:
>
> ```
> WHERE CONTAINS ("urn:schemas:contacts:o", '"Sanford And Son"')
> ```

The FORMSOF Predicate

The **FORMSOF** predicate allows you a bit of leeway. It is used as part of a **WHERE** clause to find word variations, typically within a **CONTAINS** or **FREETEXT** predicate. The basic syntax is

```
FORMSOF (<type>, "<string>" [, <some other string>])
```

In the Web Storage System the only type supported is **INFLECTIONAL**. The string can be one or more words for which the search engine is to find variations. Each word must be delimited by double quotation marks and separated by commas. For example,

```
FORMSOF (INFLECTIONAL, "fight")
```

will find items containing "fighter," "fighters," "fighting," and so on.

When **FORMSOF** is used within a **CONTAINS** or **FREETEXT** predicate, the whole **FORMSOF** predicate is considered a token, so it must be surrounded by single quotation marks:

```
WHERE CONTAINS ("urn:schemas:contacts:hobbies", _
'FORMSOF (INFLECTIONAL, "photograph", "announce")')
```

In this case all contacts that listed "photography," "photographs," "photographer," "announcer," "announcing," and so on would be returned.

The FREETEXT Predicate

The **FREETEXT** predicate is used as part of a **WHERE** clause to loosely match any item having a variation of a word or a group of words. The basic syntax is

```
FREETEXT ("<property name>" [, <some other property name>],
'<search criteria>')
```

The property name is optional. If none is specified, then only the message or document body is searched. You can also use an asterisk (*) to include all properties marked for full-text indexing. The property name must be a string surrounded by double quotation marks, such as "**urn:schemas:mailheader:to**". The asterisk does not have to be surrounded by the quotation marks.

The search specification is the string to search for, surrounded by single quotation marks and following the same rules as discussed earlier for tokens in a **WHERE** clause. You can use the AND and OR keywords and the **FORMSOF** predicate (see the previous subsection). The NOT operator is allowed only if it follows the AND keyword.

The main difference is that **FREETEXT** allows you to find one or more words specified in the search criteria. For example,

```
WHERE FREETEXT ("urn:schemas:contacts:personaltitle", 'Mr Ms Dr')
```

pulls all contacts with "Mr," "Ms," or "Dr" in their name. When you're using the **FREETEXT** predicate, a group of words can match several items. For example, in the clause that follows, any item containing "garden," "gardening," "gardener," "gardens," "rose," "roses," and so on will be returned:

```
WHERE FREETEXT ("urn:schemas:contacts:hobbies", 'garden rose')
```

The LIKE Predicate

The **LIKE** predicate is used as part of the **WHERE** clause to perform character matches. **LIKE** does a character-by-character comparison of the specified property value and the supplied characters. It essentially finds characters that match a specified string. The basic syntax is

```
WHERE "<property name>" LIKE "<value>"
```

The property name must be surrounded by double quotation marks. The value needs to be surrounded by single quotation marks. The percent character (%) matches any or no characters adjacent to the specified string. For example, "%ar%" would match "Mary":

```
WHERE ("urn:schemas:contacts:spousecn" LIKE '%ar%')
```

The GROUP BY Predicate

The **GROUP BY** predicate organizes the returned **Recordset** object according to one or more of the properties specified in the **SELECT** statement. The basic syntax is

```
GROUP BY "<property name>" [, <some more property names>]
```

Basically, you can have any number of property names surrounded by double quotation marks and separated by commas. The only catch is that the property names have to be specified in the **SELECT** clause as well:

```
SELECT "DAV:href", "urn:schemas:contacts:fileas", _
       "urn:schemas:contacts:email1", _
       "urn:schemas:contacts:st"
FROM "file://./backofficestorage/GomezaMobile.local/MBX/Administrator/
             Contacts"
GROUP BY "urn:schemas:contacts:st"
```

Getting Item Counts with GROUP BY As we'll see shortly, WSS SQL does not support **COUNT**. However, by including the **DAV:visiblecount** property in the **SELECT** statement, you can get a count of the items that you specify in the **GROUP BY** clause. The **DAV:visiblecount** property is a read-only property that returns the number of visible items in a **Recordset** object that are not folders. That is, items that have **DAV:isfolder** and **DAV:ishidden** set to True will not be counted.

For example, let's say that you want to count the number of low-importance, normal-importance, and high-importance messages in a user's inbox. Your query could go something like this:

```
SELECT "DAV:visiblecount", "urn:schemas:httpmail:importance", _
FROM "file://./backofficestorage/GomezaMobile.local/MBX/Administrator/
             Inbox"
GROUP BY "urn:schemas:httpmail:importance"
```

Let's assume that **objRecordset** is a new ADO **Recordset**, that sSQL contains the query string given in the preceding code, and that **objConn** is a valid connection to the Administrator's root mailbox folder:

```
objRecordset.Open sSQL, objConn
```

Now take the resulting **Recordset** and loop through it, checking for the **urn:schemas:httpmail:importance** field. Whenever you find it, consult the **DAV:visiblecount** property to get the total for that importance value. The code to do this would look something like this:

```
Dim sImportance As String
objRecordset.MoveFirst
Do Until objRecordset.EOF
    Select Case objRecordset("urn:schemas:httpmail:importance")
        Case 2
            sImportance = "High"
```

```
            Case 1
                sImportance = "Normal"
            Case 0
                sImportance = "Low"
        End Select
        MsgBox objRecordset("DAV:visiblecount") & " " & sImportance _
            & " importance messages."
    Loop
```

The ORDER BY Clause

The **ORDER BY** clause sorts the returned **Recordset** in ascending or descending order according to one or more of the properties specified. The basic syntax is

```
ORDER BY "<property name>" [, "<some more property names>"]
    [ASC or DESC]
```

For example,

```
SELECT "DAV:href", "urn:schemas:contacts:fileas", _
    "urn:schemas:contacts:email1", _
    "urn:schemas:contacts:st"
FROM "file://./backofficestorage/GomezaMobile.local/MBX/Administrator/
             Contacts"
ORDER BY "urn:schemas:contacts:st" ASC
```

The RANK BY Clause

Finally, there is the **RANK BY** clause. Ranking can be used to sort results on the basis of how frequently and where the queried strings appear in the indexed documents. In a nutshell, this is how Internet tools such as a search engine know how to sort the results. The basic syntax is

```
RANK BY <clause>(Mechanism, weight)
```

The value of the clause can be either **WEIGHT** or **COERSION**. The Mechanism refers to an action such as **WEIGHT**, **MULTIPLY**, or **ABSOLUTE**. The weight is the significance of the rank. See the Microsoft Exchange 2000 SDK for more information.

Some Unsupported SQL

As we said earlier, WSS SQL can be used only to query data, not to update. Although the discussion we've presented here is not an exhaustive treatment of the language, by now you should have a very good idea of what you can and cannot do with it. With this in mind, note that the following SQL statements are simply not supported in WSS SQL:

- AVG
- CONVERT (WSS SQL uses CAST instead)
- COUNT
- CREATE VIEW
- DELETE
- DROP INDEX
- INSERT
- JOINS (all kinds)
- MAX
- MIN
- SELECT DISTINCT
- SET
- SUM
- UPDATE

Summary

We hope that this chapter provided you with several new tools to add to your Exchange 2000 development belt. We discussed the theories behind Universal Data Access, introduced the enhancements to ADO for dealing with Web Storage System data, learned two ways to build a URL for any item in the Web Storage System, and studied the syntax for WSS SQL. If your organization has invested in Microsoft Exchange as a messaging, scheduling, and collaboration platform, it has a wealth of data in the form of e-mail messages, contacts, appointments, tasks, conversation threads, documents, and so on. Leveraging your prior programming experiences with ADO and "conventional" SQL, you will soon be developing robust applications for Exchange 2000 using the familiar ADO object model and writing robust WSS SQL queries against that data with the elegance and ease of a database.

Chapter 8

Using ADO and ExOLEDB: Advanced Topics

Now that we have the basics of using ADO and ExOLEDB to access Exchange data in both the public and private message stores, it's time to move on to more advanced topics. The first part of this chapter will examine how to use ADO and ExOLEDB together with COM+ and DCOM to create a scalable solution in a multi-server Exchange organization. Then we'll examine how the role-based security model to which we've become accustomed in previous versions of Exchange lends itself to the Exchange 2000 security model and how to set access permissions to files and folders in Exchange 2000 using ADO and ExOLEDB.

Using ADO and ExOLEDB to Create Scalable Solutions

To create a scalable application using Exchange 2000, you can spread the data out across multiple Exchange servers in the Exchange organization. The public and private message stores easily lend themselves to this arrangement.

If you're using the public store, you can configure Exchange to *replicate* folder schemas and their contents to other servers at periodic intervals. Figure 8.1 shows a public folder that is replicated to three Exchange servers in the organization. Depending on how often you decide to synchronize data across the organization, you will have to examine the impact of synchronization and concurrency issues. Do you want all servers always to have an updated copy of the data that has just changed? Do you want *all* servers to have a copy of *all* the folder schemas and data, or some to have just the data?

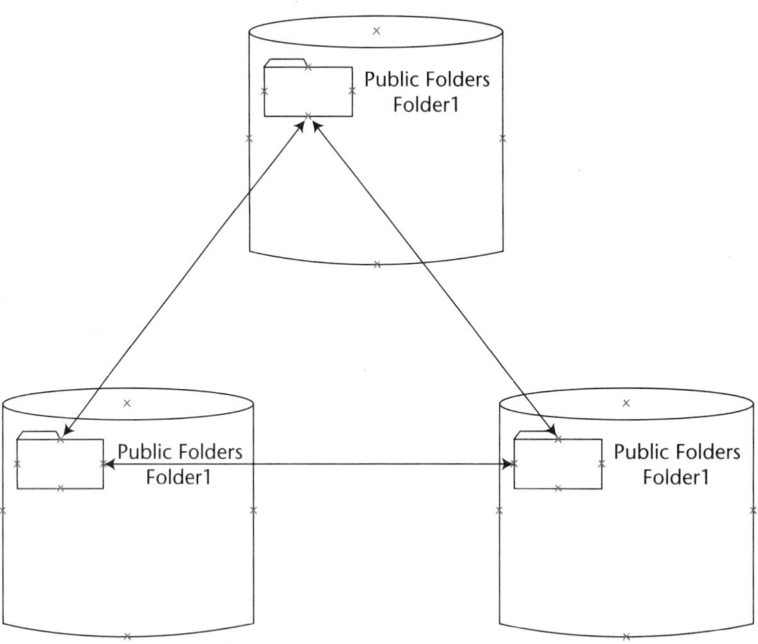

Figure 8.1 An Exchange public folder replicated among three Exchange servers

If you're considering the private mailbox store, there are different considerations. Here, Exchange uses a different scalability model. When you create an Exchange mailbox for a user, you decide the server, storage group, and database on which the mailbox will be located, and that mailbox will be located on that server *only*. Mailboxes are not replicated from server to server. Using this scenario, you can balance the load by spreading out users' mailboxes across multiple servers (see Figure 8.2).

Both scenarios have their strengths and weaknesses. Public folder replication is great for data that is updated infrequently and read frequently. If you have a situation in which documents are posted daily in a scenario of publisher and subscriber, public folder replication can allow folders to be replicated fairly infrequently to remote servers, and users can connect to any available server to read the published documents.

However, if you have a situation in which users are concurrently accessing data that are updated frequently, private folders may provide a better solution because there's only one copy of a specific file in the organization at a given time. You will need to provide users other than the mailbox owner access to a user's private folders, however.

Whichever approach you choose—public folders or the private mailbox store—note that ExOLEDB can access data only *on the same Exchange server.* This is

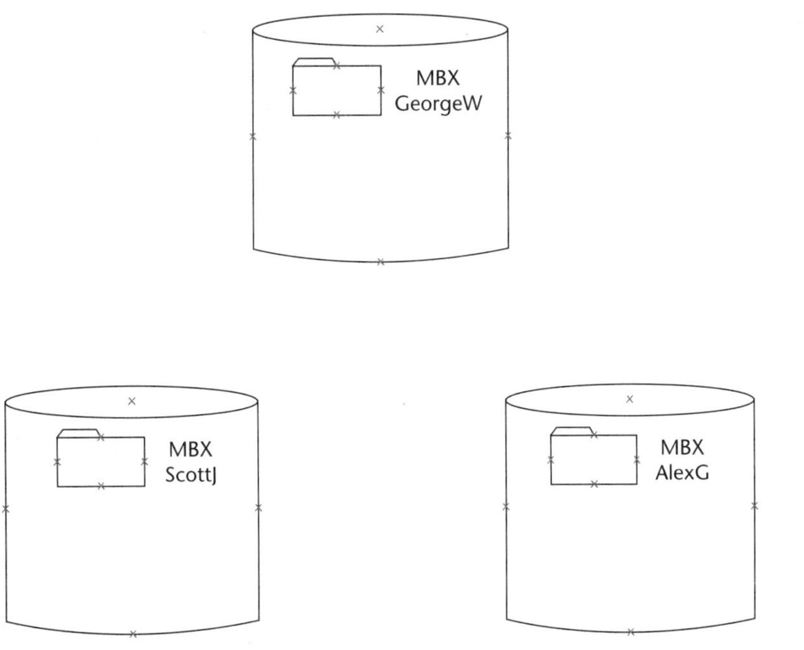

Figure 8.2 Three Exchange private mailboxes in a three-server scenario

drastically different from the client-server scenario we're all used to. If you are trying to access data that's located in a user's Exchange mailbox, the only way ExOLEDB can find it is if it is executing on the server that contains the Exchange mailbox. Similarly, ExOLEDB will access the replica of an Exchange public folder only if the local machine has a replica of the folder. If we are going to use ExOLEDB in our scalable, multiserver environment, then we'll need some additional help!

Using DCOM to Access Remote Exchange Data

There's an old saying that goes something like, "If you're stuck with a bunch of lemons, then make lemonade!" Now we're *not* saying that ADO and ExOLEDB are lemons! What we *are* saying is that because ExOLEDB is not "remotable," we will have to build in the "remoting" part ourselves. Enter DCOM.

Note: To use DCOM effectively, all your remote servers must be connected by a high-speed local network. A DCOM solution will not perform well over a slow link.

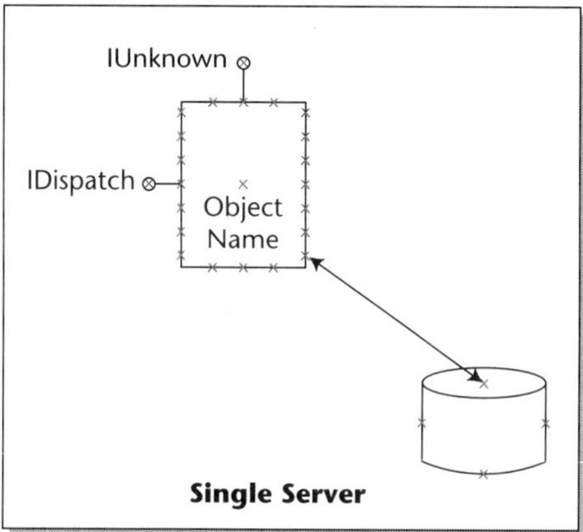

Figure 8.3 A typical in-process component

Remember that DCOM stands for Distributed Component Object Model and is nothing more than "COM over the wire." Instead of the typical scenario, in which we implement an in-process COM DLL, as shown in Figure 8.3, we'll implement a component that executes out of process and across a machine boundary using a COM proxy and stub. The machine where the component will execute is, of course, the machine where our Exchange data resides (see Figure 8.4).

The best part about implementing and using a remote component in DCOM is that you implement and call the component in exactly the same way that you'd implement and call a local, in-process component. In other words, we'll take the same code we wrote in the previous chapter, install it on the Exchange server machine and administer a COM+ server application for it, and export the proxy to the client machine. The client has no idea that the component is not located locally, but the client is really calling a component proxy and letting COM+ take care of the details of marshaling the inbound parameters to the remote server and any outbound data back to the client.

Configuring a COM+ Server Application in Windows 2000

In our example, we'll consider an in-process component implemented in Visual Basic with ADO and ExOLEDB. The component exposes one method, **GetFolder-Contents**, that takes a user name as an inbound parameter and returns the contents of the user's Exchange **Inbox** folder. The contents will be returned as a comma-delimited string of file and folder names.

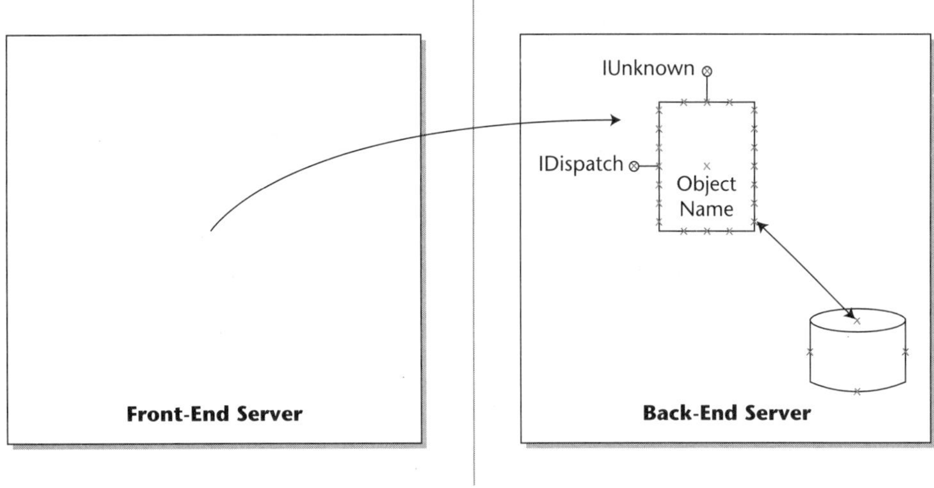

Figure 8.4 A remote COM component using a proxy and stub to access Exchange data

Once we build the DLL using Visual Basic, we'll install and register it on the Exchange server machine. Typically, we would build an installation package using the Package and Deployment wizard and deploy it on the server. Once you have the component installed and registered, you then need to configure a COM+ server application. To do this, open **Component Services** in Administrative Tools. Navigate to the **COM+ Applications** folder under **My Computer** as shown in Figure 8.5, and select **New** and then **Application** from the **Action** menu. This will start the COM Application Install wizard (Figure 8.6). Choose the second option, **Create Empty Application**, enter a name for the application, and choose the **Server application** option.

Next you need to specify the application identity—that is, the user whose context the component will assume during execution. In this case we'll need to set the identity to that of a "super user" that has access to all users' mailboxes. This is discussed in further detail in Chapter 9, but for now, assume there's a user named ExchangeSuperUser that has access to everyone's mailbox. We'll set the identity to this user as shown in Figure 8.7.

Click **Next**, then **Finish**, and you've successfully created a new COM+ server application. All that remains is to add the component to the application. To do this, expand the application you just created on the left pane, select the **Components** folder, and choose **New** and then **Application** from the **Action** menu, as shown in Figure 8.8.

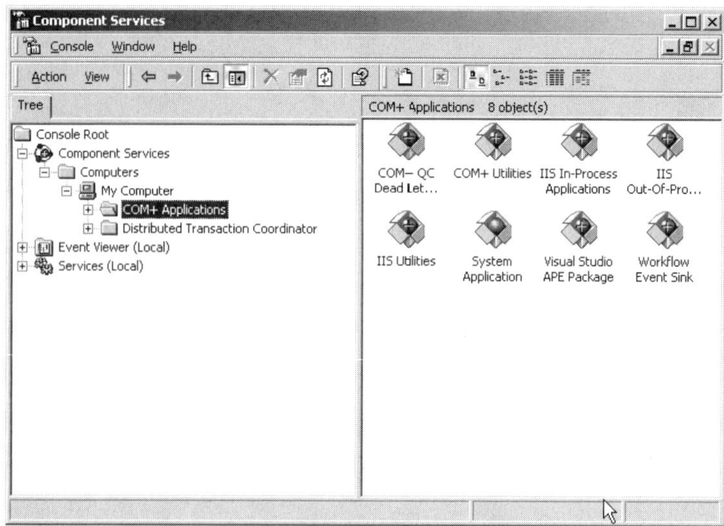

Figure 8.5 Creating a new COM+ application using Component Services

This will start the COM Component Install wizard. Select the first option, **Install New Components**, use the file common dialog to select your component DLL, click **Next**, and then **Finish**, and you have successfully configured your COM+ application on the Exchange server machine.

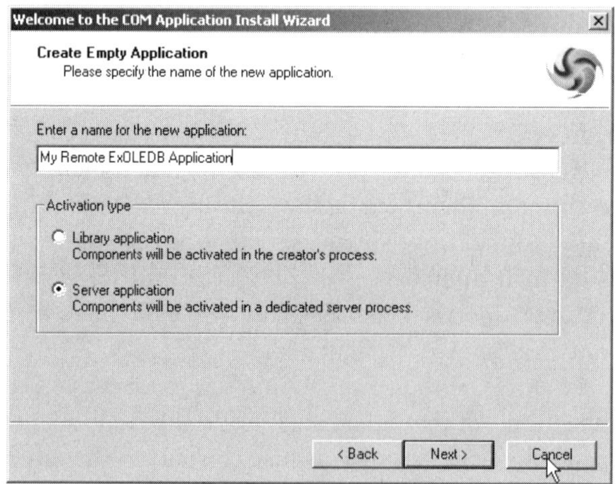

Figure 8.6 Configuring a new COM+ application as a server application using the COM Application Install wizard

Welcome to the COM Application Install Wizard

Set Application Identity
Please specify the application identity.

Account
The application identity will be set to the following account. Components in the application will run under this account. If you are creating more than one application, this setting will be applied to each application.

Interactive user - the current logged on user
This user:
User: BILLERICA\ExchangeSuperUser Browse...
Password: ********
Confirm password: ********

< Back Next > Cancel

Figure 8.7 Setting the application identity using the COM Application Install wizard

You can run the included component test harness program on the server machine and, with the **Component Services** window open, watch your component be activated and deactivated by watching the component icon (the sphere with the plus sign) rotate.

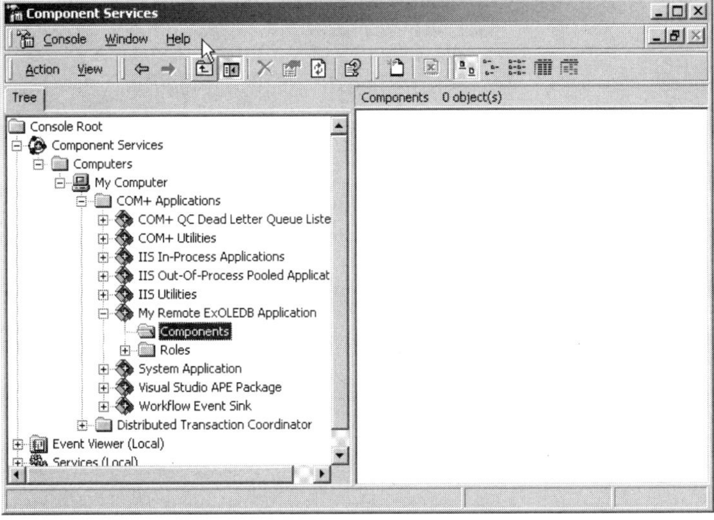

Figure 8.8 Adding a component using the COM Application Install wizard

Creating and Installing the Application Proxy Package

Now that the component is installed on the Exchange server machine as part of a COM+ server application, all we need to do is export a proxy to the client machine. To do this, select the COM+ application in the left pane in **Component Services**, and choose **Action** and then **Export...** from the menu. This will start the COM Application Export wizard. Enter the path of the desired package file you want to create (or use the **Browse** button) and choose the **Application proxy** option, as shown in Figure 8.9. Click **Finish**, and you've successfully created the proxy package.

> **Note:** In Figure 8.9, the proxy package is being saved to diskette. You may want to simply use a network share to save the package directly to the client machine where the proxy is to be installed.

All that remains is to install the proxy package on the client machine. To do this, copy the package file along with the corresponding CAB file to the client machine. (The COM Application Export wizard always creates a package file with a ".msi" file extension and a cabinet file with a ".cab" file extension.) Then execute the package by double-clicking the ".msi" file in Windows Explorer. If everything is successful, you'll notice a COM+ application with the same name that you created on the server machine in the listing of applications in the **Component Services** MMC on the client machine.

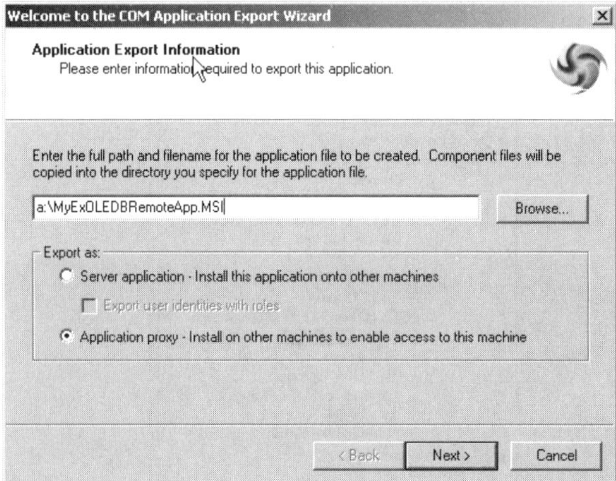

Figure 8.9 Creating an application proxy package using the COM Application Export wizard

If you now run the test harness program on the *client* machine, you can open a **Component Services** window on the *server* machine and watch your component be activated and deactivated by your client-side test harness via the proxy-and-stub mechanism.

A Proxy-and-Stub Scenario with Multiple Front-End and Back-End Servers

Once you master the proxy and stub with two servers (the proxy installed on the front-end server and the component and stub installed on the back-end), you can readily extend this design technique to use multiple front-end and back-end servers to increase scalability. The best part is that you need to do nothing more on the server (back-end) side, and you need to make only minor coding changes on the client (front-end) side.

On each back-end server, you simply need to install and register the component in the same way that you did on the first back-end server. As long as you make no modifications to the component's type library, you can easily invoke the same component from a front-end proxy on *any* back-end server machine. If you do decide to make modifications to the component's type library, you'll need to uninstall and reinstall the new version of the component on all the back-end servers.

On each front-end server, you simply need to install the same proxy package that you installed on the first front-end server. You now have a situation in which multiple front-end servers are configured to invoke a component on one of many back-end servers (Figure 8.10).

On the client side, all that remains is to come up with some sort of mechanism to determine the back-end server on which to invoke our component. Remember that in our example we are trying to access Exchange data from the private mailbox store. Therefore, we need to map the user name that we're given to the name of the back-end Exchange server that houses that user's mailbox. Since this information is stored in the Windows 2000 Active Directory, we could look there for it, or we could maintain our own SQL Server database containing this information (see Figure 8.11).

Whichever method you choose, all that the client-side code running on the front-end server needs to do is invoke the component on the desired back-end with the following line of Visual Basic code:

```
Set iFolder = CreateObject("ExIFSLib.iFolder", GEORGE002)
```

where "ExIFSLib.iFolder" is the programmatic identifier (**ProgID**) of our component and "GEORGE002" is the name of the back-end machine where our particular user's data lives.

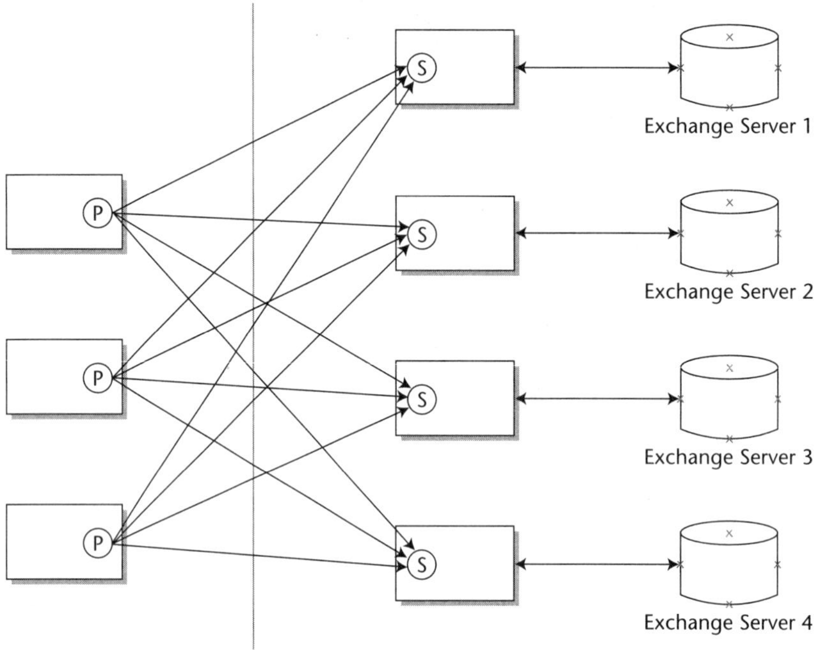

Figure 8.10 Multiple front-end servers with proxies (P) to the same component on multiple back-end servers (S)

You're probably accustomed to calling **CreateObject** without the second parameter. This parameter is optional. If you omit it, one of the following things will happen: If the component is installed locally, you will invoke the local copy of the component. If the component is not installed locally but a proxy is installed, you'll invoke the component on the remote server specified on the **Activation** tab of the COM+ Application property page in the **Component Services** MMC (Figure 8.12). Note that this is the server where you originally created the proxy package.

Therefore, in a multiserver proxy-and-stub configuration, by default you'll invoke the back-end server where you created the proxy, but you can explicitly invoke a component on a specific back-end server on the basis of the location of the Exchange data you need to access. You do, however, need an external mechanism for mapping the data you want to its actual location.

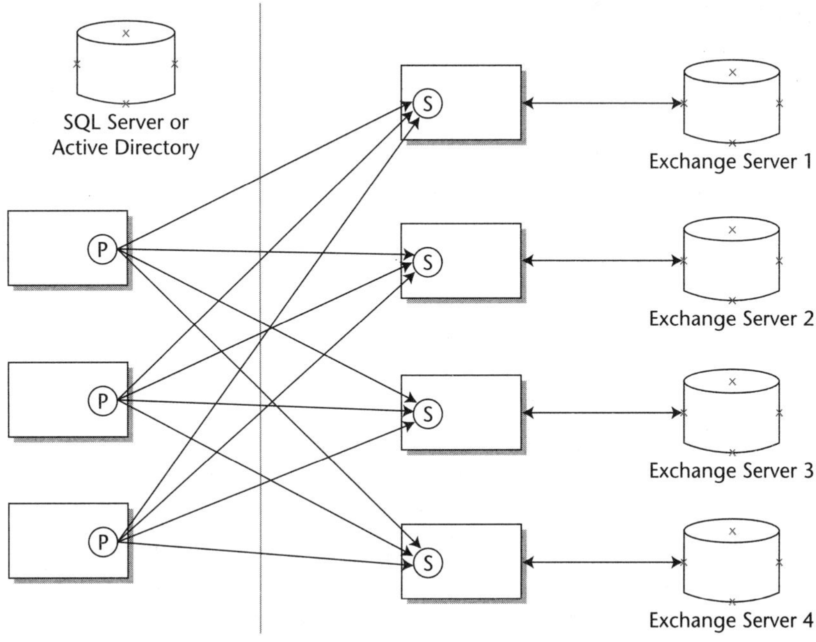

Figure 8.11 Front-end/back-end Exchange configuration with an external database to maintain location data

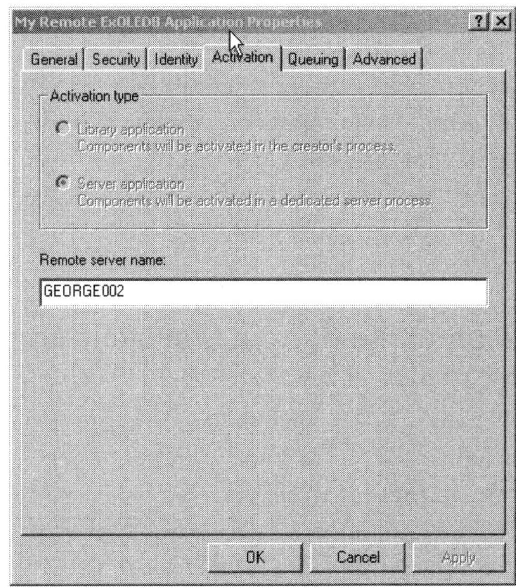

Figure 8.12 Specifying the default remote server name in Component Services

Using ADO and XML to Set Access Control Lists

Data security is a big concern when you're designing and building an enterprise application. In the previous example we had a scenario in which an Exchange "super user" was granted access to everyone's private mailbox. If you're using the public folder store, you may want to grant a certain level of access, or deny access entirely, to a specific user or a group of users. You can do this with ADO and ExOLEDB. But before we delve into some code samples, let's talk a little about Exchange 2000 security principles in general.

Exchange 2000 Pseudo-Role-Based Security

You may remember that Exchange 5.5 used the concept of *role-based security.* If you were administering a public folder store, for example, you could select a folder and choose from a list of roles that had a certain level of access on the folder and its contents. Examples of such roles include contributor, publishing editor, and author. You could also modify the access level of existing roles, effectively creating a definition of a custom role. You then assigned specific roles to specific NT users or security groups. For example, you could assign user GeorgeW the contributor role, user ScottJ and group PluralBostonDev the publishing author role, and so on.

In Exchange 2000, we can also use the concept of role-based security; however, Exchange 2000 basically uses integrated Windows 2000 security principles "under the hood" instead of its own security model. (For a brief discussion of Windows 2000 security, see Chapter 18.) Roles are mapped on top of Windows 2000 security through custom properties defined in the Exchange security schema. You then set access permissions on an item by adding an access control entry (ACE) to the item's access control list (ACL) that refers to the role properties you have defined on the item. Setting the descriptor property of the security schema using an XML format does just this.

Configuring the Custom MAPI Role Properties: Assigning Users to Roles

The following URL defines the Exchange security schema:

```
http://schemas.microsoft.com/exchange/security
```

This schema and ExOLEDB allow you to make use of the general-purpose properties listed in Table 8.1.

Table 8.1 General-Purpose Exchange Security Properties

http://schemas.microsoft.com/exchange/security/creator
http://schemas.microsoft.com/exchange/security/lastmodifier
http://schemas.microsoft.com/exchange/security/originalauthor
http://schemas.microsoft.com/exchange/security/originalsender
http://schemas.microsoft.com/exchange/security/originalsentrepresenting
http://schemas.microsoft.com/exchange/security/originator
http://schemas.microsoft.com/exchange/security/readreceiptfrom
http://schemas.microsoft.com/exchange/security/receivedby
http://schemas.microsoft.com/exchange/security/receivedrepresenting
http://schemas.microsoft.com/exchange/security/reportdestination
http://schemas.microsoft.com/exchange/security/reportfrom
http://schemas.microsoft.com/exchange/security/sender
http://schemas.microsoft.com/exchange/security/sentrepresenting

In addition, 16 custom MAPI properties are set aside for use as role properties. You can use as many of these as you wish for defining which users are members of which roles. The format of the URL for these properties is

```
http://schemas.microsoft.com/mapi/proptag/x3D250102
```

where "x3D250102" is the MAPI property tag. This property tag is further split up into the property ID, (3D25) and the property type (0102). (0102 represents the data type array of BYTEs.) The 16 MAPI properties (their property names and property IDs) reserved for use as defining roles are listed in Table 8.2.

Now that we've defined the 16 role properties to which we can assign a list of users and groups, how exactly do we make these assignments? Basically, to use a role property we need to set its value to an array of bytes representing the security IDs (SIDs) of the users that we wish to add to the role. The exact format of the role property is shown in Table 8.3.

To map a user or security group name to a SID and create the array of BYTEs described in Table 8.3, we'll need to implement a component using Visual C++ and Win32 APIs. An excellent sample of such a component can be found at **http://msdn.microsoft.com/library/techart/secroles.htm** (download the **roles.exe** sample), or,

Table 8.2 Custom MAPI Role Properties

Property Name	**Property ID**
PR_XMT_SECURITY_ROLE_1	0x3d25
PR_XMT_SECURITY_ROLE_2	0x3d26
PR_XMT_SECURITY_ROLE_3	0x3d27
PR_XMT_SECURITY_ROLE_4	0x3d28
PR_XMT_SECURITY_ROLE_5	0x3d29
PR_XMT_SECURITY_ROLE_6	0x3d2a
PR_XMT_SECURITY_ROLE_7	0x3d2b
PR_XMT_SECURITY_ROLE_8	0x3d2c
PR_NON_XMT_SECURITY_ROLE_1	0x3d7c
PR_NON_XMT_SECURITY_ROLE_2	0x3d7d
PR_NON_XMT_SECURITY_ROLE_3	0x3d7e
PR_NON_XMT_SECURITY_ROLE_4	0x3d7f
PR_NON_XMT_SECURITY_ROLE_5	0x3d80
PR_NON_XMT_SECURITY_ROLE_6	0x3d81
PR_NON_XMT_SECURITY_ROLE_7	0x3d82
PR_NON_XMT_SECURITY_ROLE_8	0x3d83

if you wish, you can use the accompanying sample "stateless" component, **RolePropLib**, that was based on this sample. The following code sample assigns the sample component to add the users GeorgeW, ScottJ, and AlexG to the **PR_XMT_SECURITY_ROLE_1** role for the public folder named **Folder1**:

```
Dim iRec As ADODB.Record
Dim iRoleProp As RolePropLib.iRoleProp
```

Table 8.3 Format of a Custom MAPI Role Property in the Exchange Security Schema

Version	**Total Byte Count**	**SIDs, Concatenated**	**Additional Information**
DWORD	DWORD	Array of BYTEs	Array of BYTEs
0	Total number of bytes used by the SIDs	SID1, SID2, ..., SIDn	Reserved for future use

```
Dim sURL As String
Dim vUserList As Variant     '/ Array of user name strings ...
Dim vRole As Variant         '/ The property value array ...

'/ Use the RolePropLib to build our Role Property value
'/ based on an array of user name strings ...
vUserList = Array("GeorgeW", "ScottJ", "AlexG")
Set iRoleProp = New RolePropLib.iRoleProp
vRole = iRoleProp.GetPropValue(vUserList)
Set iRoleProp = Nothing

'/ Open our folder and append the PR_XMT_SECURITY_ROLE_1 property ...
sURL = "file://./backofficestorage/wesolowski.george.local/public
            folders/Folder1"
Set iRec = New ADODB.Record
iRec.Open sURL, , adModeReadWriteSetting
iRec.Fields.Append "http://schemas.microsoft.com/mapi/proptag/
                       x3D250102", adVarBinary, Len(vRole), , vRole
iRec.Fields.Update
iRec.Close
Set iRec = Nothing
```

Access Permissions: Using Roles to Assign Permissions

Now that we've defined a role for a public folder and assigned users to it, all that's left to do is assign an access level for this role using XML to configure the folder's access control list (ACL). The following URL defines the property that describes the security descriptor for an item:

```
http://schemas.Microsoft.com/exchange/security/descriptor
```

The following code example grants read-only access to the **PR_XMT_SECURITY_ROLE_1** role for the **Folder1** public folder.

```
Dim iRec As ADODB.Record
Dim sURL As String
Dim sXML As String

'/ Open our folder and append the security descriptor property ...
sURL = "file://./backofficestorage/wesolowski.george.local/public
            folders/Folder1"
Set iRec = New ADODB.record
iRec.Open sURL, , adModeReadWrite
```

```
sXML = "<S:security_descriptor " & _
    "xmlns:S=""http://schemas.microsoft.com/security/""" & _
    "xmlns:D=""urn:uuid:c2f41010-65b3-11d1-a29f-00aa00c14882/""" & _
    "D:dt=""microsoft.security_descriptor"">"
sXML = sXML & "<S:dacl>"
sXML = sXML & "<S:effective_aces>"
sXML = sXML & "<S:access_allowed_ace>"
sXML = sXML & "<S:access_mask>1301BF</S:access_mask>"
sXML = sXML & "<S:role_sid>"
sXML = sXML & "<S:scope>object</S:scope>"
sXML = sXML & "<S:property_name>" & _
    "http://schemas.microsoft.com/mapi/proptag/x3D250102" & _
              "</S:property_name>"
sXML = sXML & "</S:role_sid>"
sXML = sXML & "</S:access_allowed_ace>"
sXML = sXML & "</S:effective_aces>"
sXML = sXML & "</S:dacl>"
sXML = sXML & "</S:security_descriptor>"

iRec.Fields.Append "http://schemas.microsoft.com/exchange/security/
                           descriptor", adBSTR, Len(sXML), , sXML
iRec.Fields.Update
iRec.Close
```

Note that the **access_mask** XML tag in this code sample defines read-only access. This corresponds to the **ACCESS_MASK** Win32 structure that defines a bit mask for setting more granular security settings. The basic settings are defined in Table 8.4. If you need more granularity, consult the Exchange 2000 SDK or MSDN Win32 help files for more details.

Remember that we defined **PR_XMT_SECURITY_ROLE_1** as having users GeorgeW, ScottJ, and AlexG as its members. Therefore, we've given these three users read-only access to **Folder1** by first defining a role property and then assigning a security descriptor based on the defined role property.

Table 8.4 ACCESS_MASK Values for Commonly Used Access Levels

Access Level	Hexadecimal Value	Decimal Value
Read-only	0x001200A9	1179817
Write-only	0x00100117	1048855
Read/write	0x001301BF	1245631
Full	0x001F01FF	2032127

Summary

This chapter demonstrated how to build a robust, scalable, and secure system using ADO and ExOLEDB. We first enlisted the help of DCOM and COM+ to address the "nonremotable" aspect of ExOLEDB. This allowed us to effectively use ADO and ExOLEDB in a scalable, multiserver environment. Finally, we learned how to set security descriptors using custom MAPI properties and ExOLEDB, which will help us build more scalable, robust enterprise systems.

Chapter 9

Exchange 2000 Store Events

Web Storage System events provide a mechanism by which an application can execute code in response to certain things happening in the system. For example, whenever an item is saved, deleted, copied, or modified, the server can create an event sink object to run some custom programming in response to a certain event being fired. An event sink is a creatable COM object that implements an event interface to service the event and runs out of process with respect to the process that triggered the event. It is a piece of code written in Visual Basic (VB), Visual C++ (VC++), Visual Basic Scripting Edition (VBScript) or any other language that supports COM, which is triggered by a specific event. By running out of process, the Information Store process is spared from crashes in the event sink itself.

Events come in three flavors: synchronous, asynchronous, and system. Synchronous events run at the time the operation is being performed and can therefore be used to intercept an operation before it is committed to the store. Asynchronous events run at some point after a particular operation has completed and therefore can be used not to abort the operation but merely as notification that the event occurred. System events fire when Exchange databases start up or shut down.

Event sinks interact with data in the Web Storage System using the Exchange OLE DB provider and ADO 2.5. As we saw in previous chapters, the Exchange OLE DB provider is meant only for accessing local data, which means that your event sinks must run on the server. In addition, your event sinks must be wrapped up in COM+ to work. This chapter focuses on how to use event sinks in your applications and all of the aforementioned repercussions.

Note: When writing any type of event sink in Visual Basic, include a reference to the ExOLEDB Type library in your Visual Basic Project file. This is the **exoledb.dll** usually found in the **Exchsrvr\bin** directory on the Exchange 2000 server.

System Events

System events give timed notifications or notify the event sink that Exchange databases have started up or shut down. Therefore, they can be classified as a type of asynchronous event sink. The Web Storage System is made up of public stores and mailbox stores that the Exchange 2000 Server keeps in Exchange databases (MDBs). If this sounds familiar to the Access developers in the audience, it should because an MDB on an Exchange 2000 Server is in fact a special type of Jet database. Exchange provides system event notifications by calling the following **IExStoreSystemEvents** interface event procedures:

- **OnTimer** is called after a certain period of time.
- **OnMDBStartUp** is called when an MDB is started.
- **OnMDBShutDown** is called when an MDB is shut down.

To access these event procedures, set a reference to the ExOLEDB Type library in your Visual Basic Project file and include the following line of code in your class module:

```
Implements Exoledb.IExStoreSystemEvents
```

You will now find that the following three methods appear in the right-hand drop-down list in the Visual Basic integrated development environment (IDE) (Figure 9.1).

OnTimer Event Sink

```
Private Sub IExStoreSystemEvents_OnMDBShutDown(ByVal bstrMDBGuid As _
                                              String, ByVal lFlags _
                                              As Long)
End Sub
```

The **OnTimer** event can be used for repeated calls, such as scheduling routine maintenance tasks on the server, or for a one-time event. We'll see how to specify each later, when we learn how to register for this event.

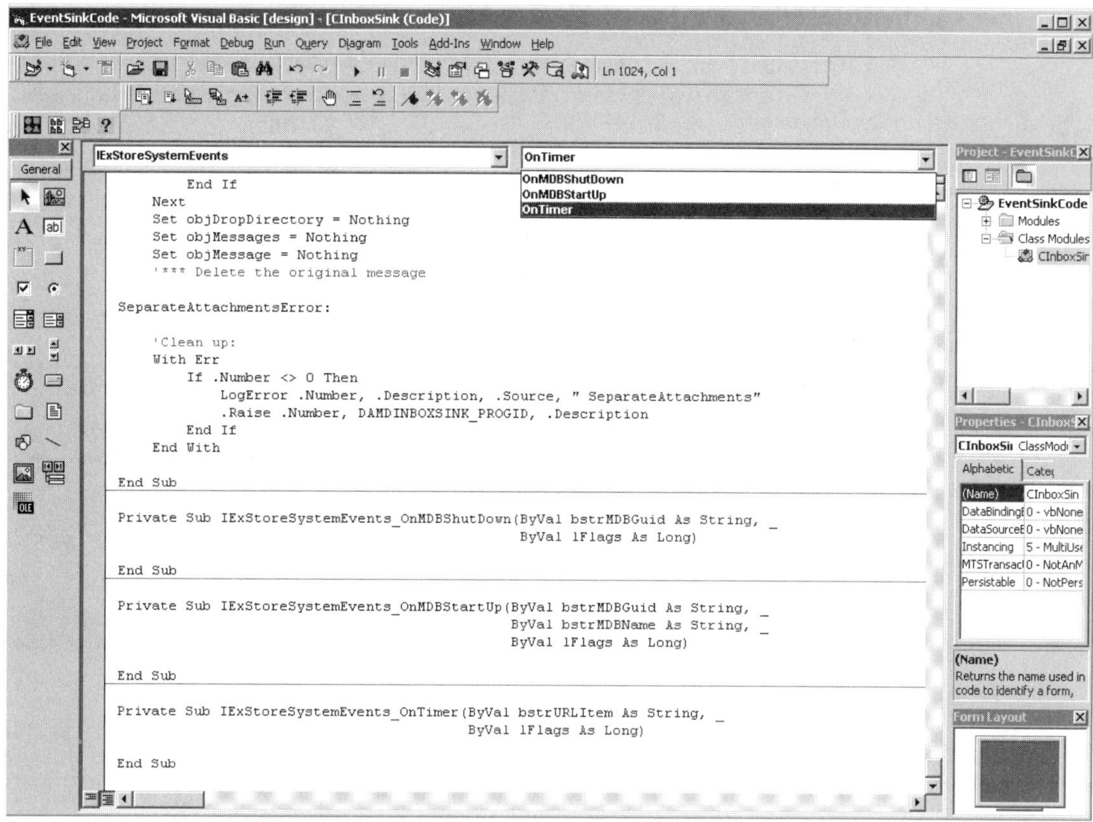

Figure 9.1 Implementing store events using the Visual Basic IDE

OnMDBStartUp Event Sink

```
Private Sub IExStoreSystemEvents_OnMDBStartUp(ByVal bstrMDBGuid As _
                                              String, ByVal _
                                              bstrMDBName As String, _
                                              ByVal lFlags As Long)
End Sub
```

The **OnMDBStartUp** event sink fires whenever an Exchange store starts functioning. The **bstrMDBGuid** string contains the GUID of the MDB being started. The **bstrMDBName** string contains the name of the MDB being started. The **lFlags** field contains bitwise AND flags.

OnMDBShutDown Event Sink

```
Private Sub IExStoreSystemEvents_OnMDBShutDown(ByVal bstrMDBGuid As _
                                              String, ByVal lFlags As _
                                              Long)
End Sub
```

The **OnMDBShutDown** event sink fires whenever an Exchange store is shut down. The **bstrMDBGuid** string contains the GUID of the MDB being stopped. The **lFlags** field contains bitwise AND flags.

> **Note:** In all three of the system events, the **lFlags** parameter supports the **EVT_INITNEW** flag. This flag is set at the first firing of the event. It is usual for initialization purposes because it is set only once during the lifetime of a created event sink. You can check whether this flag is set in the system event sink with the following code:
>
> ```
> If lFlags And EVT_INITNEW Then
> ' Insert your initialization code.
> End If
> ```

Asynchronous Events

There are a few ground rules that the developer should be aware of when dealing with asynchronous events. Since asynchronous events have been conceptually supported in prior versions of Exchange, veteran Exchange developers should not be surprised to find that when the **OnDelete** event is called, the item that caused it to fire has already been deleted. Furthermore, asynchronous events do not have any firing priority, and there is no guarantee as to how soon asynchronous event notifications are called after the event occurs. Logically, asynchronous events are not processed if a synchronous event aborts the event.

Deleting a folder does not cause events to fire on individual items in the folder, but it does cause events to fire on the subfolders. Copying a folder causes events to fire on all of the items in the folder, but moving a folder does not cause events to fire on any items in the folder.

Also note that an asynchronous event method can modify the event that caused the event notification. This modification, in turn, can fire an event for the same item, thereby causing a recursive event loop like a good science fiction time travel paradox. So, it is the responsibility of the event sink to ensure that this looping doesn't happen.

To access the asynchronous store events, set a reference to the ExOLEDB Type library in your Visual Basic Project file and include the following line of code in your class module:

```
Implements Exoledb.IExStoreAsyncEvents
```

OnSave Event Sink

```
Private Sub IExStoreAsyncEvents_OnSave(ByVal pEventInfo As _
                                       Exoledb.IExStoreEventInfo, _
                                       ByVal bstrURLItem As String, _
                                       ByVal lFlags As Long)
End Sub
```

The **OnSave** event is fired whenever a new item is saved or an existing item is saved, moved, or copied. The **bstrURLItem** is a string containing the URL of the newly saved item. The **lFlags** argument consists of a bunch of bitwise AND flags that provide further information about the newly saved item, as described in Table 9.1.

The first argument, **pEventInfo**, is an **IExStoreEventInfo** interface, which is a support interface used to retrieve event information passed to the event method. To discuss this interface in appropriate detail, we devote an entire section to it later in the chapter. Note that the information regarding the **IExStoreEventInfo** interface applies to both asynchronous and synchronous events.

Table 9.1 **OnSave** Event Sink Flags

Value	Enumeration	Description
1	EVT_NEW_ITEM	The item being saved is brand-new.
2	EVT_IS_COLLECTION	The item being saved is a collection.
4	EVT_REPLICATED_ITEM	The item is being saved as a result of replication.
8	EVT_ISDELIVERED	The item is being saved as a result of message delivery.
64	EVT_INITNEW	This flag is set at the first firing of the event. It is usual for initialization purposes because it is set only once during the lifetime of a created event sink.
256	EVT_MOVE	The item was moved over (an implicit save).
512	EVT_COPY	The item was copied over (an implicit save).

Programmatically Determining the Cause of the OnSave Event

Getting back to the **OnSave** event, the following VB code will write the cause of the **OnSave** event to a log file. Establish a reference to the Microsoft Scripting Runtime library ("C:\WINNT\System32\scrrun.dll") in your Visual Basic Project file to handle writing to a log file. Of course, you should already have the reference to the ExOLEDB Type library.

```
Private Sub IExStoreAsyncEvents_OnSave(ByVal pEventInfo _
                                       As Exoledb.IExStoreEventInfo, _
                                       ByVal bstrURLItem As String, _
                                       ByVal lFlags As Long)
'-----------------------------------------------------------------------
'   Plural
'-----------------------------------------------------------------------
'   Called by a store event when an item is saved.
'   Input:  Name        Description
'           pEventInfo  A pointer to an IExStoreEventInfo interface
'                       that can be used to obtain further information
'                       related to the event.
'           bstrURLItem A string containing a URL to the newly saved
'                       item.
'           lFlags      Bitwise AND flags providing more info on the
'                       Save event. See the Exchange SDK for more
'                       information.
'   Output: None
'-----------------------------------------------------------------------
'   Revision History:
'   Date:       Developer:      Description:
'-----------------------------------------------------------------------
'   07/28/2000  Alex Gomez      Initial Design
'-----------------------------------------------------------------------
On Error GoTo IExStoreAsyncEvents_OnSaveError
    Dim objFSO As New Scripting.FileSystemObject
    Dim EvtFile As Scripting.TextStream
    Dim sEvtLog As String

    ' Create a new log file or open it if it already exists:
    sEvtLog = Environ("SystemDrive") & "\OnSave.log"
    Set EvtFile = objFSO.OpenTextFile(sEvtLog, ForAppending, True)

    ' Determine the cause of the OnSave event:
    ' Case 1: EVT_IS_DELIVERED
    If lFlags And EVT_IS_DELIVERED Then
        ' Perform your tasks for an OnSave delivered mail item:
        EvtFile.WriteLine ("  Flag contains EVT_IS_DELIVERED bit set")
    ' Case 2: EVT_MOVE
    ElseIf lFlags And EVT_MOVE Then
```

```
            ' Perform your tasks for an OnSave moved item:
            EvtFile.WriteLine ("  Flag contains EVT_MOVE bit set")
        ' Case 3: EVT_COPY
        ElseIf lFlags And EVT_COPY Then
            ' Perform your tasks for an OnSave copied item:
            EvtFile.WriteLine ("  Flag contains EVT_COPY bit set")
        End If
        ' Check if it is a folder notification
        If lFlags And EVT_IS_COLLECTION Then
            ' Perform your tasks if the item being saved is a folder:
            EvtFile.WriteLine ("  Flag contains EVT_IS_COLLECTION bit set")
        End If

    IExStoreAsyncEvents_OnSaveError:
        ' Clean up:
        EvtFile.Close
        Set EvtFile = Nothing
        Set objFSO = Nothing
        With Err
            If .Number <> 0 Then
                ' Insert your custom error-handling code:
            End If
        End With
    End Sub
```

OnDelete Event Sink

```
Private Sub IExStoreAsyncEvents_OnDelete(ByVal pEventInfo As _
                                         Exoledb.IExStoreEventInfo, _
                                         ByVal bstrURLItem As String, _
                                         ByVal lFlags As Long)
End Sub
```

The **OnDelete** event is fired whenever an item is deleted or as the delete part of a move operation on the item. The **bstrURLItem** is a string containing the URL of the deleted item. Remember that since this is an asynchronous event, the URL cannot be used to open the item, because it has already been deleted. The **lFlags** argument consists of a bunch of bitwise AND flags that provide further information about the deleted item, as described in Table 9.2.

The **OnDelete** event uses the **EVT_HARDDELETE** and **EVT_SOFTDELETE** flags to distinguish between hard and soft deletes. A soft delete is defined as a delete that moves an item into the dumpster (the deleted subfolder within each folder). A hard delete is defined as a delete in which an item is completely removed from the store.

Table 9.2 OnDelete Event Sink Flags

Value	Enumeration	Description
2	EVT_IS_COLLECTION	The item being deleted is a collection.
4	EVT_REPLICATED_ITEM	The item is being replicated from another location.
16	EVT_SOFTDELETE	The item was moved to the dumpster (soft delete).
32	EVT_HARDDELETE	The item was permanently deleted (hard delete).
64	EVT_INITNEW	This flag is set at the first firing of the event. It is usual for initialization purposes because it is set only once during the lifetime of a created event sink.
256	EVT_MOVE	The delete was part of a move operation on the item.

The first argument, **pEventInfo**, is an **IExStoreEventInfo** interface that can be used to obtain further information related to the event, as discussed earlier.

Dummy Event Sinks

The **Implements** statement that we used earlier is how Visual Basic implements what is called polymorphism. In this object-oriented programming concept, many classes can provide the same property or method. When you add the **Implements** statement to your VB class, you are agreeing to provide an implementation for *all* of the properties and methods in the class you're implementing. If you don't, your code will not compile. For example, by adding the line

```
Implements Exoledb.IExStoreAsyncEvents
```

to your class, you must now provide code for *both* the **IExStoreAsyncEvents_OnSave** and the **IExStoreAsyncEvents_OnDelete** methods. Even if you are interested in only the **OnSave** event and don't care what happens in the **OnDelete** event, you must provide the code stub for the **OnDelete** method:

```
Private Sub IExStoreAsyncEvents_OnDelete(ByVal pEventInfo As _
                                         Exoledb.IExStoreEventInfo, _
                                         ByVal bstrURLItem As String, _
                                         ByVal lFlags As Long)
'---------------------------------------------------------------------
'   Plural
'---------------------------------------------------------------------
'   Called by a store event when an item is deleted.
```

```
'   Input:  Name         Description
'           pEventInfo   A pointer to an IExStoreEventInfo interface
'                        that can be used to obtain further information
'                        related to the event.
'           bstrURLItem  A string containing the deleted item's URL.
'                        The URL item cannot be opened because the item
'                        has already been deleted.
'           lFlags       Bitwise AND flags providing more info on the
'                        Delete event. See the Exchange SDK for more
'                        information.
'   Output: None
'----------------------------------------------------------------------
'   Revision History:
'   Date:       Developer:      Description:
'----------------------------------------------------------------------
'   07/28/2000  Alex Gomez      Initial Design
'----------------------------------------------------------------------
    '*** THERE IS NO CODE HERE BECAUSE WE DID NOT REGISTER AN ***
    '*** OnDelete EVENT. HOWEVER, WE STILL NEED TO INCLUDE THE STUB ***
    '*** HERE BECAUSE WE ARE IMPLEMENTING IExStoreAsyncEvents. ***
End Sub
```

Synchronous Events

Just as with asynchronous events, there are a few ground rules that the developer should be aware of when dealing with synchronous events. Moving a folder does not cause events to occur on any items in the folder, while copying a folder causes events to occur on all the items in the folder. Deleting a folder does not cause events to fire on individual items in the folder, but it does cause events to fire on the subfolders. Synchronous events are processed in a specific order, which is set when you register for synchronous event notification, as we'll see later in this chapter.

The item causing the event to fire is passed into the sink in the context of an OLE DB local transaction. When the event sink is processing a synchronous event, it can abort the OLE DB local transaction. If the transaction is aborted, no further synchronous event notifications will occur for that event. In addition, the synchronous events in the transaction that have already been notified are again notified that the transaction was aborted, allowing the developer to clean up data or undo activities if an event is aborted.

Aborting the transaction associated with a delete event prevents the item from being deleted. Similarly, if you abort an event that is the result of a move, both the save and the delete steps of the move are aborted, meaning that the original item is not deleted and the new item is not saved.

OnSyncSave Event Sink

```
Private Sub IExStoreSyncEvents_OnSyncSave(ByVal pEventInfo As _
                                          Exoledb.IExStoreEventInfo, _
                                          ByVal bstrURLItem As String, _
                                          ByVal lFlags As Long)

End Sub
```

The **OnSyncSave** event is fired before the item is saved. It is fired whenever a new item enters the Web Storage System and when an existing item is saved, moved, or copied. As noted earlier, the event is not fired when the item's parent folder is moved or copied. In the case of a move, aborting the transaction associated with the event aborts the entire move, meaning that the original item is not deleted and the new item is not saved.

The **bstrURLItem** is a string containing the URL of the item on which the event is occurring only if the item was created using the Exchange OLE DB provider or through DAV. The **lFlags** argument consists of a bunch of bitwise AND flags that provide further information about the event, as described in Table 9.3.

The first argument, **pEventInfo**, is an **IExStoreEventInfo** interface, which is a support interface used to retrieve event information passed to the event method and is discussed in more detail in its own section later in the chapter.

OnSyncDelete Event Sink

```
Private Sub IExStoreSyncEvents_OnSyncDelete(ByVal pEventInfo As _
                                            Exoledb.IExStoreEventInfo, _
                                           ByVal bstrURLItem As _
                                           String, ByVal lFlags As _
                                           Long)

End Sub
```

The **OnSyncDelete** event is fired when an item is being deleted in the Web Storage System. It is fired whenever an item is deleted or moved in the store. As noted earlier, the event is not fired when the item's parent folder is moved or deleted. Aborting the transaction associated with the event prevents the item from being deleted. In the case of a move, aborting the transaction associated with the event aborts the entire move, meaning that the original item is not deleted and the new item is not saved.

The **bstrURLItem** is a string containing the URL of the item that will be deleted upon successful completion of all synchronous events. The **lFlags** argu-

Table 9.3 **OnSyncSave** Event Sink Flags

Value	Enumeration	Description
1	EVT_NEW_ITEM	The item being saved is brand-new.
2	EVT_IS_COLLECTION	The item being saved is a collection.
4	EVT_REPLICATED_ITEM	The item is being saved as a result of replication.
8	EVT_ISDELIVERED	The item is being saved as a result of message delivery.
64	EVT_INITNEW	This flag is set at the first firing of the event. It is usual for initialization purposes because it is set only once during the lifetime of a created event sink.
256	EVT_MOVE	The item was moved over (an implicit save).
512	EVT_COPY	The item was copied over (an implicit save).
1024	EVT_DRAFT_CREATE	The item being saved is a newly created draft.
2048	EVT_DRAFT_SAVE	The item being saved is a draft.
4096	EVT_DRAFT_CHECKIN	The item being saved is a draft check-in.
16777216	EVT_SYNC_BEGIN	This is a synchronous begin event.
33554432	EVT_SYNC_COMMITTED	This is a synchronous commit event.
67108864	EVT_SYNC_ABORTED	This is a synchronous abort event.
536870912	EVT_INVALID_SOURCE_URL	The URL of the source item could not be obtained during a move operation.
1073741824	EVT_INVALID_URL	The URL passed to the sink is invalid.
2147483648	EVT_ERROR	An unexpected error occurred in the event.

ment consists of a bunch of bitwise AND flags that provide further information about the event, as described in Table 9.4.

The first argument, **pEventInfo**, is an **IExStoreEventInfo** interface, which is a support interface used to retrieve event information passed to the event method and is discussed in more detail in its own section shortly.

Table 9.4 OnSyncDelete Event Sink Flags

Value	Enumeration	Description
2	EVT_IS_COLLECTION	The item being deleted is a collection.
4	EVT_REPLICATED_ITEM	The item is being replicated from another location.
16	EVT_SOFTDELETE	The item has been moved to the dumpster (soft delete).
32	EVT_HARDDELETE	The item has been completely deleted from the Web Storage System (hard delete).
64	EVT_INITNEW	This flag is set at the first firing of the event. It is usual for initialization purposes because it is set only once during the lifetime of a created event sink.
256	EVT_MOVE	The item was moved over (an implicit delete).
33554432	EVT_SYNC_COMMITTED	This is a synchronous commit event.
67108864	EVT_SYNC_ABORTED	This is a synchronous abort event.
1073741824	EVT_INVALID_URL	The URL passed to the sink is invalid.
2147483648	EVT_ERROR	An unexpected error occurred in the event.

The Synchronous Event Always Rings Twice

As you may have gathered from the preceding discussions, synchronous events are always called twice. The first call is known as the begin phase. The next call is either the commit phase or the abort phase, depending on what your code decides. Therefore, it is imperative that your code determine which type of call is being made and act accordingly. To do this programmatically, you would write an **If . . . ElseIf** statement similar to the one shown earlier in the chapter (in the section Programmatically Determining the Cause of the OnSave Event). Just substitute in your code the flags that interest you from Table 9.3 or Table 9.4.

■ The IExStoreEventInfo and IExStoreDispEventInfo Support Interfaces

The **IExStoreEventInfo** interface is a support interface that is passed to every OLE DB event sink and is used to retrieve event information and control the event transaction. The **Abort**, **EventBinding**, **GetEventItem**, and **GetEventSession** methods of the **IExStoreEventInfo** interface can be used in C++ programs. If you want to use the **IExStoreEventInfo** interface in VB or VBScript programs, you must use the **IExStoreDispEventInfo** interface. The **IExStoreDispEventInfo** interface is just the OLE Automation equivalent of the **IExStoreEventInfo** interface. You simply set an **IExStoreDispEventInfo** variable equal to the **IExStoreEventInfo** variable passed into the event, as in the sample Visual Basic asynchronous save event shown here:

```
Private Sub IExStoreAsyncEvents_OnSave(ByVal pEventInfo As _
                                       Exoledb.IExStoreEventInfo, _
                                       ByVal bstrURLItem As String, _
                                       ByVal lFlags As Long)
    Dim iDispEventInfo As IExStoreDispEventInfo

    ' Just set it and forget it:
    Set iDispEventInfo = pEventInfo

End Sub
```

Let's look at the individual methods of the **IExStoreDispEventInfo** interface.

The AbortChange Method

The **AbortChange** method aborts the transaction in which the synchronous event is running. The method is not valid for asynchronous transactions. The method takes one argument—**lErrorCode**—which is a Long value and allows you to return an error code to the event source indicating the reason for the abort.

The Data Property

The **Data** property sets or retrieves data that is stored between the begin phase and the commit or abort phase of a synchronous event. In the begin phase you would set the data by assigning the **Data** property to a Long value representing a memory location. In the commit phase, you would get the data by retrieving a Long pointer to the data through the **Data** property, as in the following sample VB code:

```
Private Sub IExStoreSyncEvents_OnSyncSave(ByVal pEventInfo As _
                                          Exoledb.IExStoreEventInfo, _
                                          ByVal bstrURLItem As String, _
                                          ByVal lFlags As Long)
    Dim objDispInfo As IExStoreDispEventInfo
    Dim lValue As Long

    Set objDispInfo = pEventInfo
```

```
    ' Set the data in the Begin phase:
    objDispInfo.Data = lValue

    ' ....

    ' Retrieve the data in the commit phase:
    lValue = objDispInfo.Data

End Sub
```

The EventConnection Property

The **EventConnection** property provides you with the ADO connection object for the current event. The object is created within the security context of the default user, and access is limited to the event item. The following VB code illustrates how to use this property:

```
Private Sub IExStoreSyncEvents_OnSyncSave(ByVal pEventInfo As _
                                          Exoledb.IExStoreEventInfo, _
                                          ByVal bstrURLItem As String, _
                                          ByVal lFlags As Long)
    Dim objDispInfo As IExStoreDispEventInfo
    Dim objConn As ADODB.Connection

    Set objDispInfo = pEventInfo

    ' Get the Connection object:
    Set objConn = objDispInfo.EventConnection

End Sub
```

The EventRecord Property

The **EventRecord** property provides an ADO **Record** object bound to the item that caused the event as follows:

```
Private Sub IExStoreSyncEvents_OnSyncSave(ByVal pEventInfo As _
                                          Exoledb.IExStoreEventInfo, _
                                          ByVal bstrURLItem As String, _
                                          ByVal lFlags As Long)
    Dim objDispInfo As IExStoreDispEventInfo
    Dim objRec As ADODB.Record

    Set objDispInfo = pEventInfo

    ' Get the Connection object:
    Set objRec = objDispInfo.EventRecord

End Sub
```

The SourceURL Property

In the case of an **OnSyncSave** event that has fired during a move operation, the **SourceURL** property returns the URL of the source item that caused the event (i.e., the item that you originally wanted to move). For any other events or operations, this property will have a NULL value.

The StoreGuid Property

The **StoreGuid** property returns the globally unique identifier (GUID) of the Exchange MDB store in which the event was fired as a string.

The UserGuid Property

The **UserGuid** property returns the GUID of the user that caused the event to fire as a string.

The UserSid Property

The **UserSid** property returns the Windows security identifier (SID) of the user that caused the event to fire as a string.

The Event Registration Item

Now that you know how to write an event sink, the other task is to register that sink. You register with Exchange to receive event notifications by creating and saving **Event Registration** items. An item becomes an **Event Registration** item when its content class is set to **urn:content-class:storeeventreg**, as defined in the **http://schemas.microsoft.com/exchange/events** namespace. Table 9.5 summarizes this item's properties.

After we look at each of these properties in a bit more detail, we'll explain how you would use these to register your own event sink.

The Criteria Property

The **Criteria** property represents a Web Storage System SQL **WHERE** clause that restricts the criteria for when an event fires. It can apply to the asynchronous **OnSave** event and the synchronous **OnSyncSave** and **OnSyncDelete** events. The **Criteria** field is optional, but if it is set, then the event sink will be notified if the criteria's SQL **WHERE** condition is satisfied. The AND, OR, NOT, and EXISTS operators are supported. For more information, see Chapter 7.

Table 9.5 Properties of the **Event Registration** Item

Property Name	Comments
Criteria	A Web Storage System SQL **WHERE** clause that specifies the conditions that will cause the event to fire.
Enabled	Boolean to enable the event to be fired.
EventMethod	Property that defines which event or events cause notification.
MatchScope	Property that defines where the event will fire relative to where it is saved.
Priority	The priority of the event, in case there are several event sinks on the folder.
ScriptUrl	The name of the script if the event is a script being run by the script host sink.
Sinkclass	The class ID (**ClsID**) or programmatic ID (**ProgID**) of the object containing the event sink.
TimerExpiryTime	Time to end an **OnTimer** event.
TimerInterval	Interval, in minutes, for an **OnTimer** event.
TimerStartTime	Start time for an **OnTimer** event.

The Enabled Property

The **Enabled** property is a Boolean value that indicates if an event registration is enabled. If the property is set to False, Exchange does not provide event notifications for the registration item.

The EventMethod Property

The **EventMethod** property is a list of events to receive event notification represented as a semicolon-delimited string. For example, if we wanted to receive event notification for the asynchronous **OnSave** and **OnDelete** events, we would set this property to "OnSave;OnDelete." Using this property, you can register to receive event notifications for store events, system events, and **OnTimer** events. The property can contain names only from the same category as shown in Table 9.6.

The MatchScope Property

The **MatchScope** property defines where the event will fire relative to where it is saved and if the event is for items, folders, or both. Table 9.7 defines the scope values and the type of event where you can use each one.

Table 9.6 EventMethod Values

Event Category	Event Names
Store events	OnSave; OnDelete; OnSyncSave; OnSyncDelete
System events	OnMDBStartUp; OnMDBShutdown
OnTimer events	OnTimer

Note that DEEP can be registered only at a top-level folder—that is, a folder in an Exchange MDB that has no parent folder—a.k.a. a root folder. When an event sink is registered for a folder and its subfolders in this way, it is called a recursive event. Also note that this property is not valid for system events.

The Priority Property

The **Priority** property sets or gets the priority of the event registration with respect to other event registrations for the same events. Synchronous event sinks are notified according to a priority order, with 0 being the highest. Event registrations with the same priority are notified in a random order. Obviously this property is valid only for synchronous event sink bindings, since there is no implied order for asynchronous or system events.

The ScriptUrl Property

Only when you are using a script written in VBScript or a similar COM-compliant language do you need to set this property. The **ScriptUrl** property specifies the path or URL to the file containing the script code to execute. The URL can be a script file located in the Web Storage System or on a file system. Both the OLE DB "http://" and "file://" URL syntaxes are supported, and the script cannot be on a remote machine.

Table 9.7 MatchScope Values

Scope Value	Event Type	Definition
ANY	Synchronous	Within the scope of the Exchange MDB
DEEP	Asynchronous/synchronous	The specified folder and all subfolders
EXACT (default)	Asynchronous	The specified folder only
SHALLOW	Synchronous	The specified folder only

> **Note:** The script host sink is what makes writing script code for an event registration possible. The script host sink is provided and registered with Exchange 2000 Server for running all event methods in scripts in process. The script host resides in **exodbesh.dll** and is registered when you install Exchange 2000 as **ExOleDB. ScriptEventSink.1**.

The Sinkclass Property

The **Sinkclass** property stores the COM class identifier (**ClsID**) in registry format or the programmatic identifier (**ProgID**) of the event sink COM class. If you write a COM component to handle your event sink, this is where you specify its **ProgID** ("MyComponent.MyClass," for example). If you are using a script, set the **Sinkclass** property to the script host sink **ProgID**—namely, "ExOleDB.ScriptEventSink.1."

If you do use a **ClsID**, it has to be enclosed within brackets, as in the following example:

```
{0cfb5d5c-fafe-11d3-9ad3-00bf4d9137b7f}
```

The TimerExpiryTime Property

This property and the next two come into play only when you're dealing with the **OnTimer** event, which is the system event that is called after a specified period of time. These properties are not valid for any other event.

The **TimerExpiryTime** property is the absolute time at which Exchange no longer notifies event sinks of the **OnTimer** event. In VB it can be any valid date value. It is an optional property, and if it is not set, the binding never expires.

The TimerInterval Property

The **TimerInterval** property specifies the period (in minutes) between **OnTimer** event notifications. In VB it is expressed as an integer value. The default is 1440 (every 24 hours). If the property isn't set, Exchange notifies the event sink just once.

The TimerStartTime Property

The **TimerStartTime** property is the absolute time at which Exchange commences notifying event sinks of the **OnTimer** event. In VB it can be any valid date value. If the property isn't set, Exchange will begin notifying the event sink immediately after the **Event Registration** item has been created.

Setting Up the Exchange Super User Account

To register an event sink on a folder, it is only logical that you must be logged in as a user that has permissions on that folder. Although you are certainly free to register event sinks on your own private mail folders and certain public folders to which you have access, more often than not your application will need to register an event sink on everyone's **Incoming Faxes** private folder, for example. To pull off a task like this, your application needs to log on using an account that has access to *all* of the folders in the Exchange store.

This calls for an Exchange "super user." We can create one by promoting an existing Exchange account with an Exchange mailbox or by creating a brand-new account. The quickest way to create an account is by using the **Active Directory Users and Computers** (ADUAC) Microsoft Management Console (MMC) in the Microsoft Exchange program group. First make sure that you are logged on to the machine as a user with administrator rights; then simply click on the **Users** folder in the **ADUAC** MMC and select **New** and then **User** from the **Action** menu. Fill in the **First name**, **Last name**, and **User logon name** fields similar to the example shown in Figure 9.2 and hit the **Next** button.

Fill in the password information on the ensuing screen according to your policies and hit the **Next** button. On the resulting screen, make sure that **Create an Exchange mailbox** is checked off and hit the **Next** button when the **Alias**, **Server**,

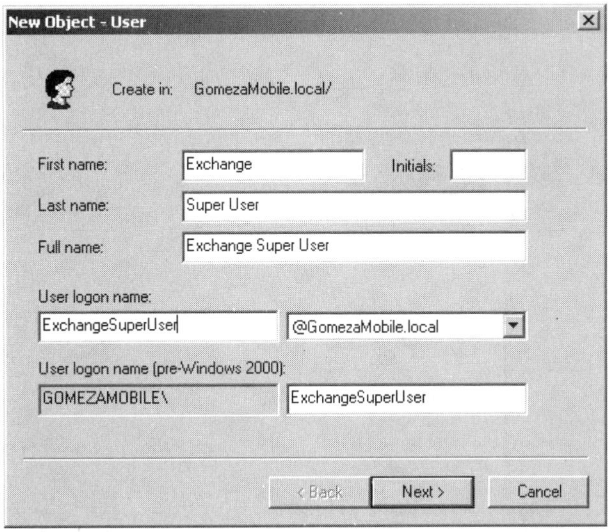

Figure 9.2 A sample Exchange user

and **Mailbox Store** fields are to your liking. Hit the **Finish** button on the summary screen to create the user and its mailbox.

Once you have the user that you want to promote, open the **Exchange System Manager** MMC in the Microsoft Exchange program group. Expand **Servers**, right-click on your Exchange server, and select **Properties** (see Figure 9.3).

Click on the **Security** tab of the **Properties** dialog box and hit the **Add** button. Find the user that you want to promote and hit the **Add** button and then the **OK** button. Voilà! You have created a "super user" (see Figure 9.4).

You should now be able to log in using this account and be able to see every folder on the Exchange server, including private mailboxes. In practice, the right to do this should be closely guarded on a production Exchange 2000 installation. This account now has the right to view, modify, and delete anyone's Exchange items. Therefore, you should treat the login name and password with the same caution as you would any other administrative account.

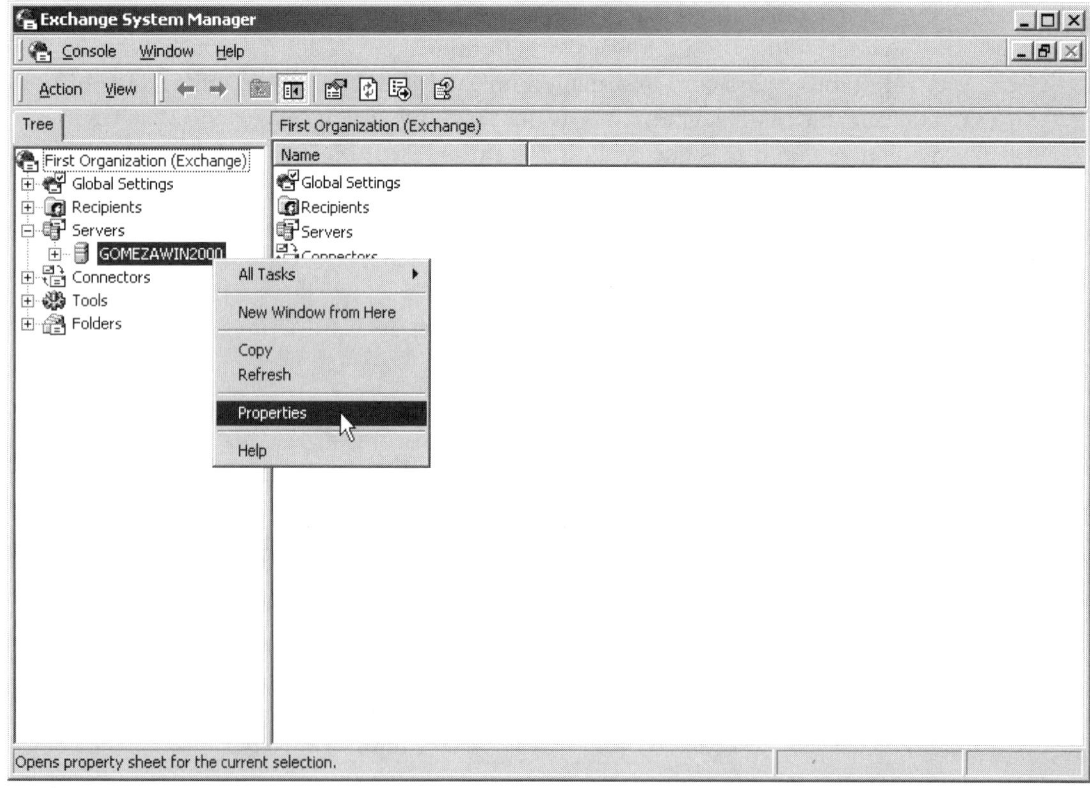

Figure 9.3 Getting the properties of your Exchange server

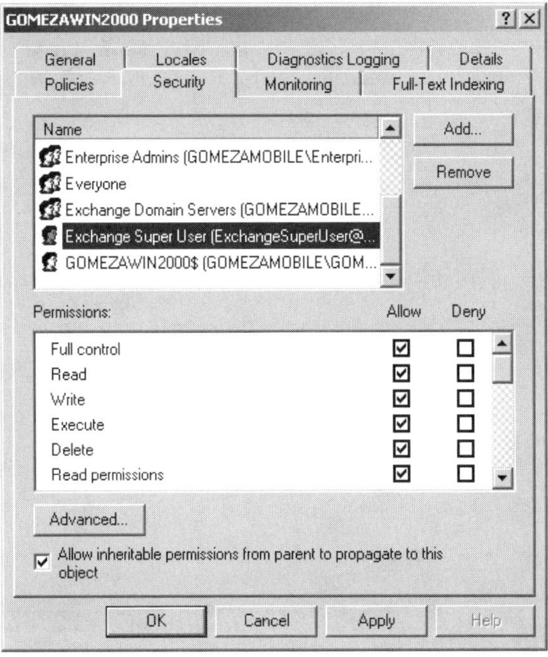

Figure 9.4 The sample Exchange user is now an Exchange "super user"

Logging On Locally

If you were not able to log on to the Windows 2000 server hosting your Exchange store, the reason may be that your account does not have permissions set to log on locally. This restriction is a clever Windows 2000 security feature, which allows only certain accounts to log on to the server. It is controlled by the "log on locally" security policy on each Windows 2000 server. To change this policy on your server, log on as a user with administrator rights and open the **Domain Security Policy** MMC in the Administrative Tools program group. Expand **Security Settings** and then **Local Policies.** Click **User Rights Assignment**, and then double-click **Log on locally** (see Figure 9.5). Hit the **Add** button to add your account and then the **Browse** button to select it from a list. Find your account, click on it, and hit **Add.** Hit **OK** three times to finish up.

Note: If your Windows 2000 server is also a primary domain controller, you also need to change this policy in the **Domain Controller Security Policy** MMC.

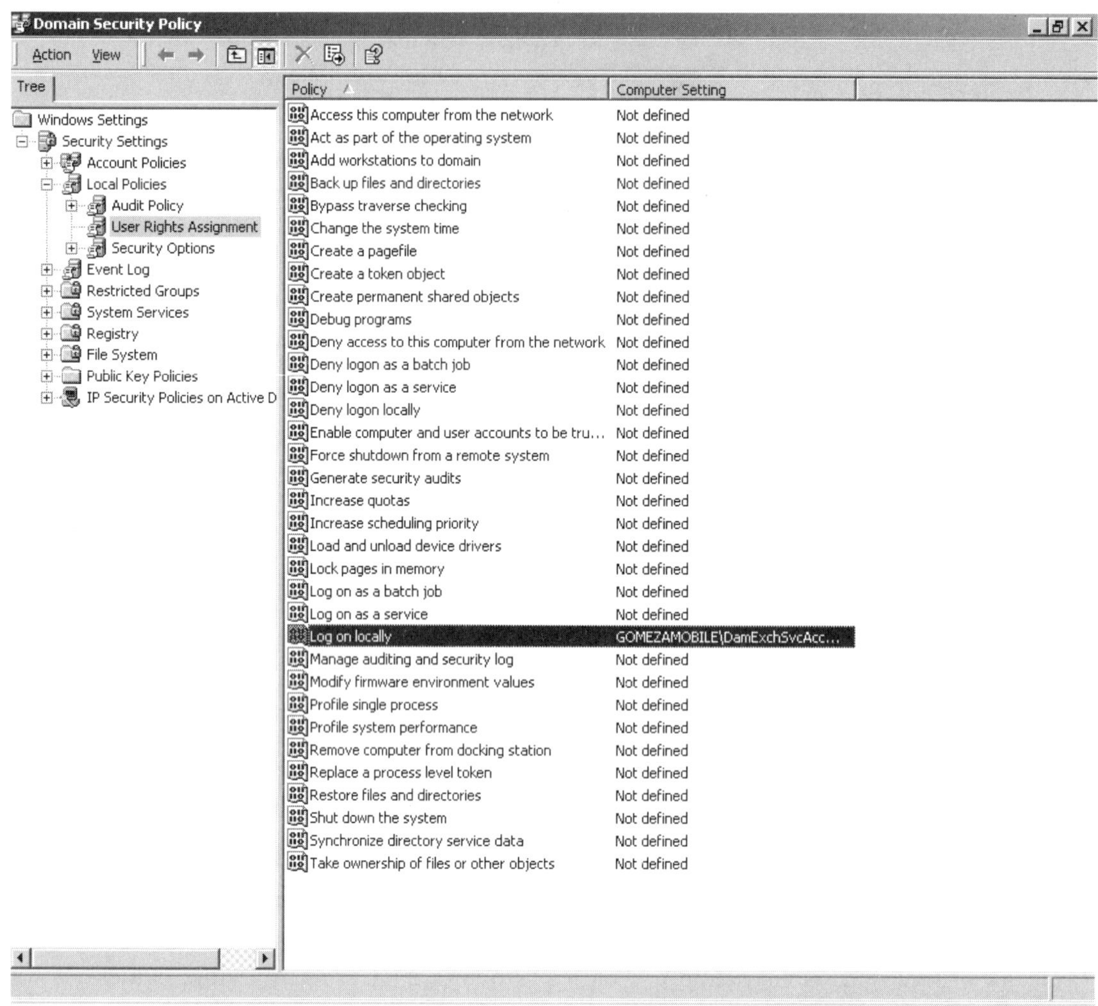

Figure 9.5 Choosing the "log on locally" policy in the **Domain Security Policy** MMC

■ Registering Events Programmatically

There are currently two options for registering your event sink: writing your own code or using the **regevent.vbs** script file.

The RegEvent Script

If you install the Exchange 2000 SDK, you will find the **regevent.vbs** file under **C:\Program Files\Exchsrvr\SDK\Support\OLEDB\Scripts**, assuming that you install it to its default directory. If you open it in Notepad (or another text editor), you can inspect the VBScript code. This script allows you to register, enumerate, and even delete event registrations, depending on the arguments you give it. Table 9.8 lists the command-line arguments for the **regevent.vbs** script.

Table 9.8 RegEvent.vbs Arguments

Argument Name	Optional?	Operation or Event Type	Description
CriteriaField	Yes	Add only	SQL **WHERE** clause specifying the conditions for notification.
EventMethod	No	Add only	The name of the store or system event should be one or more of the following: **OnSave**, **OnDelete**, **OnSyncSave**, **OnSyncDelete**, **OnMdbStartup**, **OnMdbShutDown**, or **OnTimer**. Note that the case is ignored and that multiple events can be specified in the same registration by the placement of semicolons (;) between the names of each event.
ExpiryTimer	Yes	**OnTimer** events only	When to stop the **OnTimer** event.
Interval	No	**OnTimer** events only	The time, in minutes, between each **OnTimer** event notification.
MatchScope	Yes	Add for synchronous and asynchronous notifications	The scope for the event registration: DEEP, SHALLOW, EXACT, ANY.
Priority	Yes	Add for **OnSyncSave** and **OnSyncDelete** events only	The registration's priority.
RegistrationItemName	No	Add, Delete, or Enum	The name of the **Event Registration** item.
ScriptFilePath	Yes	Add only	The full file path to the event sink script file.
ScriptURL	Yes	Add only	The full **HTTP URL** to the event sink script file.
SinkClass	No	Add only	The **ClsID** or **ProgID** of the event sink.
StartTime	No	**OnTimer** events only	When to start the **OnTimer** event.

Note: Running the **regevent.vbs** script file with no arguments returns all of its parameters and examples of use as a series of small message boxes like the one shown in Figure 9.6. If you do this, get ready to click **OK** quite a few times!

The syntax for running **regevent.vbs** is as follows:

```
cscript RegEvent.vbs Add|Delete|Enum
                            EventMethod
                            SinkClass
                            Registration Item Name(Scope)
                            StartTime
                            Interval
                            [-p Priority]
                            [-m MatchScope]
                            [-f CriteriaFilter]
                            [-file ScriptFilePath]
                            [-url ScriptUrl]
                            [-e ExpiryTime]
```

There are a few more caveats for **regevent.vbs**. You cannot register for the **OnTimer** event with any other events. You also cannot register system events and asynchronous or synchronous events in the same command. Some examples will help illustrate how to use the **RegEvent** script.

Registering Asynchronous Events

This example will add a registration for the **OnSave** event to a public folder and use a COM+ class (**MailSink.Sink**) to handle the event:

```
cscript regevent.vbs Add OnSave MailSink.Sink
"file://./backofficestorage/gomeza.local/PF1/User3/MailSink"
```

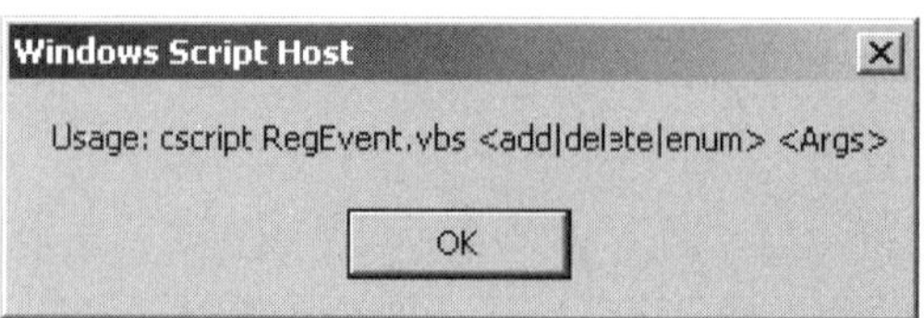

Figure 9.6 Windows Script Host dialog box

The following example will add a registration for the **OnSave** and **OnDelete** events to a user's Exchange inbox (and any subfolders) and use a VBScript file to handle the event (**d:\test.vbs**):

```
cscript RegEvent.vbs add "onsave;ondelete" Exoledb.ScriptEventSink.1
    file://./backofficestorage/gomeza.local/jetsong/Inbox/EventRegItem1
    -m deep -file d:\test.vbs
```

Registering Synchronous Events

The example will add a registration for the **OnSyncSave** event to a user's Exchange inbox and use a VBScript file to handle the event (**c:\script3.vbs**):

```
cscript RegEvent.vbs Add OnSyncSave ExOleDB.ScriptEventSink.1
    file://./backofficestorage/mydomain.com/user1/inbox/EventRegItem5
    -file c:\script3.vbs
```

Registering System Events

This example will add a registration for the **OnMDBStartup** system event using a URL to specify the VBScript file to handle the event:

```
cscript RegEvent.vbs Add OnMDBStartup ExOleDB.ScriptEventSink.1
    http://mystore/public/myfolder/startupevent
    -url http://mystore/myeventscripts/script.vbs
```

Registering OnTimer Events

This example will add to a public folder an **OnTimer** event that occurs every minute for an hour:

```
cscript RegEvent.vbs add ontimer sink1.sink1.1
    file://./backofficestorage/mydomain/public%20folders/events/
EventRegTimerItem1
    "8/4/00 01:50:00 AM" 1 -e "8/4/00 02:50:00 AM"
```

Deleting Event Registrations

Deleting event registrations is as easy as deleting the **Event Registration** item itself. The **RegEvent** script does not recursively delete events in child folders. It does allow you to delete all event registrations on a specified folder with one command, as in this example:

```
cscript regevent.vbs delete
"file://./backofficestorage/gomeza.local/pf1/Administrator" all
```

Of course, you can delete just a single item, as in the following example:

```
cscript regevent.vbs delete
"file://./backofficestorage/gomeza.local/pf1/Administrator/EvtRegA"
```

Enumerating Event Registrations

Similarly, you can get all of the event registrations on a folder:

```
cscript regevent.vbs enum
"file://./backofficestorage/gomeza.local/PF1/administrator" all
```

or just a single item:

```
cscript regevent.vbs enum
"file://./backofficestorage/gomeza.local/PF1/administrator/EvtRegB"
```

Note that **RegEvent** does not recursively enumerate events in child folders.

Sinking to New Heights

The other option is to write your own code to manipulate the registration of event sinks. This isn't very difficult. In the following example, a VB component is created to handle enabling and disabling of an event sink. To help with readability, all of these constants are defined in the general declarations section of the component:

```
' The Incoming EMail Event Sink Name:
Private Const m_sIncomingEmailEvent = "IncomingEMailEvent"

Private Const propContentclass = "DAV:contentclass"
'-----------------------------------------------------------------------
' The following is a list of the properties that can be set for the
' registration event item.
' Note that not all of these need to be set:

' An optional SQL WHERE clause that specifies the conditions that will
' cause the event to fire:
Private Const propCriteria = "http://schemas.microsoft.com/exchange/
                                        events/Criteria"

' An optional Boolean value that indicates if an event registration is
' enabled ' or not:
Private Const propEnabled = "http://schemas.microsoft.com/exchange/
                                       events/Enabled"
```

```
' Defines which events cause notification (NOT optional):
Private Const propEventMethod =
"http://schemas.microsoft.com/exchange/events/EventMethod"

' Optional String that defines where the event will be fired relative to
' where it is saved:
Private Const propMatchScope =
"http://schemas.microsoft.com/exchange/events/MatchScope"

' The optional priority of the event registration with respect to other
' event registrations (for asynchronous events only; 0 = highest):
Private Const propPriority =
"http://schemas.microsoft.com/exchange/events/Priority"

' If using the script host sink, this is the URL (path) to the file
' containing the script code to execute:
Private Const propScriptURL =
"http://schemas.microsoft.com/exchange/events/ScriptUrl"

' The COM class identifier (ClsID) in registry format, or the
' programmatic identifier (ProgID), of the event sink COM class:
Private Const propSinkClass =
"http://schemas.microsoft.com/exchange/events/SinkClass"

' The next three properties are used only for OnTimer events.
' The time to end an OnTimer event:
Private Const propTimerExpiryTime =
"http://schemas.microsoft.com/exchange/events/TimerExpiryTime"

' The interval (in minutes) for an OnTimer event:
Private Const propTimerInterval =
"http://schemas.microsoft.com/exchange/events/TimerInterval"

' The start time for an OnTimer event:
Private Const propTimerStartTime =
"http://schemas.microsoft.com/exchange/events/TimerStartTime"
'-----------------------------------------------------------------------
```

Adding an Event Registration for a Folder

We can now write a method, like the one that follows, that takes the full folder path, registers an **OnSave** event, and specifies a COM component that was written to handle the event:

```
Private Sub IEXReg_EnableIncomingMailEvent(ByVal PathToFolder As String)
'-----------------------------------------------------------------------
'   Plural
'-----------------------------------------------------------------------
```

```
'   Enables the OnSave and OnDelete Exchange 2000 events on the
'   specified folder.
'   Input:  Name            Type    Restrictions   Description
'           PathToFolder    String                 Path to the folder
'                                                  or file.
'   Output: None
'-----------------------------------------------------------------------
'   Revision History:
'   Date:       Developer:   Description:
'-----------------------------------------------------------------------
'   07/28/2000  Alex Gomez   Initial Design
'-----------------------------------------------------------------------
    Dim objEvent As ADODB.Record
    Dim objConn As ADODB.Connection
    Dim sEvent As String

    ' Create the record
    Set objEvent = New ADODB.Record

    ' Open the folder:
    ' The PathToFolder should be something like:
    ' file://./backofficestorage/gomezamobile.local/MBX/gomeza-DAV/
    ' Inbox/Boxes
    ' file://./backofficestorage/<DomainName>/MBX/<UserAlias>-DAV/
    ' Inbox/Boxes
    sEvent = PathToFolder & "/" & m_sIncomingEmailEvent

    objEvent.Open sEvent, , adModeReadWrite, adCreateNonCollection

    Set objConn = objEvent.ActiveConnection

    ' Begin a new transaction
    objConn.BeginTrans

    ' Set the properties in the item
    With objEvent.Fields
    ' Create a new Event Registration item:
      .Item(propContentclass) = "urn:content-class:storeeventreg"
    ' Register for the Save event only (if we need to register for more
    ' than one event in the future, use the syntax "OnSave;OnDelete"):
      .Item(propEventMethod) = "OnSave"
    ' ProgID of the sink class:
      .Item(propSinkClass) = "DAMDINBOXSINK_PROGID"
    ' Make sure the event is enabled:
      .Item(propEnabled) = True
    ' Register the event on this folder ONLY (and not on its subfolders):
      .Item(propMatchScope) = "SHALLOW"
```

```
    ' Fire the event only when nonhidden items are saved or deleted on
    ' the folder:
      .Item("propCriteria") = "WHERE $DAV:ishidden$ = FALSE"
      .Update
    End With

    ' Commit the transaction
    objConn.CommitTrans

    ' Close the connection and record:
    objEvent.Close
    objConn.Close

    ' Clean up:
    Set objEvent = Nothing
    Set objConn = Nothing
    End Sub
```

Removing an Event Registration for a Folder

We can also write a method, like the one that follows, that takes the full folder path and removes an event registration. Remember that removing an event registration is as simple as deleting the **Event Registration** item itself. We use ADO 2.5 to bind an ADO record to the item and then just delete the record:

```
Private Sub IEXReg_DisableIncomingMailEvent(ByVal PathToFolder _
                                             As String)
'-----------------------------------------------------------------------
'   Plural
'-----------------------------------------------------------------------
'   Disables the OnSave and OnDelete Exchange 2000 events from firing on
'   the specified folder by deleting the registration item created in
'   the EnableIncomingMailEvent method.
'   Input:  Name            Type    Restrictions    Description
'           PathToFolder    String                  Path to the folder
'                                                   or file.
'   Output: None
'-----------------------------------------------------------------------
'   Revision History:
'   Date:       Developer:      Description:
'-----------------------------------------------------------------------
'   07/28/2000  Alex Gomez      Initial Design
'-----------------------------------------------------------------------
    Dim objEvent As ADODB.Record
    Dim objConn As ADODB.Connection
    Dim sEvent As String
```

```
    ' Create the record
    Set objEvent = New ADODB.Record

    ' Open the folder:
    ' The PathToFolder should be something like:
    ' file://./backofficestorage/gomezawin2000.gomezamobile.local/MBX/
    ' gomeza-DAV/Inbox/Boxes
    ' file://./backofficestorage/<DomainName>/MBX/<UserAlias>-DAV/
    ' Inbox/Boxes
    sEvent = PathToFolder & "/" & m_sIncomingEmailEvent

    ' Open the correct record:
    objEvent.Open sEvent, , adModeReadWrite, adFailIfNotExists
    Set objConn = objEvent.ActiveConnection

    ' Begin a new transaction
    objConn.BeginTrans

    ' Delete it:
    objEvent.DeleteRecord

    ' Commit the transaction
    objConn.CommitTrans

    ' Close the connection and record:
    objEvent.Close
    objConn.Close

    ' Clean up:
    Set objEvent = Nothing
    Set objConn = Nothing
End Sub
```

Debugging

Several quirks make debugging event sinks "interesting." First, **Event Registration** items are automatically hidden when saved. If your event sink is included in a DLL, it needs to have a surrogate host defined when the object is instantiated by Exchange.

Wrapping the DLL in a COM+ application assigns the surrogate host automatically. The COM+ application provides the user context in which the event will run. The event can now access the Web Storage System with the privileges of the package's security context without having to log on.

Note: For more information on creating and maintaining a COM+ application, see the following topics in the Platform SDK: COM+ (Component Services) documentation on the MSDN CD:

- Creating a New COM+ Application
- Installing New Components
- Importing Components
- Removing a Component from a COM+ Application
- Deleting a COM+ Application

Summary

Web Storage System events provide us with a means to respond to certain events relative to a specific item or folder in the Web Storage System. These events may be handled in a synchronous or asynchronous manner. In addition to these store events, system events such as system startup and shutdown can also be programmed. All of these events are programmed by implementation of the well-known COM interfaces that are distributed with the Web Storage System.

Part IV

Collaboration Data Objects (CDO)

Chapter 10

CDO Overview

This chapter introduces the various incarnations of the Collaboration Data Objects (CDO) library. Many versions of libraries go by the term CDO. In fact, some are MAPI based, some are SMTP based, and others are OLE DB based. Table 10.1 lists the versions of CDO, the DLLs that house them, and where you get them.

> **Note:** All versions of CDO that come with Exchange 2000 are labeled as version 6.0, regardless of the actual version number shown in Table 10.1.

CDO 1.xx

This section covers the legacy versions of the Collaboration Data Objects (CDO) library. The CDO 1.xx library is the MAPI-based version of CDO that has been (and can still be) used to access information on an Exchange server. CDO 1.21, the latest version of the MAPI-based library, is a scriptable interface into MAPI with additional objects to aid in the creation of collaborative applications. The CDO library can be used either on the client side or on the server side to either a local or a remote machine. You get the CDO library (**cdo.dll**) when you install Microsoft Outlook on the client side or Microsoft Exchange Server version 5.5 (or 2000) on the server side. The version of CDO that ships with Outlook 98 and Outlook 2000 is CDO 1.21.

Table 10.1 CDO Objects: What They're Based On and How You Get Them

Version	Library Name	Full Name	Based Mainly on:	Comes with:
1.0	olemsg.dll	OLE Messaging	MAPI	Exchange 4.0
1.1	actmsg32.dll	Active Messaging	MAPI	Outlook 97 (8.01), Exchange 5.0
1.21	cdo.dll	Collaboration Data Objects	MAPI	Exchange 5.5, Exchange 2000, Outlook 98, Outlook 2000 (optional component)
1.2	cdohtml.dll	CDO Rendering Objects	MAPI, outputs HTML	Exchange 5.5, Exchange 2000
1.2	cdonts.dll	Collaboration Data Objects for Windows NT Server	SMTP	NT Option Pack 4 (IIS 4.0)
2.0	cdosys.dll	Collaboration Data Objects for Windows 2000	SMTP, NNTP	Windows 2000
3.0	cdoex.dll	Collaboration Data Objects for Exchange 2000	OLE DB	Exchange 2000
6.0	cdoexm.dll	Collaboration Data Objects for Exchange Management	OLE DB, ADSI	Exchange 2000
6.0	cdowf.dll	Collaboration Data Objects for Exchange Workflow	OLE DB	Exchange 2000

The version of the CDO library that ships with Outlook 97 (versions 8.01–8.03) and Exchange 5.0 (client and server) is CDO 1.1, which is actually called Active Messaging (**actmsg32.dll**). The prior version of the library (version 1.0) was called OLE Messaging and existed before Outlook did. OLE Messaging is an out-of-process server (**mdisp32.exe**) that shipped with Exchange 4.0 (client and server). Both versions 1.0 and 1.1 are available in 16-bit versions. However, CDO 1.21 is available only as a 32-bit COM component (and not in a 16-bit version).

Also covered in this chapter is the CDO for NT Server library (CDONTS), which provides a scriptable means of sending mail without the need for the MAPI subsystem. CDONTS was designed specifically for sending SMTP-based mail from Web-based applications on an NT Server machine. CDONTS is an in-process server (**cdonts.dll**) that runs on Windows NT 4.0 and is installed by either IIS 4.0 or Exchange 5.0 or higher.

Finally, the CDO Rendering library (**cdohtml.dll**) is also included with Microsoft Exchange Server and is installed on the server when the installation option **Active Server Components** is selected. It is used to render the information returned by the CDO objects automatically, making Web page formatting fast and simple. The CDO 1.21 Rendering library is also covered in Chapter 11.

What CDO Provides

The CDO 1.21 library provides access to a MAPI session through the use of profiles, along with access to address books, folders, and items (only e-mail, post, and calendar items). CDO does not provide access to Outlook-specific features, such as the Explorer or Inspector windows, toolbars, or the Outlook bar. For a complete reference to CDO 1.21, see Chapter 11.

CDO for NT Server (CDONTS)

Collaboration Data Objects for NT Server (CDONTS) is an SMTP-based messaging library. CDONTS is part of the overall CDO library "family," but it is not MAPI dependent like CDO 1.21 and much of the Outlook object model.

The NewMail Object

The CDONTS library is a simple way to send SMTP mail on an NT server. For example, it takes only three lines of code to create a CDONTS object, send a **NewMail** object with standard properties, and clean up the object:

```
Set objCDONTSMail = CreateObject("CDONTS.NewMail")
objCDONTSMail.Send "jamisons@plural.com","gomeza@plural.com", _
"Using CDONTS","I hope you get this message!"
Set objCDONTSMail = Nothing
```

> **Note:** The **NewMail** object becomes invalid upon successful completion of the **Send** method. You cannot reuse it for another message; trying to do so will return the error "CdoE_INVALID_OBJECT." Always set the **NewMail** object to Nothing to release its memory after use.

The syntax for sending mail with the **NewMail** object of CDONTS is as follows:

```
objNewMail.Send([From][, To][, Subject][, Body][, Importance] )
```

where

- **objNewMail** is required. This is the **NewMail** object. Use **CreateObject("CDONTS.NewMail")**.
- **From** is an optional String containing the sender's e-mail address (e.g., "info@plural.com").
- **To** is an optional String containing a list of e-mail addresses of "To" recipients. The addresses are separated by semicolons (e.g., "jamisons@plural.com; gomeza@plural.com").
- **Subject** is an optional String containing the subject line for the message.
- **Body** is an optional String containing the main text of the message.
- **Importance** is an optional Long containing the importance associated with the message: High (2), Normal (1), or Low (0).

Note: Since there's no log-on authentication when you're using CDONTS, you can send anonymous mail by simply omitting the **From** property. You can also "spoof" the From address because you must specify it yourself.

Note: You must have an SMTP server specified in order to send SMTP mail using CDONTS. To send mail from an IIS 4.0 server via your SMTP server, do the following:

1. On the IIS 4.0 server machine, open the Microsoft Management Console (MMC) and expand the Internet Information Server section.
2. In the left-hand pane, select and expand the specific IIS 4.0 server you're using.
3. In the right-hand pane, right-click **Default SMTP server** and select **Properties**.
4. Select the **Delivery** tab, and in the **Fully Qualified Domain Name** text box enter the IIS 4.0 computer name.
5. In the **Smart Host** text box, enter the name of your SMTP server.

This will enable IIS 4.0 to find your company's SMTP server and use it to send an outbound e-mail message.

When to Use CDONTS

CDO 1.21 is designed for Microsoft Exchange 5.5, so it's almost always the better choice for doing Exchange-based messaging, conversation threading, and calendaring. CDO for NT Server is a better choice for applications involving bulk e-mail or access to SMTP messages on Internet Information Server 4.0. CDO for NT Server also is more suitable for processing messages without mailboxes because Exchange supports individual inboxes and IIS 4.0 doesn't.

CDO for Windows 2000 and Exchange 2000

CDO for Windows 2000 is an SMTP SendMail version of CDO included with Windows 2000, much like that of CDONTS. CDO for Exchange 2000 (CDO 3.0) is the version of CDO that is based on OLE DB and is included with Exchange 2000.

CDO for Windows 2000

Windows 2000 includes a version of the CDO library that provides a SendMail functionality. CDO for Windows 2000 is installed *only* on computers running Windows 2000 Workstation or Windows 2000 Server. When you install Windows 2000, this version of CDO is installed by default.

> **Note:** Remember, CDO 1.21 is the library to use when communicating to a computer running Microsoft Exchange Server. CDO 1.21 is installed with either Microsoft Exchange Server 5.5 or Microsoft Outlook 98 or 2000, so it is very likely that the computer running Windows 2000 will have CDO 1.21, CDONTS (for backward compatibility), and CDO for Windows 2000 installed.

CDO for Windows 2000 introduces a new object-naming convention for the CDO objects—namely, "CDO." The following Visual Basic example shows the CDO for Windows 2000 protocol for sending a message. This example assumes you've already set a reference to the Microsoft CDO 2.0 object library:

```
Dim objMessage As New CDO.Message
With objMessage
    .From = "scott@jamison.org"
    .To = "gomeza@plural.com"
    .Subject = "Elephants and Llamas"
    .TextBody = "A stampede is imminent!"
    .Send
End With
Set objMessage = Nothing
```

CDO for Windows 2000 does not replace CDO 1.21. In fact, the two would be used together on a Windows 2000 machine. Version 1.21 would be used to access

Exchange Server data, and CDO for Windows 2000 would be used for SMTP Send-Mail, where Exchange is not required.

CDO for Exchange 2000

A superset of the Windows 2000 version of CDO is included with Exchange Server 2000. The CDO for Exchange library (**cdoex.dll**) works in conjunction with ADO and the native Exchange OLE DB provider. CDO for Exchange provides several new messaging objects and interfaces. CDO for Exchange also supports the creation of items that CDO 1.21 does not support, such as **Contact** items. The following example uses the CDO **Person** object to create a new contact and save it in the user's **Contacts** folder:

```
Dim objPerson
Set objPerson = CreateObject("CDO.Person")
With objPerson
    .FirstName = "William"
    .LastName = "Brown"
    .HomeCity = "Billerica"
    .HomeState = "MA"
    .Email = "willy@media.org"
End With
objPerson.DataSource.SaveTo _
    "file://./backofficestorage/Server/MBX/jamisons/Contacts/William
            Brown"
Set oPerson = Nothing
```

CDO for Exchange 2000 is described in much greater detail in Chapters 11 through 15.

How CDO and ADO Work Together

CDO for Exchange 2000 and ADO are designed to be used together. You will typically use ADO to navigate, search, and modify the properties of items in the Web Storage System. On the other hand, you'll use CDO to create and manage specific types of items, such as messages, contacts, appointments, messages containing meeting requests, and folders. To sum up, ADO provides raw data access to the Web Storage System. If you don't need to provide any functionality besides strict data access, you can stop here. However, if you want to perform additional functions, such as checking free/busy information, creating a reply to a message, or creating a recurring appointment, you'll want to use CDO.

Both CDO and ADO rely directly on the Exchange OLE DB provider (ExOLEDB) to access data residing in Microsoft Exchange private and public information stores.

Summary

The Collaboration Data Objects (CDO) library is an important part of building Web-enabled, collaborative applications using Exchange 2000. A summary of the core CDO libraries follows:

- **CDO 1.21** uses the MAPI subsystem.
- **CDO 2.0** uses Windows 2000 SMTP or NNTP.
- **CDO 3.0** uses the Exchange OLE DB provider to supplement messaging functionality.

Chapter 11

CDO 1.21

This chapter covers the legacy versions of the Collaboration Data Objects (CDO) library, which includes CDO 1.0, 1.1, and 1.21. The CDO 1.xx library is the MAPI-based version of CDO that has been (and can still be) used to access information on an Exchange server. The CDO 1.21 library provides access to a MAPI session through the use of profiles, along with access to address books, folders, and items (only e-mail, post, and calendar items). CDO does not provide access to Outlook-specific features, such as the Explorer or Inspector windows, toolbars, or the Outlook bar. This chapter will focus on the client-side features of CDO as well as on the object model.

> **Note:** If you're writing server-side Web code, your best bet is to use ADO 2.5 against the Web Storage System, rather than using CDO 1.21, which is provided for backward compatibility.

The CDO Objects

Generally speaking, the CDO library defines the following objects. At the top there's the **Session** object, which represents the client-server connection that CDO maintains to provide access to message stores and address books. Hence, under the **Session** object is a collection of **AddressBook** objects, as well as a collection of **InfoStore** objects. From within each information store you can access the folders and messages in the store. Figure 11.1 illustrates the structure of the CDO object model.

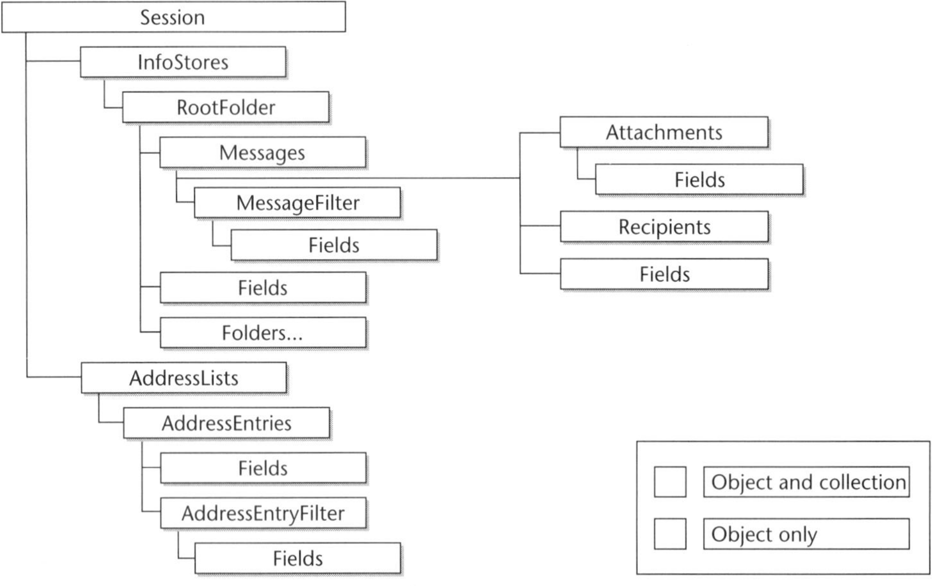

Figure 11.1 The CDO 1.21 object model

Note: Remember that although the CDO library is based on MAPI, its design does not always represent a one-to-one correspondence with MAPI objects.

At the Top: The Session Object

In CDO the only externally creatable object is the **Session** object. The **Session** object is the top-level object, roughly equivalent to Outlook's **Namespace** object. Under the **Session** object you have access to much of the same data that you would in Outlook, such as folders, items (in CDO they're called messages), and address book information.

Note: In Outlook, the top-level object is the **Application** object. A big difference between Outlook and CDO is that Outlook has a complete user interface set of objects, which creates an added level of hierarchy. This is one reason why CDO and the Outlook object model don't match up perfectly.

The key difference between the Outlook library and CDO is that Outlook provides an extensive set of user interface objects. With CDO, your application would normally provide the user interface, through either a client application or a Web interface. CDO also provides more low-level access to MAPI properties.

Getting Started with CDO

To start a CDO session you must use either the **CreateObject** statement (or a **New**). This will return a reference to a CDO **Session** object as follows:

```
Set objSession = CreateObject("MAPI.Session")
```

Note: All objects that you create using the **CreateObject** syntax are stored in the registry under **HKEY_CLASSES_ROOT**. The key "MAPI.Session" contains information on the version, file name, and unique identifier for the CDO object.

Note: You can't access any methods, properties, or other CDO objects until the **Session** object has successfully logged on. Attempting to access any object without a current session results in the "MAPI_E_NOT_INITIALIZED" error message. The only exception is the **SetLocaleIDs** method, which allows you to set locale and code page settings and must be called before the **Logon** method.

Now that you have a **Session** object, you must log on to the MAPI store using a profile. With CDO, you can do one of the following:

- Use a predefined profile
- Dynamically create a temporary profile

For a client-side application, in which users would have a list of profiles defined for normal use, you would specify one of those profiles, as in the following example:

```
Set objSession = CreateObject("MAPI.Session")
objSession.Logon profileName:="My Profile"
```

Note: When using the **Logon** method, you may get an error back from MAPI with a value of –2147221231 ("MAPI_E_LOGON_FAILED") if you didn't specify a profile and there's no current session open. You can resolve this problem by retrieving the user's default profile from the registry. On Windows 95 or 98, look under **Software\Microsoft\Windows Messaging Subsystem\Profiles\DefaultProfile**. On Windows NT, use **Software\Microsoft\Windows NT\CurrentVersion\Windows Messaging Subsystem\Profiles\DefaultProfile**.

On a server, for example, you probably don't have profiles set up for every scenario. CDO (by design) provides a way to create a temporary profile dynamically. You simply create a string with a server name and mailbox. Then you can log onto your MAPI provider using the **Logon** method:

```
strProfile = "ServerName" & vbLf & "UserName"
Set objSession = CreateObject("MAPI.Session")
objSession.Logon ,,, False,, True, strProfile
```

Note: You must insert a line feed character between the server name and the user name in your dynamic profile string. Visual Basic provides the **vbLf** constant for this purpose.

After the code has a reference to the top-level **Session** object and has secured a successful log-on, it can delve down into the rest of the CDO objects. The code will be able to access any of the information stores and address books that are listed in the profile that the code used to log on.

Session Properties

After the log-on is complete, you'll be able to access any of the **Session** object's properties. Table 11.1 gives the complete list of **Session** properties.

Note: Be careful when using the **Session** object's **Version** and **OperatingSystem** properties. The CDO help file's example claims that the CDO 1.21 **Version** property will return "1.2.1." CDO will actually return only a major and minor version number—that is, "1.21." The CDO Session's **OperatingSystem** property will return "Microsoft Windows 95(TM) 4.10" for both Windows 95 and Windows 98 operating systems. It will not return "Windows 98." For Windows NT, this property returns "Microsoft Windows NT(TM) N.k," where "N.k" represents the major and minor version numbers.

Session Methods

After the log-on is complete, you'll be able to access any of the **Session** object's methods. Table 11.2 gives the complete list of **Session** methods.

Table 11.1 Properties of the **Session** Object

Property Name	Description	Type	Access Level	1.0	1.1	1.21
AddressLists	Returns the collection of **AddressList** objects available in the current profile.	Object	Read-only		✓	✓
Application	Always returns "Collaboration Data Objects."	String	Read-only	✓	✓	✓
Class	For a session, returns **cdoSession** (0).	Long	Read-only	✓	✓	✓
CurrentUser	Returns the current user in the form of an **AddressEntry** object.	Object	Read-only	✓	✓	✓
Inbox	Returns the current user's **Inbox** folder.	Object	Read-only	✓	✓	✓
InfoStores	Returns the session's **InfoStores** collection.	Object	Read-only	✓	✓	✓
Name	Returns the profile name that was used for the current session.	String	Read-only	✓	✓	✓
OperatingSystem	Returns the current operating system in the form of a string.	String	Read-only	✓	✓	✓
Outbox	Returns the current user's **Outbox** folder.	Object	Read-only	✓	✓	✓
OutOfOffice	Returns True if this user is out of the office.	Boolean	Read/write		✓	✓
OutOfOfficeText	Returns the message text for an out-of-office response that is automatically sent if the **OutOfOffice** property is set to True.	String	Read/write		✓	✓
Parent	For a **Session** object, always returns Nothing because the **Session** is the top-level object.	Object	Read-only	✓	✓	✓
Session	Returns the current **Session** object.	Object	Read-only	✓	✓	✓
Version	Returns the CDO version number.	String	Read-only	✓	✓	✓

Table 11.2 Methods of the **Session** Object

Method Name	Description	1.0	1.1	1.21
AddressBook([recipients] [, title] [, oneAddress] [, forceResolution] [, recipLists] [, toLabel] [, ccLabel] [, bccLabel] [, parentWindow])	Displays a modal form that allows the user to select recipients from the address book. Returns a **Recipients** collection.	✓	✓	✓
CompareIDs(ID1, ID2)	Determines whether two CDO library objects are the same object.		✓	✓
CreateConversationIndex ([ParentIndex])	Creates or updates an index for a conversation thread. Useful for creating new posts on a discussion folder using code.		✓	✓
DeliverNow	Requests immediate delivery of all undelivered messages. Applies to both inbound and outbound messages.		✓	✓
GetAddressEntry(entryID)	Using the **EntryID** provided, returns the corresponding **AddressEntry** object.	✓	✓	✓
GetAddressList (ObjectType)	Returns an **AddressList** object, either the Global Address List (GAL) or the Personal Address Book (PAB). Pass one of the following: for GAL, **cdoAddressListGAL** (0); for PAB, **cdoAddressListPAB** (1).			✓
GetArticle(ArticleID, FolderID [, StoreID])	Returns a **Message** object corresponding to an article number. An article number is a Long value that uniquely identifies a message within a message store.			✓
GetDefaultFolder (ObjectType)	Returns a default **Folder** object based on the type passed in.			✓
GetFolder (folderID [, storeID])	Returns a **Folder** object based on the ID passed in.	✓	✓	✓
GetInfoStore(storeID)	Returns an **InfoStore** object based on the ID passed in.	✓	✓	✓
GetMessage(messageID [, storeID])	Returns an item based on its ID.	✓	✓	✓
GetOption(OptType)	Returns a calendar rendering option for the session. See the CDO help file for more information.			✓
Logoff	Logs off of the current session from the MAPI system.	✓	✓	✓
Logon([profileName] [, profilePassword] [, showDialog] [, newSession] [, parentWindow] [, NoMail] [, ProfileInfo])	Logs on to the MAPI system.	✓	✓	✓
SetLocaleIDs(LocaleID, CodePageID)	Sets options that define a user's locale.		✓	✓
SetOption(OptType, OptValue)	Sets a calendar rendering option for the session.			✓

The next section will cover the **InfoStore** object, which represents the message stores that can be accessed during a session.

The InfoStores Collection

The **InfoStores** collection is the list of possible message stores (places to store Outlook or Exchange items) for the current session. Each **InfoStore** object provides access to the folder hierarchy of a message store. **InfoStores** is a small collection, so its **Count** property is reliable.

About Small and Large Collections

A *large collection* is a collection for which the service provider cannot always maintain an accurate count of member objects. In such a collection the **Count** property will not necessarily return an accurate value. Large collections support get methods that enable you to access individual members of the collection. A *small collection* is a collection for which the service provider maintains an accurate count of member objects. You can rely on the **Count** property and directly access individual members of the collection using an index. The following table identifies which CDO collections are small and which are large:

Collection Name	Small Collection	Large Collection
AddressEntries		✓
AddressLists	✓	
Attachments	✓	
Columns	✓	
Fields	✓	
Folders		✓
Formats	✓	
InfoStores	✓	
Messages		✓
Patterns	✓	
Recipients	✓	
Views	✓	

InfoStores Code Example

To get a feel for what an **InfoStore** object represents, here's a code segment that runs through the **InfoStores** collection and prints out some of its key properties. It assumes that the user is already logged on:

```
Dim objSession as MAPI.Session
Dim objInfoStores as MAPI.InfoStores
Dim objInfoStore as MAPI.InfoStore
' assume I've logged on…
Debug.Print "InfoStore", "RootFolder Name", "Provider"
For n = 1 To objSession.InfoStores.Count
    Set objInfoStore = objSession.InfoStores(n)
    Debug.Print objInfoStore.Name, objInfoStore.RootFolder.Name,
        _objInfoStore.ProviderName
Next
```

The following is sample output against a profile with two message stores: an Exchange server (with a private mailbox and a set of public folders) and a personal folder:

```
InfoStore                 RootFolder Name             Provider
Scott's Personal Folder   Top of Personal Folders     Personal Folders
Mailbox - Jamison, Scott  Top of Information Store    Microsoft Exchange
                                                      Server
Public Folders            IPM_SUBTREE                 Microsoft Exchange
                                                      Server
```

InfoStore Properties

The InfoStore object exposes a set of properties such as **Name**, **RootFolder**, and **ProviderName**, among others. Table 11.3 shows the entire set of properties for the **InfoStore** object.

Determining Whether a Session Is Offline

You can use the **Fields** collection of the **InfoStore** object to determine whether the current store is logged in offline. This information can be useful when you need to access a remote database or other online-only feature. The following example shows how to use the **PR_STORE_OFFLINE** property:

```
' If you are using VBScript or late binding, the next line is needed:
CONST PR_STORE_OFFLINE = &H6632000B
Dim objSession as MAPI.Session
Dim objInfoStore as MAPI.InfoStore
```

Table 11.3 Properties of the **InfoStore** Object

Property Name	Description	Type	Access Level	1.0	1.1	1.21
Application	Always returns "Collaboration Data Objects."	String	Read-only	✓	✓	✓
Class	Returns **cdoInfoStore** (1).	Long	Read-only	✓	✓	✓
Fields	Returns the entire collection of **InfoStore** fields.	Object	Read-only		✓	✓
ID	Returns the **EntryID** for this **InfoStore** object.	String	Read-only	✓	✓	✓
Index	Returns the index number for this **InfoStore** object within the parent **InfoStores** collection.	Long	Read-only	✓	✓	✓
Name	Returns the **InfoStore** name.	String	Read-only	✓	✓	✓
Parent	Returns the parent **InfoStores** collection.	Object	Read-only	✓	✓	✓
ProviderName	Returns the name of the **InfoStore** object's message store provider—for example, "Personal Folders."	String	Read-only	✓	✓	✓
RootFolder	Returns the root folder for this **InfoStore**.	Object	Read-only	✓	✓	✓
Session	Returns the current **Session** object.	Object	Read-only	✓	✓	✓

```
Set objSession = CreateObject("MAPI.Session")
objSession.Logon
Set objInfoStore = objSession.InfoStores("Public Folders")
If objInfoStore.Fields(PR_STORE_OFFLINE).Value Then
    ' Value is TRUE -> we are offline
    MsgBox "Store is offline"
Else
    MsgBox "Store is online"
End If
```

Note: Be careful when using this technique with a personal folder store. If you try to use this field on a non-Exchange InfoStore, you will get a "MAPI_E_NOT_FOUND" error, because the **STORE_OFFLINE** field does not exist.

The InfoStore Method: IsSameAs

The **InfoStore** object allows you to compare two objects to determine if they're the same by calling the **IsSameAs** method (see Table 11.4).

Table 11.4 The Method of the **InfoStore** Object

Method Name	Description	1.0	1.1	1.21
IsSameAs(objInfoStore2)	Returns True if the two InfoStore objects are the same.		✓	✓

Accessing Folders

Folders are organized in a hierarchy, allowing access to folders within other folders. Subfolders appear in the **Folders** collection and are returned by the **Folders** property.

In CDO, there are several ways to access folders:

- Getting a default folder directly. CDO allows you to get any one of the default Outlook folders.
- Traversing through folders using the **Folders** collection's get methods.
- Obtaining a folder using its **EntryID** by calling the **Session** object's **GetFolder** method.
- Getting a reference to **Public Folders** using the **InfoStore** object's **RootFolder** method.
- Using a **Message** object's **Parent** property, which is the folder in which the message is stored.
- Using a folder name as a parameter to the **Folders** collection—for example, **Folders("MyFolder")**.

> **Warning:** When using the folder name parameter technique, the **Folders** collection must be sorted first or unpredictable results will occur. For example, **Session.InfoStores(1).Folders("Public Folders")** will always return "Favorites" unless the collection is sorted.

Getting a Default Folder

CDO 1.21 provides two ways to get standard folders. The **Session** object has **Inbox** and **Outbox** properties, which return the respective folders for the current session. The **GetDefaultFolder** method also returns a **Folder** object. Table 11.5 lists the possible values you can use to return a default folder. For example, the following code returns the default **Calendar** folder:

```
Set objSession = CreateObject("MAPI.Session")
objSession.Logon
objFolder = objSession.GetDefaultFolder(cdoDefaultFolderCalendar)
```

Table 11.5 cdoDefaultFolderTypes Constants

Folder	Constant	Value
Calendar	cdoDefaultFolderCalendar	0
Contacts	cdoDefaultFolderContacts	5
Deleted Items	cdoDefaultFolderDeletedItems	4
Inbox	cdoDefaultFolderInbox	1
Journal	cdoDefaultFolderJournal	6
Notes	cdoDefaultFolderNotes	7
Outbox	cdoDefaultFolderOutbox	2
Sent Items	cdoDefaultFolderSentMail	3
Tasks	cdoDefaultFolderTasks	8

Note: If you're also using the Outlook objects, be careful when using **GetDefault-Folder**. The numeric values that you pass to specify the folder are different for CDO and Outlook.

Traversing Folders

CDO allows you to iterate through the **Folders** collection to get its subfolders. The best way to get a subfolder, however, is to reference it directly. The following example starts with the Inbox and retrieves a subfolder called **Pending**:

```
Set objSession = CreateObject("MAPI.Session")
objSession.Logon
objFolder = objSession.GetDefaultFolder(cdoDefaultFolderInbox)
Set objSubFolder = objFolder.Folders("Pending")
If Not objSubFolder Is Nothing Then
    MsgBox "Folder not found."
Else
    ' objSubFolder contains a reference to the folder we want
    MsgBox "Folder was found."
End If
```

Using the GetFolder Method

When you know the unique identifier for the folder you're looking for, call the **Session** object's **GetFolder** method. The unique identifier for the folder, established at the time the folder is created and saved, is stored in its **ID** property.

Note: In Outlook, you'd use a **GetFolderFromID** method call to retrieve a folder in this way. Outlook's **MAPIFolder** object defines this property as the **EntryID**. In any case, both properties refer to the MAPI property **PR_ENTRYID**.

The following code saves the ID for a folder and then uses a **GetFolder** call to get the folder back:

```
Set objSession = CreateObject("MAPI.Session")
objSession.Logon
' Get the user's inbox
Set objFolder = objSession.Inbox
' Save the current Entry ID
strFolderEntryID = objFolder.ID
MsgBox "Current Folder ID = " & strFolderID
' Clear the object out
Set objFolder = Nothing
' Use GetFolder to get it back
Set objFolder = objSession.GetFolder(strFolderID)
If objFolder Is Nothing Then
    MsgBox "Unable to retrieve folder using ID"
Else
    MsgBox "objFolder is set to " & objFolder.Name
End If
```

Note: When using the **GetFolder** method call (as well as **GetMessage**), you have the option to also pass a **StoreID** parameter. By default, CDO assumes you want to look in the store of the private mailbox. **StoreID** is therefore necessary when you want to access a folder or message from another store, such as a PST (Personal Store) or public folder. If you don't pass in a **StoreID**, be sure to pass in NULL instead.

Using the RootFolder Object to Access Public Folders

To retrieve data in a public folder, CDO provides a collection under the **Session** object called the **InfoStores** collection—a collection of **InfoStore** objects, each of which provides access to the folder hierarchy of a message store. By using the **RootFolder** object of an **InfoStore**, you get to the IPM subtree—the hierarchy of folders for all interpersonal messages (IPMs). The following code example uses the **Fields** collection of the **Public Folders InfoStore** object to get a specific item (**All Public Folders**) using a special property tag: **PR_IPM_PUBLIC_FOLDERS_ENTRYID.**

Warning: "Public Folders" is a localized string. Trying to search for this string in non-English versions of Outlook will result in the public folder hierarchy not being found.

```
Set objInfoStores = objSession.InfoStores
For i = 1 to objInfoStores.Count
    If objInfoStores.Item(i) = _
        "Public Folders" Then
        Set objInfoStore = _
            objInfoStores.Item(i)
        Exit For
    End If
Next
' Find Top Folder
strPublicRootID = _
    objInfoStore.Fields.Item(PR_IPM_PUBLIC_FOLDERS_ENTRYID).Value
Set objTopFolder = _
    objSession.GetFolder(strPublicRootID, _
    objInfoStore.ID)
Set objFolders = objTopFolder.Folders
Set objFolder = objInfoStore.RootFolder
```

By continuing down the folder hierarchy using the **Folders** collection, you can search the folders until you arrive at the folder that interests you.

Using a Message Object's FolderID Property

You can also obtain a reference to a folder by using the **FolderID** property of a Message object in conjunction with the **GetFolder** method. The **FolderID** property will return the ID of the folder in which the **Message** is stored. The following example demonstrates the **FolderID** property:

```
Set objFolder = objSession.Inbox
' Get the first message in the folder
Set objMessage = objFolder.Messages.GetFirst
' Get its parent folder ID
sFolderID = objMessage.FolderID
Set objParentFolder = _
    objSession.GetFolder(sFolderID, objMessage.StoreID)
MsgBox "The parent folder is " & objParentFolder.Name
```

Folder Properties

The **Folder** object, which corresponds to Outlook's **MAPIFolder** object, exposes many of the same properties, such as **Name.** Rather than having an **Items** collection (as Outlook does), CDO has a **Messages** collection. Table 11.6 lists the properties of the **Folder** object.

Folder Methods

The methods of the CDO **Folder** object are listed in Table 11.7.

Table 11.6 Properties of the **Folder** Object

Property Name	Description	Type	Access Level	1.0	1.1	1.21
Application	Always returns "Collaboration Data Objects."	Object	Read-only	✓	✓	✓
Class	Returns **cdoFolder** (2).	Long	Read-only	✓	✓	✓
Fields	Returns the collection of folder-specific fields.	Collection	Read-only	✓	✓	✓
FolderID	Returns this folder's *parent* folder's **EntryID.**	String	Read-only	✓	✓	✓
Folders	Returns a collection of the subfolders.	Collection	Read-only	✓	✓	✓
HiddenMessages	Returns a collection of hidden messages in this folder.	Collection	Read-only			✓
ID	Returns the **EntryID** for this folder.	String	Read-only	✓	✓	✓
Messages	Returns a collection of all messages in this folder.	Collection	Read-only	✓	✓	✓
Name	Returns the folder name.	String	Read/write	✓	✓	✓
Parent	Returns this folder's parent. For **Inbox** and **Outbox**, CDO will return the **Session** object. For other folders, a **Folder** object will be returned, unless it is a top-level folder, in which case an **InfoStore** object will be returned.	Object	Read-only	✓	✓	✓
Session	Returns the current **Session** object.	Object	Read-only	✓	✓	✓
StoreID	Returns the unique identifier of the **InfoStore** object in which the **Folder** object resides.	String	Read-only	✓	✓	✓

Table 11.7 Methods of the **Folder** Object

Method Name	Description	1.0	1.1	1.21
CopyTo(folderID [, storeID] [, name] [, copySubfolders])	Copies the folder (and all contents) to another folder hierarchy location.		✓	✓
Delete	Deletes the folder.	✓	✓	✓
IsSameAs(objFolder2)	Returns True if the two folder objects are the same.		✓	✓
MoveTo(folderID [, storeID])	Moves the folder (and all contents) to another folder hierarchy location.		✓	✓
Update([makePermanent] [, refreshObject])	Saves changes to the **Folder** object in the MAPI system. Changes to **Folder** objects are not permanently saved until you call the **Update** method with **makePermanent** set to True.	✓	✓	✓

Retrieving Messages

The Messages Collection

Every folder contains a collection of items. In CDO this collection is called the **Messages** collection. You can access all messages in the folder by using the **GetFirst**, **GetNext**, **GetPrevious**, and **GetLast** methods. The following example prints out a list of all messages in the inbox:

```
Dim objMessage as MAPI.Message
Dim objMessages as MAPI.Messages
Dim objFolder as MAPI.Folder
Dim objSession as MAPI.Session
Set objSession = CreateObject("MAPI.Session")
objSession.Logon
Set objFolder = objSession.Inbox
Set objMessages = objFolder.Messages
Set objMessage = objMessages.GetFirst
If objMessage Is Nothing Then
    MsgBox "Folder is empty."
Else
' Loop through all the messages in the collection
    Do While Not objMessage Is Nothing
        Debug.Print objMessage.Subject
        Set objMessage = objMessages.GetNext
    Loop
End If
Set objMessage = Nothing
```

```
Set objMessages = Nothing
Set objFolder = Nothing
Set objSession = Nothing
```

The HiddenMessages Collection

The **HiddenMessages** property returns a **Messages** collection object of hidden messages in a folder. The messages in the collection returned by the **HiddenMessages** property are not visible through Outlook. These hidden messages correspond to the folder-associated information kept in a folder by MAPI. Some messaging clients use hidden messages for various tasks, such as Inbox rules or routing information. You can use the **HiddenMessages** collection to store public folder or other settings. You can view the **HiddenMessages** collection with the Exchange 2000 property inspector (ADO Explorer) featured in Chapter 20.

> **Note:** Be careful when using the **HiddenMessages** collection. Outlook and Exchange store information such as custom views, custom forms, and other types of information that you should never change.

The **Messages** within the **HiddenMessages** collection can be accessed in the normal manner (through its **Add** and **Delete** methods), and the properties on its member **Message** objects retain their respective read/write or read-only accessibility.

> **Note:** Only the owner of a folder can add or delete items in the **HiddenMessages** collection (and these additions and deletions can be done only through code).

Using the HiddenMessages Collection

One of the things that the **HiddenMessages** collection stores is the list of form definition messages for the folder. A form definition message is a custom form that has been published to the folder. The following code will allow you to remove a published form from a folder using the CDO object model:

```
Set objFolder = <set a reference to the folder here>
Set objHiddenMessages = objFolder.HiddenMessages
' Passing a message class value to GetFirst will create a filter:
Set objMessage = _
   objHiddenMessages.GetFirst("IPM.Microsoft.FolderDesign.
                               FormsDescription")
```

```
' Loop through all forms
Do Until objMessage Is Nothing
    sFormName = "Form Name: " & objMessage.Fields(cdoPR_DISPLAY_NAME)
    If MsgBox(sFormName, vbYesNo, "Delete?") = vbYes Then
        objMessage.Delete
    End If
    Set objMessage = objHiddenMessages.GetNext
Loop
Set objFolder = Nothing
Set objHiddenMessages = Nothing
Set objMessage = Nothing
```

Sorting a Messages Collection

If you want the messages in the collection to be returned in a particular order, you can use the **Messages** collection's **Sort** method. The **Sort** method sorts the collection on the specified property according to the specified sort order. Its format is as follows:

```
objMessages.Sort( [SortOrder] [, PropTag or name] )
```

SortOrder can be either **cdoAscending** (1) or **cdoDescending** (2). **PropTag** is the property tag value for the MAPI property to be used for the sort. Or instead of using a property tag, you can use the **Name** parameter, which is the property name of a MAPI-named property.

> **Note:** You can use the same technique to sort the **Folders** and **AddressEntries** collections.

For example, if you wanted to print out your inbox **Messages** collection sorted by **Subject**, you could add the following single line of code:

```
objMessages.Sort(cdoAscending, PR_SUBJECT)
```

Your code would then look like this:

```
Dim objMessage as MAPI.Message
Dim objMessages as MAPI.Messages
Dim objFolder as MAPI.Folder
Dim objSession as MAPI.Session
Set objSession = CreateObject("MAPI.Session")
```

```
objSession.Logon
Set objFolder = objSession.Inbox
Set objMessages = objFolder.Messages
objMessages.Sort(cdoAscending, PR_SUBJECT)
Set objMessage = objMessages.GetFirst
If objMessage Is Nothing Then
    MsgBox "Folder is empty."
Else
' Loop through all the messages in the collection
    Do While Not objMessage Is Nothing
        Debug.Print objMessage.Subject
        Set objMessage = objMessages.GetNext
    Loop
End If
Set objMessage = Nothing
Set objMessages = Nothing
Set objFolder = Nothing
Set objSession = Nothing
```

Note: You cannot sort a collection of **AppointmentItem** objects on any property other than start date. CDO will return the error "cdoE_TOO_COMPLEX." However, since **MeetingItem** objects are really enhanced e-mail messages, you can sort **MeetingItems** by other criteria.

MessageFilter

Often you don't want to return all of the messages in a folder. For example, you may want messages from only a specific person. You could loop through and check every item in the folder, returning only the ones you want. However, a more efficient way is to filter the **Messages** collection using a **MessageFilter.** You can create a filter that will return only those **Messages** that match a list of criteria. The format of a **MessageFilter** is as follows:

```
Set objMessageFilter = objMessages.Filter
objMessageFilter.(field name) = "(value to filter by)"
```

Getting back to the example, say you want only unread messages that were sent by Scott Jamison. The following example sets a reference to the **Messages** collection's **MessageFilter** and sets the **Unread** and **Sender** properties. The resulting collection will consist of only those messages that match the criteria.

Note: As soon as you set your **MessageFilter** property, your associated collection is filtered appropriately. See the comments in the code for more details.

```
Dim objSession As MAPI.Session
Dim objFolder As MAPI.Folder
Dim objMessages As MAPI.Messages
Dim objMessageFilter As MAPI.MessageFilter
Dim objMessage As Message
' Create a CDO session
Set objSession = CreateObject("MAPI.Session")
' Log on to the session
objSession.Logon
' Get a reference to the folder we want to filter
Set objFolder = objSession.Inbox
' Get the collection of messages in the folder
Set objMessages = objInbox.Messages
' Use the next line to see the number of messages (before)
' MsgBox objMessages.Count
' Assign a message filter to the messages collection
Set objMessageFilter = objMessages.Filter
' Set our first filter setting
' NOTE: As soon as this line is executed, objMessages
' will NOT contain all messages in the folder anymore.
' Instead, it will contain just the filtered list.
objMessageFilter.Sender = "Jamison, Scott"
' Filter the messages some more
objMessageFilter.Unread = True
' Use the next line to see the number of messages (after)
' MsgBox objMessages.Count
Set objMessage = objMessages.GetFirst
If objMessage Is Nothing Then
    MsgBox "Folder is empty."
Else
' Loop through all the messages in the collection
    Do While Not objMessage Is Nothing
        Debug.Print objMessage.Subject
        Set objMessage = objMessages.GetNext
    Loop
End If
Set objMessageFilter = Nothing
Set objMessage = Nothing
Set objMessages = Nothing
Set objFolder = Nothing
Set objSession = Nothing
```

> **Note:** You can also pass a message class string to the **GetFirst** method to create a filtered **Messages** collection automatically, as shown in the **HiddenMessages** example.

You can also use the **Not** property to create negated filters. Say you wanted to create a filter that returned all messages that were *not* from Scott Jamison. You would create your filter in the same way, except that you would set the **Not** property to True:

```
Set objMessageFilter = objSession.Inbox.Messages.Filter
objMessageFilter.Not = True ' negate all results
objMessageFilter.Sender = "Simpson, Homer"
```

You cannot, however, create filters that "NOT" specific properties. For example, you cannot filter like this:

```
Field1 = "text" AND NOT(Field2 = "text")
```

This won't work because the **Not** property negates all filter values in the message filter.

> **Note:** You cannot filter on custom fields or keyword fields.

MessageFilter Properties

Table 11.8 gives the complete list of **MessageFilter** properties.

The MessageFilter Method: IsSameAs

The only method provided by the **MessageFilter** object is the **IsSameAs** method (see Table 11.9), which allows you to test whether two **MessageFilter** objects are the same underlying object.

The Message Object

Once you have the collection of messages you're looking for, you can use the **Message** object to retrieve properties of existing messages, or simply to create new ones.

Table 11.8 Properties of the **MessageFilter** Object

Property Name	Description	Type	Access Level	1.0	1.1	1.21
Application	Always returns "Collaboration Data Objects."	Object	Read-only		✓	✓
Class	Returns **cdoMessageFilter** (10).	Long	Read-only		✓	✓
Conversation	Sets filtering on the message's **ConversationTopic** property.	String	Read/write		✓	✓
Fields	Returns the entire collection of **MessageFilter** fields. Use this collection when the field on which you wish to filter is not defined as a property.	Collection	Read-only		✓	✓
Importance	Sets filtering on the importance of a message.	Long	Read-only		✓	✓
Not	Specifies that all restriction values are to be negated before being ANDed or ORed.	Boolean	Read/write		✓	✓
Or	Specifies that the restriction values are to be ORed instead of ANDed.	Boolean	Read/write		✓	✓
Parent	Returns the parent **Messages** collection.	Collection	Read-only		✓	✓
Recipients	Sets filtering on whether the message's recipients include at least one recipient with a particular name. Note that this is *not* a **Recipients** collection.	String	Read/write		✓	✓
Sender	Sets filtering on the name of a message's sender.	String	Read/write		✓	✓
Sent	Sets filtering on whether this message was sent or posted. This value is True if it was sent through the MAPI system and False if it was posted or saved directly.	Boolean	Read/write		✓	✓
Session	Returns the current **Session** object.	Object	Read-only		✓	✓
Size	Sets filtering on the approximate total size of a message, in bytes.	Long	Read/write		✓	✓
Subject	Sets filtering on the subject of a message.	String	Read/write		✓	✓
Text	Sets filtering on the main text (body) of a message. The filter will look for the specified text as a substring of the entire message body.	String	Read/write		✓	✓

Continued on next page.

Table 11.8 Properties of the **MessageFilter** Object *(continued)*

Property Name	Description	Type	Access Level	1.0	1.1	1.21
TimeFirst	Sets filtering on whether a message was received since the specified date and time.	Date	Read/write			
TimeLast	Sets filtering on whether a message was received before the specified date and time.	Date	Read/write		✓	✓
Type	Sets filtering on the message class of a message.	String	Read/write		✓	✓
Unread	Sets filtering on whether or not a message has been read.	Boolean	Read/write		✓	✓

Message Properties

The **Message** object corresponds to Outlook's **Item** object. Table 11.10 lists the entire set of properties of the CDO **Message** object.

Message Methods

Many of the methods of the **Message** object are similar to those of the Outlook item objects. Table 11.11 lists the available methods.

> **Note:** The **Reply** and **ReplyAll** methods do not copy the **Text** property to the new message, nor do they copy any attachments from the original message.

Entry IDs versus Article IDs

As described throughout the book, every message (and Outlook item) has a property called **EntryID** (or just **ID**) that is a string of hexadecimal characters. This string uniquely identifies a message within a given message store. If you know a message's **EntryID** value, you can use the **GetMessage** method to access the message directly.

Table 11.9 The Method of the **MessageFilter** Object

Method Name	Description	1.0	1.1	1.21
IsSameAs(objMessageFilter)	Returns True if the two **MessageFilter** objects are the same.		✓	✓

Table 11.10 Properties of the **Message** Object

Property Name	Description	Type	Access Level	1.0	1.1	1.21
Application	Always returns "Collaboration Data Objects."	Object	Read-only	✓	✓	✓
Attachments	Returns the attachments for this item.	Object or Collection	Read-only	✓	✓	✓
Categories	Returns a variant array of the categories associated with this item.	Array of Strings	Read/write			✓
Class	Returns **cdoMsg** (3).	Long	Read-only	✓	✓	✓
Conversation	This property is outdated; do not use it. Instead use **ConversationTopic** or **ConversationIndex.**	—	—	—	—	—
ConversationIndex	Returns a hexidecimal value indicating its discussion-ordering placement that is unique to the message (see the section titled Discussion Group Support later in this chapter).	String	Read/write	✓	✓	✓
ConversationTopic	Returns the human-readable name of the conversation (usually the subject of the initial message) (see the section titled Discussion Group Support later in this chapter).	String	Read/write	✓	✓	✓
DeliveryReceipt	If set to True, obtains a notification message when each recipient receives your message. The default setting is False.	Boolean	Read/write	✓	✓	✓
Encrypted	If set to True, represents a request for encryption. CDO does not encrypt or digitally sign the item itself.	Boolean	Read/write	✓	✓	✓
Fields	Returns the collection of field values for this item.	Collection	Read-only	✓	✓	✓
FolderID	Returns the **EntryID** of this item's parent folder.	String	Read-only	✓	✓	✓
ID	Returns the **EntryID** of this item.	String	Read-only	✓	✓	✓
Importance	Can be **cdoLow** (0), **cdoNormal** (1), or **cdoHigh** (2). The default is **cdoNormal.**	Long	Read/write	✓	✓	✓
Parent	Returns the parent **Messages** collection for this item.	Collection	Read-only	✓	✓	✓
ReadReceipt	Returns True if a read receipt is requested.	Boolean	Read/write	✓	✓	✓

Continued on next page.

Table 11.10 Properties of the **Message** Object *(continued)*

Property Name	Description	Type	Access Level	1.0	1.1	1.21
Recipients	Returns the list of "To," "Cc," and "Bcc" recipients for this item.	Collection	Read/write	✓	✓	✓
Sender	Returns the **From** value of the message. You can change the **Sender** property before a message is either sent or saved.	Object	Read/write	✓	✓	✓
Sensitivity	Can be **cdoNoSensitivity** (0), **cdoPersonal** (1), **cdoPrivate** (2), or **cdoConfidential** (3). The default is **cdoNoSensitivity**.	Long	Read/write			✓
Sent	Returns True if sent.	Boolean	Read/write	✓	✓	✓
Session	Returns the current **Session** object.	Object	Read-only	✓	✓	✓
Signed	Returns True if digital signature is present.	Boolean	Read/write	✓	✓	✓
Size	Returns the size of the item in bytes. Unsaved messages have a size of zero.	Long	Read-only	✓	✓	✓
StoreID	Returns the ID of the message store. Use with get methods.	String	Read-only	✓	✓	✓
Subject	Returns the subject of the message (default property).	String	Read/write	✓	✓	✓
Submitted	States whether the item has been submitted to the subsystem.	Boolean	Read/write	✓	✓	✓
Text	Returns the body of the message. Corresponds to the **Body** property of an Outlook item.	String	Read/write	✓	✓	✓
TimeCreated	Returns the date and time that the item was first saved.	Date	Read-only			✓
TimeExpired	Returns the date and time that the item becomes invalid.	Date	Read/write			✓
TimeLastModified	Returns the date and time that the item was last saved.	Date	Read-only			✓
TimeReceived	Returns the date and time that the item was received (through e-mail, this property is set automatically).	Date	Read/write	✓	✓	✓
TimeSent	Returns the date and time that the item was sent (through e-mail, this property is set automatically).	Date	Read/write	✓	✓	✓

Table 11.10 Properties of the **Message** Object *(continued)*

Property Name	Description	Type	Access Level	1.0	1.1	1.21
Type	Returns the message class for this item. Corresponds to the **MessageClass** property of an Outlook item.	String	Read/write	✓	✓	✓
Unread	Returns True if the item has not been read. For public folders, Exchange maintains separate values for each client.	Boolean	Read/write	✓	✓	✓

Table 11.11 Methods of the **Message** Object

Method Name	Description	1.0	1.1	1.21
CopyTo (folderID [, storeID])	Makes a copy of the item in another folder.		✓	✓
Delete ([DeletedItems])	Removes the item. If you set the **DeletedItems** parameter to True, **Delete** moves the item to the **Deleted Items** folder. To delete an item permanently that is already in the **Deleted Items** folder, call **Delete** without supplying **DeletedItems.**	✓	✓	✓
Forward	Returns a new **Message** object that can be used to forward the current message.			✓
IsSameAs (objMessage)	Returns True if the two **Message** objects are the same.		✓	✓
MoveTo (folderID [, storeID])	Moves the item to another folder.		✓	✓
Options	Shows a dialog box that allows the user to configure options on the message. Note: This method does not work on ".pst" files.	✓	✓	✓
Reply	Returns a new **Message** object that can be used to reply to the sender of the current message.			✓
ReplyAll	Returns a new **Message** object that can be used to reply to the sender and all recipients of the current message.			✓
Send ([saveCopy] [, showDialog] [, parentWindow])	Sends the message to the recipients through the MAPI system.	✓	✓	✓
Update ([makePermanent] [, refreshObject])	Saves the message to a message store.	✓	✓	✓

Table 11.12 Comparing the **EntryID** and **ArticleID** Properties

Feature	EntryID	ArticleID
How to access its value?	objMessage.ID	objMessage.Fields(cdoPR_INTER-NET_ ARTICLE_NUMBER)
Description	Unique value for message in a store	Unique value for message in a folder
Data type	String (70+ characters)	Long (32 bits)
Get method for message	GetMessage(EntryID)	GetArticle(ArticleID, FolderID)
Other data needed for the get?	No other information needed (other than optional store ID)	Need to also pass folder's EntryID (and optional store ID)
Use when...	You don't know the folder ID You don't mind storing a large string	You know the folder ID You need to save space when storing the message ID

Another way to identify a message in CDO uniquely is to use its article number. An article number is a long integer associated with all items in a message store. The store sets the article number on each item as it is added to a folder. The advantage of an article number is that it is only 32 bits long, as opposed to the item's unique identifier in its ID property, which is typically on the order of 70 bytes. One advantage of using the article ID is that if you are constructing a URL to reference an item, you can make the URL much shorter by using the item's article number instead of its unique identifier. Another advantage is that if you're using a single folder, you can store Long values instead of huge strings. Table 11.12 summarizes the **EntryID** and **ArticleID** values.

The Fields Collection

Perhaps the most important property of the **Message** object is the **Fields** collection, which provides access to any field in a message. The **Fields** collection allows you to iterate through all fields in a message. It also allows you to access fields directly using a property tag. The **Fields** property returns one or all of the fields associated with a **Message** object. Each field typically corresponds to a MAPI property. For the most part, data types are preserved. The only exception is that binary properties are converted to and from character strings representing hexadecimal digits (e.g., **EntryID** and **ConversationIndex**).

The **Fields** property provides a generic access mechanism that allows developers to retrieve the value of a MAPI property using either its name or its MAPI property tag. For access with the property tag, use **objMessage.Fields(proptag)**, where "proptag" is the 32-bit MAPI property tag associated with the property, such as "cdoPR_Subject." To access a custom property, use **objMessage.Fields(<name of property>)**, where "<name of property>" is a string that represents the custom property name.

You can also iterate through the fields of an item, which is something you cannot do using the Outlook object model. The following example shows how to iterate through all fields of the first item in the current user's inbox. Typically, only custom properties will show their name:

```
Set objMessage = objSession.Inbox.Messages.GetFirst
Set objFields = objMessage.Fields
Debug.Print, "Name", "ID", "Value"
For Each objField In objFields
    Debug.Print objField.Name, objField.ID, objField.Value
Next
```

Discussion Group Support

CDO supports the use of messages that are saved directly in a folder, typically for threaded discussions. Such a discussion is sometimes referred to as a *conversation*. A conversation is a group of related messages that have the same **ConversationTopic** property value. The conversation topic is typically the subject text of the first message in a thread. In a discussion application, users typically save the original message and responses to the original message. Figure 11.2 shows a threaded discussion.

All messages are tagged with a field called **ConversationIndex**, which is used to order the messages within the conversation. When the first message in a thread is created, MAPI creates a 44-character field that is stored in the **ConversationIndex** field. When a message is replied to, the child message is assigned a **ConversationIndex** value that is its parent's **ConversationIndex** plus a 10-character time stamp value. For illustration, look at the following code, which sorts a **Messages** collection by its **ConversationIndex** value, loops through the collection, and then prints out the **Subject** text in the manner of a conversation thread:

```
' Get a public folder
Set objFolder = objRootFolder.Folders("Microsoft Word Discussion")
' Get the Messages collection
Set objMessages = objFolder.Messages
' Sort the messages by conversation index
objMessages.Sort cdoAscending, mapi.cdoPR_CONVERSATION_INDEX
```

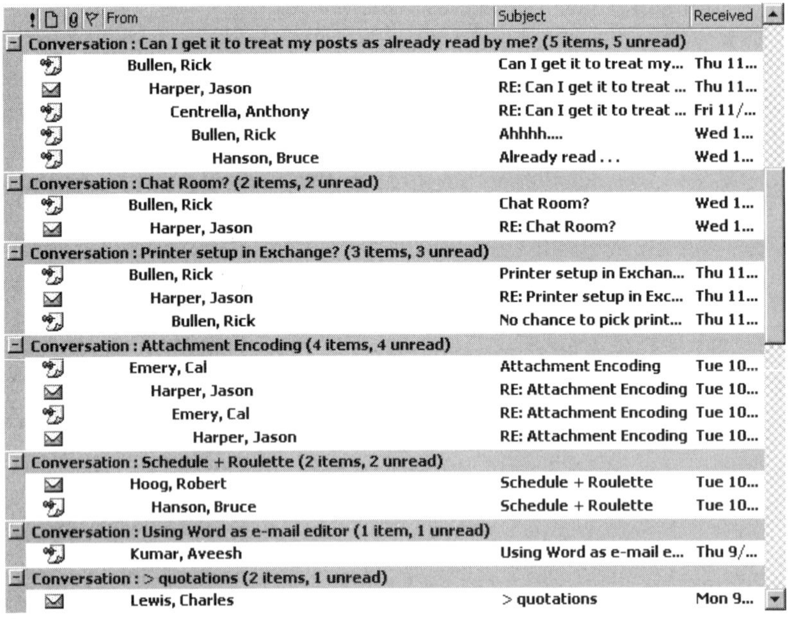

Figure 11.2 A threaded discussion

```
' Loop through the sorted messages
For Each objMessage In objMessages
    ' Depending on the size of the conversation index, indent the subject
    With objMessage
        sTemp = ""
        hLen = ((Len(.ConversationIndex) - 44) / 10)
        For I = 1 to hLen
            sTemp = sTemp & "--"
        Next
        sTemp = sTemp & .Subject
        Debug.Print sTemp
    End With
Next
```

The output looks something like this:

```
Outlook 2000
--Re: Outlook 2000
----Re: Re: Outlook 2000
----Re: Re: Outlook 2000
------Another Outlook Question
--Re: Outlook 2000
```

Try replacing the **Debug.Print sTemp** statement with **Debug.Print .ConversationIndex.** You'll see the **ConversationIndex** string values, which will look something like this:

```
01BE752C882CB15DF5B8E0F511D290A00080C7AC5ABF
01BE752C882CB15DF5B8E0F511D290A00080C7AC5ABF0000009D20
01BE752C882CB15DF5B8E0F511D290A00080C7AC5ABF0000009D20000001EA20
01BE752C882CB15DF5B8E0F511D290A00080C7AC5ABF0000009D20000001EA200042384610
|---- Original message index --------------|1st reply|2nd reply|3rd reply|
```

The **Session** object provides the **CreateConversationIndex** method to create or update a conversation index. This method allows you to create new **ConversationIndex** values properly.

> **Note:** The **ConversationIndex** property is actually a string that represents a hexadecimal number. Valid characters within the string include the numbers 0 through 9 and the letters A through F (uppercase or lowercase).

> **Note:** The CDO help file suggests using the **Util_GetEightByteTimeStamp** function to create an Exchange-compatible conversation index. You don't need to do that because the **CreateConversationIndex** method was added to CDO in version 1.2 and works fine.

For example, the following code segment illustrates how you would use the **CreateConversationIndex** method. It assumes you have a valid session and a reference to a folder:

```
' ...Assume we have a valid Session object and a Folder object
' Extract a message from the folder
Set objMessage = objFolder.GetFirst
' Use its index to make a new conversation index
' CDO creates it for us automatically
' See how we pass the parent's index?  CDO uses it to
' generate a child index based on the one we passed it
sIndex = objSession.CreateConversationIndex _
    (objMessage.ConversationIndex)
Set objReply = objFolder.Messages.Add ' generate reply
With objReply
     .ConversationIndex = sIndex
     .ConversationTopic = objMessage.ConversationTopic
     .Subject = "RE: " & objMessage.Subject
```

```
    .Text = "I agree with your message."
    .Update
End With
```

Note: The **ConversationIndex** property can be inspected like this only in CDO. In Outlook, this property is an unreadable value.

Calendar Support

CDO supports two calendar item types: **MeetingItems** and **AppointmentItems**. CDO also supports retrieval of free/busy information through the **AddressEntry** and **Recipient** objects. In CDO, an **AppointmentItem** object is distinguished from a **Message** object by a value of **IPM.Appointment** (its message class) in its **Type** property. You create an **AppointmentItem** object by using the **Add** method on a **Messages** collection obtained only from a calendar **Folder** object. For example,

```
Dim objSession As MAPI.Session
Dim objFolder As MAPI.Folder
Dim objMessages As MAPI.Messages
Dim objAppointmentItem As MAPI.AppointmentItem
Set objCalendarFolder = objSession.GetDefaultFolder _
                        (cdoDefaultFolderCalendar)
Set objMessages = objFolder.Messages
Set objAppointment = objMessages.Add
```

Note: In this example, all types are defined explicitly (e.g., **MAPI.AppointmentItem**). You could leave off the "MAPI" part of the statement, but then you could run into confusion as to whether it should be an **Outlook.AppointmentItem** or a **MAPI.AppointmentItem** (CDO). We recommend using an explicit typing convention.

Note: You cannot use CDO to access another user's **Calendar** folder. You must use the **GetSharedDefaultFolder** method in Outlook.

Address Books

Like Outlook, CDO can be used to access address lists such as the Global Address List, Personal Address Book, and the Outlook Contacts Address Book Provider. In

CDO, the simplest way to use the address books is to use the **Session** object's **AddressBook** method, which allows a user to select "To," "Cc" (carbon copy), and "Bcc" (blind carbon copy) recipients from a customizable user interface. Add the following code behind a button to allow the user to select a list of recipients:

```
Private Sub cmdRecipients_Click()
    On Error GoTo Err_cmdRecipients
    Set objRecipients = objSession.AddressBook( _
        Title:="Select CDO Recipients", _
        forceResolution:=True, _
        recipLists:=3, _
        toLabel:="&To", _
        ccLabel:="&Carbon Copies", _
        bccLabel:="&Blind Copies")
    Exit Sub
Err_cmdRecipients:
    If Err.Number = cdoE_USER_CANCEL Then
        MsgBox "User canceled."
    Else
        MsgBox "An error has occurred."
    End If
End Sub
```

With this code the user will get a dialog box like the one in Figure 11.3.

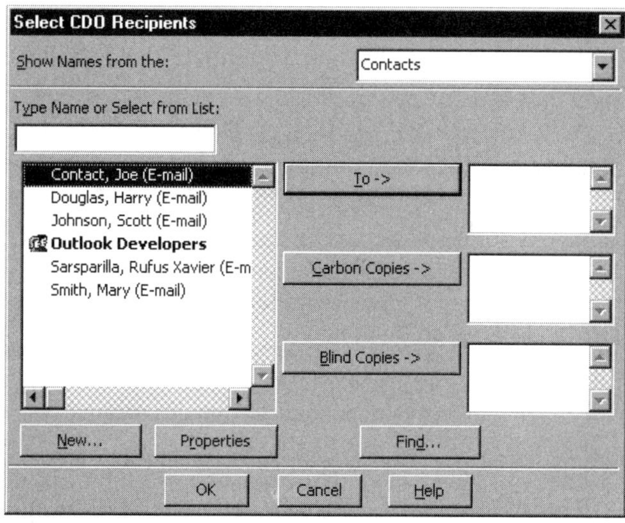

Figure 11.3 The address book recipient selection dialog box

The **AddressBook** method takes a list of optional parameters and returns a **Recipients** collection object. The syntax is as follows:

```
Set objRecipients = objSession.AddressBook( [recipients] [, title]
[, oneAddress] [, forceResolution] [, recipLists] [, toLabel]
[, ccLabel] [, bccLabel] [, parentWindow] )
```

where

- **recipients** represents the **Recipients** object. A **Recipients** collection object can be provided that gives initial values for the recipient list boxes in the address book dialog box.
- **title** is a String that contains the title or caption of the address book dialog box. The default value is an empty string.
- **oneAddress** is a Boolean parameter that lets the user select only one address entry at a time. The default value is False.
- **forceResolution** is a Boolean parameter that attempts to resolve all names before closing the address book and will prompt the user to resolve any ambiguous names. The default value is True.
- **recipLists** is a Long parameter representing the number of recipient list boxes to display in the address book dialog box according to one of the values in Table 11.13. No constants are defined in CDO for these values, so you'll have to use the values directly.
- **toLabel** is a String containing the caption for the button associated with the first recipient list box. If omitted, the default value "To:" is displayed.

Table 11.13 Valid Values for the **recipLists** Optional Parameter

Value	Action
–1	Displays three list boxes with default captions and without resolution. (i.e., a shortcut for **forceResolution=False**, **recipLists=3**, with the default **To:**, **Cc:**, and **Bcc:** button captions).
0	Displays no list boxes. The user can interact with the address book dialog box, but no recipients are returned by this method.
1	Displays one list box for **cdoTo** recipients.
2	Displays two list boxes for **cdoTo** and **cdoCc** recipients.
3	Displays three list boxes for **cdoTo**, **cdoCc**, and **cdoBcc** recipients.

- **ccLabel** is a String containing the caption for the button associated with the second recipient list box. If omitted, the default value "Cc:" is displayed.
- **bccLabel** is a String containing the caption for the button associated with the third recipient list box. If omitted, the default value "Bcc:" is displayed.
- **parentWindow** is a Long parameter representing the parent window handle for the address book dialog box. A value of zero (the default) specifies that the dialog box should be application-modal.

> **Note:** The **AddressBook** method displays an application-modal dialog box, which means that the user must select **OK** or **Cancel** before the application will continue. This method is useful for selecting recipients from an address book in Outlook because the Outlook object model does not have such a feature.

The AddressBook Object

Rather than using the **AddressBook** method to select recipients visually, you can traverse the CDO object model to view, add, and delete entries in the address books. The **AddressLists** collection provides access to the root of the MAPI address book hierarchy for the current session. Only address books that are listed in the current session's profile can be accessed through these objects. You obtain the collection through the parent **Session** object's **AddressLists** property as follows:

```
Set objSession  = CreateObject("MAPI.Session")
objSession.Logon
Set objAddressList = objSession.AddressLists("Global Address List")
```

> **Warning:** "Global Address List" is a localized string.

You can also obtain either the Global Address List (GAL) or the Personal Address Book (PAB) using the **GetAddressList** method:

```
Set objAddressList = objSession.GetAddressList(cdoAddressListGAL)
```

From here you can obtain the individual entries in the address book.

> **Note:** CDO does not support addition, deletion, or modification of members of a distribution list in the Global Address List. You must use ADSI to manipulate distribution lists in the GAL.

The AddressEntry Object

AddressEntry objects are items that exist in an **AddressList**, such as the Global Address List or a Personal Address Book. Say you want to fill a drop-down list with distribution lists in the Global Address List. The following code segment shows how to do this incrementally. First get a reference to the GAL as follows:

```
Set objAddressList = objSession.GetAddressList(cdoAddressListGAL)
```

Next use the **AddressEntries** property to obtain the entire list of users and distribution lists in the GAL:

```
Set objAddressEntries = objAddressList.AddressEntries
```

Finally, walk the collection of entries, selecting only those that are distribution lists. Make sure to call the **GetFirst** method to obtain the first entry in the collection, and then loop through using the **GetNext** method until you reach the end. Table 11.14 gives a complete list of **AddressList** display types.

To make sure you add only distribution lists to the drop-down list, check the **DisplayType** property for **cdoDistList** (1):

```
Dim objAddressEntry As MAPI.AddressEntry
    Set objAddressEntry = objAddressEntries.GetFirst
    Do Until (objAddressEntry Is Nothing)
        If objAddressEntry.DisplayType = cdoDistList Then
            cboDistList.AddItem objAddressEntry.Name
        End If
        Set objAddressEntry = objAddressEntries.GetNext
    Loop
    Set objAddressEntry = Nothing
```

Table 11.14 cdoDisplayType Address List Constants

Display Type	Constant	Value
User	cdoUser	0
Public Distribution List	cdoDistList	1
Forum (Public Folder)	cdoForum	2
Agent	cdoAgent	3
Organization	cdoOrganization	4
Private Distribution List	cdoPrivateDistList	5
Remote User	cdoRemoteUser	6

Address List Entries

If a distribution list is chosen, you'll need to extract the users for the selected list. The **Members** property of the distribution list will return a collection of address entries (list of users or other distribution lists). Use the **GetFirst/GetNext** combination to loop through the collection, this time checking to make sure **DisplayType** is **cdoUser** (0):

```
Dim objDistList As MAPI.AddressEntry
Dim objMembers As MAPI.AddressEntries
Dim objAddressEntry As MAPI.AddressEntry

Set objDistList = gobjGALEntries(cboDistList.Text)
Set objMembers = objDistList.Members
Set objAddressEntry = objMembers.GetFirst
    Do Until (objAddressEntry Is Nothing)
        If objAddressEntry.DisplayType = cdoUser Then
            cboAttendee.AddItem objAddressEntry.Name
        End If
        Set objAddressEntry = objMembers.GetNext
    Loop
Set objDistList = Nothing
Set objMembers = Nothing
Set objAddressEntry = Nothing
```

You now have a list of recipients from the chosen distribution list, and a user can select a particular recipient if desired.

Table 11.15 lists all **AddressEntry** properties.

> **Note:** To retrieve the address entry's e-mail address in the form "jamison@plural.com," use the following syntax: "objAddressEntry.Fields(&H39FE001E)." Be careful, however, because this will not work offline.

Table 11.16 gives the complete list of **AddressEntry** methods.

AddressEntryFilter

Sometimes you don't want all of the address entries in an address book. For example, you may want only address entries for a specific office, or with a first name of Scott. You could loop through and check every entry in the collection, keeping only the ones you want. However, a more efficient way is to filter the **AddressEntries** collection using an **AddressEntryFilter** object. You can create a filter that will return only those entries that match a list of criteria. The format of an **AddressEntryFilter** is as follows:

```
Set objAddrEntFilter = objAddressEntries.Filter
objAddrEntFilter.(field name) = "(value to filter by)"
```

Table 11.15 Properties of the **AddressEntry** Object

Property Name	Description	Type	Access Level	1.0	1.1	1.21
Address	Returns the fully qualified e-mail address of the recipient. Save this value for later use to guarantee recipient resolution.	String	Read/write	✓	✓	✓
Application	Always returns "Collaboration Data Objects."	String	Read-only	✓	✓	✓
Class	Returns **cdoAddressEntry** (8).	Long	Read-only	✓	✓	✓
DisplayType	Describes the kind of address entry. Can be **cdoUser** (0), **cdoDistList** (1), **cdoForum** (2), **cdoAgent** (3), **cdoOrganization** (4), **cdoPrivateDistList** (5), or **cdoRemoteUser** (6).	Long	Read-only	✓	✓	✓
Fields	Returns a collection of fields in the address entry.	Object	Read-only	✓	✓	✓
ID	Returns the unique ID of the object assigned by the transport provider.	String	Read-only	✓	✓	✓
Manager	Returns the address entry's manager. This is actually a reference to another **AddressEntry** object.	Object	Read/write		✓	✓
Members	Returns an **AddressEntries** collection representing the members of a distribution list in an address book. Valid only for **AddressEntry** objects of **DisplayType cdoDistList** (1) or **cdoPrivateDistList** (5).	Collection	Read-only		✓	✓
Name	Returns the name of the address entry.	String	Read/write	✓	✓	✓
Parent	Returns the parent **AddressEntries** collection.	Object	Read-only	✓	✓	✓
Session	Returns the **Namespace** object for the current session.	Object	Read-only	✓	✓	✓
Type	Returns the **AddressEntry** type, such as "SMTP" or "EX."	String	Read/write	✓	✓	✓

Table 11.16 Methods of the **AddressEntry** Object

Method Name	Description	1.0	1.1	1.21
Delete	Removes the item from the **AddressEntries** collection.	✓	✓	✓
Details([HWnd])	Displays a modal dialog box that provides detailed information about this **AddressEntry** object.	✓	✓	✓
GetFreeBusy(StartDate, Interval, [CompleteFormat])	Returns a string representing one month of free/busy information, starting at midnight of the start date. If **CompleteFormat** = False, **GetFreeBusy** returns 0 for free, 1 for busy. If **CompleteFormat** = True, **GetFreeBusy** returns one of the **cdoBusyStatus** constant values: **cdoFree** (0), **cdoTentative** (1), **cdoBusy** (2), or **cdoOutOfOffice** (3).			✓
IsSameAs (objAddressEntry)	Compares this **AddressEntry** with another **AddressEntry** object and returns True if they are the same.		✓	✓
Update ([makePermanent], [refreshObject])	Saves a change to the **AddressEntry** object. makePermanent will persist the change to storage, while **refreshObject** will reload the cache.	✓	✓	✓

Say you want to retrieve only those entries with a last name of Jamison. The following example sets a reference to the address entry collection's **AddressEntry-Filter** and sets the **Name** property. The resulting collection will consist of only those messages that match the criteria:

```
Dim objSession As MAPI.Session
Dim objAddrEntFilter As MAPI.AddressEntryFilter
Dim objAddressEntries As MAPI.AddressEntries
Dim objAddressEntry As MAPI.AddressEntry
Dim objGAL As MAPI.AddressList
Set objGAL = objSession.GetAddressList(cdoAddressListGAL)
Set objAddressEntries = objGAL.AddressEntries
Set objAddrEntFilter = objAddressEntries.Filter
objAddrEntFilter.Name = "Jamison"
For Each objAddressEntry In objAddressEntries
    Debug.Print objAddressEntry.Name
Next
Set objAddressEntry = Nothing
Set objAddressEntries = Nothing
Set objAddrEntFilter = Nothing
Set objGAL = Nothing
```

Table 11.17 gives the complete list of **AddressEntryFilter** properties.

Table 11.17 Properties of the **AddressEntryFilter** Object

Property Name	Description	Type	Access Level	1.0	1.1	1.21
Application	Always returns "Collaboration Data Objects."	String	Read-only		✓	✓
Class	Returns **cdoMessageFilter** (10).	Long	Read-only		✓	✓
Conversation	Sets filtering on the **ConversationTopic** property.	String	Read/write		✓	✓
Fields	Use this when the field you want to filter on is not defined as a property.	Collection	Read-only		✓	✓
Importance	Sets filtering on the importance of a message.	Long	Read-only		✓	✓
Not	Specifies that all restriction values be negated before being ANDed or ORed.	Boolean	Read/write		✓	✓
Or	Specifies that the restriction values are to be ORed instead of ANDed.	Boolean	Read/write		✓	✓
Parent	Returns the parent **Messages** collection.	Object	Read-only		✓	✓
Recipients	Sets filtering on whether the message's recipients include at least one recipient with a particular name. Note that this is not a **Recipients** collection.	String	Read/write		✓	✓
Sender	Sets filtering on the name of a message's sender.	String	Read/write		✓	✓
Sent	Sets filtering on whether this message was sent (rather than simply posted).	Boolean	Read/write		✓	✓
Session	Returns the current **Session** object.	Object	Read-only		✓	✓
Size	Sets filtering on the size of a message, in bytes.	Long	Read/write		✓	✓
Subject	Sets filtering on the subject of a message.	String	Read/write		✓	✓
Text	Sets filtering on the main text (body) of a message. The filter will look for the text as a substring of the entire message body.	String	Read/write		✓	✓
TimeFirst	Sets filtering on whether a message was received since the specified date and time.	Date	Read/write		✓	✓
TimeLast	Sets filtering on whether a message was received before the specified date and time.	Date	Read/write		✓	✓
Type	Sets filtering on the message class.	String	Read/write		✓	✓
Unread	Sets filtering on whether or not a message has been read.	Boolean	Read/write		✓	✓

Table 11.18 The Method of the **AddressEntryFilter** Object

Method Name	Description	1.0	1.1	1.21
IsSameAs (objAddressEntryFilter)	Returns True if the two **AddressEntryFilter** objects are the same.		✓	✓

The only method provided by the **AddressEntryFilter** object is the **IsSameAs** method (see Table 11.18).

Summary

This chapter covered the complete list of objects for the Collaboration Data Objects library (CDO 1.21), including how to log on using a **Session** object, how to access data using the **InfoStores** collection, and how to use **Message** and **AddressBook** objects. CDO 1.21, which uses the MAPI subsystem, is still a valid way to access data in Exchange 2000. In fact, since the Exchange OLE DB provider (and by extension, CDO 3.0) cannot be used on the client side, CDO 1.21 will continue to be a common way to access data and create collaborative applications, especially for Outlook 2000–based applications.

Chapter 12

CDO for Messaging

This chapter introduces the messaging-enabled aspects of the Collaboration Data Objects (CDO) for Exchange 2000 library. The primary component interface, **IMessage**, defines methods and properties that provide messaging functionality.

Many applications require automated communication through electronic mail. There are several ways to send and receive automated messages in Exchange 2000, including Simple Mail Transport Protocol (SMTP), Network News Transfer Protocol (NNTP), Internet Message Access Protocol (IMAP), and the Messaging Application Programmers Interface (MAPI). Users receive messages in their private mailbox folders in the Web Storage System, which can be accessed through HTTP/WebDAV, Post Office Protocol version 3 (POP3), IMAP, OLE DB, and MAPI. Messages in the Exchange 2000 Web Storage System are natively stored in RFC 822 and MIME formats.

This chapter will focus on CDO for Exchange 2000, the component library that provides a set of COM classes you can use in your application to create, access, modify, and send messages in Internet standard formats. CDO messaging objects can bind directly to messages in the Web Storage System by using the Web Storage System OLE DB provider, and they can send messages using a variety of tools, including SMTP and NNTP, and directly by using the Web Storage System OLE DB provider. Specifically, this chapter will show you how to

- Send an e-mail message programmatically
- Add attachments to messages
- Retrieve a list of messages from a user's inbox

Tech Info: CDO for Exchange Messaging

Item type:	Message
Content class:	urn:content-classes:message
COM ProgID:	CDO.Message
Outlook equivalent:	Outlook.MailItem

Supported Internet Standards

RFC 822

The Internet Request for Comments (RFC) 822 specification defines an electronic message format consisting of header fields and an optional message body. The header fields contain information about the message, such as the sender, the recipient, and the subject. If a message body is included, it is separated from the header fields by an empty line ("\r\n"). The following example illustrates a message in the RFC 822 message format:

```
From: jamisons@plural.com
To: someone@plural.com
Subject: This is a message in RFC 822 format

This is the message (in plain text). Note that there must be a blank
line between the header information and the body of the message.
```

MIME Format

The Multipurpose Internet Mail Extensions (MIME) specification enables the exchange of messages with more complex content than RFC 822 does. The body of a MIME-formatted message is subdivided into *body parts*. Body parts contain various parts of a message, such as an image, a spreadsheet, some text formatted as HTML, and so on. The MIME specification also defines additional mail header fields to describe aspects of each message body part. MIME header fields allow you to specify

- The type of content within the body part, such as an image, an application file, or another data blob
- The class of content within the body part, which describes the content's format and purpose
- The encoding for each content part when encoding is necessary—for example, in a binary file

- A character-encoding scheme other than United States (US) ASCII for each separate text body part
- The intended disposition of a body part—for example, inline or attachment

Body parts can be organized into groups formed in a hierarchy. With this hierarchy you can relate multiple body parts in the body of a message.

More about Body Parts

A MIME body part content type can be either single or multipart. A single body part represents a single entity, such as text or an image. A multipart body part consists of child body parts, thereby providing multiple representations of the same message, such as plain text, HTML, and audio.

Uuencode

Another message format is uuencode, which stands for the Unix-to-Unix encode format. This format was (and still is) one of the ways to add attachments to messages. In the uuencode format, attachments are appended to the message body after being encoded with a special algorithm. Each attachment is prefixed with the file name and the encoding end string. Multiple attachments are individually appended in sequence and separated by a blank line. In the uuencode attachment format, the message body consists of only two basic parts: the message text and the message attachments.

The uuencode format is not described at length here, but you can use CDO to save attachments that are in uuencode format.

Techniques and Code Examples

This section describes the coding techniques you're likely to use when developing messaging applications. Each of these code samples is contained in the CDO helper class sample project (see this book's companion Web site, at **http://www.plural.com/outlookexchange.asp**), which wraps the CDO objects into stateless components that you can use in your Web applications.

Sending an E-mail

The simplest thing to do is to send an e-mail. Using the CDO library to send an e-mail is very straightforward. You simply specify one or more recipients for the "To," "Cc" (carbon copy), and "Bcc" (blind carbon copy) addresses. Next you specify subject and body text. Then you use the **Send** method to transport the e-mail. The following code encapsulates the process into a single stateless routine:

> **Note:** The **TextBody** property is analogous to CDO 1.21's **Text** property and the Outlook object model's **Body** property. They have been conflated to the **TextBody** property.

```
Sub SendEmail(ByVal FromAddress As String, _
              ByVal ToAddress As String, _
              ByVal CcAddress As String, _
              ByVal BccAddress As String, _
              ByVal Subject As String, _
              ByVal TextBody As String)
'
' Sends a simple message using CDO
'
    Dim objCDOMessage As CDO.Message
    Set objCDOMessage = CreateObject("CDO.Message")
    With objCDOMessage
        ' Set the properties of the message
        .From = FromAddress
        .To = ToAddress
        .Cc = CcAddress
        .Bcc = BccAddress
        .Subject = Subject
        .TextBody = TextBody

        ' Send the message
        .Send
    End With
    Set objCDOMessage = Nothing
End Sub
```

> **Note:** When sending an e-mail within your organization, you can elect simply to use the alias of the recipient rather than the full e-mail address. For example, rather than specifying "jamisons@plural.com," you could specify just "jamisons."

Attachments

One of the most common uses of e-mail is to send one or more files to a set of recipients. CDO makes it pretty easy to send files with your e-mail: You simply use the **AddAttachment** method of the **Message** object. Behind the scenes, **AddAttachment** adds a **BodyPart** object to the message. The **AddAttachment** method takes one parameter: the name of the file and path to be attached (as a string). The format of this file path can be a file system or a Web page. Table 12.1 shows some examples.

Table 12.1 Sample File Paths for Use with the **AddAttachment** Method

URL Type	Example
Local file system	C:\My Documents\Resume.doc
Network file system	\\Computer_01\Docs\SharedFile.txt
Web Storage System file	http://MyServer/exchange/jamisons/inbox/MyEmail.eml
Web site	http://www.plural.com/logo.gif

Sending an E-mail with Attachments

To use **AddAttachment** in code, simply send an e-mail as you normally would, but before sending it, call the **AddAttachment** routine for each file you wish to add. The following routine creates and sends an e-mail with one or more attachments:

```
Sub SendEmailWithAttachment(ByVal FromAddress As String, _
                            ByVal ToAddress As String, _
                            ByVal CcAddress As String, _
                            ByVal BccAddress As String, _
                            ByVal Subject As String, _
                            ByVal TextBody As String, _
                            ByVal AttachmentList As String)
'
' Sends a simple message (with attachments) using CDO
' Attachment list is passed in as a comma-delimited list of file paths
'
    On Error GoTo Exit_Handler

    Dim n As Long
    Dim vAttachmentList As Variant

    Dim objCDOMessage As CDO.Message
    Set objCDOMessage = CreateObject("CDO.Message")
    With objCDOMessage
        ' Set the properties of the message
        .From = FromAddress
        .To = ToAddress
        .CC = CcAddress
        .BCC = BccAddress
        .Subject = Subject
        .TextBody = TextBody

        ' Split out the attachment list
```

```
        vAttachmentList = Split(AttachmentList, ",")
        For n = 0 To UBound(vAttachmentList)
            .AddAttachment vAttachmentList(n)
        Next 'n

        ' Send the message
        .Send
    End With

Exit_Handler:
    If Err.Number <> 0 Then
MsgBox "An error has occurred."
    End If
    Set objCDOMessage = Nothing
End Sub
```

> **Note:** If CDO can't find the file at the specified path, it will throw the following error: "80070002 - The system cannot find the file specified."

Determining Whether Attachments Exist

If you're simply interested in checking to see whether attachments exist in a given message, you can check the **urn:schemas:httpmail:hasattachment** property. This property returns True if the message has attachments. The following example, which uses ADO, is a fast way to filter out any messages that do not contain attachments:

```
Function DoAttachmentsExist(sEmailURL As String) As Boolean
    Dim objRec As ADODB.Record
    ' Example URL = "file://./backofficestorage/DOMAIN.local/MBX/
                            jamisons/Inbox/MyEmail.eml"
    Set objRec = CreateObject("ADODB.Record")
    objRec.Open sEmailURL
    DoAttachmentsExist = objRec.Fields("urn:schemas:httpmail:
                         hasattachment")
    objRec.Close
    Set objRec = Nothing
End Function
```

Saving an Attachment to a File

Once you've determined that attachments exist, you'll often want to save them to a file system. You can do this by using the **SaveToFile** method of the **Message** object. The following code illustrates how to use this method:

```
Sub SaveAttachmentsToFile(EmailURL As String, SaveToPath As String)
    Dim objCDOMessage As CDO.Message
    Dim objAttachment As CDO.IBodyPart

    ' Example URL = "file://./backofficestorage/DOMAIN.local/MBX/
                        jamisons/Inbox/MyEmail.eml"

    ' Open and bind to the record using CDO

    Set objCDOMessage = CreateObject("CDO.Message")
    objCDOMessage.DataSource.Open EmailURL

    With objCDOMessage
        If .Attachments.Count > 0 Then
            For Each objAttachment In .Attachments
                objAttachment.SaveToFile SaveToPath &
                    objAttachment.FileName
            Next
        End If
    End With

    Set objAttachment = Nothing
    Set objCDOMessage = Nothing
End Sub
```

How Attachments Are Formatted

Attachments are stored as body parts in the message's **BodyPart** hierarchy. Typically, attachments are described in MIME-formatted messages by having the MIME header **Content-Disposition** set to "attachment." However, the status of a given body part as an attachment depends on the implementation.

Reading Through a User's Inbox

On the flip side of creating messages is retrieving them. Although this chapter is on CDO, we can obtain all of the information we need by using ADO and the OLE DB provider. The following code sample uses a **SELECT** statement to return a stream of **Inbox** information:

```
Function GetInboxItems(Username As String) As String
    Dim objRec As ADODB.Record
    Dim objInboxRec As ADODB.Record
    Dim objRS  As ADODB.Recordset
    Dim sURLInbox As String
    Dim sSQL As String
```

```
    On Error GoTo Exit_Handler

    Set objRec = CreateObject("ADODB.Record")
    Set objInboxRec = CreateObject("ADODB.Record")
    Set objRS = CreateObject("ADODB.Recordset")

    sURLInbox = "file://./backofficestorage/" & DOMAIN_NAME & "/MBX/"
                      & Username
    objRec.Open sURLInbox

    ' Get URL for inbox by using the Inbox property
    sURLInbox = objRec.Fields("urn:schemas:httpmail:inbox")
    objRec.Close

    ' Open the mailbox
    objInboxRec.Open sURLInbox, objRec.ActiveConnection

    sSQL = "SELECT " _
    & "  ""DAV:href""" _
    & ", ""DAV:content-class""" _
    & ", ""urn:schemas:httpmail:datereceived""" _
    & ", ""DAV:isfolder""" _
    & ", ""DAV:getcontentlength""" _
    & ", ""urn:schemas:httpmail:from""" _
    & ", ""urn:schemas:httpmail:subject""" _
    & ", ""urn:schemas:mailheader:importance""" _
    & ", ""urn:schemas:httpmail:hasattachment""" _
    & ", ""urn:schemas:httpmail:read""" _
    & " from scope ('shallow traversal of """ _
    & sURLInbox & """') " _
    & " WHERE ""DAV:isfolder"" = false AND ""DAV:ishidden"" = false" _
    & " ORDER BY ""urn:schemas:httpmail:datereceived"" DESC"

    objRS.Open sSQL, objRec.ActiveConnection
    objInboxRec.Close

    If objRS.RecordCount = 0 Then
        ' No items in inbox
        GetInboxItems = "No Records Found"
    Else
        GetInboxItems = objRS.GetString(, , "</Col>", "</Row>")
    End If

Exit_Handler:

    Set objRec = Nothing
    Set objInboxRec = Nothing
    Set objRS = Nothing
```

```
        If Err.Number <> 0 Then
            Err.Raise Err.Number, Err.Source, Err.Description
        End If

    End Function
```

Summary

The Collaboration Data Objects (CDO) library for Exchange 2000 Server offers various features for building Web-enabled messaging applications. This chapter covered the format of RFC 822 and MIME message types, how to send an e-mail message programmatically, how to add attachments to messages, and how to obtain information from a user's inbox. For more information on CDO for messaging, see the Exchange 2000 SDK, available on the Microsoft Developer Network (**http://msdn.microsoft.com/library**).

Chapter 13

CDO for Calendaring

When it comes to organizing a busy life, one important tool comes to mind: Outlook calendar. Calendaring is an important part of collaborative software because scheduling, meetings, and time management are key aspects of working together. This chapter introduces the calendar-enabled aspects of the Collaboration Data Objects (CDO) for Exchange 2000 library, which allow you to tap into the power of the Exchange 2000 calendar features.

Tech Info: CDO for Exchange Calendaring

Item type:	Appointment
Content class:	urn:content-classes:appointment
COM ProgID:	CDO.Appointment
Outlook equivalent:	Outlook.AppointmentItem
CDO 1.21 equivalent:	MAPI.AppointmentItem

Working with Appointment Items

Let's take a look at a typical **Appointment** item. Figure 13.1 shows an Exchange 2000 **Appointment** item as displayed by Outlook Web Access. As you can see, the item is more complex than a simple e-mail message because it contains additional appointment-specific information, such as the location of the appointment, as well as start and end times.

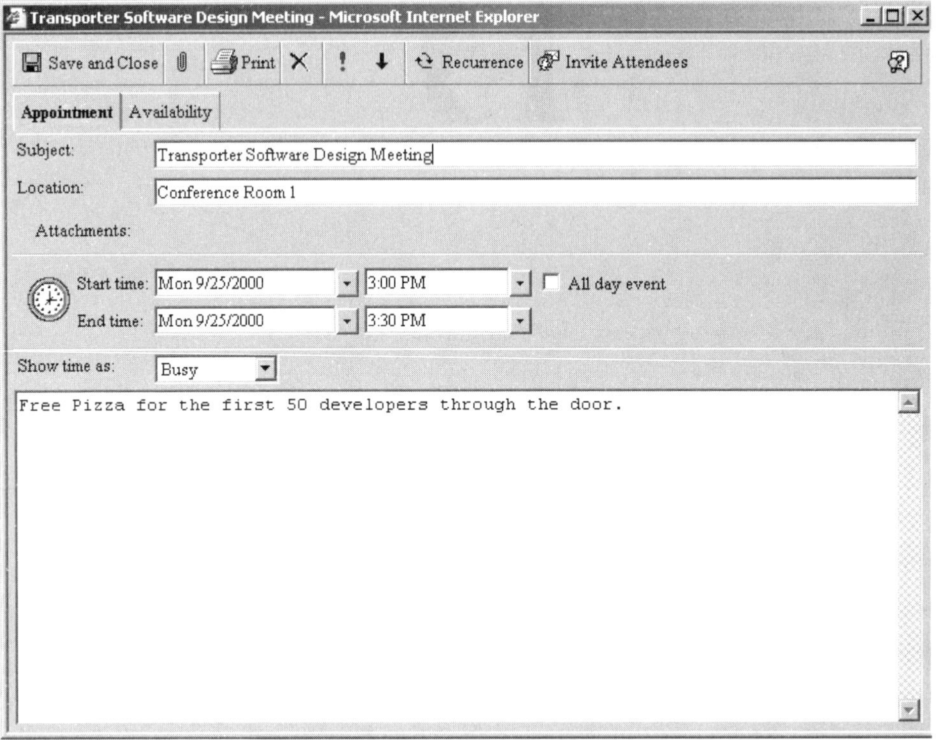

Figure 13.1 An Exchange 2000 **Appointment** item, as displayed by Outlook Web Access

A standard **Appointment** item is based on the **urn:content-classes:appointment** content class. To jump-start things, let's look at a brief example of some typical code used to create and store an item in a default calendar folder.

Creating an Appointment in a User's Private Calendar Folder

The simplest way to create an appointment object is to create a new CDO **Appointment** object, fill out applicable properties, and use the **SaveToContainer** method to save the item to the specified calendar folder. For the following example, make sure you set references to both the Microsoft ActiveX Data Objects 2.5 library and the Microsoft CDO for Exchange 2000 library. You'll also need to replace "<domain>" and "<user>" with actual values that pertain to your environment:

```
Dim objCDOAppt As CDO.Appointment
Dim sURL As String
```

```
' Create a new CDO Appointment object
Set objCDOAppt = CreateObject("CDO.Appointment")
With objCDOAppt
   ' Set the start and end times
   .StartTime = #8/27/2001 1:00:00 PM#
   .EndTime = #8/27/2001 2:00:00 PM#
   ' Set the subject and location
   .Subject = "Nice Dinner"
   .Location = "Top of the Hub"
   ' Save the item to the user's calendar URL
   sURL = "file://./backofficestorage/<Domain>/MBX/<User>/Calendar"
   .DataSource.SaveToContainer sURL
End With
Set objCDOAppt = Nothing
```

Before we get into other code examples, let's review some concepts and explore the object libraries related to calendars.

Appointments and Meetings

An *appointment* is the name given to a period of time that is blocked off in an Exchange calendar folder. Sometimes other people from your organization are able to join you during your blocked-off time. When an **Appointment** item is updated to include other people, it is called a meeting. To get other people (the *attendees*) to become aware of your meeting, you send a *meeting request* to those people (in this case, we call them *addressees* because they are part of an e-mail message). In CDO for Exchange, all of the italicized items listed here are represented by programmable objects, each of which we will discuss in the subsections that follow.

Appointments

At the core of the calendaring objects is the CDO **Appointment** object, an abstraction for a simple block of time. This is the object that was used in the first example. It's also the object that we'll focus on the most because the other calendar-related objects are often initiated from the **Appointment** object.

Attendees and Addressees

A CDO **Attendee** object is the abstraction that is used to represent a person who is planning to attend a meeting. As we stated just a moment ago, an appointment has a single attendee: the calendar owner. For meetings, there are additional attendees who may or may not actually attend the meeting.

A CDO **Addressee** object represents the recipient of a message. The distinction between an **Attendee** and an **Addressee** is that the **Addressee** provides address resolution and free/busy information. We'll discuss free/busy information later in this chapter.

How Appointments and Calendar Messages Work Together

When a user creates an **Appointment** item, Exchange supplies the item with a content class of **urn:content-classes:appointment**. After a prospective attendee is invited to the meeting and the appointment is saved, a meeting request is sent out to the user. The user receives a **Meeting** item (**urn:content-classes:calendarmessage**) in his or her **Inbox** (mail) folder. After opening the item, the user typically responds to the meeting request with "Accept," "Decline," or "Tentative." Each of these actions sends a **Meeting** item with a content class of **urn:content-classes:calendarmessage** with the response (specified within the message) back to the originator.

If the meeting was either accepted or tentatively accepted, an **Appointment** item is created in the attendee's default **Calendar** folder. If the originator decides to cancel an appointment, he or she sends out an item of the type **urn:content-classes:calendarmessage** (flagged as canceled), which, when read by attendees (and the **Remove from calendar** button is pressed), removes the related appointment from the user's calendar.

Now that the relationships between objects have been established, let's look at some code examples to see how they are used together.

■ Programming Examples

As you saw in the first example in this chapter, to create an appointment you simply create a new CDO object of type **Appointment**, set properties, and save the item using the **SaveToContainer** method of the **DataSource** property. You can adapt this basic set of code to achieve other goals, such as adding appointments to public folders.

Creating an Appointment in a Public Folder

To create an **Appointment** object in a public folder, all you need to do is change the URL to point to a public folder. The following code sample, which simply has a new "save to" URL, will create a new appointment in the **TeamCalendar** public folder:

```
Dim objCDOAppt As CDO.Appointment
Dim sURL As String
```

```
Dim sDomain As String
' Create a new CDO Appointment object
Set objCDOAppt = CreateObject("CDO.Appointment")
With objCDOAppt
    ' Set the start and end times
    .StartTime = #7/27/2001 1:00:00 PM#
    .EndTime = #7/27/2001 2:00:00 PM#
    ' Set the subject and location
    .Subject = "Team Meeting"
    .Location = "Conf Room 3"
    ' Save the item to a public folder calendar URL
    sDomain = txtDomain.Text
    sURL = "file://./backofficestorage/" & sDomain & _
          "/public folders/TeamCalendar"
    .DataSource.SaveToContainer sURL
End With
Set objCDOAppt = Nothing
```

Altering this set of code for virtually any URL will work, provided that your security context allows you write access to the folder in question.

Sending a Meeting Request

If you prefer to have your meetings with other people, you can invite them through code. To do so, you need to take an **Appointment** item (either an existing one or a newly created one) and add attendees. Each of the attendees will receive a meeting request that they can then decide to accept, tentatively accept, or decline. The following example creates a new appointment and then invites two people to it—one as required and one as optional:

```
Dim objCDOAppt   As CDO.Appointment
Dim objCalMsg    As CDO.CalendarMessage
Dim objAttendee  As CDO.Attendee
Dim objConfig    As CDO.Configuration
Dim objPerson    As CDO.Person
Dim objMailbox   As CDO.IMailbox
Dim objInfo      As ActiveDs.ADSystemInfo
Dim objNTInfo    As ActiveDs.WinNTSystemInfo

Dim sURL As String
Dim sMBXURL As String

' Create an Active Directory Information object
Set objInfo = New ActiveDs.ADSystemInfo
```

```
' Create a Windows NT Information object
Set objNTInfo = New ActiveDs.WinNTSystemInfo

' Create an appointment and save it
Set objCDOAppt = CreateObject("CDO.Appointment")
With objCDOAppt
    ' Set the start and end times
    .StartTime = #8/23/2001 1:00:00 PM#
    .EndTime = #8/23/2001 2:00:00 PM#
    ' Set the subject and location
    .Subject = "Team Meeting"
    .Location = "Conf Room 1"
    ' Save the item to the user's calendar URL
    sURL = "file://./backofficestorage/" & objInfo.DomainDNSName & _
           "/MBX/" & objNTInfo.UserName & "/Calendar"
    .DataSource.SaveToContainer sURL

    ' Open a CDO Person object to current user
    Set objPerson = CreateObject("CDO.Person")
    objPerson.DataSource.Open "LDAP://" & objInfo.DomainDNSName & _
                              "/" & objInfo.UserName
    ' Get the current user's contact
    Set objMailbox = objPerson

    ' Set the configuration fields for e-mail and base folder properties
    Set objConfig = CreateObject("CDO.Configuration")
    objConfig.Fields(cdoSendEmailAddress) = objPerson.Email
    objConfig.Fields(cdoMailboxURL) = objMailbox.BaseFolder
    objConfig.Fields.Update

    ' Attach the Configuration object to the appointment
    .Configuration = objConfig

    ' Add a required attendee to the appointment
    Set objAttendee = .Attendees.Add
    objAttendee.Address = "gomeza@plural.com"
    objAttendee.Role = cdoRequiredParticipant

    ' Add an optional attendee to the appointment
    Set objAttendee = .Attendees.Add
    objAttendee.Address = "wesolowskig@plural.com"
    objAttendee.Role = cdoOptionalParticipant

    ' Create the calendar message and send it
    Set objCalMsg = .CreateRequest

    ' Save the changes to the appointment
    .DataSource.Save
```

```
        objCalMsg.Message.Send
    End With

    Set objCDOAppt = Nothing
    Set objCalMsg = Nothing
    Set objAttendee = Nothing
    Set objConfig = Nothing

    Set objPerson = Nothing
    Set objMailbox = Nothing
    Set objInfo = Nothing
    Set objNTInfo = Nothing
```

IAppointment Reference

Now that you understand how the flow of **Appointment** and **CalendarMessage** items works, let's dig into the **IAppointment** properties and methods and how they can be used.

Properties of the Appointment Object

The **Appointment** object provides numerous values, all of which are COM-based properties that provide access to the underlying ADO **Fields** collection. Table 13.1 summarizes the properties of the CDO **Appointment** object.

The AllDayEvent Property

To create an all-day appointment (one that runs for an entire day), set this property to True. For appointments that are less than a full day, set this field to False. For an all-day appointment, the **Duration** property value remains zero.

> **Note:** The **AllDayEvent** property is not created until it is set, meaning that it will almost never be False, but instead missing. When you set the **AllDayEvent** to True in Exchange 2000, the start and end times remain unchanged, causing Outlook 2000 to ignore the **AllDayEvent** indicator. This is a new "feature" over previous calendaring libraries; in Outlook 2000 and CDO 1.21, setting the **AllDayEvent** property automatically sets the start and end times to 0:00 and the duration to 1440 (the number of minutes in a full day).

Table 13.1 Properties of the **Appointment** Object

Property Name	Type	Access Level	Description
AllDayEvent	Boolean	Read/write	Returns True if the appointment is for a full day.
Attachments	IBodyParts collection	Read-only	Returns the collection of attachments associated with the **Appointment** item.
Attendees	IAttendees collection	Read-only	Returns the collection of attendees associated with the **Appointment** item.
BodyPart	IBodyPart object	Read-only	Returns the **IBodyPart** interface for this item.
BusyStatus	String	Read/write	Describes how the appointment will appear in a free/busy status view.
Configuration	IConfiguration object	Read/write	References the **Configuration** object that defines the configuration information used by the **Appointment** object.
Contact	String	Read/write	Returns a person's name as a contact for this appointment.
ContactURL	String	Read/write	Returns a URL that points to contact information.
DataSource	IDataSource object	Read-only	Returns the **IDataSource** interface on the object.
Duration	Long	Read/write	Returns the duration of the appointment in seconds.
EndTime	Date/time	Read/write	Returns the ending date and time for the appointment.
Exceptions	IExceptions collection	Read-only	Returns an **IExceptions** collection of "one-off" changes (see text for explanation) to a recurring appointment schedule.
Fields	ADODB.Fields collection	Read-only	Returns an ADO **Fields** collection.
GEOLatitude	Long	Read/write	Returns the geographical latitude of the appointment's location.
GEOLongitude	Long	Read/write	Returns the geographical longitude of the appointment's location.

Table 13.1 Properties of the **Appointment** Object *(continued)*

Property Name	**Type**	**Access Level**	**Description**
Keywords	Variant	Read/write	Contains keywords for this appointment.
Location	String	Read/write	Returns the location in free-form text.
LocationURL	String	Read/write	Returns a URL that specifies the meeting location as an alternative to the location string property.
MeetingStatus	String	Read/write	Contains "Tentative," "Confirmed," or "Canceled."
Priority	Long	Read/write	Contains Normal (0), Urgent (1), or Nonurgent (–1).
RecurrencePatterns	IRecurrencePatterns collection	Read-only	Returns an **IRecurrencePatterns** collection of information for a recurring appointment.
ReplyTime	Date/time	Read-only	Returns the time that a recipient replied to a meeting request.
Resources	String	Read/write	Contains a delimited list of resources for the appointment.
ResponseRequested	Boolean	Read/write	If set to True, indicates that a response is requested for the appointment.
Sensitivity	Long	Read/write	Contains None (0), Personal (1), Private (2), or Company-Confidential (3).
StartTime	Date/time	Read/write	Returns the start date and time for the appointment.
Subject	String	Read/write	Contains the subject or topic of the appointment.
TextBody	String	Read/write	Contains a text description of the appointment.
Transparent	String	Read/write	If the value is "Opaque" or blank, the appointment appears in the free/busy string; if the value is "Transparent," the appointment will not appear in a free/busy string.

In the following example, an appointment is created with a start and end date and time; then the **AllDayEvent** flag is set:

```
Dim objCDOAppt As CDO.Appointment
Dim sURL As String

Dim sDomain As String
Dim sUser As String

sDomain = txtDomain.Text
sUser = txtUser.Text

Set objCDOAppt = CreateObject("CDO.Appointment")
With objCDOAppt
    .StartTime = #6/27/2001 1:00:00 PM#
    .EndTime = #6/27/2001 2:00:00 PM#
    .Subject = "Will this be an all-day thing?"

    sURL = "file://./backofficestorage/" & sDomain & "/MBX/" & _
           sUser & "/Calendar"
    .DataSource.SaveToContainer sURL

    ' First, AllDayEvent property will *not* exist
    ' ** Be careful - an error will occur here **
    MsgBox "AllDayEvent = " & .AllDayEvent

    ' Show times, duration
    MsgBox "StartTime = " & Format(.StartTime, "mm/dd/yy hh:mm")
    MsgBox "EndTime = " & Format(.EndTime, "mm/dd/yy hh:mm")

    ' Unlike Outlook 2000 and CDO 1.21, Duration property is still zero
    MsgBox "Duration = " & .Duration
    .DataSource.Save

    ' Now set the AllDayEvent flag, unlike Outlook 2000 and CDO 1.21,
    ' Duration property is still zero
    .AllDayEvent = True
    .DataSource.Save

    ' Unlike Outlook 2000 and CDO 1.21, start and end dates are NOT
    ' automatically changed, and AllDayEvent flag is ignored
    MsgBox "Start = " & Format(.StartTime, "mm/dd/yy hh:mm")
    MsgBox "end = " & Format(.EndTime, "mm/dd/yy hh:mm")
    MsgBox "Duration = " & .Duration
End With
Set objCDOAppt = Nothing
```

The Attachments Property

The **Attachments** collection provides a way to access the list of file attachments for the appointment. For more information on attaching files to and saving files from items, see Chapter 12, which describes how to use the **Attachments** collection.

The Attendees Property

The **Attendees** collection provides a way to access the list of persons that are planning to attend the meeting. See the section titled Sending a Meeting Request earlier in this chapter for an example.

The BodyPart Property

The **BodyPart** property returns an **IBodyPart** interface that enables you to access the entire collection of body parts, as well as the attributes of the **IBodyPart** interface. Using the **BodyPart** object, you can save the item's stream directly. This object is used later in the chapter to view an appointment in **iCalendar** format.

The BusyStatus Property

The **BusyStatus** property indicates how the appointment you've booked will be blocked out on your availability information. This value, which is a string, can be set to "Free," "Busy," "Tentative," or "OOF" (out of office). The values are summarized in Table 13.2.

> **Note:** Availability information will come in handy when another user wants to check whether there's free time to schedule an appointment. Information on how to retrieve free/busy information will be discussed later in this chapter.

Table 13.2 cdoBusyStatusValues Constants

Availability	Constant	Value
Free	cdoFree	Free
Tentative	cdoTentative	Tentative
Busy	cdoBusy	Busy
Out of office	cdoOOF	OOF

The following example creates an **Appointment** item and changes the busy status from busy ("Busy") to out of office ("OOF"):

```
Dim objCDOAppt As CDO.Appointment
Dim sURL As String
Set objCDOAppt = CreateObject("CDO.Appointment")
With objCDOAppt
    .StartTime = #6/27/2001 1:00:00 PM#
    .EndTime = #6/27/2001 2:00:00 PM#
    .Subject = "Tour of the Lowell canals"
    .Location = "Lowell, MA"
    sURL = "file://./backofficestorage/EXCHDOM.local/MBX/" &
           "Administrator/Calendar"
    .DataSource.SaveToContainer sURL

    ' First, BusyStatus will be cdoBusy
    ' (the default for non-all-day appointments)
    MsgBox "BusyStatus = " & .BusyStatus
    ' Now set the AllDayEvent flag
    .AllDayEvent = True
    .DataSource.Save
    ' The BusyStatus is *NOT* automatically changed to cdoFree,
    ' as it was in Outlook 2000 and CDO 1.21
    MsgBox "BusyStatus = " & .BusyStatus
    ' Now set the BusyStatus to olOutOfOffice
    .BusyStatus = cdoOOF
    MsgBox "BusyStatus = " & .BusyStatus
    .DataSource.Save
End With
Set objCDOAppt = Nothing
```

The Configuration Property

The **Configuration** property returns a reference to a **Configuration** object. A CDO **Configuration** object has one property: an ADO **Fields** collection that stores configuration information regarding a particular CDO object as defined in the **http://schemas.microsoft.com/cdo/configuration** namespace. In the case of an **Appointment** item, we have seven values (see Table 13.3).

Table 13.4 summarizes all of the possible values for **urn:schemas:calendar:timezoneid** as defined in the **cdoTimeZoneID** constants. This field allows you to set appropriate time zone values for your appointments. You can also create your own time zones (see the Exchange 2000 SDK in MSDN for more information).

The Contact Property

The **Contact** property contains a free-form text field that can be used to store a contact's name for this appointment. A typical value would be a name, like "Joe Smith."

Table 13.3 Appointment Item Configuration Values

Name	Description	Possible Value
http://schemas.microsoft.com/cdo/configuration/languagecode	Contains the language code for user message response text, as specified in RFC 1766.	en-us
http://schemas.microsoft.com/cdo/configuration/nntpserverpickupdirectory	Contains the full path to the NNTP service pickup directory, if the **postusing** field is set to 1.	C:\inetpub\nntpfile\pickup
http://schemas.microsoft.com/cdo/configuration/postusing	Indicates how a message is being posted.	1 (cdoPostUsingPickup—if NNTP installed), 2 (cdoPostUsingPort), or 3 (cdoPostUsingExchange—if Exchange 2000 installed)
http://schemas.microsoft.com/cdo/configuration/sendusing	Indicates how a message is being sent.	1 (cdoPostUsingPickup—if NNTP installed), 2 (cdoPostUsingPort), or 3 (cdoPostUsingExchange—if Exchange 2000 installed)
http://schemas.microsoft.com/cdo/configuration/smtpserverpickupdirectory	Contains the full path to the local SMTP service pickup directory, if the **sendusing** field is set to 1.	C:\Program Files\Exchsrvr\Mailroot\vsi 1\PickUp
http://schemas.microsoft.com/cdo/configuration/usemessageresponsetext	Indicates whether response text is inserted when replying to or forwarding messages.	True (default)
urn:schemas:calendar:timezoneid	Contains the time zone (see Table 13.4).	10

The ContactURL Property

The **ContactURL** field is a free-form text field intended for holding a URL that points to a contact, something like "http://www.plural.com/contacts/Joe_Smith."

The DataSource Property

The **DataSource** property returns the **IDataSource** interface to the CDO **Appointment** item. Like the other CDO objects, you can use it to access or save a particular appointment in code such as this:

```
objAppointment.DataSource.Open sURL   ' Open an Appointment item
objAppointment.DataSource.Save        ' Save an Appointment item
```

Table 13.4 cdoTimeZoneID Values

Name	Value	Description
cdoUTC	0	Coordinated Universal Time (UTC)
cdoGMT	1	Greenwich Mean Time (same as UTC)
cdoLisbon	2	Dublin, Edinburgh, Lisbon, London (UTC + 0:00)
cdoParis	3	Brussels, Copenhagen, Madrid, Paris, Vilnius (UTC + 1:00)
cdoBerlin	4	Amsterdam, Berlin, Bern, Rome, Stockholm, Vienna (UTC + 1:00)
cdoEasternEurope	5	Eastern Europe (UTC + 2:00)
cdoPrague	6	Belgrade, Bratislava, Budapest, Ljubljana, Prague (UTC + 1:00)
cdoAthens	7	Athens, Istanbul, Minsk (UTC + 2:00)
cdoBrasilia	8	Brasilia (UTC – 3:00)
cdoAtlanticCanada	9	Atlantic time (UTC – 4:00)
cdoEastern	10	Eastern time (UTC – 5:00)
cdoCentral	11	Central time (UTC – 6:00)
cdoMountain	12	Mountain time (UTC – 7:00)
cdoPacific	13	Pacific time (UTC – 8:00)
cdoAlaska	14	Alaska (UTC – 9:00)
cdoHawaii	15	Hawaii (UTC – 10:00)
cdoMidwayIsland	16	Midway Island, Samoa (UTC – 11:00)
cdoWellington	17	Auckland, Wellington (UTC + 12:00)
cdoBrisbane	18	Brisbane (UTC + 10:00)
cdoAdelaide	19	Adelaide (UTC + 9:30)
cdoTokyo	20	Osaka, Sapporo, Tokyo (UTC + 9:00)
cdoHongKong	21	Hong Kong (UTC + 8:00)
cdoBangkok	22	Bangkok, Hanoi, Jakarta (UTC + 7:00)
cdoBombay	23	Bombay, Calcutta, Madras, New Delhi (UTC + 5:30)
cdoAbuDhabi	24	Abu Dhabi, Muscat (UTC + 4:00)
cdoTehran	25	Tehran (UTC + 3:30)
cdoBaghdad	26	Baghdad, Kuwait, Riyadh (UTC + 3:00)
cdoIsrael	27	Israel (UTC + 2:00)
cdoNewfoundland	28	Newfoundland (UTC – 3:30)
cdoAzores	29	Azores, Cape Verde Islands (UTC – 1:00)

Table 13.4 cdoTimeZoneID Values *(continued)*

Name	Value	Description
cdoMidAtlantic	30	Mid-Atlantic (UTC – 2:00)
cdoMonrovia	31	Casablanca, Monrovia (UTC + 0:00)
cdoBuenosAires	32	Buenos Aires, Georgetown (UTC – 3:00)
cdoCaracas	33	Caracas, La Paz (UTC – 4:00)
cdoIndiana	34	Indiana (UTC – 5:00)
cdoBogota	35	Bogota, Lima, Quito (UTC – 5:00)
cdoSaskatchewan	36	Saskatchewan (UTC – 6:00)
cdoMexicoCity	37	Mexico City, Tegucigalpa (UTC – 6:00)
cdoArizona	38	Arizona (UTC – 7:00)
cdoEniwetok	39	Eniwetok, Kwajalein (UTC – 12:00)
cdoFiji	40	Fiji, Kamchatka, Marshall Islands (UTC + 12:00)
cdoMagadan	41	Magadan, Solomon Islands, New Caledonia (UTC + 11:00)
cdoHobart	42	Hobart (UTC + 10:00)
cdoGuam	43	Guam, Port Moresby (UTC + 10:00)
cdoDarwin	44	Darwin (UTC + 9:30)
cdoBeijing	45	Beijing, Chongqing, Urumqi (UTC + 8:00)
cdoAlmaty	46	Akmola, Almaty, Dhaka (UTC + 6:00)
cdoIslamabad	47	Islamabad, Karachi, Tashkent (UTC + 5:00)
cdoKabul	48	Kabul (UTC + 4:30)
cdoCairo	49	Cairo (UTC + 2:00)
cdoHarare	50	Harare, Pretoria (UTC + 2:00)
cdoMoscow	51	Moscow, St. Petersburg, Volgograd (UTC + 3:00)
cdoInvalidTimeZone	52	Invalid time zone

For more information on the other properties and methods of the IDataSource interface, see the Exchange 2000 SDK.

The Duration Property

The **Duration** property is the length (in seconds) of the appointment. This value is normally the difference between the start and end times. Either a duration or an end time value is required. If an end time is specified, the **Duration** property is ignored.

> **Note:** In Outlook 2000 and CDO 1.21, the duration was stored in minutes instead of seconds. In addition, those libraries changed the duration to 1440 (the equivalent of 24 hours in minutes) for an all-day event. The **Duration** property is ignored in Exchange 2000 for all-day events.

The EndTime Property

The **EndTime** property is a date/time field that represents the ending time of the appointment or meeting. This value must be set if the **Duration** property has not been set.

The Exceptions Property

The **Exceptions** collection allows you to create one-off changes to a recurring meeting. For example, say you're taking a class every Monday evening from 6:00 to 9:00 PM for 15 weeks. You could schedule one recurring meeting for the class. Then if you got one of the classes off (maybe because of a holiday), you would want to delete only that instance of the appointment. This is where an **Exception** would come in handy. For more information, see the section titled Recurring Appointments later in this chapter.

The Fields Property

The **Fields** property returns a read-only ADO **Fields** collection of appointment information from the Exchange 2000 schema as defined in the **urn:schemas:appointment namespace**. The **Name** property of each ADO **Field** object is always a string; the **Value** property depends on its definition in the schema.

The GEOLatitude and GEOLongitude Properties

These properties enable you to specify the location of a meeting in a very precise way. Rather than simply providing a street address or building number, you specify the latitude and longitude in whole degrees. Use positive values from 0 to 90 for degrees north latitude, negative values from 0 to –90 for degrees south latitude. For east longitude, use positive values from 0 to 180; for west longitude, negative values from 0 to –180.

> **Note:** You must set both **GEOLatitude** and **GEOLongitude** for either of these properties to be saved. If you set only one of the two properties, the value is ignored.

The Keywords Property

The **Keywords** property is a Variant value that contains a list of keywords associated with this appointment, delimited by commas.

Note: The **Keywords** property is used primarily by Outlook clients.

The Location Property

The **Location** field is simply a free-form string that describes where the meeting will be held. Typically, you should set both the subject and location, since they both appear at the top of an appointment's inspector window. An example of a location is "Main Conference Room."

The LocationURL Property

The **LocationURL** field is a free-form text field intended for holding a URL that points to a location. It is up to the developer to make sure **Location** and **LocationURL** match from a logical perspective.

The MeetingStatus Property

The **MeetingStatus** property indicates whether a meeting has been accepted by you, tentatively accepted by you, or canceled. Interestingly, the default value for standard appointments is "Tentative." See Table 13.5 for a complete list of **cdoMeetingStatusValues** constants.

Where Did the MessageClass Property Go?

Typically, the next property you'd see here is **MessageClass**. However, **MessageClass** is no longer exposed as a standard property in CDO for Exchange 2000. The **MessageClass** property is used in MAPI to link an item to the format on which it is based. When an item is opened, Outlook uses the message class of the item to locate the form for display purposes. For this purpose, Exchange 2000 uses the content class value instead. For a complete listing of how message classes map into content classes, see Chapter 3.

Table 13.5 **cdoMeetingStatusValues** Constants

Status	Constant	Value
Accepted (confirmed)	cdoMeetingStatusConfirmed	Confirmed
Tentatively accepted	cdoMeetingStatusTentative	Tentative (default)
Canceled	cdoMeetingStatusCanceled	Canceled

The Priority Property

The **Priority** property indicates the priority of the meeting as Normal, Urgent, or Nonurgent (low). The default value is 0 (Normal). Table 13.6 shows the **cdoPriorityValues** constants.

> **Note:** For incoming **ICalendar** meeting requests, a priority of 5 is converted to Normal, with lesser values converted to Urgent and higher values converted to Nonurgent. For outgoing **ICalendar** meeting requests, Urgent is converted to 1, Normal to 5, and Nonurgent to 9.

The RecurrencePatterns Property

An object closely related to appointments is the **RecurrencePattern** object, which is used to set how often an appointment will recur. By using the **RecurrencePattern** object (described further in the section titled Recurring Appointments later in this chapter), you can assign an appointment to happen daily, weekly, or monthly rather than just once.

The ReplyTime Property

The **ReplyTime** property returns the time at which a recipient replied to a meeting request. This value is updated by CDO when the user accepts, tentatively accepts, or declines a meeting request. This value is good for determining which response is the most recent if an attendee sends more than one response to a meeting request.

The Resources Property

The **Resources** property contains a comma-delimited list of resources that will be used at this meeting. A resource is usually a conference room or a piece of equipment (e.g., a video projector). An example of a value is “Projector P-13, Computer C-6.”

The ResponseRequested Property

The **ResponseRequested** property indicates whether a response is requested for an appointment. According to MSDN, this property is set to True automatically after

Table 13.6 **cdoPriorityValues** Constants

Priority Level	Constant	Value
Nonurgent (low)	cdoPriorityNonUrgent	–1
Normal	cdoPriorityNormal	0 (default)
Urgent	cdoPriorityUrgent	1

you convert an appointment to a meeting by inviting at least one attendee. However, it is our experience that this value is always set to True, even for appointments that have not been converted to meetings.

The Sensitivity Property

The **Sensitivity** property contains the status for the sensitivity level of an appointment, which can be None, Company-Confidential, Personal, or Private. Table 13.7 summarizes the sensitivity value constants.

> **Note:** In Exchange 2000, the default value for appointments is Personal. In Outlook 2000 and CDO 1.21, the default for appointments was None.

The StartTime Property

The **StartTime** property is a date/time field that represents the starting time of the appointment or meeting. This value *must* be set.

> **Note:** The **StartTime** needs to be a date and time value. If a date is specified without a time, the time is assumed to be midnight.

The Subject Property

The **Subject** field is simply a free-form string that briefly describes the topic of the meeting. You should always set both the subject and the location, although neither value is required. An example of a subject is "Team Meeting to Discuss Project."

> **Note:** If you do not specify a **Subject** value, your subject line will be filled in for you with a GUID that looks something like this:
>
> {E6414426-04AF-44B6-A15E-4346ABDDAE8D}.EML

Table 13.7 cdoSensitivityValues Constants

Priority Level	Constant	Value
None	cdoSensitivityNone	0
Personal	cdoPersonal	1
Private	cdoPrivate	2
Company-confidential	cdoCompanyConfidential	3

The TextBody Property

The **TextBody** property is an optional text description of the appointment. A detailed description of the appointment would be stored here.

The Transparent Property

The **Transparent** property indicates whether the appointment should appear in a free/busy string returned by the addressee's **GetFreeBusy** method. If the value of this property is "Transparent," the appointment does not appear in the free/busy string.

More about Calendars

This section delves into some additional topics related to calendars, such as checking whether a user is busy and creating recurring meetings and appointments.

Resolving an Addressee

Before we get into how to check other people's calendars for availability, we need to know how to retrieve a person's information from the active directory. When you first create an **Addressee** object, it is in an unresolved state. After you specify known information (which can be the display name, the directory URL, or the e-mail address), call the **CheckName** method to attempt to resolve the **Addressee**. If the object is located and uniquely matches the specified criteria, the object is resolved (see Table 13.8 for all possible states). If nothing is found, it remains in an unresolved state. If multiple directory objects match the criteria, the object is referred to as ambiguous. You can then check the **objAddressee.AmbiguousNames** record set, which contains information about each object that matched the criteria for the resolution attempt. The following code illustrates the process:

```
Dim objAddressee As CDO.Addressee
Dim objInfo      As ActiveDs.ADSystemInfo
Dim n            As Integer

' Create an Active Directory Information object
' This will help us get the local domain's DNS name
```

Table 13.8 cdoResolvedStatus Constants

Status	Constant	Value
Unresolved or not yet resolved (default)	cdoUnresolved	0
Resolved	cdoResolved	1
Ambiguous	cdoAmbiguous	2

```
Set objInfo = New ActiveDs.ADSystemInfo
' Create a new Addressee object
Set objAddressee = CreateObject("CDO.Addressee")

' Set known info on the person, which can be either the
' e-mail address, display name, or directory URL
objAddressee.EmailAddress = "mike@exchdom.local"
' Display the ResolvedStatus property, which will be zero
' (cdoUnresolved)
Debug.Print objAddressee.ResolvedStatus

' Call the CheckName method, passing the directory to use for resolution
' This will resolve the name for us if it can
objAddressee.CheckName "LDAP://" & objInfo.DomainDNSName
' Check the Resolved status for success or failure
Select Case objAddressee.ResolvedStatus
Case cdoUnresolved
    Debug.Print "Error: Unsuccessful resolution for " & _
                 objAddressee.EmailAddress
Case cdoResolved
    Debug.Print "Successful resolution for " &
                 objAddressee.EmailAddress
    Debug.Print "Display Name: " & objAddressee.DisplayName
    Debug.Print "Directory URL: " & objAddressee.DirURL
    ' Next line will get an error
    ' (the Fields collection is not implemented for Addressee objects)
    For n = 1 To objAddressee.Fields.Count
        Debug.Print objAddressee.Fields.Item(n).Name & ": " & _
                    objAddressee.Fields.Item(n).Value
    Next
Case cdoAmbiguous
    Debug.Print "Resolution for " & objAddressee.EmailAddress & _
                " turned up the following names: "
    For n = 1 To objAddressee.AmbiguousNames.Count
        Debug.Print objAddressee.AmbiguousNames.Item(n).DisplayName
    Next
End Select
Set objInfo = Nothing
Set objAddressee = Nothing
```

Running this code block in an environment with a person named Mike in the active directory produces the following output:

```
Successful resolution for mike@EXCHDOM.local
Display Name: Mike Daddeo
Directory URL: LDAP://EXCHDOM.local/
                      CN=Mike Daddeo,CN=Users,DC=EXCHDOM,DC=local
```

Determining the Status of a User's Calendar (Free/Busy Information)

To determine whether a user is available at the desired date and time, Exchange Server stores information known as free/busy information. This information is stored in a hidden public folder on a user's home Exchange server. The information is then replicated to other Exchange servers, providing a fast way to check availability. Figure 13.2 shows Outlook's way of showing free/busy information when a user schedules a meeting.

A single CDO for Exchange 2000 method allows you to check the free/busy status of a user's calendar, thereby allowing you to check availability information without having to explicitly open every **Appointment** item in every calendar. In fact, checking free/busy information is up to a thousand times faster than opening each item individually. For fast access to a user's availability, we use the **GetFreeBusy** method, which we call by using an **IAddressee** object.

> **Note:** Outlook 2000 users will want to know that this method works just like the **GetFreeBusy** methods of Outlook 2000 and CDO 1.21, which are part of the **AddressEntry** object.

The **GetFreeBusy** method returns a string representing a time interval of availability information, with one character in the string for each time interval. The characters in the returned string correspond logically with the values in Table 13.2, which shows the four possible types of availability. However, rather than returning "Free" or "Busy," the **GetFreeBusy** method returns an integer value (see Table 13.9).

The following example illustrates calling the **GetFreeBusy** method on a user's calendar. Let's look at a particular date—say, August 3, 2001. If the user has a two-hour appointment scheduled at 9:00 AM (marked as Busy) and is out of the office after 4:00 PM, a call to **GetFreeBusy** (#8/3/2001 5:00 AM#, #8/3/2001 8:00

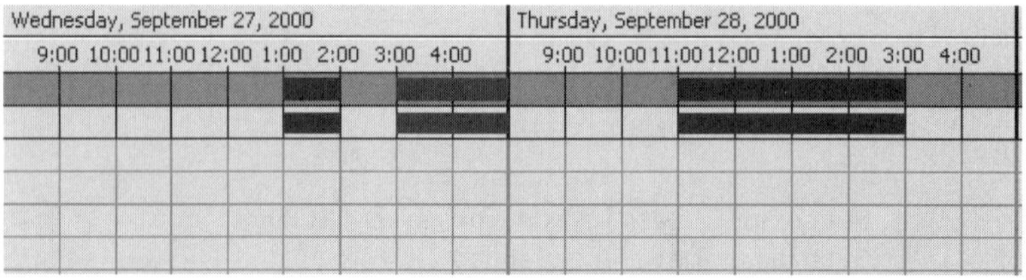

Figure 13.2 Outlook automatically updates free/busy information for meeting requests

Table 13.9 Values Returned by **GetFreeBusy**

Value	Meaning
0	Free
1	Tentative
2	Busy
3	Out of office (OOF)
4	No free/busy information available

PM#, 30) would return the following string, denoting the free time before and after the meeting:

```
00000000222200000000000333333333
|       |             |
5:00AM  9:00AM        4:00 PM
```

Note: The syntax for **GetFreeBusy** is as follows:

```
sFreeBusy = objAddressee.FreeBusy(StartDate, EndDate, Interval)
```

where

- **objAddressee** is a valid CDO **Addressee** object that *has been resolved* (see the previous discussion).
- **StartDate** is a valid date and time.
- **EndDate** is a valid date and time that is later than **StartDate**.
- **Interval** is an integer value representing the number of minutes that each character should represent.

Let's look at some code showing the **GetFreeBusy** method in action. The following example checks to see if a user is available after 1:00 PM on September 27. The code uses an interval value of 60, so each character represents a one-hour block:

```
Dim objAddressee As CDO.Addressee
Dim sFreeBusy    As String
Dim objInfo      As ADSystemInfo

Dim n            As Integer
Dim sFreeOrBusy  As String

Set objInfo = New ADSystemInfo
```

```
Set objAddressee = CreateObject("CDO.Addressee")
objAddressee.EmailAddress = "administrator@exchdom.local"

' Be sure to resolve the name
If Not objAddressee.CheckName("LDAP://" & objInfo.DomainDNSName) Then
    MsgBox "Cannot resolve " & objAddressee.EmailAddress
End If

' Get the free/busy status in 60-minute intervals
' from 9/27/2000 1:00 PM to 9/27/2000 11:00 PM
sFreeBusy = objAddressee.GetFreeBusy(#9/27/2000 1:00:00 PM#, #9/27/2000
           11:00:00 PM#, 60)
Debug.Print sFreeBusy

For n = 1 To 10
    Select Case Mid$(sFreeBusy, n, 1)
    Case "0"
        sFreeOrBusy = "Free"
    Case "1"
        sFreeOrBusy = "Tentative"
    Case "2"
        sFreeOrBusy = "Busy"
    Case "3"
        sFreeOrBusy = "OOF"
    Case "4"
        sFreeOrBusy = "Unavailable"
    End Select
    Debug.Print n & ":00 to " & n + 1 & ":00 is " & sFreeOrBusy
Next

Set objAddressee = Nothing
Set objInfo = Nothing
```

When this code block is run against the user's calendar shown in Figure 13.3, the following is the result:

```
Complete Free/Busy String:  2033301000
1:00 to 2:00 is Busy
2:00 to 3:00 is Free
3:00 to 4:00 is OOF
4:00 to 5:00 is OOF
5:00 to 6:00 is OOF
6:00 to 7:00 is Free
7:00 to 8:00 is Tentative
8:00 to 9:00 is Free
9:00 to 10:00 is Free
10:00 to 11:00 is Free
```

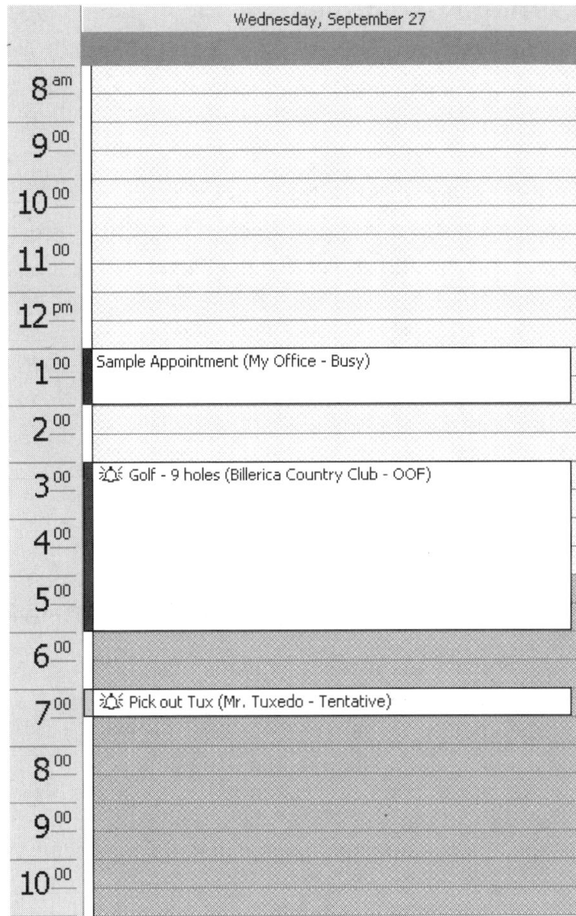

Figure 13.3 A user's calendar, as displayed by Outlook 2000

Note: The free/busy status is not updated immediately when a meeting is added to a user's calendar. When a user creates an **Appointment** item using Outlook, the free/busy information on the Exchange server is updated according to the settings under **Tools | Options | Calendar Options | Free/Busy Options**. These settings default to publish three months of future free/busy information, updated to the server at 15-minute intervals. For Exchange users who don't use Outlook, an automated process in Exchange 2000 Server periodically updates the free/busy status of users.

Recurring Appointments

Recurring appointments and meetings occur more than once and follow a pattern. For example, a team meeting on the third Monday of each month would be defined as a recurring meeting.

Creating Recurring Appointments

To create a recurring appointment or meeting, create the item as you would normally and then add a **RecurrencePattern** object to the item, as in the following example:

```
Dim objCDOAppt As CDO.Appointment
Dim objRecurrencePattern As CDO.IRecurrencePattern
Dim sURL As String

Dim sDomain As String
Dim sUser As String

' Create a new CDO Appointment object
Set objCDOAppt = CreateObject("CDO.Appointment")
With objCDOAppt
    ' Set the start and end times
    .StartTime = #8/27/2001 1:00:00 PM#
    .EndTime = #8/27/2001 2:00:00 PM#
    ' Set the subject and location
    .Subject = "Nice Dinner"
    .Location = "Top of the Hub"
    ' Save the item to the user's calendar URL
    sDomain = txtDomain.Text
    sUser = txtUser.Text

    ' Create the RecurrencePattern object
    Set objRecurrencePattern = .RecurrencePatterns.Add("Add")
    ' Define the recurrence pattern
    ' Frequency, such as cdoWeekly, cdoDaily, or cdoMonthly
    objRecurrencePattern.Frequency = cdoDaily
    ' Interval (every n days, in this case 2)
    objRecurrencePattern.Interval = 2
    ' Set the pattern end date
    objRecurrencePattern.PatternEndDate = #11/1/2001#
    sURL = "file://./backofficestorage/" & sDomain & _
           "/MBX/" & sUser & "/Calendar"
    .DataSource.SaveToContainer sURL
End With
Set objRecurrencePattern = Nothing
Set objCDOAppt = Nothing
```

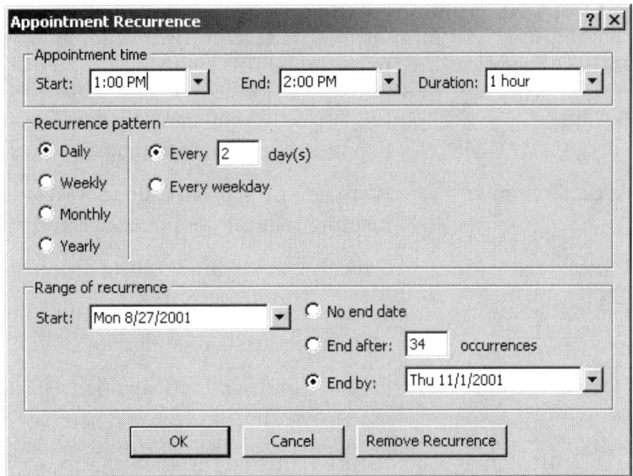

Figure 13.4 Recurring appointment information, as displayed by Outlook 2000

Figure 13.4 shows how the appointment is displayed in Outlook. The settings, such as the frequency and end date, are recognized and displayed.

Exceptions to a Recurring Appointment

Say you have a recurring appointment like the one described in the previous section. Often the meeting won't take place on one of the regularly scheduled days. For these items you can use the **Exceptions** collection, which is a list of one-off changes to a recurring appointment schedule. For example, the following code snippet shows how to modify a recurring appointment with a deleted occurrence:

```
' First, create an appointment with a recurrence as usual
' (see preceding block of code)...
' When you want to delete an appointment instance,
' you add an exception of type "Delete"
  Set objException = objAppt.Exceptions.Add("Delete")
' The ID is the start time of the appointment instance being deleted
  objException.RecurrenceID = #8/29/2001#
' Then, save the appointment as usual (see preceding block of code)
```

IAppointment Methods

There are other actions that you can take when using Exchange calendaring solutions. Table 13.10 gives the complete list of methods that apply to the CDO **Appointment** object.

Table 13.10 Methods of the **Appointment** Object

Method Name	Description
Accept	Prepares and sends a **CalendarMessage** object. Used to respond to a meeting request with acceptance.
AcceptTentative	Prepares and sends a **CalendarMessage** object. Used to respond to a meeting request with tentative acceptance.
Cancel	Cancels an existing meeting for one or more (or all) attendees.
CreateRequest	Turns an **Appointment** item into a meeting by creating and sending meeting requests to attendees.
Decline	Prepares and sends a **CalendarMessage** object. Used to decline a meeting request.
GetFirstInstance	Returns the first instance of a recurring meeting.
GetInterface	Helper method that enables scripting languages to get a reference to a dual interface.
GetNextInstance	Returns the next instance of a recurring meeting.
GetRecurringMaster	Returns the recurrence master (or exception) for a recurring meeting.
Invite	Returns a **CalendarMessage** object that is used to send a meeting request, immediately adding the recipient(s) to the **Attendees** collection.
Publish	Allows you to send a meeting to multiple recipients; however, there is no **Attendees** collection for published appointments.

The ICalendar Standard

Using Internet standards, you can send meeting requests to users who have non-Exchange-based calendaring systems. The **iCalendar** specification, which is specified in RFC 2445, defines the format of calendar information that is supported by various calendaring systems. You can use Collaboration Data Objects (CDO) to send calendar information to any system that complies with the **iCalendar** specification because Exchange 2000 Server supports the **iCalendar** specification as an interchange format:

```
Dim objCDOAppt As CDO.Appointment
Dim objStream As ADODB.Stream
Dim sURL As String
```

```
Dim sDomain As String
Dim sUser As String

' Create a new CDO Appointment object
Set objCDOAppt = CreateObject("CDO.Appointment")
With objCDOAppt
    ' Set the start and end times
    .StartTime = #9/27/2001 11:00:00 AM#
    .EndTime = #9/27/2001 2:00:00 PM#
    ' Set the subject and location
    .Subject = "Internet Appointment"
    .Location = "My Home Office"
    ' Save the item to the user's calendar URL
    sDomain = txtDomain.Text
    sUser = txtUser.Text
    sURL = "file://./backofficestorage/" & sDomain & "/MBX/" & sUser &
           "/Calendar"
    .DataSource.SaveToContainer sURL

    ' Display the appointment in iCalendar format by accessing its
        stream
    Debug.Print .BodyPart.GetDecodedContentStream.ReadText
End With

Set objCDOAppt = Nothing
```

CDO also creates a plain-text representation of calendar messages. When you send a meeting request or response to users who do not have an **iCalendar**-compliant e-mail client, they see the plain-text version of the meeting, including the start and end times, location, subject, and meeting description.

The following is the output of the sample meeting, natively formatted in **iCalendar** format. This format can be interpreted by any system following RFC 2445:

```
BEGIN:VCALENDAR
METHOD:REQUEST
PRODID:Microsoft CDO for Microsoft Exchange
VERSION:2.0
BEGIN:VTIMEZONE
TZID:Eastern Time (US & Canada)
X-MICROSOFT-CDO-TZID:10
BEGIN:STANDARD
DTSTART:16010101T020000
TZOFFSETFROM:-0400
TZOFFSETTO:-0500
RRULE:FREQ=YEARLY;WKST=MO;INTERVAL=1;BYMONTH=10;BYDAY=-1SU
END:STANDARD
```

```
BEGIN:DAYLIGHT
DTSTART:16010101T020000
TZOFFSETFROM:-0500
TZOFFSETTO:-0400
RRULE:FREQ=YEARLY;WKST=MO;INTERVAL=1;BYMONTH=4;BYDAY=1SU
END:DAYLIGHT
END:VTIMEZONE
BEGIN:VEVENT
DTSTAMP:20000922T180411Z
DTSTART;TZID="Eastern Time (US & Canada)":20010927T110000
SUMMARY:Internet Appointment
UID:{7D86C7E0-F4DF-406A-B5FE-BC05F29ED50B}
LOCATION:My Home Office
DTEND;TZID="Eastern Time (US & Canada)":20010927T140000
SEQUENCE:0
PRIORITY:5
CLASS:Personal
CREATED:20000922T180411Z
LAST-MODIFIED:20000922T180415Z
STATUS:TENTATIVE
TRANSP:OPAQUE
X-MICROSOFT-CDO-BUSYSTATUS:BUSY
X-MICROSOFT-CDO-INSTTYPE:0
END:VEVENT
END:VCALENDAR
```

Note: For more information on the **iCalendar** format, see RFC 2445, which can be found at **http://www.ietf.org/rfc/rfc2445.txt**.

Summary

The Collaboration Data Objects (CDO) library for Exchange 2000 Server offers various features for building Web-enabled calendaring applications. This chapter covered the format of calendar items, how to schedule appointments, and how to send meeting invitations as e-mail requests programmatically. For additional code examples, see the sample application in Chapter 21 (gradebook 2001), which uses CDO for calendaring for maintaining student schedules. For more information on CDO calendaring, see the Exchange 2000 SDK, available in MSDN.

Chapter 14

CDO for Contacts

At the core of most e-mail applications is the concept of a contact. Like cards on a Rolodex, each contact is a collection of information about a person or company such as an address, phone number, e-mail address, pager number, and so on.

Prior to Exchange 2000, contacts were only programmatically accessible through the Outlook object model. This meant that a developer could write only client-side code to manipulate a contact. The reason for this limitation was CDO 1.21's lack of direct support for contacts (CDO 1.21 is the library designed to access information via MAPI; see Chapter 11). Although CDO 1.21 had the notion of a **Recipient** object, a developer had to use the Outlook object model to access all of the non-address book properties of a standard contact, such as the one shown in Figure 14.1. Installing Outlook on a server is taboo (and completely unsupported by Microsoft), so there was no way to write code that would run directly on the Exchange server and access an Outlook contact in a supported fashion.

Tech Info: CDO for Exchange Contacts

Item type:	Contact
Content class:	urn:content-classes:person
COM ProgID:	CDO.Person
Outlook equivalent:	Outlook.ContactItem
CDO 1.21 equivalent:	N/A

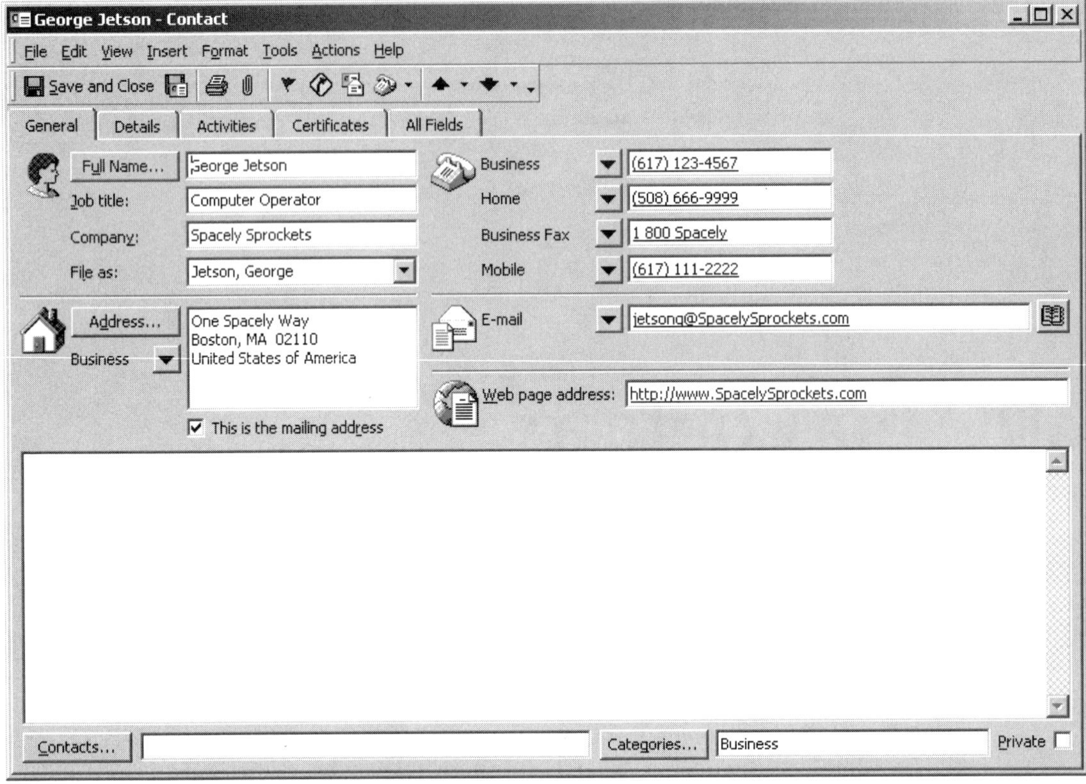

Figure 14.1 A standard Outlook 2000 contact

Luckily, Microsoft CDO for Exchange 2000 has direct support for contacts as part of the **Person** object. Using the CDO **Person** object, the collaborative application developer can store contact information on both the Web Storage System and the Windows 2000 Active Directory. The developer can now write components that execute on the Exchange 2000 server and can be called from a Web application to manipulate contact information. To begin working with the **Person** object and follow along on your own computer, set references in your standard VB Project file to the Microsoft CDO for Exchange 2000 library and the Microsoft ActiveX Data Objects 2.5 library as shown in Figure 14.2.

But without further ADO, let's create a contact.

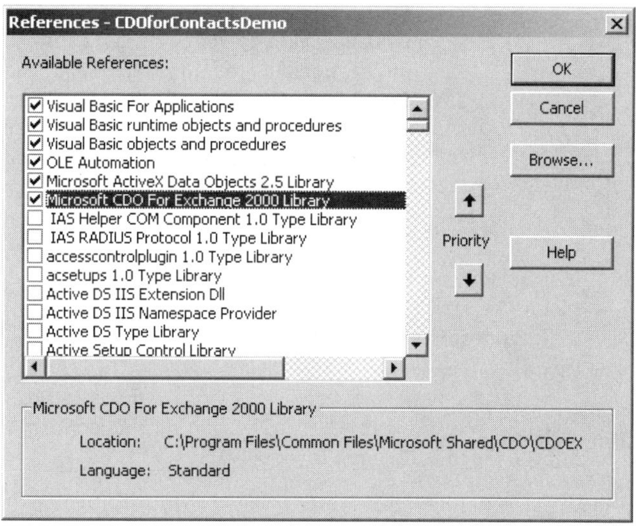

Figure 14.2 Setting a reference to the CDO for Exchange 2000 library

Creating a Contact in the Web Storage System

Creating a contact in the Web Storage System involves creating a new CDO **Person** object, setting the desired properties on this **Person** object, and saving it using the Exchange OLE DB provider. Consider the following subroutine written in Visual Basic:

```
Option Explicit
Public Const ONE_SPACE As String = " "
Public Const TWO_SPACES As String = "  "
Sub CreateContact(ByVal UserMailbox As String, ByVal Company As String, _
                  ByVal EMail As String, ByVal EMail2 As String, _
                  ByVal EMail3 As String, ByVal FirstName As String, _
                  ByVal HomeCity As String, ByVal HomeCountry As String, _
                  ByVal HomeFax As String, ByVal HomePhone As String, _
                  ByVal HomePostalCode As String, ByVal HomePostOfficeBox _
                                                  As String, _
                  ByVal HomeState As String, ByVal HomeStreet As String, _
                  ByVal LastName As String, ByVal MiddleName As String, _
                  ByVal MobilePhone As String, ByVal NamePrefix As String, _
```

```
                    ByVal NameSuffix As String, ByVal Title As String, _
                    ByVal WorkCity As String, ByVal WorkCountry As String, _
                    ByVal WorkFax As String, ByVal WorkPager As String, _
                    ByVal WorkPhone As String, ByVal WorkPostalCode _
                                               As String, _
                    ByVal WorkPostOfficeBox As String, ByVal WorkState _
                                               As String, _
                    ByVal WorkStreet As String)

    Dim objPerson As New CDO.Person
    Dim sURL As String
    Dim sContactName As String
    Dim objInfo As Object

    ' Need this to get the fully qualified domain name for the URL:
    Set objInfo = CreateObject("ADSystemInfo")

    ' Set the name of the item containing our contact:
    sContactName = FirstName & ONE_SPACE & MiddleName & ONE_SPACE & _
                   LastName &  ONE_SPACE & NameSuffix
    sContactName = Trim(Replace(sContactName, TWO_SPACES, ONE_SPACE))

    ' Fill in the contact values:
    objPerson.Company = Trim(Company)
    objPerson.EMail = Trim(EMail)
    objPerson.EMail2 = Trim(EMail2)
    objPerson.EMail3 = Trim(EMail3)
    objPerson.NamePrefix = Trim(NamePrefix)
    objPerson.FirstName = Trim(FirstName)
    objPerson.MiddleName = Trim(MiddleName)
    objPerson.LastName = Trim(LastName)
    objPerson.NameSuffix = Trim(NameSuffix)
    objPerson.HomeCity = Trim(HomeCity)
    objPerson.HomeCountry = Trim(HomeCountry)
    objPerson.HomeFax = Trim(HomeFax)
    objPerson.HomePhone = Trim(HomePhone)
    objPerson.HomePostalCode = Trim(HomePostalCode)
    objPerson.HomePostOfficeBox = Trim(HomePostOfficeBox)
    objPerson.HomeState = Trim(HomeState)
    objPerson.HomeStreet = Trim(HomeStreet)
    objPerson.MobilePhone = Trim(MobilePhone)
    objPerson.Title = Trim(Title)
    objPerson.WorkCity = Trim(WorkCity)
    objPerson.WorkCountry = Trim(WorkCountry)
    objPerson.WorkFax = Trim(WorkFax)
    objPerson.WorkPager = Trim(WorkPager)
    objPerson.WorkPhone = Trim(WorkPhone)
```

```
    objPerson.WorkPostalCode = Trim(WorkPostalCode)
    objPerson.WorkPostOfficeBox = Trim(WorkPostOfficeBox)
    objPerson.WorkState = Trim(WorkState)
    objPerson.WorkStreet = Trim(WorkStreet)

    ' By default, a CDO Person object creates a user.
    ' Need to set this, to create a contact:
    objPerson.Fields("objectClass").Value = "contact"
    objPerson.Fields.Update

    ' Set up the URL to save the contact using the Exchange OLE DB provider:
    ' The URL should be something like:
' file://./backofficestorage/GomezaMobile.local/MBX/Administrator/Contacts/
'       J.EML
    sURL = "file://./backofficestorage/" & objInfo.DomainDNSName & "/MBX/" & _
                & UserMailbox & "/Contacts/" & sContactName & ".EML"

    ' Save the contact to Web Storage System:
    objPerson.DataSource.SaveTo sURL

    ' Clean up:
    Set objPerson = Nothing
    Set objInfo = Nothing

End Sub
```

As you can see, this subroutine takes most of the values that you would want to set for a contact as arguments. We declare **objPerson** as a new CDO **Person** object with the following line of code:

```
Dim objPerson As New CDO.Person
```

We then fill in the properties of the **Person** object using the arguments passed into the subroutine. A new CDO **Person** object creates a user by default, so we need to specify "contact" as the object class in the ADO **Fields** collection of our CDO **Person** object and use its **Update** method to create the contact:

```
objPerson.Fields("objectClass").Value = "contact"
objPerson.Fields.Update
```

The final step is saving the contact to the Web Storage System. We do this by constructing a valid URL for it. Note that in the code we create an Active Directory System Information object (**ADSystemInfo**). We use the **DomainDNSName** property of this object to get the domain of the server we're on for the URL. We also need to give our contact a name. We concatenate the contact's first name, middle name, last name, and suffix (removing spaces if any of these values are missing). We use this concatenation to give our contact a name with a ".EML" extension so that Outlook will recognize it as one of its own:

```
sURL = "file://./backofficestorage/" & objInfo.DomainDNSName & "/MBX/" & _
            & UserMailbox & "/Contacts/" & sContactName & ".EML"
```

For example, a valid URL for a contact could be something like the following:

```
file://./backofficestorage/GomezaMobile.local/MBX/Administrator/
       Contacts/ _JoeBlack.EML
```

where "GomezaMobile.local" is the name of the domain on the user's laptop and "Joe Black" is the name of a contact the user just created.

If we call this subroutine with the proper values (and we have logged in as a user with the proper rights), we can create contacts such as the one shown in Chapter 5.

Creating a Contact in the Active Directory

We can also create contacts in the Active Directory. Whereas items in the Web Storage System are referenced by file URLs, items in the Active Directory are referenced by the Active Directory Service Interfaces (ADSI). Contacts that exist in the Active Directory can be saved to the Web Storage System and vice versa. CDO handles the underlying mapping between ADSI and the Web Storage System schema. To use ADSI, we construct an LDAP (Lightweight Directory Access Protocol) URL to reference a particular item. An LDAP URL consists of prefixes and distinguished names for the contact that address its placement in the Active Directory hierarchy. The prefix "cn" is used for common names, "dc" for domain and subdomain names, and "o" and "ou" for organizations and organizational units. For example, if Joe Black is a person with an Exchange mailbox in the domain **adomain.plural.com** and the name of the Exchange 2000 server is "BigBadServer," then the LDAP URL would be

```
LDAP://BigBadServer/cn=joeblack,cn=users,dc=adomain,dc=plural,dc=com
```

To use the previously defined **CreateContact** subroutine to save a contact to the Active Directory rather than to the Web Storage System, the only modification you would need to make is to use an LDAP URL when setting the **sURL** variable. You would need some underlying logic to break up the domain name returned by the **objInfo.DomainDNSName** property into its various pieces for use in the LDAP URL (e.g., "GomezaMobile.local" would need to be "dc=GomezaMobile,dc=local" for use in the LDAP URL). We leave this to you as an exercise.

> **Note:** For more information on ADSI and LDAP, see the Exchange 2000 documentation or the Microsoft Developer Network (**http://msdn.microsoft.com/default.asp**).

At the center of the code to create a contact and any other code that manipulates contacts in Exchange 2000 is the CDO **Person** object. Let's take a good look at the properties and methods of this object.

The CDO Person Object

The CDO **Person** object defines properties and methods for managing contacts in the Web Storage System or Active Directory.

Properties of the Person Object

Table 14.1 summarizes the properties of the CDO **Person** object.

The Company Property

The **Company** property stores the contact's company name (e.g., Plural, Microsoft, Spacely Sprockets) as an updatable string value.

The Configuration Property

The **Configuration** property returns a reference to a **Configuration** object. A CDO **Configuration** object has one property: an ADO **Fields** collection that stores configuration information regarding a particular CDO object as defined in the **http://schemas.microsoft.com/cdo/configuration** namespace. In the case of a contact item, we have seven values (see Table 14.2).

Table 14.3 shows some values for **urn:schemas:calendar:timezoneid**, as defined in the **cdoTimeZoneID** constants. For a complete list of the time zone values, see Table 13.4.

Table 14.1 Properties of the **Person** Object

Property Name	Type	Access Level	Description
Company	String	Read/write	Contains the company name.
Configuration	Configuration object	Read-only	Contains a reference to the **Configuration** object that defines the configuration information used by the contact.
DataSource	IDataSource object	Read-only	Returns the **IDataSource** interface on the object.
Email	String	Read/write	Contains the contact's primary e-mail address.
Email2	String	Read/write	Contains the contact's secondary e-mail address.
Email3	String	Read/write	Contains the contact's tertiary e-mail address.
EmailAddresses	Variant	Read/write	Contains a list of valid e-mail addresses for the contact.
Fields	ADODB. Fields	Read-only	Returns the ADO **Fields** object for the contact.
FileAs	String	Read/write	Defines how to display the contact.
FileAsMapping	String	Read/write	Defines how to construct the **FileAs** property.
FirstName	String	Read/write	Contains the contact's first name.
HomeCity	String	Read/write	Contains the contact's home city.
HomeCountry	String	Read/write	Contains the contact's home country.
HomeFax	String	Read/write	Contains the contact's home fax number.
HomePhone	String	Read/write	Contains the contact's home telephone number.
HomePostalAddress	String	Read-only	Contains the concatenation of the **HomeStreet**, **HomeCity**, **HomeState**, and **HomePostalCode** properties.
HomePostalCode	String	Read/write	Contains the contact's home postal (zip) code.
HomePostOfficeBox	String	Read/write	Contains the contact's post office box number.
HomeState	String	Read/write	Contains the contact's home state.
HomeStreet	String	Read/write	Contains the contact's home street.
Initials	String	Read/write	Contains the contact's initials.
LastName	String	Read/write	Contains the contact's last name.
MailingAddress	String	Read-only	Contains the contact's mailing address.
MailingAddressID	String	Read/write	Defines how to construct the **MailingAddress** property.

Table 14.1 Properties of the **Person** Object *(continued)*

Property Name	Type	Access Level	Description
MiddleName	String	Read/write	Contains the contact's middle name.
MobilePhone	String	Read/write	Contains the contact's mobile telephone number.
NamePrefix	String	Read/write	Contains the title to precede the contact's name.
NameSuffix	String	Read/write	Contains the title to follow the contact's name.
Title	String	Read/write	Contains the contact's job title.
WorkCity	String	Read/write	Contains the contact's work city.
WorkCountry	String	Read/write	Contains the contact's work country.
WorkFax	String	Read/write	Contains the contact's work fax number.
WorkPager	String	Read/write	Contains the contact's work pager number.
WorkPhone	String	Read/write	Contains the contact's work telephone number.
WorkPostalAddress	String	Read-only	Contains the concatenation of the **WorkStreet**, **WorkCity**, **WorkState**, **WorkPostalCode**, and **WorkCountry** properties.
WorkPostalCode	String	Read/write	Contains the contact's work postal (zip) code.
WorkPostOfficeBox	String	Read/write	Contains the contact's work post office number.
WorkState	String	Read/write	Contains the contact's work state.
WorkStreet	String	Read/write	Contains the contact's work street.

Table 14.2 Contact Configuration Values

Name	Description	Possible Value
http://schemas.microsoft.com/cdo/configuration/languagecode	Contains the language code for user message response text, as specified in RFC 1766.	en-us
http://schemas.microsoft.com/cdo/configuration/nntpserverpickupdirectory	Contains the full path to the NNTP service pickup directory, if the **postusing** field is set to 1.	C:\inetpub\nntpfile\pickup
http://schemas.microsoft.com/cdo/configuration/postusing	Indicates how a message is being posted.	1 (cdoPostUsingPickup—if NNTP installed), 2 (cdoPostUsingPort), or 3 (cdoPostUsingExchange—if Exchange 2000 installed)

Continued on next page.

Table 14.2 Contact Configuration Values *(continued)*

Name	Description	Possible Value
http://schemas.microsoft.com/cdo/configuration/sendusing	Indicates how a message is being sent.	1 (cdoPostUsingPickup—if NNTP installed), 2 (cdoPostUsingPort), or 3 (cdoPostUsingExchange—if Exchange 2000 installed)
http://schemas.microsoft.com/cdo/configuration/smtpserverpickupdirectory	Contains the full path to the local SMTP service pickup directory, if the **sendusing** field is set to 1.	C:\Program Files\Exchsrvr\Mailroot\vsi 1\PickUp
http://schemas.microsoft.com/cdo/configuration/usemessageresponsetext	Indicates whether response text is inserted when replying to or forwarding messages.	True (default)
urn:schemas:calendar:timezoneid	Contains the local time zone (see Table 13.4).	10

Table 14.3 U.S. **cdoTimeZoneID** Values

Name	Value	Description
cdoEastern	10	Eastern time (UTC – 5:00)
cdoCentral	11	Central time (UTC – 6:00)
cdoMountain	12	Mountain time (UTC – 7:00)
cdoPacific	13	Pacific time (UTC – 8:00)

Accessing a Contact's Configuration Information How do we get at these configuration properties? The following Visual Basic function returns the configuration information for a specified contact in a user's **Contacts** folder as a one-dimensional variant array showing both the name and the value of each configuration property:

```
Public Function ViewConfiguration(ByVal ExchangeAlias As String, _
                                  ByVal ContactName As String) As _
                                  Variant
    Dim objPerson As New CDO.Person
    Dim sURL As String
    Dim sContactName As String
    Dim objInfo As New ADSystemInfo
    Dim objConfigFields As ADODB.Fields
```

```
    Dim vaConfiguration() As Variant
    Dim nCounter As Integer

    ' Assume failure:
    ViewConfiguration = ""

' Set up the URL to retrieve the contact using the Exchange OLE DB
' provider: The URL should be something like:
' file://./backofficestorage/GomezaMobile.local/MBX/Administrator/
        Contacts/JoeBlack.EML
sURL = "file://./backofficestorage/" & objInfo.DomainDNSName & "/MBX/" _
            & Trim(ExchangeAlias) & "/Contacts/"
            & Trim(ContactName) & ".EML"

    ' Get the contact:
    objPerson.DataSource.Open sURL

    Set objConfigFields = objPerson.Configuration.Fields
    ReDim vaConfiguration(objConfigFields.Count - 1)
    For nCounter = LBound(vaConfiguration) To UBound(vaConfiguration)
        vaConfiguration(nCounter) =
            objConfigFields.Item(nCounter).Name _& " " & _
            objConfigFields.Item(nCounter).Value
    Next

    ' Return it:
    ViewConfiguration = vaConfiguration

    ' Clean up:
    Set objPerson = Nothing
    Set objInfo = Nothing
    Set objConfigFields = Nothing

End Function
```

The function takes an Exchange user alias and the name of a contact and builds a valid URL to the **Contact** item in the Web Storage System after deducing the local domain name. It uses this URL to open the contact in the following line of code:

```
objPerson.DataSource.Open sURL
```

We declare an ADO **Fields** collection and set it to the Fields collection of the CDO **Person** object's **Configuration** property like so:

```
Dim objConfigFields As ADODB.Fields
Set objConfigFields = objPerson.Configuration.Fields
```

We then resize a variant array and loop through the **Configuration** item's names and values to fill the array before returning it to the calling procedure. If the calling procedure loops through this array, it will get values similar to those in the first and last columns of Table 14.2.

The DataSource Property

The **DataSource** property returns the **IDataSource** interface to the CDO contact. We've been using it all along to access a particular contact in code:

```
objPerson.DataSource.Open sURL
```

For more information on the other properties and methods of the **IDataSource** interface, see the Exchange 2000 SDK.

The Email Property

A **Contact** item can have up to three different e-mail addresses associated with it. The **Email** property stores the contact's primary e-mail address (e.g., **gomeza@plural.com**, **jetsone@LittleDipper.edu**, **jetsonjudy@OrbitHS.edu**) as an updatable string value.

The Email2 Property

The **Email2** property stores the contact's secondary e-mail address as an updatable string value.

The Email3 Property

The **Email3** property stores the contact's tertiary e-mail address as an updatable string value.

The EmailAddresses Property

The **EmailAddresses** property contains a Variant array of valid e-mail addresses for the contact. It consists of the values in the **Email**, **Email2**, and **Email3** properties. For example, if all three fields are filled in on the CDO **Person** object bound to **objPerson**, then:

```
objPerson.EmailAddresses(0)
' might contain: SMTP:jetsong@SpacelySprockets.com
objPerson.EmailAddresses(1)
' might contain: smtp:rorge_jetson@aol.com
objPerson.EmailAddresses(2)
' might contain: smtp:GeorgeJetson@hotmail.com
```

The capital "SMTP" in the first address makes this the primary e-mail address for the contact. Be sure always to check the upper bound of this array:

```
UBound(objPerson.EmailAddresses)
```

when looping through it in your code. The array will be big enough to hold only the number of e-mail addresses specified for the contact. For example, if only the **Email** property is filled in, **EmailAddresses** will be big enough to contain only the one element. The **EmailAddresses** property is recalculated whenever the **Email**, **Email2**, or **Email3** property is updated.

The Fields Property

The **Fields** property returns a read-only ADO **Fields** collection of contact information from the Exchange 2000 schema as defined in the **urn:schemas:contacts** namespace. The **Name** property of each ADO **Field** object is always a string, but the type of the **Value** property depends on its definition in the schema.

Accessing a Contact's Fields Let's assume **objPerson** is a valid CDO **Person** object bound to a **Contact** item in the Web Storage System by means of a URL, a situation we have seen in several earlier examples. The following Visual Basic function returns a Variant array containing the field names and their values, if possible:

```
Public Function ViewFields(ByVal ExchangeAlias As String, _
                           ByVal ContactName As String) As Variant
    Dim objPerson As New CDO.Person
    Dim sURL As String
    Dim sContactName As String
    Dim objInfo As New ADSystemInfo
    Dim objFields As ADODB.Fields
    Dim vaFields() As Variant
    Dim nCounter As Integer

    ' Assume failure:
    ViewFields = ""

' Set up the URL to retrieve the contact using the Exchange OLE DB
' provider: The URL should be something like:
' file://./backofficestorage/GomezaMobile.local/MBX/Administrator/
'        Contacts/JoeBlack.EML
sURL = "file://./backofficestorage/" & objInfo.DomainDNSName & "/MBX/" & _
               Trim(ExchangeAlias) & "/Contacts/" & _
               Trim(ContactName) & ".EML"
```

```
        ' Get the contact:
        objPerson.DataSource.Open sURL

        Set objFields = objPerson.Fields
        ReDim vaFields(objFields.Count - 1)
        For nCounter = LBound(vaFields) To UBound(vaFields)
            If objFields.Item(nCounter).Name = "DAV:supportedlock" Or _
               objFields.Item(nCounter).Name = _
                   "http://schemas.microsoft.com/exchange/
                   keywords-utf8" Or _
               objFields.Item(nCounter).Name = _
                   "urn:schemas-microsoft-com:office:office#Keywords" Then
                   vaFields(nCounter) = objFields.Item(nCounter).Name
            ElseIf objFields.Item(nCounter).Name = _
                   "urn:schemas:contacts:proxyaddresses" Then
                   vaFields(nCounter) = objFields.Item(nCounter).Name
                   & " " & _Join(objFields.Item(nCounter).Value, ",")
            Else
                vaFields(nCounter) = objFields.Item(nCounter).Name & " " & _
                   objFields.Item(nCounter).Value
            End If
        Next

    ' Return it:
        ViewFields = vaFields

    ' Clean up:
        Set objPerson = Nothing
        Set objInfo = Nothing
        Set objFields = Nothing

    End Function
```

Note the special processing for **DAV:supportedlock**, **http://schemas.microsoft.com/exchange/keywords-utf8**, **urn:schemas-microsoft-com:office:office#Keywords**, and **urn:schemas:contacts:proxyaddresses**. These are not simple string values, so we avoid a type mismatch by omitting their values in the array (after all, this is just pedagogical demo code), with the exception of the proxy addresses. This is a Variant array of client e-mail addresses that we can convert to a single comma-separated string value using the **Join** function like so:

```
Join(objFields.Item(nCounter).Value, ",")
```

> **Note:** For more information on the **Join** function, see the section titled "The Join Function" in the Microsoft Office 2000/Visual Basic Programmer's Guide on MSDN (**http://msdn.microsoft.com/library/officedev/odeopg/deconthejoin-function.htm**).

The FileAs Property

The **FileAs** property defines how a contact is displayed and consequently its order in the folder view in Outlook. The **FileAs** property is usually a concatenation of the **LastName**, **FirstName**, **MiddleName**, **NameSuffix**, and/or **Company** properties according to a pattern specified by the **FileAsMapping** property. As Figure 14.3 shows, our contacts are filed as "LastName, FirstName MiddleName."

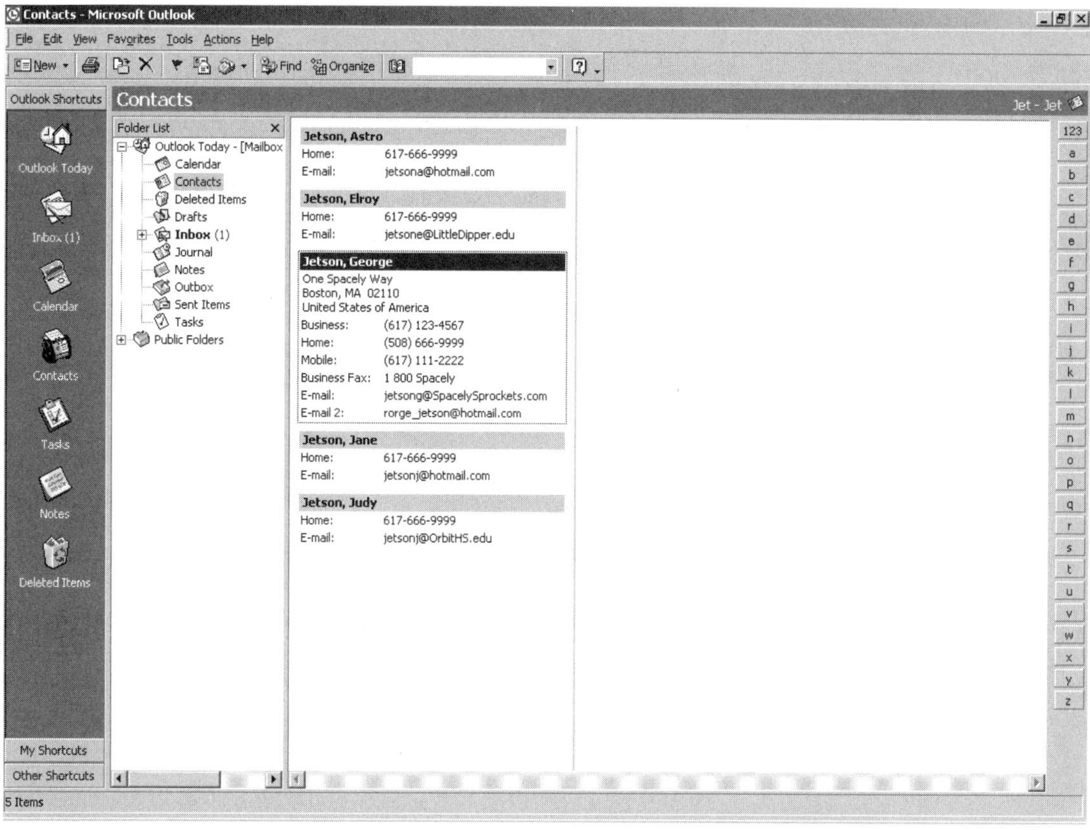

Figure 14.3 Outlook 2000 address card view of contacts sorted by the **FileAs** property

The default is to sort the contacts alphabetically, so things would have been pretty different if we had chosen to file our contacts as "FirstName MiddleName LastName NameSuffix." You can view all of the **FileAs** options of a contact in the **File as:** drop-down list, such as the one shown on the contact in Figure 14.4.

The FileAsMapping Property

Going hand in hand with the **FileAs** property is the **FileAsMapping** property. If you don't explicitly set the **FileAs** property in your code, the value in the **FileAsMapping** property defines how the **FileAs** property will be created from the other contact fields. If you do explicitly set the **FileAs** property, the **FileAsMapping** property is set to 0 (**cdoMapToNone**). The values for the **FileAsMapping** property are defined by the **cdoFileAsMappingID** constants (see Table 14.4).

Note that updating the **FileAsMapping** property (or one of the **FileAs** constituent values, such as **LastName**) on a contact will dynamically update the **FileAs** property.

The FirstName Property

The **FirstName** property stores the contact's first name as an updatable string value.

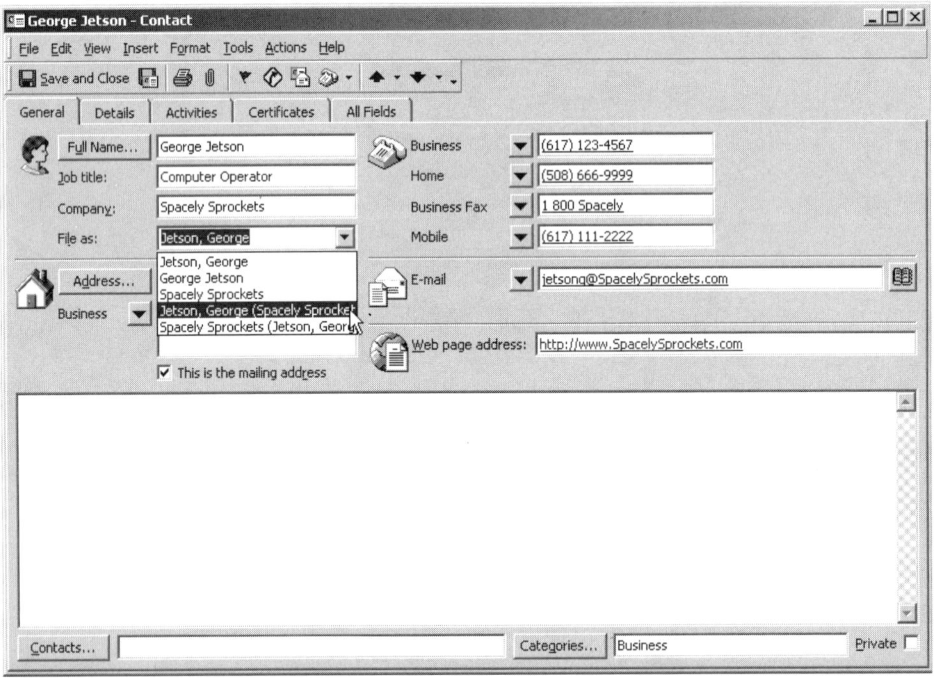

Figure 14.4 The **FileAs** property of a contact

Table 14.4 cdoFileAsMappingID Values

Name	Value	Description	Example
cdoMapToNone	0	No construction. The **FileAs** property is not generated and must be set explicitly.	Future father
cdoMapToLastFirst	1	LastName, FirstName MiddleName.	Jetson, George R.
cdoMapToFirstLast	2	FirstName MiddleName LastName NameSuffix.	George R. Jetson I
cdoMapToOrg	3	Company.	Spacely Sprockets
cdoMapToLastFirstOrg	4	**LastName**, **FirstName MiddleName** (**Company**).	Jetson, George R. (Spacely Sprockets)
cdoMapToOrgLastFirst	5	**Company** (**LastName**, **FirstName MiddleName**).	Spacely Sprockets (Jetson, George R.)

The HomeCity Property

The **HomeCity** property stores the city part of a contact's home postal address as an updatable string value.

The HomeCountry Property

The **HomeCountry** property stores the country part of a contact's home postal address as an updatable string value.

The HomeFax Property

The **HomeFax** property stores the contact's home fax number as an updatable string value.

The HomePhone Property

The **HomePhone** property stores the contact's home phone number as an updatable string value.

The HomePostalAddress Property

The **HomePostalAddress** property is the concatenation of the **HomeStreet**, **HomeCity**, **HomeState**, **HomePostalCode**, and **HomeCountry** properties. Changing any one of these constituent properties dynamically updates the **HomePostalAddress** property, so it is a read-only property.

The HomePostalCode Property

The **HomePostalCode** property stores the postal code (zip code) part of a contact's home postal address as an updatable string value.

The HomePostOfficeBox Property

The **HomePostOfficeBox** property stores the contact's post office box number as an updatable string value.

The HomeState Property

The **HomeState** property stores the state part of a contact's home postal address as an updatable string value.

The HomeStreet Property

The **HomeStreet** property stores the street part of a contact's home postal address as an updatable string value.

The Initials Property

The **Initials** property stores the contact's initials as an updatable string value. The Web Storage System calculates the initials using the first capitalized letters of the **FirstName**, **MiddleName**, and **LastName** properties separated by a period. However, you can explicitly set the **Initials** property in code to be any string up to six characters long.

For contacts stored in the Active Directory, the initial is the capitalized first letter of the **MiddleName** property followed by a period. However, you can explicitly set the Initials property in code to be any string up to four characters long.

The LastName Property

The **LastName** property stores the contact's last name as an updatable string value.

The MailingAddress Property

The **MailingAddress** property is the concatenation of the contact's home, work, or other address properties and is considered the postal mailing address for the contact. This property is functionally equivalent to the **This is the mailing address** check box on a standard Outlook **Contact** form (see Figure 14.1). The **MailingAddressID** property defines how the **MailingAddress** property is generated.

The MailingAddressID Property

The **MailingAddressID** property identifies which address is the mailing address for the contact. It specifies the other contact properties from which the **MailingAddress** object is created. The **MailingAddressID** property can contain one of the **cdoMailingAddressIDValues** values shown in Table 14.5.

So, for example, if the **MailingAddressID** has a value of 1, then the **MailingAddress** is made up of the **HomeStreet**, **HomeCity**, **HomeState**, **HomePostalCode**, and **HomeCountry** properties.

Table 14.5 **cdoMailingAddressIDValues** Values

Name	Value	Description
cdoNoAddress	0	The **MailingAddress** property is not automatically generated and must be set manually.
cdoHomeAddress	1	The **MailingAddress** property is constructed from the home address properties.
cdoBusinessAddress	2	The **MailingAddress** property is constructed from the work address properties.
cdoOtherAddress	3	The **MailingAddress** property is constructed from the other address associated with the contact.

The MiddleName Property

The **MiddleName** property stores the contact's middle name as an updatable string value.

The MobilePhone Property

The **MobilePhone** property stores the contact's mobile telephone number as an updatable string value.

The NamePrefix Property

The **NamePrefix** property stores the title that precedes the contact's name (e.g., Mr., Ms., Dr.) as an updatable string value.

The NameSuffix Property

The **NameSuffix** property stores the title that follows the contact's name (e.g., III, The Great, Jr.) as an updatable string value.

The Title Property

The **Title** property stores the contact's job title as an updatable string value.

The WorkCity Property

The **WorkCity** property stores the city part of the contact's work postal address as an updatable string value.

The WorkCountry Property

The **WorkCountry** property stores the country part of the contact's work postal address as an updatable string value.

The WorkFax Property

The **WorkFax** property stores the contact's work fax number as an updatable string value.

The WorkPager Property

The **WorkPager** property stores the contact's work pager number as an updatable string value.

The WorkPhone Property

The **WorkPhone** property stores the contact's work telephone number as an updatable string value.

The WorkPostalAddress Property

The **WorkPostalAddress** property is the concatenation of the **WorkStreet**, **WorkCity**, **WorkState**, **WorkPostalCode**, and **WorkCountry** properties. Changing any one of these constituent properties dynamically updates the **WorkPostalAddress** property, so it is a read-only property.

The WorkPostalCode Property

The **WorkPostalCode** property stores the postal code part (e.g., 90210) of the contact's work postal address as an updatable string value.

The WorkPostOfficeBox Property

The **WorkPostOfficeBox** property stores the contact's post office box number as an updatable string value.

The WorkState Property

The **WorkState** property stores the state part of a contact's work postal address as an updatable string value.

The WorkStreet Property

The **WorkStreet** property stores the street part of a contact's work postal address as an updatable string value.

Methods of the Person Object

The CDO **Person** object sports two methods: **GetInterface** and **GetVCardStream**.

The GetInterface Method

The **GetInterface** method is designed to support script languages (such as VBScript) by returning the specified interface. Remember that everything is a Variant in VBScript, so declaring a variable as a **CDO.IDataSource** is not supported. What we can do instead is use the **GetInterface** method to get the **IDataSource** interface, as in the following VBScript code:

```
Dim objPerson
Set objPerson = CreateObject("CDO.Person")
Dim objDataSource
Set objDataSource = objPerson.GetInterface("IDataSource")
```

After executing this code, your VBScript program would have access to all of the properties and methods of the **IDataSource** interface through the **objDataSource** variable. Had you been writing a Visual Basic program, you could have just accessed the **DataSource** property of the CDO **Person** object as shown earlier. As you can see, the **GetInterface** method takes a string identifying the desired interface and returns it if it is exposed. Several CDO objects feature a **GetInterface** method.

Using a CDO Person Object to Get the IMailbox Interface Lest you think that you can use the **GetInterface** method only to access interfaces that are returned as properties of the CDO **Person** object (as was the case with **DataSource**), let's get the **IMailbox** interface. The **IMailbox** interface is supported by CDO and contains URLs to an Exchange user's major private folders. In the following VBScript code we create a CDO **Person** object and bind it to the currently logged-on user, using the Active Directory System Information object (**ADSystemInfo**). We then use that **Person** object to get the **IMailbox** interface:

```
Dim objInfo
Dim objPerson
Dim objMailbox
Set objInfo = CreateObject("ADSystemInfo")
Set objPerson = CreateObject("CDO.Person")
objPerson.DataSource.Open "LDAP://" & objInfo.UserName
Set objMailbox = objPerson.GetInterface("IMailbox")
```

We can now use the **objMailbox** variable to access all of the user's folders. For example, we can open a connection to the user's inbox with the following additional lines of VBScript code:

```
Dim objConn
Set objConn = CreateObject("ADODB.Connection")
objConn.Provider = "ExOLEDB.DataSource"
objConn.Open objMailbox.Inbox
```

As we shall see in Chapter 16, when we create a mailbox-enabled recipient we can use the **GetInterface** method to access interfaces in other CDO libraries. For example, we can get the **IMailboxStore** interface, which is in the CDO for Exchange Management library using a simple CDO **Person** object.

The GetVCardStream Method

vCard is the Internet standard for creating and sharing virtual business card information. The **GetVCardStream** method returns an ADO **Stream** object containing the vCard information from your CDO contact. You can then save this stream as a vCard file and share it with any other contact management system that can accept contact information in vCard format. The **GetVCardStreamMethod** takes no arguments and returns an ADO **Stream** object.

Creating a vCard from a Contact The following Visual Basic code is the functional equivalent of opening up a **Contact** in Outlook 2000, selecting **Save As...** from its **File** menu, and saving it as a vCard file, as depicted in Figure 14.5.

```
Public Sub SaveVCardFile(ByVal ExchangeAlias As String, _
                         ByVal ContactName As String)
    Dim objPerson As New CDO.Person
    Dim sURL As String
```

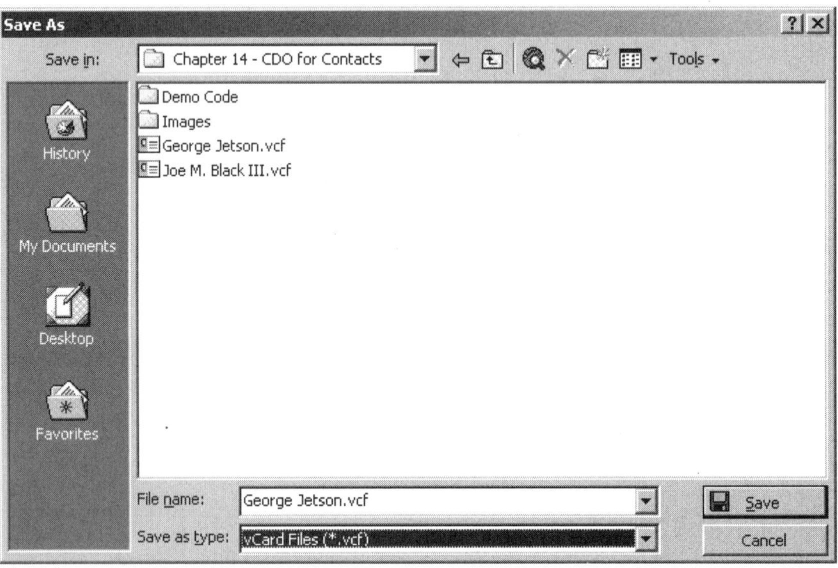

Figure 14.5 Saving an Outlook 2000 contact as a vCard file

```
    Dim sContactName As String
    Dim objInfo As New ADSystemInfo

' Set up the URL to retrieve the contact using the Exchange OLE DB
' provider: The URL should be something like:
' file://./backofficestorage/GomezaMobile.local/MBX/Administrator/
'        Contacts/JoeBlack.EML
sURL = "file://./backofficestorage/" & objInfo.DomainDNSName
            & "/MBX/" & _Trim(ExchangeAlias) & "/Contacts/"
            & Trim(ContactName) & ".EML"

    ' Get the contact:
    objPerson.DataSource.Open sURL

    ' Save the vCard file:
    objPerson.GetVCardStream.SaveToFile "C:\Work\" & ContactName _
        & ".vcf", _adSaveCreateOverWrite

    ' Clean up:
    Set objPerson = Nothing
    Set objInfo = Nothing

End Sub
```

We open up a valid contact in the Web Storage System using the tried-and-true code that we have used all along. The interesting part is in the following line of code, which uses the ADO **Stream SaveToFile** method directly to save the vCard file in one fell swoop:

```
objPerson.GetVCardStream.SaveToFile "C:\Work\" & ContactName & ".vcf", _
    adSaveCreateOverWrite
```

For the more verbose programmers, we could have also declared an ADO **Stream** object, set it to the returned vCard stream from the **Person** object, and then used the **SaveToFile** method:

```
Dim objStream As New ADODB.Stream
Set objStream = objPerson.GetVCardStream
objStream.SaveToFile "C:\Work\" & ContactName & ".vcf", _
    adSaveCreateOverWrite
```

Figure 14.6 shows what a vCard file looks like.

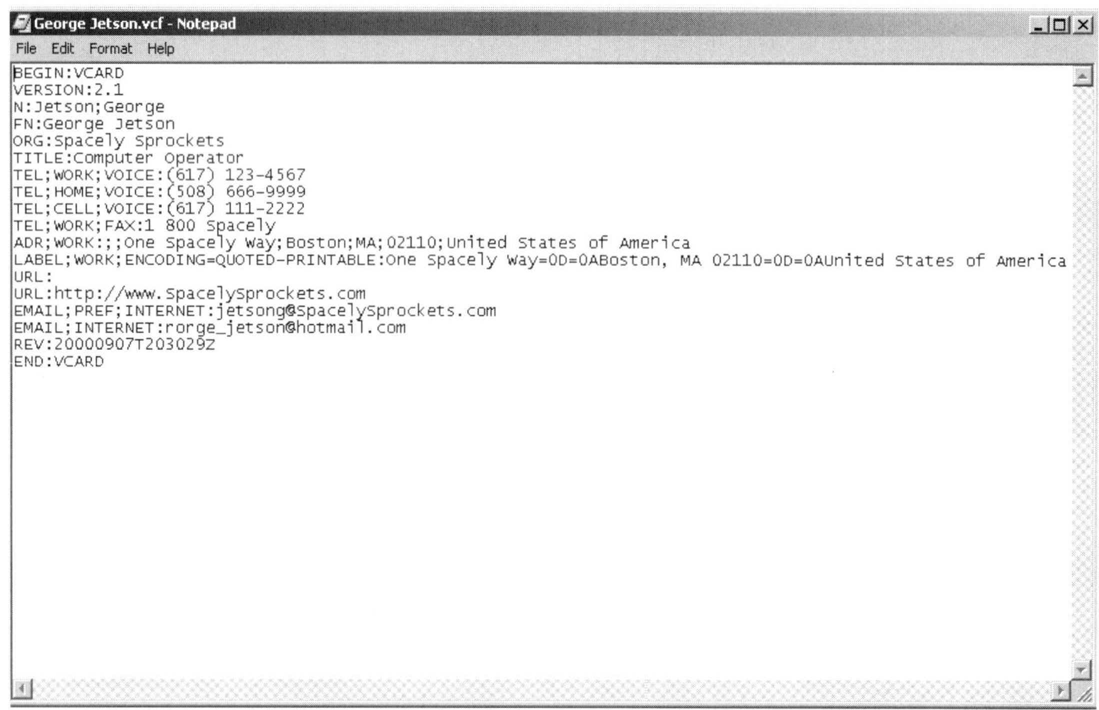

```
BEGIN:VCARD
VERSION:2.1
N:Jetson;George
FN:George Jetson
ORG:Spacely Sprockets
TITLE:Computer Operator
TEL;WORK;VOICE:(617) 123-4567
TEL;HOME;VOICE:(508) 666-9999
TEL;CELL;VOICE:(617) 111-2222
TEL;WORK;FAX:1 800 Spacely
ADR;WORK:;;One Spacely Way;Boston;MA;02110;United States of America
LABEL;WORK;ENCODING=QUOTED-PRINTABLE:One Spacely Way=0D=0ABoston, MA 02110=0D=0AUnited States of America
URL:
URL:http://www.SpacelySprockets.com
EMAIL;PREF;INTERNET:jetsong@SpacelySprockets.com
EMAIL;INTERNET:rorge_jetson@hotmail.com
REV:20000907T203029Z
END:VCARD
```

Figure 14.6 A sample vCard file in Notepad

■ The urn:schemas:contacts Namespace

As we learned in Chapter 3, several default namespaces are defined in the Web Storage System. These namespaces explicitly define a property of the schema by providing it with a scope. For example, both an HTTP mail item and a mail header have a **To** property. We can distinguish these properties in code by referring to each one by its full name—**urn:schemas:httpmail:to** and **urn:schemas:mailheader:to.**

What does all this have to do with contacts? Microsoft provides the **urn:schemas:contacts** namespace, which defines properties for managing contacts. The CDO **Person** object exposes several, but not all, of these properties. To perform certain programming tasks, such as using Web Storage System SQL to query **Contact** items, you need to know the properties in the **urn:schemas:contacts** namespace. The CDO library also has a module called **cdoContacts** (you can see it in the VB object browser) that defines all of these properties for ease of use in your code. The value of the constant is a string equal to the full name of the property. With all of this in mind, we offer Table 14.6.

Table 14.6 The **urn:schemas:contacts** Namespace

Full Name	CDO Constant?	Type	CDO Person Equivalent	Description
urn:schemas:con-tacts:account	cdoAccount	String		An account number associated with the contact.
urn:schemas:con-tacts:authorig	cdoOriginalAuthor	String		The name of the person that created the contact.
urn:schemas:con-tacts:bday	cdoBirthday	Date		The contact's birthday.
urn:schemas:con-tacts:billinginformation		String		Any billing information associated with the contact.
urn:schemas:con-tacts:businesshomepage		String		The URL to the contact's business Web site.
urn:schemas:contacts:c	cdoWorkCountry-Abbreviation	String		The contact's work country code (e.g., USA).
urn:schemas:con-tacts:callbackphone	cdoCallbackPhone	String		The contact's callback telephone number in international dialing format.
urn:schemas:con-tacts:childrensname	cdoChildrensName	String		A semicolon-separated string of the names of the contact's children (e.g., Karen; Alex; Juan Carlos).
urn:schemas:contacts:cn	cdoCommonName	String		The contact's friendly name (e.g., Al), which can be a maximum of 20 characters and should not be the same as a user's name on the Exchange 2000 server.
urn:schemas:contacts:co	cdoWorkCountry	String	Work-Country	The name of the contact's work country. If you specify a value for this field, you must also specify a value for the **urn:schemas:contacts:c** property for the object to be saved correctly in the Active Directory.

Continued on next page.

Table 14.6 The **urn:schemas:contacts** Namespace (*continued*)

Full Name	CDO Constant?	Type	CDO Person Equivalent	Description
urn:schemas:contacts:computernetworkname	cdoComputerNetworkName	String		The name of the computer network that the contact is on (e.g., plural.com).
urn:schemas:contacts:customerid	cdoCustomerID	String		A customer ID associated with the contact.
urn:schemas:contacts:department	cdoDepartment	String		The name of the contact's department.
urn:schemas:contacts:dn	cdoDistinguishedName	String		The X.500 distinguished name of the contact (e.g., **cn=Andy, dc=myDomain, dc=test, dc=plural, dc=com**).
urn:schemas:contacts:email1	cdoEmail1Address	String	Email	The contact's primary e-mail address.
urn:schemas:contacts:email2	cdoEmail2Address	String	Email2	The contact's secondary e-mail address.
urn:schemas:contacts:email3	cdoEmail3Address	String	Email3	The contact's tertiary e-mail address.
urn:schemas:contacts:employeenumber	cdoEmployeeNumber	String		An employee number associated with the contact.
urn:schemas:contacts:facsimiletelephonenumber	cdoWorkFax	String	WorkFax	The contact's work fax number.
urn:schemas:contacts:fileas	cdoFileAs	String	FileAs	How the contact name is displayed. See the discussion of the **FileAs** and **FileAsID** properties of the CDO **Person** object earlier in the chapter.
urn:schemas:contacts:fileasid	cdoFileAsId	Long	FileAsMapping	How the **urn:schemas:contacts:fileas** property is displayed. See the discussion of the **FileAs** and **FileAsID** properties of the CDO **Person** object earlier in the chapter.
urn:schemas:contacts:ftpsite	cdoFtpSite	String		The URL to the contact's FTP site.

Table 14.6 The **urn:schemas:contacts** Namespace *(continued)*

Full Name	CDO Constant?	Type	CDO Person Equivalent	Description
urn:schemas:contacts:gender	cdoGender	Integer		The contact's gender. Can be one of the following **cdoGenderValues: cdoGenderUnspecified** (0), **cdoFemale** (1), or **cdoMale** (2).
urn:schemas:contacts:givenname	cdoFirstName	String	FirstName	The contact's first name.
urn:schemas:contacts:governmentid	cdoGovernmentId	String		A government ID associated with the contact. In the United States, this is typically the contact's Social Security number.
urn:schemas:contacts:hobbies	cdoHobbies	String		A semicolon-delimited string containing the contact's hobbies (e.g., soccer; hockey; music).
urn:schemas:contacts:homecity	cdoHomeCity	String	HomeCity	The contact's home city.
urn:schemas:contacts:homecountry	cdoHomeCountry	String	HomeCountry	The contact's home country.
urn:schemas:contacts:homefax	cdoHomeFax	String	HomeFax	The contact's home fax number.
urn:schemas:contacts:homelatitude	cdoHomeLatitude	Double		The latitude of the contact's home (e.g., 47.6457).
urn:schemas:contacts:homelongitude	cdoHomeLongitude	Double		The longitude of the contact's home (e.g., –122.1151).
urn:schemas:contacts:homephone	cdoHomePhone	String	HomePhone	The contact's home telephone number in international dialing format.
urn:schemas:contacts:homephone2	cdoHomePhone2	String		The contact's alternate home telephone number in international dialing format.
urn:schemas:contacts:homepostaladdress	cdoHomePostalAddress	String	HomePostalAddress	Read-only concatenation of the **HomeStreet**, **HomeCity**, **HomeState**, and **HomePostalCode** fields.

Continued on next page.

Table 14.6 The **urn:schemas:contacts** Namespace *(continued)*

Full Name	CDO Constant?	Type	CDO Person Equivalent	Description
urn:schemas:contacts:homepostalcode	cdoHomePostalCode	String	HomePostalCode	The contact's postal (zip) code.
urn:schemas:contacts:homepostofficebox	cdoHomePostOfficeBox	String	HomePostOfficeBox	The contact's post office box number.
urn:schemas:contacts:homestate	cdoHomeState	String	HomeState	The contact's home state.
urn:schemas:contacts:homestreet	cdoHomeStreet	String	HomeStreet	The contact's home street address.
urn:schemas:contacts:hometimezone	cdoHomeTimeZone	String		The contact's home time zone (e.g., GMT + 8.00).
urn:schemas:contacts:initials	cdoInitials	String	Initials	The contact's initials, made up of the capitalized concatenation of the first letters in the contact's full name.
urn:schemas:contacts:internationalisdnnumber	cdoInternationalISDNNumber	String		The contact's ISDN (Integrated Services Digital Network) number in international dialing format.
urn:schemas:contacts:l	cdoWorkCity	String	WorkCity	The contact's work city.
urn:schemas:contacts:language	cdoLanguage	String		The contact's language in ISO 639 format (e.g., en).
urn:schemas:contacts:location		String		The contact's location (e.g., Northeast).
urn:schemas:contacts:mailingaddressid	cdoMailingAddressId	String	MailingAddressID	Properties from which the contact's mailing address is derived. See the CDO **Person MailingAddressID** property.
urn:schemas:contacts:mailingcity	cdoMailingCity	String		The read-only city portion of the contact's mailing address.
urn:schemas:contacts:mailingcountry	cdoMailingCountry	String		The read-only country portion of the contact's mailing address.
urn:schemas:contacts:mailingpostaladdress	cdoMailingPostalAddress	String	MailingAddress	The read-only postal address portion of the contact's mailing address.

Table 14.6 The **urn:schemas:contacts** Namespace *(continued)*

Full Name	CDO Constant?	Type	CDO Person Equivalent	Description
urn:schemas:contacts:mailingpostalcode	cdoMailingPostalCode	String		The read-only postal (zip) code portion of the contact's mailing address.
urn:schemas:contacts:mailingpostofficebox	cdoMailingPostOfficeBox	String		The read-only post office box portion of the contact's mailing address.
urn:schemas:contacts:mailingstate	cdoMailingState	String		The read-only state portion of the contact's mailing address.
urn:schemas:contacts:mailingstreet	cdoMailingStreet	String		The read-only street portion of the contact's mailing address.
urn:schemas:contacts:manager	cdoManager	String		The distinguished name of the contact's manager (e.g., **cn=Rob, cn=users, dc=subdomain, dc=somewhere, dc=plural, dc=com**).
urn:schemas:contacts:mapurl	cdoMapURL	String		The read-only URL to the map of the user's address on Microsoft's Web site.
urn:schemas:contacts:members		String		The members of a group contact (*reserved for future use*).
urn:schemas:contacts:middlename	cdoMiddleName	String	MiddleName	The contact's middle name.
urn:schemas:contacts:mobile	cdoWorkMobilePhone	String	MobilePhone	The contact's mobile work telephone number in international dialing format.
urn:schemas:contacts:namesuffix	cdoNameSuffix	String	NameSuffix	The title displayed after the contact's name (e.g., Jr., The Great).
urn:schemas:contacts:nickname	cdoNickname	String		The contact's nickname (e.g., El Guapo).
urn:schemas:contacts:o	cdoOrganizationName	String	Company	The name of the contact's organization or company (e.g., Plural).

Continued on next page.

Table 14.6 The **urn:schemas:contacts** Namespace *(continued)*

Full Name	CDO Constant?	Type	CDO Person Equivalent	Description
urn:schemas:contacts:officetelephonenumber		String		The contact's primary office telephone number.
urn:schemas:contacts:office2telephonenumber		String		The contact's secondary office telephone number.
urn:schemas:contacts:organizationmainphone		String		The main telephone number for the contact's company.
urn:schemas:contacts:othercity	cdoOtherCity	String		An alternative city for the contact.
urn:schemas:contacts:othercountry	cdoOtherCountry	String		An alternative country for the contact.
urn:schemas:contacts:othercountrycode	cdoOtherCountryCode	String		The two-letter country code for the contact's alternative country.
urn:schemas:contacts:otherfax	cdoOtherFax	String		An alternative work fax number for the contact, in international dialing format.
urn:schemas:contacts:othermobile	cdoOtherMobile	String		An alternative work mobile phone number for the contact, in international dialing format.
urn:schemas:contacts:otherpager	cdoOtherPager	String		An alternative work pager number for the contact, in international dialing format.
urn:schemas:contacts:otherpostaladdress	cdoOtherPostalAddress	String		A read-only generated string containing the concatenation of the contact's other address fields.
urn:schemas:contacts:otherpostalcode	cdoOtherPostalCode	String		An alternative postal (zip) code for the contact.
urn:schemas:contacts:otherpostofficebox	cdoOtherPostOfficeBox	String		An alternative post office box number for the contact.
urn:schemas:contacts:otherstate	cdoOtherState	String		An alternative state, province, or parish for the contact.

Table 14.6 The **urn:schemas:contacts** Namespace *(continued)*

Full Name	CDO Constant?	Type	CDO Person Equivalent	Description
urn:schemas:contacts:otherstreet	cdoOtherStreet	String		An alternative work street address for the contact.
urn:schemas:contacts:othertelephone	cdoOtherTelephone	String		An alternative work telephone number for the contact.
urn:schemas:contacts:othertimezone	cdoOtherTimeZone	String		An alternative work time zone for the contact (e.g., EST).
urn:schemas:contacts:pager	cdoWorkPager	String	WorkPager	The work pager number of the contact, in international dialing format.
urn:schemas:contacts:personalhomepage	cdoPersonalURL	String		The URL of the contact's personal home page (e.g., "http://www.tiac.net/gomeza").
urn:schemas:contacts:personaltitle	cdoNamePrefix	String	NamePrefix	The prefix to the contact's name (e.g., Mr., Ms., Sr., Srta.).
urn:schemas:contacts:postalcode	cdoWorkPostalCode	String	WorkPostalCode	The contact's work postal (zip) code.
urn:schemas:contacts:postofficebox	cdoWorkPostOfficeBox	String	WorkPostOfficeBox	The contact's work post office box number.
urn:schemas:contacts:profession	cdoProfession	String		The contact's profession (e.g., Software Tycoon).
urn:schemas:contacts:proxyaddresses	cdoProxyAddresses	Variant	EmailAddresses	The contact's e-mail addresses stored as an array of variants.
urn:schemas:contacts:referredby		String		The full name of the person who referred the contact.
urn:schemas:contacts:roomnumber	cdoRoomNumber	String		The contact's room number.
urn:schemas:contacts:secretary	cdoSecretary	String		The full name of the contact's administrative assistant (e.g., Ms. Nicole Reihl).
urn:schemas:contacts:secretarycn	cdoSecretaryCommonName	String		The friendly name of the contact's administrative assistant (e.g., Nikki).

Continued on next page.

Table 14.6 The **urn:schemas:contacts** Namespace (*continued*)

Full Name	CDO Constant?	Type	CDO Person Equivalent	Description
urn:schemas:contacts:secretaryphone		String		The phone number of the contact's administrative assistant.
urn:schemas:contacts:secretaryurl	cdoSecretaryURL	String		The URL of the home page of the contact's administrative assistant.
urn:schemas:contacts:sn	cdoLastName	String	LastName	The contact's last name.
urn:schemas:contacts:sourceurl	cdoSourceURL	String		The source URL for the contact.
urn:schemas:contacts:spousecn	cdoSpouseCommonName	String		The friendly name of the contact's spouse (e.g., Vero).
urn:schemas:contacts:st	cdoWorkState	String	WorkState	The contact's work state.
urn:schemas:contacts:street	cdoWorkStreet	String	WorkStreet	The contact's work street.
urn:schemas:contacts:submissioncontlength	cdoSubmissionContLength	Long		The maximum length, in kilobytes (K), of a message that can be sent to the contact.
urn:schemas:contacts:telephonenumber	cdoWorkPhone	String	WorkPhone	The contact's work telephone number in international dialing format.
urn:schemas:contacts:telephonenumber2	cdoWorkPhone	String		The contact's alternative work telephone number in international dialing format.
urn:schemas:contacts:telexnumber	cdoTelexNumber	String		The contact's work telex number in international dialing format.
urn:schemas:contacts:title	cdoTitle	String	Title	The contact's work title or job position.
urn:schemas:contacts:ttytddphone		String		A TTY/TDD phone associated with the contact.
urn:schemas:contacts:unauthorig		String		E-mail addresses that cannot send mail to this user (*reserved for future use*).

Table 14.6 The **urn:schemas:contacts** Namespace *(continued)*

Full Name	CDO Constant?	Type	CDO Person Equivalent	Description
urn:schemas:contacts:usercertificate	cdoUserCertificate	Bytes		The certificate used to authorize the contact.
urn:schemas:contacts:weddinganniversary	cdoWeddingAnniversary	Date		The date of the contact's wedding anniversary.
urn:schemas:contacts:workaddress	cdoWorkAddress	String		A read-only generated string containing the concatenation of the contact's work address fields.

Let's assume that **objPerson** is a valid CDO **Person** object bound to a contact, as we have shown in several earlier examples. The following three lines of code are equivalent:

```
objPerson.Title
objPerson.Fields("urn:schemas:contacts:title").Value
objPerson.Fields(cdoTitle).Value
```

The first gets the **Title** property of the CDO **Person** object. The second uses the name of the equivalent Exchange 2000 schema field in the **urn:schemas:contacts** namespace. Remember that the **Fields** collection of the CDO **Person** object will give you all of the **Contact** fields in the **urn:schemas:contacts** namespace—not just the ones directly supported by properties in the CDO **Person** object. The third line uses the **cdoTitle** constant, which is equal to **urn:schemas:contacts:title.** All three lines return the value "Vice President" (assuming that your contact is George Jetson and he caught Mr. Spacely on a good day).

Getting a User's Contacts Folder

To work with contacts, you usually have to get a user's **Contacts** folder. We can do this through the CDO **IMailbox** interface. It's quite simple, and with it you can get the URL to any of the folders in a user's private mailbox. For example, let's get the **Contacts** folder of the currently logged-on user. The following code assumes that you are logged into Windows 2000 using an account that has an Exchange mailbox:

```
Dim objMailbox As CDO.IMailbox
Dim objPerson As New CDO.Person
Dim objInfo As New ActiveDS.ADSystemInfo

' Get the currently logged-on user:
' UserName should be something like:
' cn=Administrator,cn=Users,dc=GomezaMobile,dc=local
objPerson.DataSource.Open "LDAP://" & objInfo.UserName

' Get his or her mailbox:
Set objMailbox = objPerson
objMailbox.Contacts
```

We start off by using the **UserName** property of the **ADSystemInfo** object. As we have seen before, this object gives us all sorts of useful information about our environment (like the name of our computer). All we have to do is declare it. We utilize the **UserName** property to bind to the currently logged-on Exchange user. We then set our CDO **IMailbox** object to the CDO **Person** object. Period. We now have all of the needed URLs. So, for example, **objMailbox.Contacts** contains the following string:

```
file://./backofficestorage/GomezaMobile.local/MBX/Administrator/
      Contacts
```

Searching for a Contact

Now that we are familiar with the properties of the **urn:schemas:contacts** namespace, we can get the **Contacts** folder of the currently logged-on user, and we know all about the CDO **IMailbox** and CDO **Person** objects, so let's put this knowledge to good use. The next example will use Web Storage System SQL, which we discussed in Chapter 7, to query a user's **Contacts** folder. The **Search-Contacts** function is written in Visual Basic and returns an ADO **Recordset** object containing all of the contacts that matched the criteria in the **WHERE** clause, which is taken as an argument. The trick is that the **WHERE** clause that you pass into the method must be in valid Web Storage System SQL syntax. The following **WHERE** clause can be typed in directly, as is, on the VB form:

```
WHERE ("urn:schemas:contacts:title" = '"Vice President"')
```

Note: Again, for a refresher on valid Web Storage System SQL syntax, see Chapter 7.

So the function goes a little something like this:

```
Public Function SearchContacts(ByVal sWhereClause As String) As _
    ADODB.Recordset
    Dim objMailbox As CDO.IMailbox
    Dim objPerson As New CDO.Person
    Dim objInfo As New ActiveDS.ADSystemInfo
    Dim objConn As ADODB.Connection
    Dim sSQL As String

    Dim objRs As New ADODB.Recordset
    Set objConn = LocalExchangeLogin()

    ' Get the currently logged-on user:
    ' UserName should be something like:
    ' cn=Administrator,cn=Users,dc=GomezaMobile,dc=local
    objPerson.DataSource.Open "LDAP://" & objInfo.UserName

    ' Get his or her mailbox:
    Set objMailbox = objPerson

    sSQL = "select ""DAV:href"", " & _
               """urn:schemas:contacts:fileas"", " & _
               """urn:schemas:contacts:email1""" & _
               " from "

    sSQL = sSQL & """" & objMailbox.Contacts & """ "

    ' The WHERE clause should be something like:
    ' WHERE ("urn:schemas:contacts:title" = '"Vice President"')
    sSQL = sSQL & sWhereClause

    objRs.Open sSQL, objConn

    ' Set the return value:
    Set SearchContacts = objRs

    ' Clean up:
    Set objMailbox = Nothing
    Set objPerson = Nothing
    Set objInfo = Nothing

End Function
```

The code that called the **SearchContacts** function now has an ADO record set. One more point: For the ADO record set to work correctly, we had to establish an explicit connection to the Exchange server. To that end we wrote the little auxiliary function **LocalExchangeLogin** referenced in the preceding code. It simply returns an ADO **Connection** object to the currently logged-on user's mailbox. We then take this **Connection** object and use it to open the **RecordSet** object. The code for **LocalExchangeLogin** is as follows:

```
Public Function LocalExchangeLogin() As ADODB.Connection
    Dim objConn As New ADODB.Connection
    Dim objInfo As New ADSystemInfo
    Dim objInfoNT As New WinNTSystemInfo
    Dim sMailboxURL As String

    sMailboxURL = "http://" & LCase(objInfoNT.ComputerName) & "." & _
                      objInfo.DomainDNSName & "/Exchange/" & _
                      objInfoNT.UserName

    ' Connect to the local Exchange server:
    objConn.Provider = gblsExchangeProvider
    objConn.Open sMailboxURL

    Set LocalExchangeLogin = objConn
End Function
```

Again, note how we use the **ADSystemInfo** object (and its sister the **WinNT-SystemInfo** object) to our advantage when building our URL.

Summary

This chapter covered the new CDO **Person** object, which allows you to create contacts in either a contacts folder or the Active Directory. In Chapter 16 we will combine the powers of the CDO **Person** object with the CDO for Exchange Management object to show how you can accomplish tasks such as creating mailboxes and managing users.

Chapter 15

CDO for Workflow and the Exchange Workflow Designer

Developing effective strategies for implementing business processes quickly and with little cost is crucial in today's fast-moving business world. Automating and consolidating recurring projects is what allows some businesses to operate more smoothly than others. Tasks such as form routing and approval, document review and publishing, issue tracking, and expense report validation all involve an item's passage through a series of states before being considered complete. One way to manage this flow of data is to implement a workflow process. A typical workflow process enables a group of users to create, review, and approve information according to a predefined set of business rules. This process can help speed data and decisions through an organization.

In this chapter we present the tools that Exchange 2000 provides developers for implementing workflow solutions. We take a look at a new tool that can be used to create a workflow process for the Microsoft Exchange 2000 Server platform. The Microsoft Workflow Designer for the Exchange 2000 Server allows a developer to quickly add back-end workflow processes to an Exchange folder through an intuitive graphical user interface that models a state transition diagram. We take an in-depth look at the CDO Workflow Objects library and how to successfully prepare and deploy workflow applications.

Without a workflow process, the Exchange folder is just a container. With a workflow process, you can connect your folder to events and manage the flow of information throughout your organization.

What Are Workflow Applications?

In general, workflow applications model real-life business processes in which an item goes through a series of states before being considered completed. Form approval and routing, document review and publishing, and issue tracking are problems that lend themselves to a workflow solution. A workflow process is made up of a series of states, the order in which they must occur, and the actions to take for each state. Conceptually a workflow process can be modeled with states, actions, and transitions:

- A **state** defines the current status of an item in a workflow process.
- An **action** defines the operations that can be performed on an item.
- A **transition** is a type of action that moves an item from one state to another. Typically, when creating a transition you also need to specify the next state that the item will be in.

To use an example that is dear to a developer's heart, let's think of a bug-tracking application. When an application tester first reports a bug, its initial state is New. An action taken on a new bug is to send it to a developer so that he or she can fix it. The bug has now made the transition from New to Assigned.

Seven types of actions can be used in a workflow process: **Create**, **Enter**, **Exit**, **Delete**, **Change**, **Receive**, and **Expiry**. We'll talk more about how these actions are used later in the chapter.

Why Exchange 2000?

Although you can implement workflow applications in nearly any programming language or development environment, you can simplify the task by using a workflow engine and specialized workflow modeling tools. Otherwise you, as a developer, would have to keep track of the state of every item, constantly check for state changes, route messages along, take action when an item changes state, and much, much more.

In Exchange 2000 parlance, a workflow process is a set of business rules enforced on items in an Exchange folder. Workflow components are installed automatically with Exchange 2000 Server. CDO Workflow Objects for Microsoft Exchange provides a built-in workflow engine and an object model for programming that engine (**cdowf.dll**). An in-process server implements the workflow engine, which controls the state changes to documents in your workflow folder. You can use the object model to create process definitions, consisting of a table of actions, or rules, that define the business process. At runtime, the application calls the workflow engine to create and manage process instances. The workflow engine evaluates the process definition to see which actions should be run and in turn executes either Microsoft VBScript code or compiled COM objects to perform application-specific business logic.

Exchange 2000 Server also includes a workflow event sink, which you can register in a folder. The workflow event sink (**cdowfevt.dll**) calls the workflow engine when an event fires in your workflow folder. The event sink also hooks into system timer events to automate expiring items, overdue work, or other cleanup tasks.

Au Revoir Routing Objects

Seasoned collaborative application developers may remember Microsoft Routing Objects. This technology has been around since the turn of the century (twenty-first, that is), when it was introduced with Microsoft Exchange Server 5.5 Service Pack 1. It is based on Exchange 5.5 agents and server-side scripting. Although they are similar in concept to the new CDO Workflow Objects, routing objects were designed only for MAPI-based e-mail routing applications, and they don't take advantage of any new Web Storage System features. So instead of adding features to routing objects, Microsoft came up with a completely new library in CDO for workflow.

However, Exchange 2000 Server is still backward compatible with existing MAPI applications, including Routing Objects. If you need to build a routing application that runs on both Microsoft Exchange 5.5 and Exchange 2000 Server servers, use MAPI and the Routing Objects libraries. If you want to write Web-based workflow applications or use new Web Storage System features, you should focus on Exchange 2000 Server and CDO Workflow Objects.

Getting Started

This section acts as a security checklist for developers to ensure that all of the needed security rights are in place before embarking on the development of a workflow application. After a few hours of trying in vain to debug your workflow application, it is pretty frustrating to find out that your application was right all along and you were just lacking the permissions to run it properly. We hope this section helps you avoid this type of mistake.

Let's start with the obvious. A workflow process enforces a set of business rules on all of the items in a particular folder. From a security standpoint, only the owners of a folder can modify application design elements, such as schema, forms, views, and workflow, of a folder. If you are not a folder owner, you won't be able to use the workflow designer or save workflow information in the folder. Folder owner permissions can be granted from the Exchange 2000 System Manager or from Microsoft Outlook.

Also don't forget your users. Users who are going to modify, edit, or approve items in the workflow process must have write permissions to those items. Permissions can be assigned at the folder level or item level programmatically through Microsoft Outlook or the Exchange 2000 System Manager. In addition, all workflow application users need at least read permissions to open the contents of items, follow a URL to an item, or view the workflow items in a window.

Adding the Workflow System Account

Although the Exchange 2000 setup program installs the workflow components by default, you still need to add a workflow system account for the workflow engine, which has administrator privileges to most of the Exchange 2000 Server's resources. Here are the steps required to set up the account:

1. Using the **Active Directory Users and Computers** (ADUAC) MMC in the Microsoft Exchange program group, select an existing account from your Windows 2000 domain or create a new one. For our illustration, we will create a new account with the name "Workflow Account." To create a brand-new account, right-click the **Users** folder and select **New** and then **User** (see Figure 15.1). In the **New Object – User** New wizard dialog box, fill in the information as shown in Figure 15.2 and hit **Next.**
2. Type in the account password and check the **Password Never Expires** box. Hit **Next.**
3. Ensure that the workflow system account has an Exchange mailbox by making sure that **Create an Exchange mailbox** is selected (see Figure 15.3), and hit **Next.** Hit the **Finish** button to generate the account.
4. Make **Workflow Account** a member of the Windows 2000 group named "Domain EXServers." This will allow the CDO workflow event sink to execute with proper privileges. Simply right-click on the **Domain EXServers** security group in the **ADUAC** dialog box and select **Properties.** In the **Members** tab of the resulting dialog box, hit the **Add** button and add the new workflow system account as shown in Figure 15.4.
5. Bring up the **Component Services** MMC from the Administrative Tools program group. Under **Component Services**, select your computer. Then select

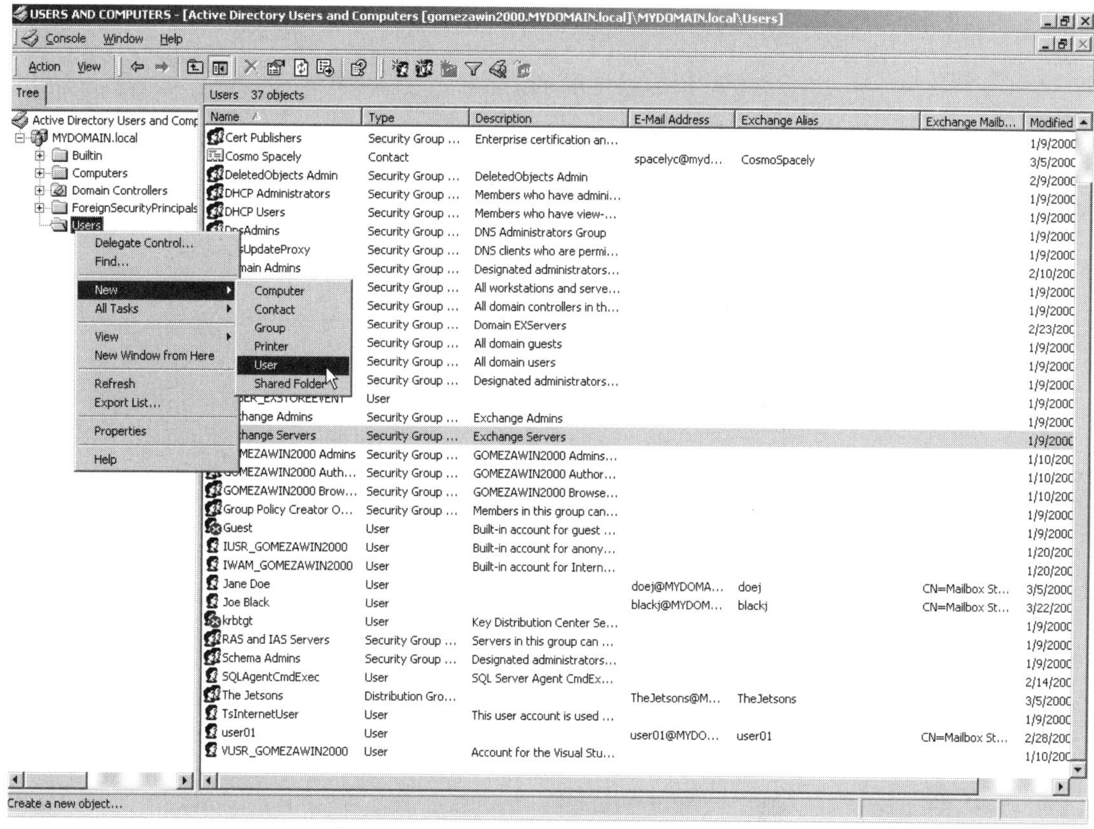

Figure 15.1 Creating a new workflow account: Part 1

the COM+ application named Workflow Event Sink (see Figure 15.5). Select **Properties** from the **Action** menu.

6. Choose the **Identity** tab. Click **This user** and enter the name and password for the workflow system account you have created (see Figure 15.6). Hit **OK.**

7. Finally, bring up the **Domain Controller Security Policy** dialog box from the Administrative Tools program group (Figure 15.7). Under **Security Settings**, expand **Local Policies** and click **User Rights Assignment.** Double-click on the **Act as part of the operating system** policy. Hit the **Add** button to add the workflow system account, and then hit **OK.**

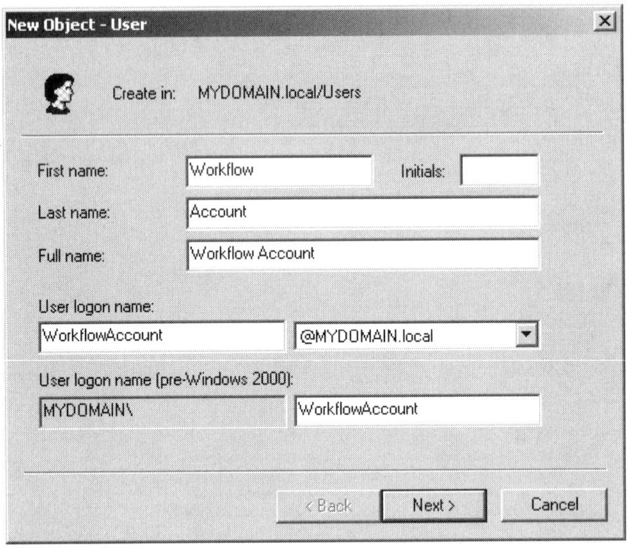

Figure 15.2 Creating a new workflow account: Part 2

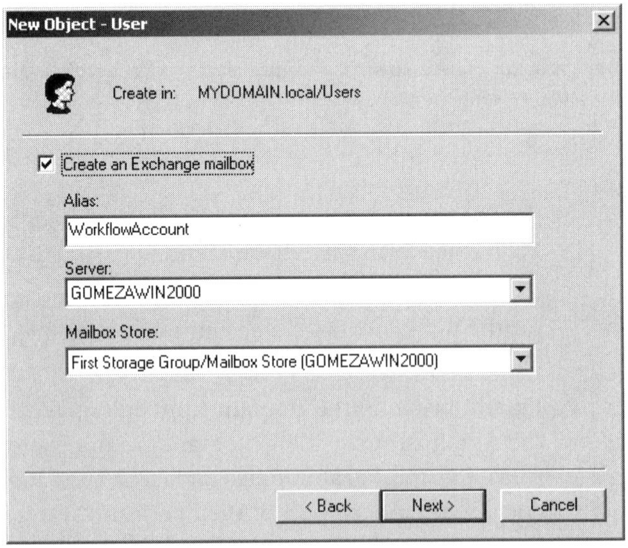

Figure 15.3 Ensuring that the new account has an Exchange mailbox

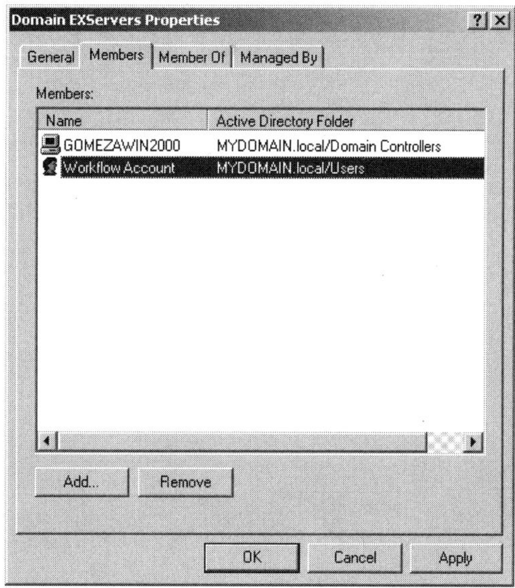

Figure 15.4 The **Domain EXServers Properties** dialog box

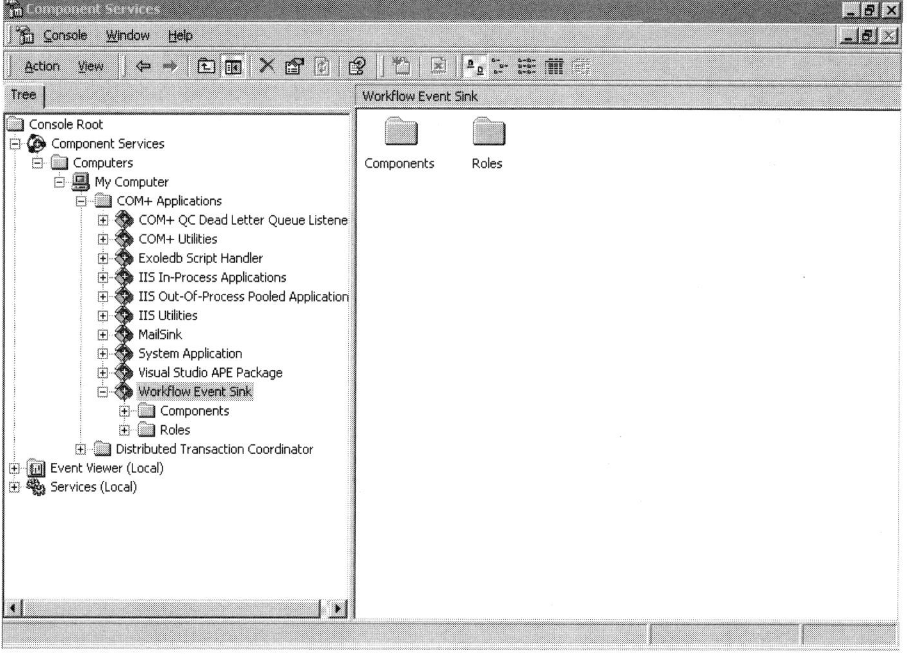

Figure 15.5 Selecting the Workflow Event Sink COM+ application

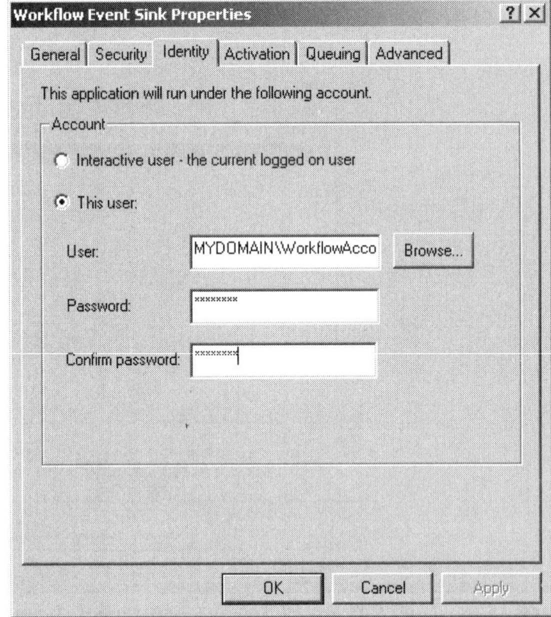

Figure 15.6 Entering the user name and password for the workflow account

Allowing a User to Register Workflows

The workflow application developer needs permission to register workflows. Only users and groups that are members of the **Can Register Workflow** role on a particular server can register the CDO workflow event sink. Follow these steps to add a user to this role:

1. Bring up the **Component Services** MMC in the Administrative Tools program group.
2. Drill down by expanding **Component Services**, **Computers**, **My Computer**, **COM+ Applications**, **Workflow Event Sink**, **Roles**, and finally **Can Register Workflow** (see Figure 15.8).
3. Right-click **Users** and select **New User**.
4. In the **Select Users or Groups** dialog box, select the users you want to be able to register workflows and hit the **Add** button. Hit **OK** to apply the changes.

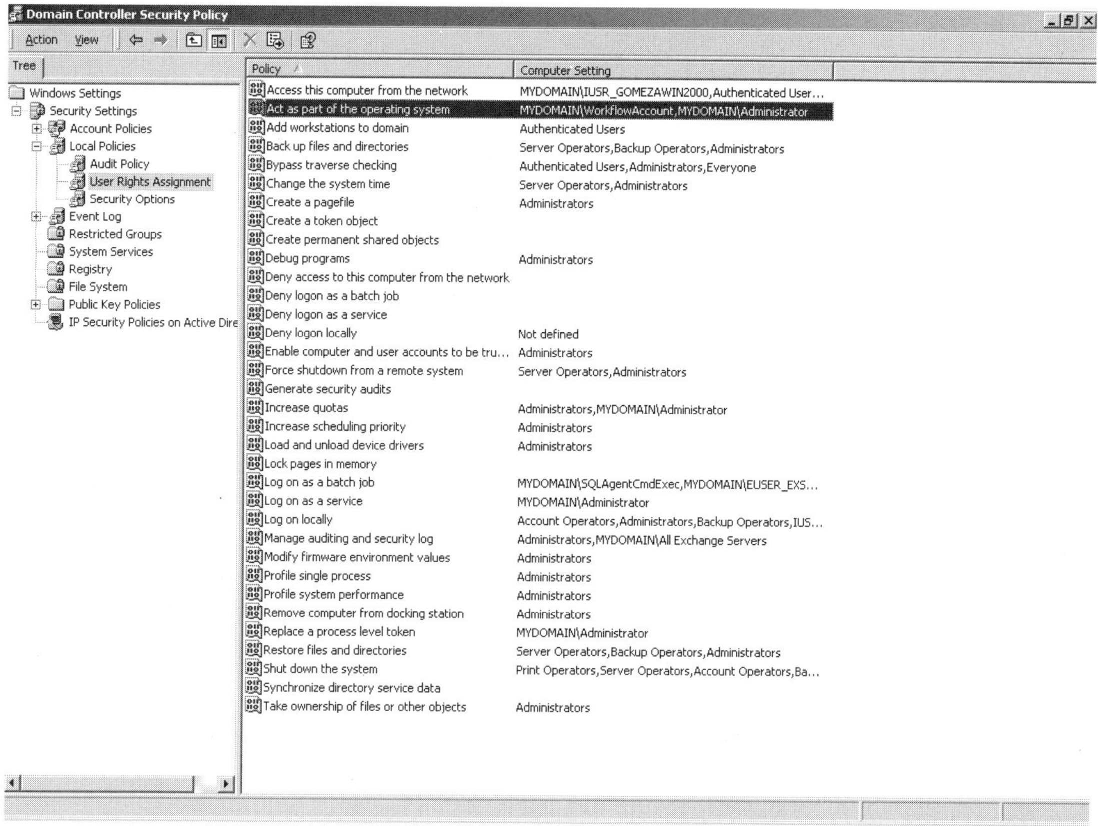

Figure 15.7 Be careful when adjusting domain policies

Restricted versus Privileged Mode

Workflow processes run in either restricted mode or privileged mode. The default is restricted mode. In restricted mode, all of the workflow code is limited to safe, nonthreatening actions such as modifying properties of the workflow document, sending notification e-mails, and writing to the audit trail. The script engine is not even allowed to create any other COM objects.

In privileged mode, by contrast, the script engine can create any registered COM objects, thereby allowing you to integrate with other systems, such as SQL databases and other business applications, that provide COM components. You can also use LDAP and the Active Directory in privileged mode, and COM objects may

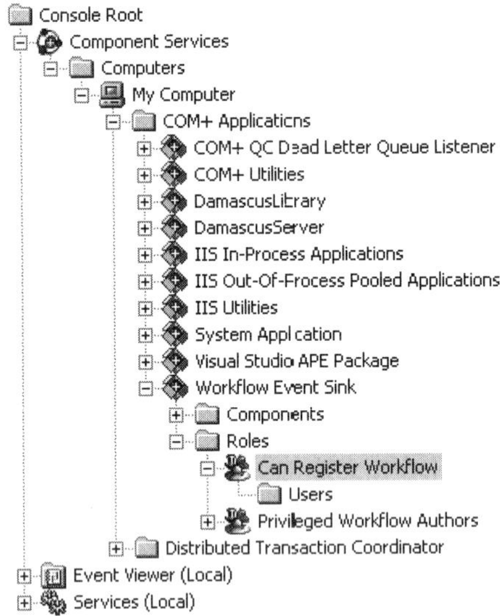

Figure 15.8 Finding the **Can Register Workflow** node in the **Component Services** MMC

also be used in place of script for workflow actions. The code will execute under the same Windows 2000 security context as the workflow engine itself—typically the workflow system account defined earlier.

Adding a User to the Privileged Workflow Authors Role

To execute workflow processes in privileged mode, either you or the group in which you are registered must be a member of the Privileged Workflow Authors group. To add a user to this role, follow these steps:

1. Bring up the **Component Services** MMC in the Administrative Tools program group.
2. Drill down by expanding **Component Services, Computers, My Computer, COM+ Applications, Workflow Event Sink, Roles,** and finally **Privileged Workflow Authors** (see Figure 15.9).
3. Right-click **Users** and select **New User.**
4. In the **Select Users or Groups** dialog box, select the users you want to be able to run workflow processes in privileged mode and hit the **Add** button. Hit **OK** to apply the changes.

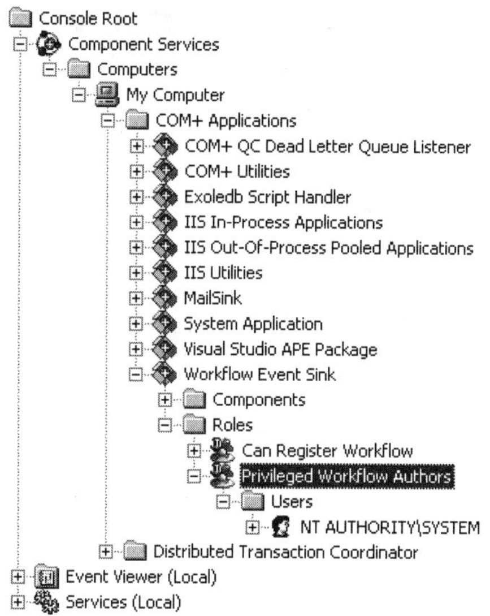

Figure 15.9 Finding the **Privileged Workflow Authors** node in the Component Services MMC

CDO Workflow Objects for Microsoft Exchange

The CDO Workflow object model is fairly simple, with three key objects: **WorkflowSession**, **ProcessDefinition**, and **ProcessInstance**. In addition, a few ancillary objects help define some of the properties of the previously mentioned objects. Let's take a look at each in more detail.

Adding a Reference to Visual Basic

If you plan to use Visual Basic to create a workflow application, you need to add a reference to the CDO Workflow type library in your Visual Basic Project file. From the VB **Project** menu, select **References** and then scroll down and check **Microsoft CDO Workflow Objects for Microsoft Exchange** (see Figure 15.10). The type library name is CDOWF, and the component library is **cdowf.dll**, which can be found in the Exchange binary files directory.

The WorkflowSession Object

Typical workflow application developers use the **WorkflowSession** object primarily for running scripts that they have added with the Workflow Designer tool.

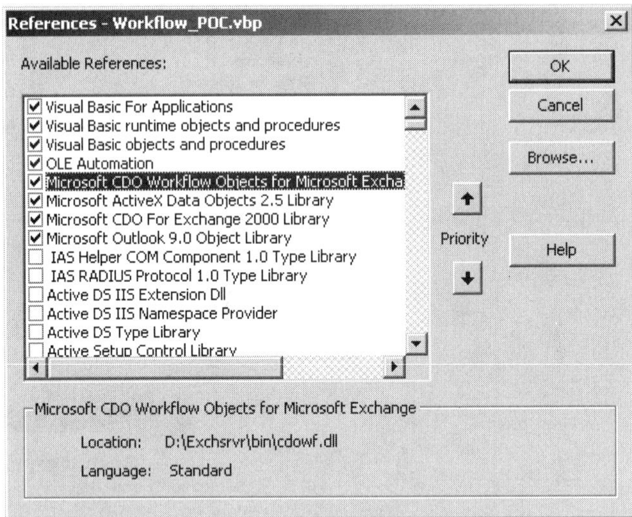

Figure 15.10 Setting a reference to the CDO Workflow object library

The extended object model for the CDO **WorkflowSession** object is shown in Figure 15.11.

IWorkflowSession, the formal name of the COM interface for the **WorkflowSession** object, specifies the intrinsic object passed to your action and condition scripts. This object provides runtime communication among the workflow engine, your scripts, and the current **ProcessInstance** object. Your script can pass errors back to the **IWorkflowSession** object, and they will be logged by your audit-logging tool. The **IWorkflowSession** object also provides a method for tracking notifications and responses correlated with a specific **ProcessInstance** object in its **TrackingTable** property, which returns an ADO **Recordset** object for easy data manipulation.

Properties of the WorkflowSession Object

The ActiveConnection Property The **ActiveConnection** property is represented in your Visual Basic or VBScript code as an ADO 2.5 **Connection** object (**ADODB.Connection**). The **ActiveConnection** property is a read-only property that contains the **Session** object of the user that initiated the event. Your workflow script can use this property to access the Web Storage System in which your **ProcessInstance** object is running. You can perform transactions in that Web Storage System only, according to the rights of the user under which your application is running. If a workflow transition fails, any changes made with the **ActiveConnection** property are rolled back. The **ActiveConnection** property is valid only for the Web Storage

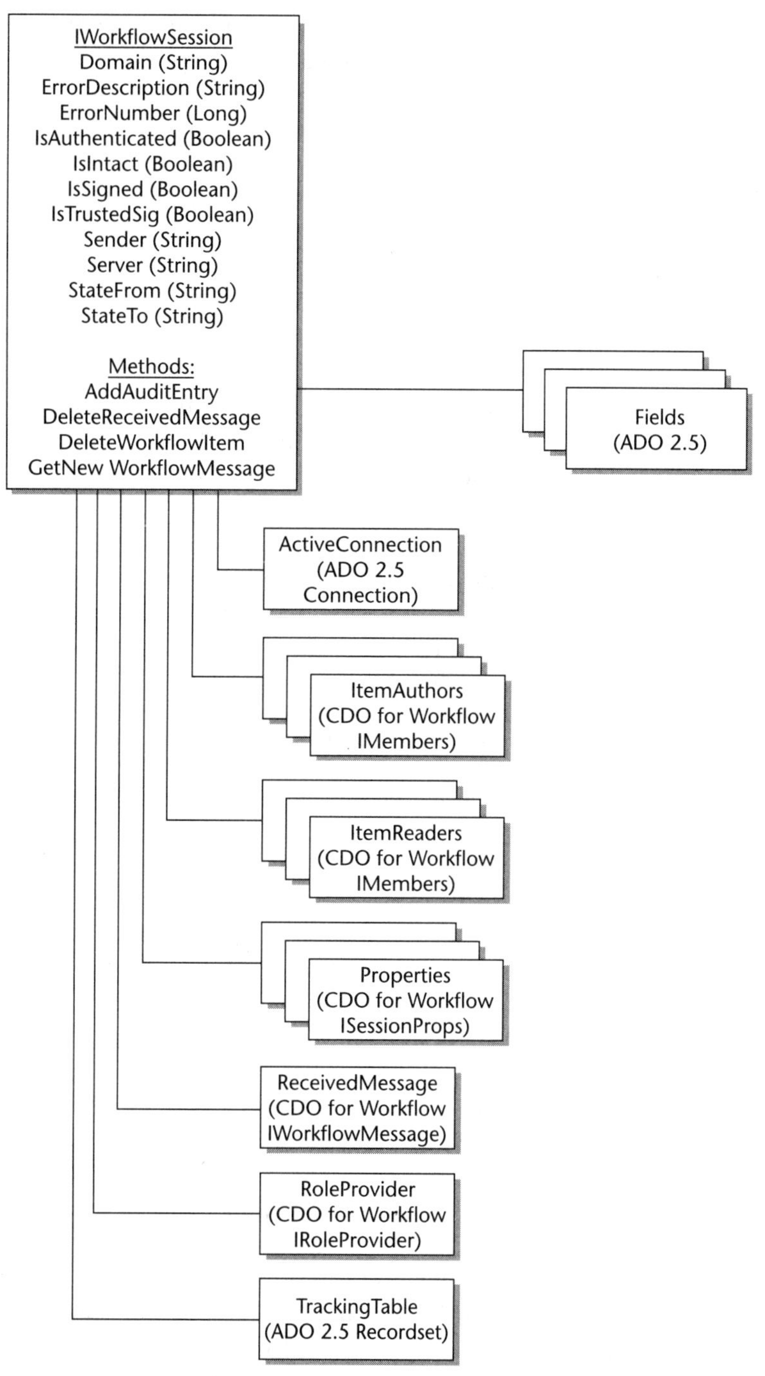

Figure 15.11 The **WorkflowSession** object model

System in which the event occurred. You cannot use the **ActiveConnection** property for a public folder event to access a user's inbox. In addition, you cannot use the **SendUsingExchange** method in CDO for Exchange 2000 to send a message as the user with an **ActiveConnection** to a public folder, because you must have access to the user's outbox.

The most important point to remember is that this property can be used only if you are running in privileged mode, as defined earlier. Your script will get an error message if you attempt to use this property in restricted mode.

The following VB code binds the ADO **Record** object to a document in a folder in the user's public folder tree. The **Record** object in your code inherits all of the access rights of the user that initiated the state transition. For example, if someone just created **PrivateUserDocument.doc** in the workflow folder, the code would now have write access to the document. This is pretty useful if the code has to approve the document in some way and pass it along to the next workflow state. Note that in this example we use **WorkflowSession** instead of **IWorkflowSession.** The reason is that the workflow engine returns an intrinsic **Session** object to us. If we wanted to create our own object, we would use **IWorkflowSession** instead.

```
' Create an ADO Record object:
Dim objRec As ADODB.Record
Set objRec = New ADODB.Record
objRec.Open "file://./backofficestorage/" & WorkflowSession.Domain & _
"/Public Folders/Bug Flow/PrivateUserDocument.doc", _
WorkflowSession.ActiveConnection, adModeReadWrite, adFailIfNotExists
```

The Domain Property The **Domain** property is a read-only string containing the server's domain name. You can use it in your code to construct HTTP, file, or LDAP URLs, as we saw in the preceding code example for the **ActiveConnection** property.

The ErrorDescription Property The **ErrorDescription** property is a string containing the details of an error to be reported back to the audit trail (the workflow debugging log, which we will see later in the chapter). This property is used in conjunction with the **ErrorNumber** property. If the **ErrorNumber** property is set to a negative value, the workflow engine looks for an error description in the **ErrorDescription** property. If the **ErrorNumber** property is not set or is set to a value greater than or equal to zero, nothing happens. The VBScript code that follows causes the item workflow transition to terminate with an error if the user failed to use the **Vote** button in the custom Web form to enter a value in this field. The workflow engine adds an entry to the audit trail with the specified error number and description. It then uses the **SendMail** subroutine to send a message back to the user who initiated the workflow with "Please Vote" on the subject line.

```
If (WorkflowSession.ReceivedMessage.Fields("VoteButton").Value = "")
Then
    WorkflowSession.ErrorNumber = &H80004005
    WorkflowSession.ErrorDescription = "Form not completed."
End If
Sub SendMail(strSubject)
    Dim objWFMsg
    Set objWFMsg = WorkflowSession.GetNewWorkflowMessage()
    objWFMsg.From = WorkflowSession.Sender
    objWFMsg.To = WorkflowSession.Sender
    objWFMsg.Subject = strSubject
    objWFMsg.TextBody = WorkflowSession.StateFrom & " -> " & _
        WorkflowSession.StateTo
    objWFMsg.SendWorkflowMessage 0       'cdowfNoTracking
End Sub
```

The ErrorNumber Property The **ErrorNumber** property is a Long value that contains the error number to be reported back to the calling client and logged to the audit trail. The workflow engine automatically looks for an error number in this property upon exiting a script. You can terminate a workflow state transition by passing a negative number back to the workflow engine in this property. If you set **ErrorNumber** to a positive number (or fail to set it at all), the workflow engine will just ignore it. The **ErrorNumber** property is used in conjunction with the **ErrorDescription** property to specify an error description to the audit trail as shown in the preceding sample code, in which we set both properties.

The Fields Property The **Fields** property is an ADO 2.5 **Fields** collection (**ADODB.Fields**) representing the property collection for the **ProcessInstance** object that initiated the workflow session. A **ProcessInstance** object, as we'll learn a bit later, represents a document in a workflow folder. The **WorkflowSession Fields** collection maps directly to the **ProcessInstance Fields** collection and can be used to read and write properties only for the **ProcessInstance** that initiated the session. It cannot be used to get the **Fields** collection for any other **ProcessInstance** item.

In addition, you can't use the **WorkflowSession Fields** collection to modify certain **ProcessInstance** schema properties protected by the workflow engine, including:

- **http://schemas.microsoft.com/cdo/workflow/currentstate**
- **http://schemas.microsoft.com/cdo/workflow/expirytime**
- **http://schemas.microsoft.com/cdo/workflow/processdefinition**
- **http://schemas.microsoft.com/cdo/workflow/trackingtablexml**

You can use the **WorkflowSession Fields** collection in an assignment statement only when dealing with your own custom properties, as in the following example:

```
WorkflowSession.Fields("YourNamespace://workflow/YourCustomProperty") =
                                            "YourValue"
```

The ItemAuthors Property The **ItemAuthors** property is a collection of users allowed to modify and delete an item. The **ItemAuthors** property is implemented as a CDOWF **IMembers** collection object. This is a collection of CDOWF **IMember** objects, which, as we will see later, represent users or roles.

You can use the **ItemAuthors** collection to maintain, modify, and delete rights on individual items. When the collection has members, only these members can modify or delete the item. When the collection is empty, only the default author privileges defined on the folder apply. This property allows you to give certain users or groups temporary exclusive author access to a workflow item. The following code traverses the **ItemAuthors** collection:

```
    Dim objcolMembers As CDOWF.IMembers
    Dim objMember As CDOWF.Imember

    Set objcolMembers = WorkflowSession.ItemAuthors
    For Each objMember In objcolMembers
        MsgBox objMember.Name
    Next

' Clean up:
    Set objcolMembers = Nothing
    Set objMember = Nothing
```

The ItemReaders Property The **ItemReaders** property is a collection of users allowed exclusive read access to an item. The **ItemReaders** property is implemented as a CDOWF **IMembers** collection object. This is a collection of CDOWF **IMember** objects, which, as we will see later, represent users or roles.

You can use the **ItemReaders** collection to maintain read rights on individual items. When the collection has members, only these members can read the item. When the collection is empty, only the default read privileges defined on the folder apply. This property allows you to give certain users or groups temporary exclusive read access to a workflow item. The following code traverses the **ItemReaders** collection:

```
    Dim objcolMembers As CDOWF.IMembers
    Dim objMember As CDOWF.Imember
```

```
        Set objcolMembers = WorkflowSession.ItemReaders
        For Each objMember In objcolMembers
            MsgBox objMember.Name
        Next

    ' Clean up:
        Set objcolMembers = Nothing
        Set objMember = Nothing
```

The Properties Property The **Properties** property returns the CDOWF **ISessionProps** interface for the **WorkflowSession** object. The **ISessionProps** interface is used for persisting custom properties within a session. You can use the interface to read and write properties to the underlying **ProcessInstance** row in the Exchange Web Storage System, enabling you to access those properties between function calls within a session. A session lasts for only one **ProcessInstance** transaction. For example, the following VBScript code retrieves the specified custom property:

```
Function GetCustomProperty (sPropName)
    GetCustomProperty = WorkflowSession.Properties.Get (sPropName)
End Function
```

The ReceivedMessage Property The **ReceivedMessage** property returns a pointer to the CDOWF **IWorkflowMessage** interface for correlated messages that initiate state transitions in the workflow process. **IWorkflowMessage** is simply an interface to a workflow message.

When a message arrives in a folder in response to an existing workflow process, the workflow engine correlates it with the ongoing process and makes an entry in the **TrackingTable** object. **TrackingTable** is also a member of the CDO Workflow object library. In this case, the **ReceivedMessage** property returns a pointer to the message. On the other hand, if a new workflow is initiated by e-mail, the workflow engine creates a new **ProcessInstance** object and our **ReceivedMessage** property returns nothing.

Let's say we have a custom Web form registered on our workflow folder with a custom property called **SomeCustomProperty.** Let's also say that our workflow process is in full swing, so the **SomeCustomProperty** value is already being tracked in the "custom0" column of the tracking table. A new message arrives in our workflow folder. The following VBScript procedure would update the custom property in the tracking table:

```
Sub UpdateWorkflowItem()
    WorkflowSession.TrackingTable.Fields("custom0") = _
WorkflowSession.ReceivedMessage.Fields("SomeCustomProperty").Value
    WorkflowSession.TrackingTable.Fields.Update
End Sub
```

The Sender Property The **Sender** property is a read-only string containing the SMTP address of the user who initiated the state transition. The following VBScript code uses this property to address a brand-new workflow message:

```
Sub SendWorkflowMessage (sSubject)
    Dim objWFMsg   'As CDOWF.IWorkflowMessage
    Set objWFMsg = WorkflowSession.GetNewWorkflowMessage()
    With objWFMsg
        .From = WorkflowSession.Sender
        .To = WorkflowSession.Sender
        .Subject = sSubject
        .TextBody = WorkflowSession.StateFrom & " -> " & _
         WorkflowSession.StateTo
        .SendWorkflowMesssage 0      'cdowfNoTracking
    End With
    Set objWFMsg = Nothing
End Sub
```

The Server Property The **Server** property is a read-only string containing the name of the server on which the workflow process is running. You can use this property in your script to construct HTTP, file, or LDAP URLs like so:

```
"http://" + WorkflowSession.Server + "." + WorkflowSession.Domain
```

The StateFrom Property The **StateFrom** property is a read-only string containing the name of the state from which the workflow item has just made a transition. The value of the property might be NULL, depending on the situation. The sample VBScript function uses the **StateFrom** property to determine if a transition has caused a state change:

```
Function CheckNewState()
    If WorkflowSession.StateFrom <> WorkflowSession.StateTo Then
        CheckNewState = True
    Else
        CheckNewState = False
    End If
End Function
```

The StateTo Property The **StateTo** property is a read-only string containing the name of the state to which the workflow item has just made a transition. The value of the property might be NULL, depending on the situation. One of our previous VBScript examples used the **StateTo** property to build a workflow message showing the state transition. Recall that the workflow engine passes the **WorkflowSession** intrinsic object to the script host, so the developer does not need to create it:

```
Sub SendWorkflowMessage (sSubject)
    Dim objWFMsg        'As CDOWF.IWorkflowMessage
    Set objWFMsg = WorkflowSession.GetNewWorkflowMessage()
    With objWFMsg
        .From = WorkflowSession.Sender
        .To = WorkflowSession.Sender
        .Subject = sSubject
        .TextBody = WorkflowSession.StateFrom & " -> " & _
         WorkflowSession.StateTo
        .SendWorkflowMesssage 0      'cdowfNoTracking
    End With
    Set objWFMsg = Nothing
End Sub
```

The TrackingTable Property The **TrackingTable** property returns an ADO 2.5 **Recordset** object (**ADODB.Recordset**) containing e-mail data related to the process instance that initiated the state transition. The workflow engine uses a tracking table to store information regarding e-mails correlated with a **ProcessInstance** object. The tracking table record set contains the following fields, all of which are character fields with a maximum size of 512 characters:

- **e-mail** contains the address in the **To** field of outgoing forms or messages. The value of this field cannot be NULL.
- **trackingid** contains a GUID created by the workflow engine when you use the **IWorkflowMessage.SendWorkflowMessage** method. The workflow engine uses this GUID to correlate all subsequent messages associated with the **ProcessInstance** object.
- **date** is the sent time for outgoing messages and the received time for incoming messages. This field cannot be NULL.
- **flags** contains one of the following values—"cdowfStrict," "cdowfAdd," or "cdowfNoTracking." These correspond to the names of the **cdowfSendFlags** values (**cdowfStrict** = 2, **cdowfAdd** = 1, **cdowfNoTracking** = 0) which are used as parameters for the **IWorkflowMessage.SendWorkflowMessage** method. For example, if you were to use "IWorkflowMessage.SendWorkflowMessage 2" in your VBScript code, the workflow engine would put "cdowfStrict" in the **flags** field. The value of this field cannot be NULL.
- **response** specifies the column into which the workflow engine automatically copies the value of the form field **http://schemas.microsoft.com/cdo/workflow/response**, with no developer intervention.
- **custom0 through custom9** are 10 fields that allow you to store additional properties that you want to track from your form. You need to write the script code to copy the data to the tracking table.

The following sample VBScript code traverses all of the records in the tracking table looking for a match between the user that initiated the state transition (**WorkflowSession.Sender**) and the e-mail field of the tracking table. If it finds one, it checks to see if the value in the tracking table's state field is "In Progress." If so, the subroutine adds a value to the first custom property field in the tracking table:

```
Sub AddCustomPropToTrackingTable()
    ' Remember it's just a Recordset object:
    WorkflowSession.TrackingTable.MoveFirst
    For nCounter = 0 To WorkflowSession.TrackingTable.RecordCount - 1
                Step 1
        If WorkflowSession.Sender = _
            WorkflowSession.TrackingTable.Fields("email").Value Then
            ' Make a note of it in the log:
            WorkflowSession.AddAuditEntry "email address matched"
            If WorkflowSession.TrackingTable.Fields("state").Value = _
                "In Progress" Then
                WorkflowSession.AddAuditEntry "state matched"
                WorkflowSession.TrackingTable.Fields.Item("custom0")_
                .Value = _
                WorkflowSession.ReceivedMessage.Fields("ACustProp")_
                .Value
                WorkflowSession.TrackingTable.Update
            End If
        End If
        WorkflowSession.TrackingTable.MoveNext
    Next
    WorkflowSession.DeleteReceivedMessage
End Sub
```

Methods of the WorkflowSession Object

The AddAuditEntry Method The **AddAuditEntry** method is used to add an entry to your audit trail. An audit trail is simply an event log for debugging your workflow application. The **AddAuditEntry** method takes a string with the description that you want to write out to the log and optionally a Long value that holds the result of the operation being logged (the **hResult**). A negative **hResult** indicates an error. The following VBScript code calls this method to write a message to the audit log:

```
WorkflowSession.AddAuditEntry "Aw, man my workflow application didn't
    work!"
```

As we'll see later, CDO for workflow provides an interface to the audit trail called **IAuditTrail** with an **AddEntry** method. The **AddAuditEntry** method of the

WorkflowSession object tells the workflow engine to call **IAuditTrail.AddEntry**, which writes the description string to the current audit trail provider.

The DeleteReceivedMessage Method The **DeleteReceivedMessage** method deletes the message correlated with the **ProcessInstance** item. This method can be called only for the **OnReceive** event, as in the following sample VBScript:

```
WorkflowSession.DeleteReceivedMessage
```

We will see all of the event types later when we discuss the **ActionTable** object.

The DeleteWorkflowItem Method The **DeleteWorkflowItem** method deletes the **ProcessInstance** row from the Exchange Web Storage System. Note that the workflow event sink will not invoke the workflow engine with an **OnDelete** event just because you call this method in your code. If you want to take special action when deleting a **ProcessInstance**, do it before or after calling **DeleteWorkflowItem**. You can call the **DeleteWorkflowItem** method only in the **OnChange**, **OnCreate**, **OnDelete**, and **OnExpiry** event procedures, like so:

```
WorkflowSession.DeleteWorkflowItem
```

The GetNewWorkflowMessage Method The **GetNewWorkflowMessage** method returns a new **WorkflowMessage** object. The **WorkflowMessage** object provides message sending and tracking ability through its **SendWorkflowMessage** method.

In the VBScript example that follows, the **GetNewWorkflowMessage** returns a **WorkflowMessage** object. As a result, the workflow script can use the **IWorkflowMessage** interface to set the **From**, **To**, **Subject**, and **TextBody** fields, as well as to send the message:

```
Sub SendMail (sSubject)
    Set objWFMsg = WorkflowSession.GetNewWorkflowMessage
    With objWFMsg
        .From = WorkflowSession.Sender
        .To = WorkflowSession.Sender
        .Subject = sSubject
        .TextBody = WorkflowSession.StateFrom & " -> " & _
            WorkflowSession.StateTo
        .SendWorkflowMessage 0      'cdowfNoTracking
    End With
    Set objWFMsg = Nothing
End Sub
```

The GetUserProperty Method The **GetUserProperty** method gets a directory attribute property of an Active Directory object. It takes three arguments:

- **bsUser** is a string containing either the distinguished name of an Active Directory object if the **bIsEmail** argument is **cdowfDistinguishedName** (1) or an e-mail address if the **bIsEmail** argument is **cdowfUserEmailAddress** (0).
- **bsAttrName** is a string containing the name of the attribute to retrieve.
- **bIsEmail** contains **cdowfUserEmailAddress** (0) if the **bsUser** argument is an e-mail address or **cdowfDistinguishedName** (1) if the **bsUser** argument is a distinguished name from the Active Directory.

For example, the following VBScript function uses the **GetUserProperty** method to retrieve the e-mail address of a user's manager:

```
Function GetUserManager (sUserAddress)
    With WorkflowSession
        sManagerDN = .GetUserProperty(sUserAddress, "manager", 0)
        GetUserManager = .GetUserProperty(sManagerDN, "mail", 1)
    End With
End Function
' Meanwhile somewhere in your action script:
sManagerEmail = GetUserManager("gomeza@plural.com")
```

The IsUserInRole Method The **IsUserInRole** method returns True if a user is in a specified folder role, False otherwise. The method takes two arguments: a string containing the user's principal name and a string containing the name of the role against which you want to check the user. There are 16 valid fixed strings that you can use here ("Role1," "Role2," . . . , "Role16"). For example, the following VBScript code checks to see if the user was in Role1 and writes the correct message to the audit trail log.

```
If WorkflowSession.IsUserInRole("gomeza@plural.com", "Role1") Then
    WorkflowSession.AddAuditEntry "The user was in Role1."
Else
    WorkflowSession.AddAuditEntry "The user was NOT in Role1."
End If
```

The ProcessDefinition Object

The **ProcessDefinition** object is the meat of your workflow application. It encapsulates the business logic and policies of a workflow application. It defines how the workflow engine will advance a workflow item, the privileges under which the

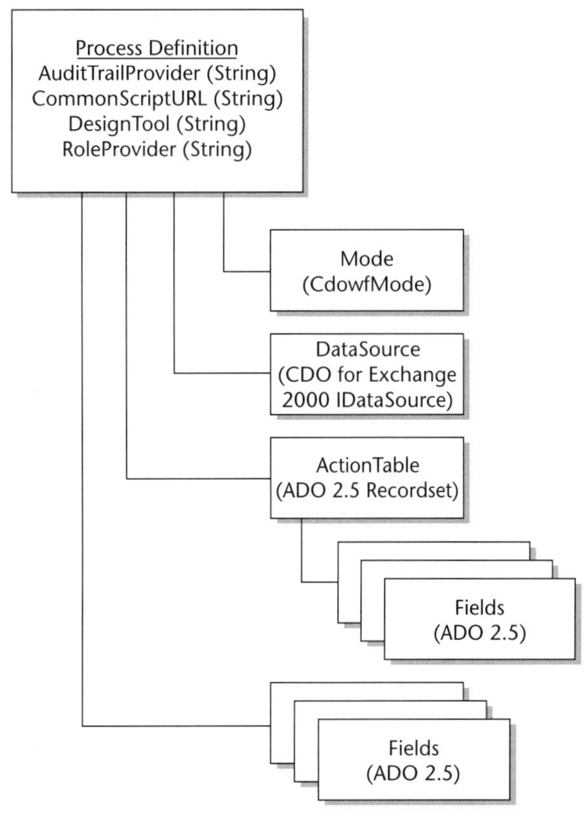

Figure 15.12 The **ProcessDefinition** object model

workflow scripts will run, and the audit trail that the workflow engine will use. The **ProcessDefinition** object is stored as an item in a public folder. Figure 15.12 shows the extended object model for the CDO workflow **ProcessDefinition** object.

Before delving into the properties of the **ProcessDefinition** object, let's see a bit of high-level code that creates a process instance. The Visual Basic code that follows creates a new **ProcessDefinition** object and an ADO 2.5 **Connection** object. It uses the **Connection** object to bind to the workflow folder and set the desired properties on the **ProcessDefinition** object:

```
Dim objPD As New CDOWF.ProcessDefinition
Dim objADOConn As New ADODB.Connection
Dim sDomainURL As String
Dim sFolderURL As String
Dim sFolderName As String
```

```
Dim sProcDefURL As String
Dim sProcDef As String

' The folder name and the process definition are hard-coded for
'   illustrative purposes:
sFolderName = "MyWorkflowFolder"
sProcDef = "MyWorkflowProcDef"

' Build the needed fully qualified paths:
sDomainURL = "file://./backofficestorage/" & Environ("USERDNSDOMAIN") & _
             "/Public Folders/"
sFolderURL = sDomainURL & sFolderName
sProcDefURL = sFolderURL & "/" sProcDef

' Open an ADO Connection to your Exchange server and bind to your workflow
'   folder:
objADOConn.Provider = "ExOLEDB.DataSource"
objADOConn.Open sFolderURL
objADOConn.BeginTrans

' Fill in the process definition fields:
With objPD
    ' objRS is an open ADO record set built prior to hitting this code:
    .ActionTable = objRS
    .AuditTrailProvider = "CDOWF.AuditTrailEventLog"
    .CommonScriptURL = sCommonScriptURL
    .Mode = cdowfPrivilegedMode
    .Fields("DAV:ishidden") = True
End With

' Save it:
objPD.DataSource.SaveTo sProcDefURL, objADOConn, adModeReadWrite, _
    adCreateOverwrite Or adcreateNonCollection
objADOConn.CommitTrans
```

Let's examine the **ProcessDefinition** properties, especially the mysterious ADO **Recordset** object that was built behind the scenes and used as an action table.

Properties of the ProcessDefinition Object

The ActionTable Property The **ActionTable** property contains the state transition rules for a workflow process definition stored as an ADO **Recordset** object. An action table is a set of rules that define how workflow items can change state. Each row in the action table represents a possible state transition in the workflow; the columns define the properties that the workflow engine uses to advance the workflow. For example, in a bug-tracking workflow application, one row in the table defines how a bug goes from Submitted to Assigned. Another row could define how a bug goes from Assigned to Fixed.

Creating action table columns is the first of two steps needed to create an action table. You do this by creating an ADO **Recordset** object and appending the action table fields to the **Fields** collection of the new **Recordset** object using the **Recordset** object's **Append** method. In the **Append** method, you give the name of the field and its type. You must do this before opening the **Recordset** object or an ADO **Connection** object. The workflow engine requires the 14 fields listed in Table 15.1 to be in the action table.

Now that we know what all the field values represent, let's look at some sample Visual Basic code to create the columns of the action table using ADO as described earlier:

```
Dim objRs As ADODB.Recordset
Set objRs = New ADODB.Recordset

With objRs.Fields
    .Append "ID", adBSTR
    .Append "Caption", adBSTR
    .Append "State", adBSTR
    .Append "NewState", adBSTR
    .Append "EventType", adBSTR
    .Append "Condition", adBSTR
    .Append "EvaluationOrder", adBSTR
    .Append "Action", adBSTR
    .Append "ExpiryInterval", adBSTR
    .Append "RowACL", adBSTR
    .Append "TransitionACL", adBSTR
    .Append "DesignToolFields", adBSTR
    .Append "CompensatingAction", adBSTR
    .Append "Flags", adBSTR
End With

Dim varColumnNames As Variant

VarColumnNames = Array(objRs.Fields.Item(0).Name, _
                 objRs.Fields.Item(1).Name, _
                 objRs.Fields.Item(2).Name, _
                 objRs.Fields.Item(3).Name, _
                 objRs.Fields.Item(4).Name, _
                 objRs.Fields.Item(5).Name, _
                 objRs.Fields.Item(6).Name, _
                 objRs.Fields.Item(7).Name, _
                 objRs.Fields.Item(8).Name, _
                 objRs.Fields.Item(9).Name, _
                 objRs.Fields.Item(10).Name, _
                 objRs.Fields.Item(11).Name, _
                 objRs.Fields.Item(12).Name, _
                 objRs.Fields.Item(13).Name)
```

Table 15.1 Action Table Fields

Field Name	Type	Description
Action	String	A script expression, common script call, or COM object **ProgID** that executes if the action table row matches the process instance and the **Condition** column is True.
Caption	String	An optional display name for the step. We recommend filling it in for readability.
CompensatingAction	String	A script expression, common script call, or COM object **ProgID** that runs if the workflow transaction is aborted.
Condition	String	A script expression, common script call, or COM object **ProgID** with a Boolean result. An empty **Condition** column causes an error. If the workflow engine does not find a row in the action table for the **EventType** (see above) it is looking for and an expression that evaluates to True in the **Condition** column, then it returns the failure code "CDOWF_NO_CONDS_MATCHED."
DesignToolFields	String	Optional field reserved for future use by design tools such as the Microsoft Workflow Designer for Exchange 2000 Server (which will be discussed later in the chapter).
EvaluationOrder	String	If there are multiple matching rows in a call to advance, then this is the order in which those matching rows will be evaluated. If the **EvaluationOrder** column is blank, no order is guaranteed.
EventType	String	The type of event that this step represents. The valid **cdowfEventType** values are as follows: **cdowfOnCreate**: A value of 1, meaning that the document was created. **cdowfOnChange**: A value of 2, meaning that the document was modified. **cdowfOnDelete**: A value of 3, meaning that the document was deleted. **cdowfOnExpiry**: A value of 4, meaning that the document has been in the current state too long. **cdowfOnReceive**: A value of 5, meaning that the folder has received an e-mail response correlating to the document.
ExpiryInterval	String	The number of minutes that the item should remain in the new state before triggering an **OnExpiry** event. This is used only with the **OnEnter** event type.
Flags	String	Bitwise OR of **cdowfTransitionFlags** that indicates which columns in the action table contain COM object **ProgIDs** and which will contain script. Use zero (0x00) if this row contains only script conditions and actions. The valid **cdowfTransitionFlag** values are as follows: **cdowfActnObject:** A value of 0x01, meaning that the **Action** column is an object. **cdowfCondObject**: A value of 0x02, meaning that the **Condition** column is an object.

Table 15.1 Action Table Fields *(continued)*

Field Name	Type	Description
Flags	String	**cdowfCompObject**: A value of 0x04, meaning that the **CompensatingAction** column is an object. **cdowfEndState**: A value of 0x08, indicating that the state being entered is the last state of the workflow.
ID	String	An optional identifier for the row. For readability, you may want to consider numbering the rows of the action table in your code as in our example.
NewState	String	The new state of the **ProcessInstance** object upon successful completion of this step.
RowACL	String	Reserved for future use. An empty value is required for now.
State	String	The current state of the **ProcessInstance** object.
TransitionACL	String	You can define an access control list (ACL) for the transition, which will override the default ACL on the folder. Valid roles are "Role1," "Role2," . . . , "Role16."

After you have your ADO **Recordset** object with all of the columns required by the workflow engine, you can add records representing the rows in the action table. To do this, you first open the **Recordset** object with the appended columns you just built and use its **AddNew** method to add the records. The specific syntax is shown in the following sample Visual Basic code:

```
objRs.Open
With objRs
    .AddNew varColumnNames, Array("1", "OnCreate", "", "Submitted", _
        "OnCreate", "true", "", "sendmail(""new ProcessInstance"")", _
        "", "", "", "", "", "0")
    .AddNew varColumnNames, Array("2", "OnEnter", "", "Submitted", _
        "OnEnter", "true", "", "sendmail(""entered submitted state"")", _
        "", "", "", "", "", "0")
    .AddNew varColumnNames, Array("3", "OnExpiry", "Submitted", _
        "Submitted", "OnExpiry", "true", "", "sendmail(""submitted state _
        expired"")", "", "", "", "", "", "0")
    .AddNew varColumnNames, Array("4", "OnDelete", "Submitted", "", _
        "OnDelete", "true", "", "sendmail(""deleted ProcessInstance"")", _
        "", "", "", "", "", "0")
   End With
End With
```

You can now assign the **Recordset** object to the **ActionTable** property of the **ProcessDefinition** object as we showed in the sample VB code at the beginning of this section on the **ProcessDefinition** object.

The workflow engine performs various consistency checks as it processes a transition. Table 15.2 summarizes the errors the workflow engine returns for failed consistency checks as a result of errors in the action table.

The AuditTrailProvider Property The **AuditTrailProvider** property contains the **ProgID** of the COM class to use for logging events in your workflow application. The following VB code uses the built-in audit trail provider that comes with CDO Workflow Objects. The **AuditTrailEventLog** writes directly to the Windows 2000 event log:

```
SomeProcessDefinitionObject.AuditTrailProvider = _
    "CDOWF.AuditTrailEventLog"
```

Note: You can write your own audit trail provider, as long as you implement the **IAuditTrail** interface. See the Exchange 2000 Server Platform SDK documentation for more details. We leave this difficult task to you as an exercise.

The CommonScriptURL Property The **CommonScriptURL** property contains a URL to an item containing the shared script functions that you referenced in the **Condition** and **Action** columns of your action table. You can implement this feature by coding the needed routines in VBScript and saving them as a single text file at the location that you will specify in the URL. You can use either an absolute or a relative URL for this property. If you use a relative URL, it must refer to a text file in the same folder or a subfolder of where the workflow application is registered. The following sample VB code sets this property using an absolute URL:

```
Dim sDomainName As String
Dim sFolderName As String
Dim sCommonScriptItem As String

' Hard-coded for illustrative purposes only:
sDomainName = "mydomain.local"
sFolderName = "MyWorkflowFolder"
sCommonScriptItem = "MyCommonScript.txt"

Dim sURL As String
sURL = "file://./backofficestorage/" & sDomainName & _
       "/Public Folders/" & _
       sFolderName & "/" & sCommonScriptItem
```

Table 15.2 Workflow Action Table Consistency Check Errors

Value	Error Code	Meaning
–2147219930 (&H80040626)	CDOWF_E_BAD_ACTIONTABLE	A column is missing, the data type isn't a string, or the workflow engine is encountering other trouble in reading the action table row.
–2147219925 (&H8004062B)	CDOWF_E_DUPLICATE_ORDER	The **EvaluationOrder** column has a duplicate order entry, the entry is not a number, or the sequence is otherwise not logical.
–2147219951 (&H80040611)	CDOWF_E_EMPTY_CURSTATE	The **State** column is empty when it shouldn't be.
–2147219947 (&H80040615)	CDOWF_E_EMPTY_EVENTTYPE	The **EventType** column is empty.
–2147219953 (&H8004060F)	CDOWF_E_EMPTY_NEWSTATE	The **NewState** column is empty when it shouldn't be.
–2147219949 (&H80040613)	CDOWF_E_INVALID_EVENTTYPE	The value in the **EventType** column isn't valid.
–2147219950 (&H80040612)	CDOWF_E_NONEMPTY_CURSTATE	The **State** column has something in it when it should be empty (as is the case when the event type is **OnCreate** or **OnEnter**).
–2147219952 (&H80040610)	CDOWF_E_NONEMPTY_NEWSTATE	The **NewState** column has something in it when it should be empty.
–2147219924 (&H8004062C)	CDOWF_E_ROW_DUPLICATE_ORDER	The **EvaluationOrder** column sequence is not logical.
–2147219945 (&H80040617)	CDOWF_E_ROW_INVALID_FLAGS	The **Flags** column is empty or contains invalid values.
–2147219923 (&H8004062D)	CDOWF_E_ROW_INVALID_SEQUENCE_NUMBER	The **EvaluationOrder** column sequence is not logical.
–2147219922 (&H8004062E)	CDOWF_E_ROW_INVALID_SEQUENCING	The **EvaluationOrder** column sequence is not logical.

Continued on next page.

Table 15.2 Workflow Action Table Consistency Check Errors *(continued)*

Value	Error Code	Meaning
–2147219932 (&H80040624)	CDOWF_E_TRANSACTIONACL_NO_USE_ONEXPIRY	A transition ACL is used in an **OnExpiry** event. The **OnExpiry** event doesn't really have a current user, so transition ACLs don't make sense in this case.
–2147219940 (&H8004061C)	CDOWF_EMPTY_ACTIONTABLE	The action table is empty.
–2147219909 (&H8004063B)	CDOWF_INVALID_EVALUATION_ORDER	The **EvaluationOrder** column sequence is not logical.

```
Dim objPD As CDOWF.ProcessDefinition
Set objPD = New CDOWF.ProcessDefinition
objPD.CommonScriptURL = sURL
```

The DataSource Property The **DataSource** property returns the **IDataSource** interface from the CDO for Exchange 2000 object library. As you may recall seeing in the sample code to create a process definition at the beginning of this section, this allows us to save our **ProcessDefinition** object using the **SaveTo** method of the **DataSource** object.

The DesignTool Property The **DesignTool** property contains a string describing the workflow design tool (if any) used to create this process definition. This property is purely for informational purposes and doesn't affect the execution of a workflow. You can use this property if you are writing a workflow design tool of your own to keep track of which workflow designs are compatible with your tool.

As we'll see shortly, Microsoft Workflow Designer for Exchange 2000 Server uses ".wfd" files to store process definitions. The following sample VB code uses an **IDataSource** interface to bind to one such file and set the property:

```
Dim objPD As New CDOWF.ProcessDefinition
Dim objDS As IDataSource

Set objDS = objPD.DataSource

Dim sURL As String
sURL = "file://./backofficestorage" & Environ("USERDNSDOMAIN") & _
       "/Public Folders/MyWorkflowFolder/MyWorkflowDefinition.wfd"
objDS.Open sURL
```

```
Dim sToolName As String
sToolName = "Microsoft Workflow Designer for Exchange 2000
            Server 1.0.27"
objPD.DesignTool = sToolName
objDS.Save
```

Microsoft Exchange Workflow Designer

With all that said, the most efficient tool to leverage the built-in workflow features of Exchange 2000 is Microsoft Workflow Designer for Exchange 2000. It essentially persists your workflow process as a document in the Exchange store. In fact, if you view the public folder where you installed your workflow process, you will notice a **.wfd file**. The workflow designer creates and edits this document to maintain your workflow process definition. The workflow process definition consists of four elements, all of which can be managed through the workflow designer: an action table, a common script URL, a security mode, and an audit trail provider.

The action table is a table of valid state transitions in which the conditions and actions are VBScript routines stored in the common script URL. The workflow engine evaluates the conditions in the table and executes the appropriate actions already discussed. The security mode is categorized as either restricted or privileged, as defined earlier. The audit trail provider is simply a property of the **ProcessDefinition** object used for debugging your workflow application. You can set the audit trail provider to write to the Windows 2000 event log, to a column in the process instance row, or to a column in the workflow folder row.

The workflow designer is a visual tool for constructing a state transition diagram that is automatically translated by the tool into an action table. With the workflow designer you can model the workflow logic, add script actions and conditions to the logic, and save the process definition in a workflow folder.

This tool shares the same user interface as the Access 2000 Workflow Designer. However, the Exchange 2000 version of the designer uses Collaboration Data Objects (CDO) Workflow Objects, which comes with Exchange 2000. When you create a workflow process, the workflow designer creates a set of rules, called a process definition, within a given folder using CDO for workflow.

In addition, the tool creates an event registration that is tied to the CDO workflow event sink. What is an event sink? Events occur when Web Storage System items are saved or deleted, when an information store is starting or stopping, or when a time interval has elapsed. You can register to be notified of these events, through COM event sink classes. The sink class can then respond to these notifications programmatically. In workflow applications, you can have three types of event sinks: those that respond when an item is saved to the workflow folder

(**OnSyncSave**), those that respond when an item is deleted from the workflow folder (**OnSyncDelete**), and those that fire every few minutes (**OnTimer**).

Installation

The Exchange Workflow Designer is part of the Exchange 2000 Software Development Kit (SDK) that comes with the Exchange 2000 installation CD. Its setup program is separate from that of the Exchange 2000 Server itself. You can access the setup program by browsing the installation CD and navigating to **E:\support\SDK\EX2KSDK.MSI**, where "E:" is the CD drive on your computer.

Note: For details on installing the Exchange SDK, see Chapter 2.

Startup

When you first start up the Exchange Workflow Designer, you need to specify the name of the Exchange 2000 server and the folder where you want to install the workflow application in the **Open Folder** dialog box (Figure 15.13). You can select a public folder from the list of available folders in the **Select Exchange Folder** dialog box by hitting the mysterious "**...**" button. The folder needs to be created before you run the workflow designer, and it needs to have the permissions described earlier. For our example, we created a public folder called Bug Flow (see Figure 15.14) to begin developing a bug-tracking workflow application. Hit the **OK** button to get the ball rolling and bring up the workflow designer window.

The Folder Pane **General** Tab

The workflow designer window is divided into two panes: the **Process List** pane on the left and a set of tabbed options (titled **General**), which vary based on the item

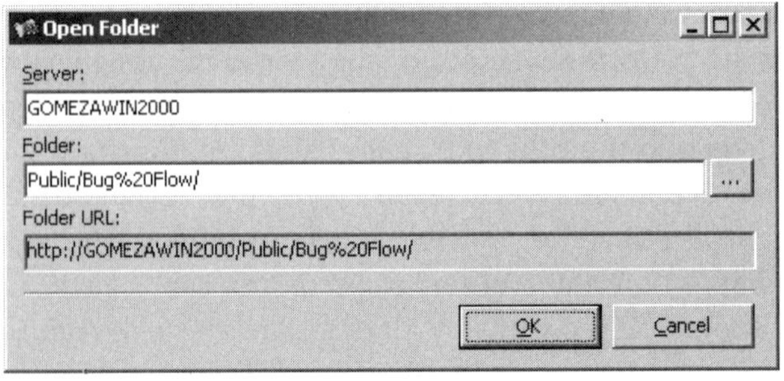

Figure 15.13 Specifying the folder in which to install the workflow designer

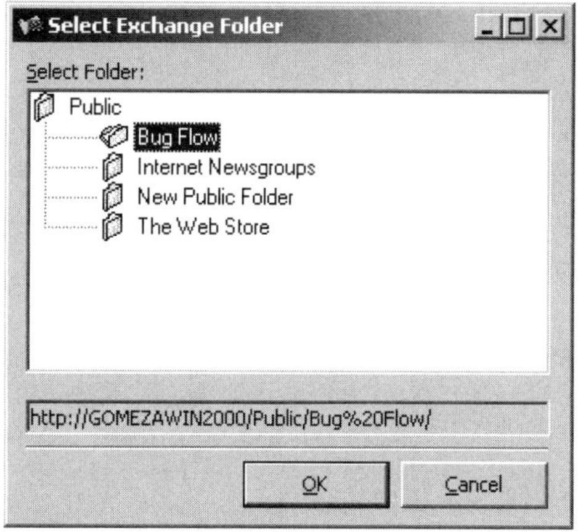

Figure 15.14 Browsing for a public folder

selected in the process list, on the right. As soon as the workflow designer comes up, you will be prompted for additional information about the folder by the **General** tab (see Figure 15.15). The **General** tab consists of the following objects:

- **Folder Name.** A read-only text box that contains the folder's URL.
- **Folder is Workflow Enabled.** A check box indicating whether a default workflow process is registered for this folder.
- **Activated.** A radio button that is available only if the folder is workflow enabled. If a workflow process is inactive, select this option to activate the workflow engine.
- **Deactivated.** A radio button that is available only if the folder is workflow enabled. If a workflow process is active, select this option to deactivate the workflow engine.
- **External Default Workflow Process?** If you have not set a default workflow process for this folder, you can select this check box and use the text box beneath it to specify a workflow process residing in another folder. The trick is that the workflow designer cannot validate the other folder you choose or its workflow process. Therefore, this option is not recommended.
- **Ad-Hoc Allowed?** This check box sets the **AllowAdhoc** property. If this property is set to True, the underlying workflow engine makes it possible for individual items in the folder to utilize workflow processes other than the default workflow process.

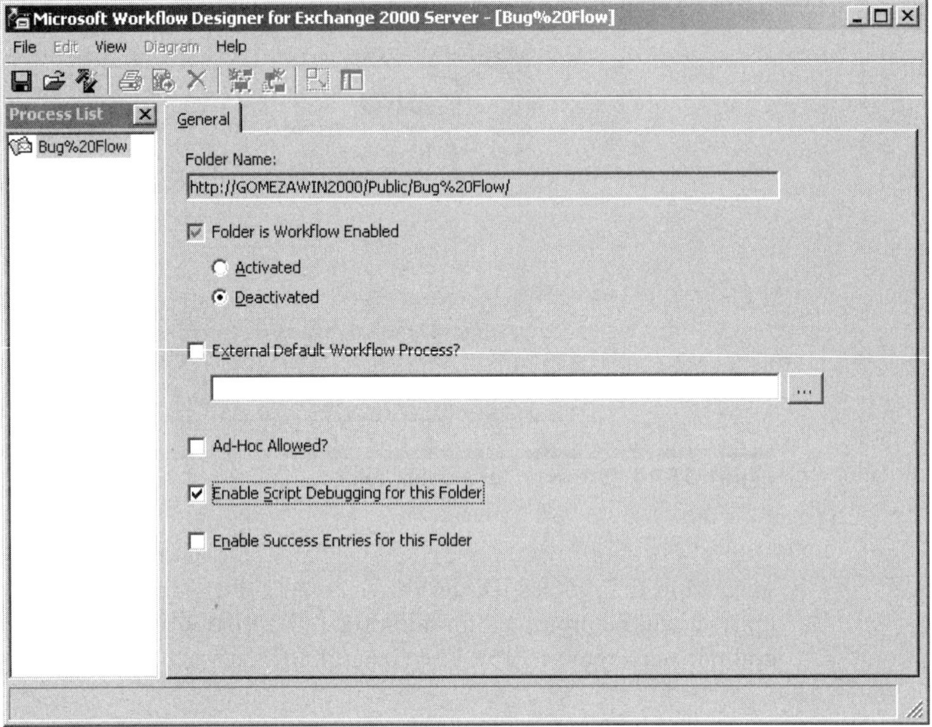

Figure 15.15 The **General** tab prompts for additional information

- **Enable Script Debugging for this Folder.** If this option is enabled, you can use Microsoft Script Debugger on the server console.
- **Enable Success Entries for this Folder.** This option is not explained in the documentation.

Workflow Actions

As mentioned earlier, a workflow process can be modeled in the workflow designer as a combination of states, actions, and transitions. When a new workflow process is created, the developer must define a single state. **Create** and **Delete** actions are added to this state automatically. The **Create** action appears in the workflow process diagram as a transition from the starting block, and the **Delete** action appears as a transition to the ending block.

Seven types of actions, listed in Table 15.3, can be used in a workflow process.

Table 15.3 Workflow Actions

Action	Description
Create	Triggered when a new item is created in the folder.
Enter	Triggered when the transition is made into a given state. The **Enter** action also starts the clock ticking for the **Expiry** action. The time between the **Enter** action and the **Expiry** action is designated in days, hours, or minutes. The minimum duration is 15 minutes.
Exit	Triggered when the transition is made out of a given state.
Delete	Triggered when an item is deleted.
Change	Triggered when an item is changed.
Receive	Triggered when an e-mail item, which is an update to an existing item participating in the workflow process, is received in the folder.
Expiry	Triggered when the time defined for the **Enter** action has elapsed. **Expiry** is a time-based action. For example, if an item remains at a certain state for more than a specified length of time, an action can be triggered to mark that item as overdue.

Each state can be assigned only one **Enter**, **Exit**, **Create**, and **Delete** action, but multiple **Change**, **Expiry**, and **Receive** actions. **Change**, **Expiry**, and **Receive** actions can all be used to create state transitions. A single state can have multiple transitions, but you can have only a single transition between any two states for each action type.

Creating a New Workflow Process

Choose **New Workflow Process** from the **File** menu. You will be prompted for a name for your workflow process (Figure 15.16). Enter a name and hit **OK**. You will now be challenged to come up with a better name than "First State" for the initial state of an item in your workflow process. In our example, a new bug reported into the system will have an initial state of New (see Figure 15.17).

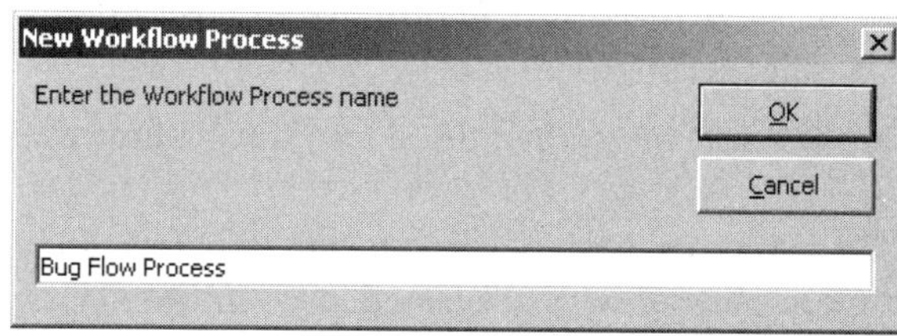

Figure 15.16 Give your workflow process a meaningful name

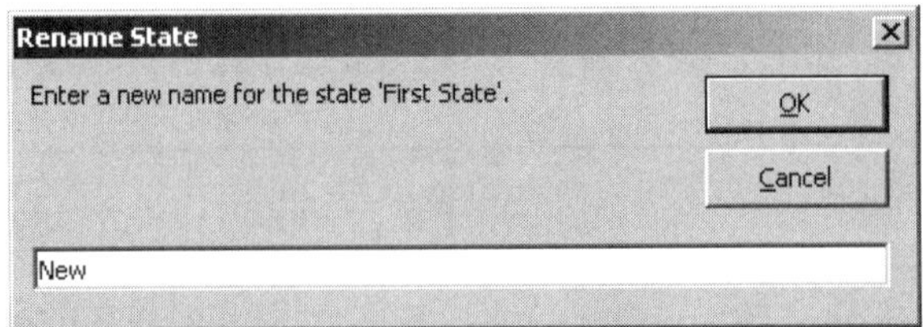

Figure 15.17 Provide a name for each state of the workflow

The Workflow Process Pane Design Tab

You now have access to the three-tab workflow process pane. The **Design** tab (shown in Figure 15.18) displays the workflow diagram and the actions related to the selected state in the diagram. The **Design** tab itself is divided into three working sections: the workflow diagram area, the **Actions List**, and the **Condition Expression/ Action Script Procedure** area. The workflow diagram displays the workflow process as a graphical series of states with actions that link them together. States are represented as boxes, and the actions that cause the transition from state to state are represented as lines with arrows.

Right-clicking on the workflow diagram's background allows you to perform the following actions (Figure 15.19):

- Add a new state to the workflow process with the **Insert State** menu command. When you select a state, the **Actions List** (see Figure 15.18) displays all actions associated with it.
- Expand or shrink the workflow diagram with the **Zoom** menu command. You can expand the diagram up to 200 percent or shrink it to 10 percent of the original size.
- Arrange, expand, center, or print the diagram.

Right-clicking on an object in the workflow diagram allows you to

- Display the **Insert Action** dialog box, where you can add an action to the selected state
- Rename or remove the selected workflow diagram object

The **Actions List** of the **Design** tab (see Figure 15.18) displays all of the actions associated with a selected state in the diagram. The **Condition Expression** text box is the first script to be evaluated and typically is used for data validation. By default, the condition expression returns a value of True. You can modify this

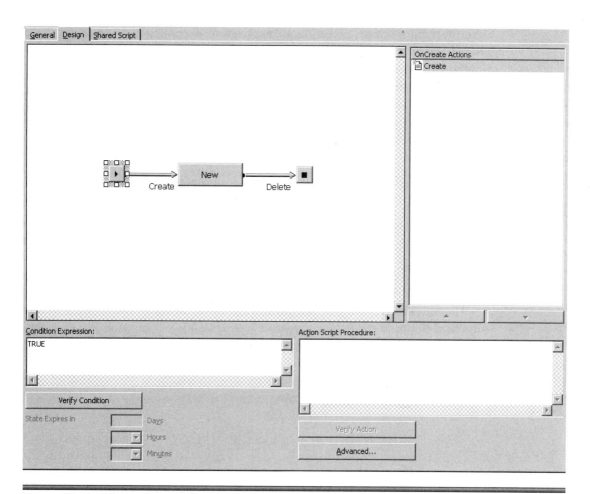

Figure 15.18 The **Design** tab displays the workflow diagram and actions related to the selected state

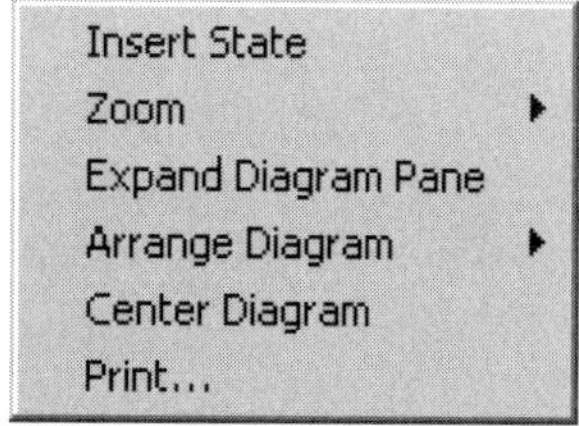

Figure 15.19 Right-clicking on the background brings up a context menu like this

value by typing "False," creating an expression, or calling a function from the **Shared Script** tab to perform a more complex evaluation. If the condition expression returns False, the action and any associated action script procedures are not executed. You can use the **Verify Condition** button (see Figure 15.18) to validate the script in the **Condition Expression** text box and report any errors.

The **State Expires In** settings are enabled only for **Enter** actions and are used to set the expiration time for the **Expiry** action. The **Days** text box sets the time in days, ranging from 0 through 999999 days. The **Hours** drop-down list sets the time in hours, ranging from 0 to 23 hours, and the **Minutes** drop-down list sets the time in minutes.

The **Action Script Procedure** text box is where you insert script code to execute. For example, if you want to send e-mail, post a message, make an appointment, or delete items, all of these activities are accomplished by action script procedures. Action script procedures are executed only if the condition expression returns a value of True. You can use the **Verify Action** button (see Figure 15.18) to validate the script in the **Action Script Procedure** text box and report any errors.

The **Advanced...** button (see Figure 15.18) is used to bring up the **Action Advanced Settings** dialog box shown in Figure 15.20. When a transaction is canceled, the workflow engine fires the **OnAbort** method that runs compensating action

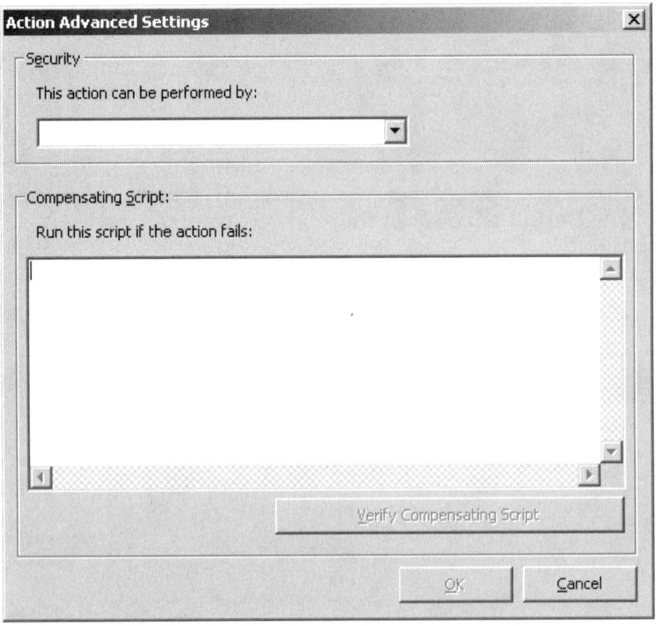

Figure 15.20 The **Action Advanced Settings** dialog box

scripts defined here. You can use the **Verify Compensating Script** button to validate the script in this text box and report any errors.

The Workflow Process Pane General Tab

The **General** tab of the workflow process pane (Figure 15.21) displays information about the selected workflow process and consists of the following:

- **Workflow Process Name.** A read-only text box that displays the file name of the workflow process.
- **Default Workflow Process for this Folder.** A check box indicating whether the selected workflow process is applied to items in the workflow-enabled folder automatically.
- **Run as Privileged?** A check box indicating the level of security for scripts associated with the workflow actions. Recall that scripts can run in either restricted or privileged mode and that you must be a member of the Privileged Workflow Authors role to execute scripts in privileged mode.
- **Advanced.** Clicking the **Advanced...** button displays the **Workflow Process Advanced Settings** dialog box (Figure 15.22). Here **Audit Trail Provider** is a drop-down list of all the audit trail providers installed on the server. Checking the **External Shared Script?** check box allows you to specify a script URL in the text box below it.

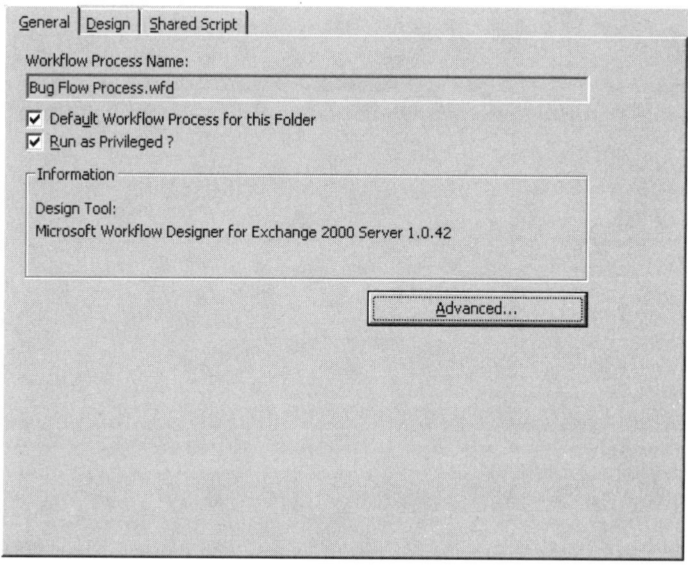

Figure 15.21 The **General** tab displays information about the current workflow

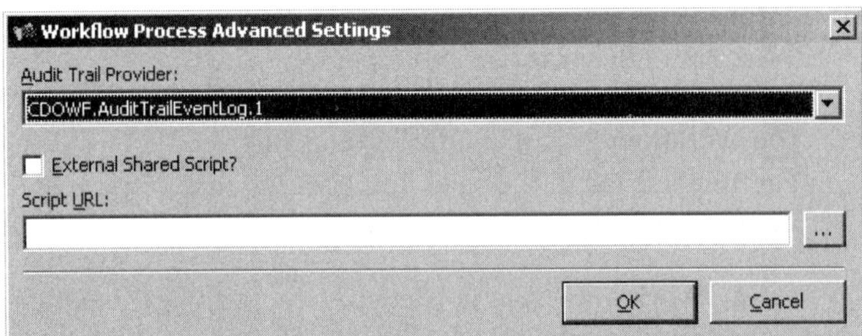

Figure 15.22 The **Workflow Process Advanced Settings** dialog box provides additional settings

> **Note:** At design time, the Exchange Workflow Designer does not check that you have the appropriate permissions to run scripts in privileged mode.

The Workflow Process Pane Shared Script Tab

The **Shared Script** tab (Figure 15.23) should be used when you have a procedure or a function that you want to use several times in your workflow process. You can write all of your code in the code pane and hit the **Verify Script** button to validate

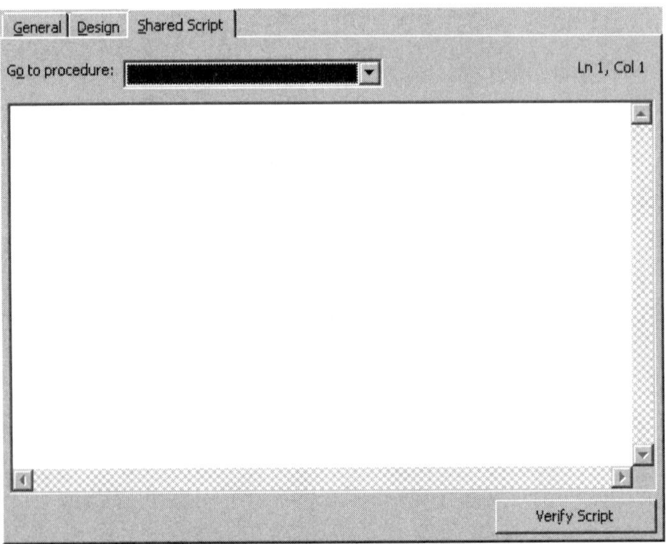

Figure 15.23 The **Shared Script** tab enables you to enter code snippets destined for reuse

it and report any errors. The **Go to procedure** drop-down list helps you navigate the script procedures in the code pane.

XML Support

The workflow designer natively supports exporting the workflow action table as XML and importing and exporting the entire workflow process definition as an XML file. Thus you can share your workflow processes with other applications in a standardized format. Simply go into the **File** menu and select **Import Workflow Process from XML...**, **Export Workflow Process to XML...**, or **Export Action Table to XML....**

Summary

The workflow designer uses CDO Workflow Objects behind the scenes to create, maintain, and register the workflow process. Developers can write their own workflow applications without using the workflow designer by making direct calls to the **ProcessDefinition** object using CDO Workflow Objects and ActiveX Data Objects (ADO 2.5) to create the necessary data bindings. You can also write your own workflow event sink, for calling the workflow engine directly, using the **IProcessInstance** object.

So what does the workflow designer buy the developer? To write your own event sink, you must define an action table, write some script functions or custom COM objects, create a process definition, and register the workflow event sink in the workflow folder. In other words, you save your workflow design as an item in a public folder and create an association between the workflow event sink and system and Web Storage System events in the folder all through some pretty nontrivial code. So go with the flow and try to use the workflow designer whenever possible to save some development time.

Chapter 16

CDO for Exchange Management

CDO for Exchange Management (CDOEXM) is a COM library that allows you to develop tools to manage your Exchange 2000 server, its databases, recipients, and their mailboxes. If we were to draw a loose analogy between Exchange 2000 and SQL Server, then CDOEXM would be comparable to SQL-DMO. SQL-DMO (which stands for SQL Server Distributed Management Objects) exposes the standard internal SQL Server objects to allow for automation of database management tasks. Similarly, CDOEXM allows Exchange administrators to automate tasks such as periodically archiving MDB files, monitoring performance, automatically creating users and their mailboxes, managing data in public folder stores, and even managing e-mail.

This chapter introduces the CDOEXM object model and explores how to use CDOEXM to perform several basic administrative tasks programmatically. Since we use the CDO **Person** object in conjunction with CDOEXM to manage Exchange 2000 recipients, this chapter builds on the lessons learned in Chapter 14, which focused on the role that the CDO **Person** object plays in contact management.

Let's start by looking at some code examples that illustrate the CDOEXM object model. We'll cover a couple of common scenarios, such as gathering information about your system and creating user mailboxes.

Server Management

CDOEXM allows you to perform various *server management* tasks, such as creating storage groups, public and private stores, and top-level folders. The server management objects also enable you to gather information about your environment, as in the example that follows shortly.

In addition to Microsoft CDO for Exchange Management, you'll want to set a reference in your VB project to the Microsoft ActiveX Data Objects 2.5 library and the Microsoft CDO for Exchange 2000 library because you will also need to create objects from these libraries to accomplish most tasks (see Figure 16.1).

Enumerating Storage Groups and Web Storage System Stores

The following code snippet loops through all server properties, storage groups, and stores, displaying relevant properties for your system. This routine is useful for gathering information about an Exchange 2000 environment:

```
Dim objCDOEXMServer As New CDOEXM.ExchangeServer
Dim objCDOEXMStorageGroup As New CDOEXM.StorageGroup
Dim objCDOEXMPubDB As New CDOEXM.PublicStoreDB
Dim objCDOEXMPrivDB As New CDOEXM.MailboxStoreDB
```

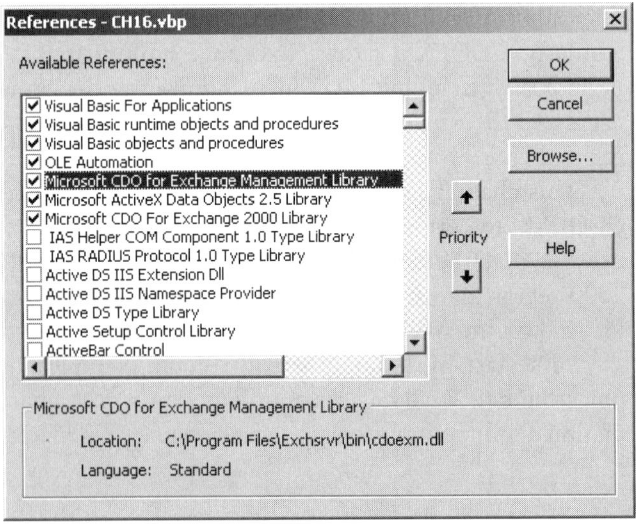

Figure 16.1 Selecting the CDO for Exchange Management library in the **References** dialog box

```
Dim objCDOEXMFolderTree As New CDOEXM.FolderTree

Dim objCDOEXMDS2 As CDOEXM.IDataSource2
Dim sServerName As String

Dim objStorageGroup As Variant
Dim objPublicStore As Variant
Dim objPrivateStore As Variant

Dim n As Long

Set objCDOEXMDS2 = objCDOEXMServer

' Get the name of the current Exchange server
sServerName = Environ("COMPUTERNAME")

' Open an Exchange Server object, passing the local server name
objCDOEXMDS2.Open sServerName

' Enumerate properties
With objCDOEXMServer
    Debug.Print "Name                    = " & .Name
    Debug.Print "ServerType (BE=0, FE=1) = " & .ServerType
    Debug.Print "DirectoryServer         = " & .DirectoryServer
    Debug.Print "ExchangeVersion         = " & .ExchangeVersion
    Debug.Print "DaysBeforeLogFileRemoval = "
        & .DaysBeforeLogFileRemoval

    ' Enumerate fields
    On Error Resume Next
    For n = 1 To .Fields.Count
        Debug.Print .Fields.Item(n).Name & " = "
            & .Fields.Item(n).Value
    Next
End With

' Enumerate storage groups
For Each objStorageGroup In objCDOEXMServer.StorageGroups
    Debug.Print vbCrLf
    Debug.Print "StorageGroup    = " & objStorageGroup & vbCrLf
    objCDOEXMStorageGroup.DataSource.Open objStorageGroup

    ' Enumerate all public stores within the storage group
For Each objPublicStore In objCDOEXMStorageGroup.PublicStoreDBs

    Debug.Print "Public Store    = " & objPublicStore
    objCDOEXMPubDB.DataSource.Open objPublicStore
    Debug.Print "Name            = " & objCDOEXMPubDB.Name & vbCrLf
```

```
        Debug.Print "FolderTree      = " & objCDOEXMPubDB.FolderTree
        objCDOEXMFolderTree.DataSource.Open objCDOEXMPubDB.FolderTree
        Debug.Print "RootFolderURL  = " & objCDOEXMFolderTree.RootFolderURL
        Debug.Print "Name           = " & objCDOEXMFolderTree.Name & vbCrLf

    Next

    ' Enumerate all private stores (mailbox stores) within the storage
    '   group
    For Each objPrivateStore In objCDOEXMStorageGroup.MailboxStoreDBs

        Debug.Print "Mailbox        = " & objPrivateStore
        objCDOEXMPrivDB.DataSource.Open objPrivateStore
        Debug.Print "Name           = " & objCDOEXMPrivDB.Name & vbCrLf

    Next

Next 'storage group

' Clean up
Set objCDOEXMServer = Nothing
Set objCDOEXMStorageGroup = Nothing
Set objCDOEXMPubDB = Nothing
Set objCDOEXMPrivDB = Nothing
Set objCDOEXMFolderTree = Nothing
```

By using the objects contained in this sample code, you can create all sorts of useful tools. Your best bet is to play with the objects to get a better feel for their power.

Since this is a developer reference and not an administrative reference, we will limit our discussion of server management components. The Exchange 2000 SDK contains an excellent reference for the server management components.

Note: Interestingly, it is possible to administer Exchange 2000 using CDOEXM from a remote machine because CDOEXM does not rely on ExOLEDB (as do the other CDO components). CDOEXM instead uses ADSI. Therefore, you are not limited by the "local access only" restriction that befalls the rest of CDO for Exchange 2000.

Recipient Management

CDOEXM also enables you to perform some *recipient management* tasks, such as creating users and moving mailboxes. In addition, the recipient management objects enable you to gather information about your recipient list.

Creating a Mailbox for a User

Our token recipient-based example (which follows) shows how to create a mailbox for a user. To do so, you'll need to specify the LDAP path for the mailbox. An LDAP path is the fully qualified URL to the Exchange Information Store. To find the appropriate path for your environment, you can use either the Active Directory **Sites and Services** MMC, or for even greater control over the Active Directory, you can use the ADSIEdit tool, available in the optional Windows 2000 Support Tools.

```
' Create a user account and mailbox
Dim objCDOPerson As CDO.Person
Dim objCDOEXMMailbox As CDOEXM.IMailboxStore
Dim sFirstName As String
Dim sLastName As String
Dim sAlias As String
Dim sLDAP As String

sFirstName = "George"
sLastName = "Wesolowski"
sAlias = "Wesolowskig"

' LDAP URL to the new user
sLDAP = "LDAP://server/cn=" & sFirstName & " " & sLastName
sLDAP = sLDAP & ",ou=users,dc=domain,dc=local"

' Create the new user account
Set objCDOPerson = New CDO.Person
With objCDOPerson
    .FirstName = sFirstName
    .LastName = sLastName
    .Fields("userAccountControl") = 512 'ADS_UF_NORMAL_ACCOUNT
    .Fields.Update
    .DataSource.SaveTo sLDAP
End With

' Create a new mailbox for the new user
Set objCDOEXMMailbox = objCDOPerson
' First, construct the LDAP path
sLDAP = "LDAP://server/cn=Mailbox Store (server)," & _
    "cn=First Storage Group,cn=InformationStore," & _
    "cn=server,cn=Servers,cn=First Administrative Group," & _
    "cn=Administrative Groups,cn=First Organization," & _
    "cn=Microsoft Exchange,cn=Services,cn=Configuration," & _
    "dc=domain,dc=local"

objCDOEXMMailbox.CreateMailbox sLDAP
```

```
' To set an e-mail address, be sure to disable the Recipient Update
'   Service
    With objCDOPerson
    .Email = "SMTP:" & sAlias & "@exchdom.local"
    .Fields("mailnickname") = sAlias
    .Fields.Update
    .DataSource.Save
End With

' Clean up
Set objCDOEXMMailbox = Nothing
Set objCDOPerson = Nothing
```

The Exchange 2000 SDK contains an excellent reference for the recipient management components, with examples of how to move and delete mailboxes, among many other tasks. Rather than repeating that sample code here, we'll move on to providing a reference.

CDOEXM Reference

Figure 16.2 shows the CDOEXM object model. The next few sections will provide a tour of the major properties and methods of this model. The quick reference format we will use to present this material will be helpful when you are coding tools and, if you so desire, creating custom MMC snap-ins.

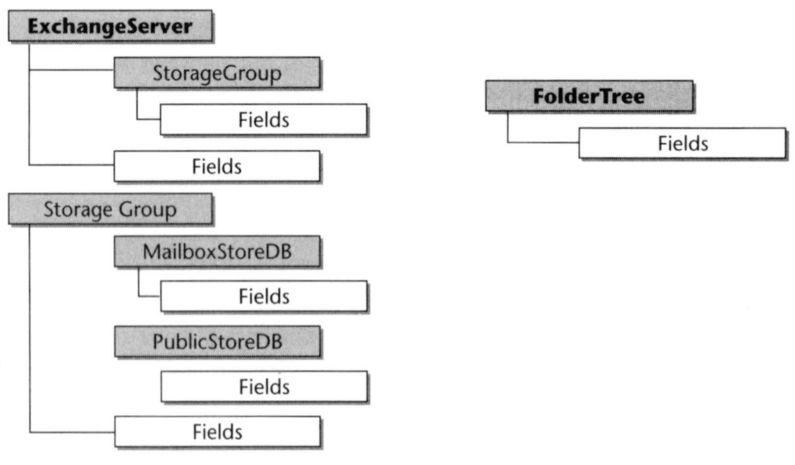

Figure 16.2 The CDO for Exchange Management object model

The ExchangeServer Object

The **ExchangeServer** object encapsulates several properties of an Exchange 2000 server, which are summarized in Table 16.1.

Table 16.1 Properties of the **ExchangeServer** Object

Property Name	Type	Values	Access Level	Description
DataSource	IDataSource2	See **IDataSource2** documentation later in this chapter.	Read-only	Returns the **IDataSource** interface on the object.
DaysBeforeLogFileRemoval	Long	Default is –1 ("No Removal").	Read/write	Gets or sets the number of days that log files are kept on the Exchange server.
DirectoryServer	String	"GOMEZAWIN2000," for example.	Read-only	Returns the domain controller used by services on the local machine.
ExchangeVersion	String	"Version 6.0 (Build 4250.8)," for example.	Read-only	Contains the version of Exchange installed on the server.
Fields	ADODB.Fields		Read-only	Contains the **Fields** collection for the object.
MessageTrackingEnabled	Boolean	True means that message tracking is enabled. That is, the subject will be viewable in the message-tracking logs and in the queue viewer in the Exchange System Manager.	Read/write	Indicates whether message tracking is enabled for the server.
Name	String	"GOMEZAWIN2000," for example.	Read-only	Returns the name of the server.
ServerType	CDOEXM-ServerType	See Table 16.2.	Read/write	Gets or sets the Exchange Server type.
StorageGroups	Variant	A list of URLs.	Read-only	Returns a list of storage groups on the local Exchange server.
SubjectLoggingEnabled	Boolean	Subject logging is enabled when the property is set to True.	Read/write	Indicates whether subject logging and display are enabled for the local Exchange server.

Table 16.2 CDOEXMServerType Values

Name	Value
cdoexmBackEnd	0
cdoexmFrontEnd	1

Table 16.2 summarizes the **CDOEXMServerType** values used in the **ServerType** property. These values indicate whether the Exchange 2000 server is a front-end or back-end server. Front-end servers are visible to HTTP, POP, or IMAP clients. The front-end servers proxy requests to back-end Exchange servers, which function as the actual data stores. Exchange 2000 servers are back-end servers by default.

> **Note:** Changing an Exchange server to a front-end server cannot be undone. See the Exchange 2000 Server documentation for more information.

The GetInterface Method for CDOEXM

The **ExchangeServer** object has one method—the **GetInterface** method—which returns the specified interface. The **GetInterface** method is intended primarily for use in scripting languages (such as VBScript), which do not support interface navigation directly. For example, the following VBScript code uses the **GetInterface** method to return the **IDataSource2** interface of an **ExchangeServer** object:

```
Dim objExchangeServer
Dim objDataSource
Set objExchangeServer = CreateObject("CDOEXM.ExchangeServer")
Set objDataSource = objExchangeServer.GetInterface("IDataSource2")
```

The interface arguments that **GetInterface** can take are defined in CDOEXM by the **CDOEXMInterfaces** constant values summarized in Table 16.3.

To use these in a scripting language (such as VBScript) you must cut and paste the definitions into your code because scripting languages do not recognize library references. Of course, feel free to use them by name as is in VB because they are automatically pulled in when you set the reference to the CDOEXM library in your project.

Table 16.3 CDOEXMInterfaces (Interfaces Supported by CDOEXM)

Name	Value
cdoexmIADs	IADs
cdoexmIDistributionList	IDistributionList
cdoexmIExchangeServer	IExchangeServer
cdoexmIFolderAdmin	IFolderAdmin
cdoexmIFolderTree	IFolderTree
cdoexmIMailboxStore	IMailboxStore
cdoexmIMailboxStoreDB	IMailboxStoreDB
cdoexmIMailRecipient	IMailRecipient
cdoexmIPublicStoreDB	IPublicStoreDB
cdoexmIStorageGroup	IStorageGroup

Note: The reason that this section is titled "The GetInterface Method for CDOEXM" rather than "The GetInterface Method for the ExchangeServer Object" is that the **GetInterface** method is also available in the **FolderTree, MailboxStoreDB, PublicStoreDB,** and **StorageGroup** objects in CDOEXM. Because all the **GetInterface** methods work in exactly the same way, the method is presented here only once; this method allows you to get to any other interface in script code no matter what CDOEXM object you have. Therefore, we will reference this section when introducing the **GetInterface** method in the other CDOEXM objects.

The FolderTree Object

The **FolderTree** object allows you to create and modify top-level folders in Exchange 2000 MDB files. It has only the **GetInterface** method discussed in the previous section. Its properties are summarized in Table 16.4.

Table 16.5 summarizes the **CDOEXMFolderTreeType** values used in the **TreeType** property. They give the programmer a quick flag to check whether the public folder tree is a MAPI public folder tree. As we learned in the Web Storage System SQL discussion in Chapter 7, this is important because you cannot perform a deep traversal on a MAPI public folder tree.

Table 16.4 Properties of the **FolderTree** Object

Property Name	Type	Values	Access Level	Description
DataSource	IDataSource2	See **IDataSource2** documentation later in the chapter.	Read-only	Returns the **IDataSource** interface on the object.
Fields	ADODB.Fields		Read-only	Contains the **Fields** collection for the object
Name	String	"MyTLH," for example.	Read/ write	Returns or sets the name of the folder tree.
RootFolderURL	String	"http:// gomezawin2000. gomezamobile. local/public," for example.	Read-only	Contains the URL of the root folder of the tree.
StoreDBs	Variant	A list of URLs.	Read-only	Returns the list of URLs of public store databases that contain replicas of the folder tree.
TreeType	CDOEXMFolderTreeType	See Table 16.5.	Read-only	Gets the folder type for the folder tree.

Table 16.5 **CDOEXMFolderTreeType** Values

Name	Value	Description
cdoexmGeneralPurpose	0	Non-MAPI public folder tree
cdoexmMAPI	1	MAPI public folder tree
cdoexmNNTPOnly	2	NNTP folder tree

The IDataSource2 Interface

The **IDataSource2** interface allows CDOEXM to open, manage, and delete Exchange-related Active Directory objects. Its properties are summarized in Table 16.6.

The **IDataSource2** methods are summarized in Table 16.7.

Table 16.6 Properties of the **IDataSource2** Object

Property Name	Type	Values	Access Level	Description
ActiveConnection	ADODB.Connection	See the ADO 2.5 documentation.	Read-only	Returns the currently active ADO connection.
IsDirty	Boolean	Set to False whenever the local data is saved back into the bound object.	Read/write	Specifies whether the local data has been changed since the last save.
Source	Object	Any valid object.	Read-only	Contains a reference to the currently bound object.
SourceClass	String	"IBodyPart," for example. If the **SourceClass** and **SourceURL** properties return an empty string, then the object is not currently bound.	Read-only	Returns the name of the interface used to bind the object.
SourceClassURL	String	A valid URL.	Read-only	Returns the URL of the currently bound item within the Active Directory or the Web Storage System.

The IDistributionList Interface

IDistributionList is a simple interface that allows you to control whether or not a distribution list is displayed. It has one Boolean property, **HideDLMembership.** When this property is set to True, it hides the membership list on a distribution list.

The IMailboxStore Interface

The **IMailboxStore** interface provides access to the administrative properties of a mailbox-enabled recipient, as well as methods to create, move, and delete mailboxes. Its administrative properties are summarized in Table 16.8.

Table 16.7 Methods of the **IDataSource2** Object

Method Name	Arguments	Description
Delete	None	Deletes the currently bound object.
MoveToContainer	ContainerURL As String	Moves the currently bound object to the new container specified by the URL.
Open	SourceURL As String, [ActiveConnection As Object], [Mode As ConnectionModeEnum], [CreateOptions As RecordCreateOptionsEnum], [Options As RecordOpenOptionsEnum], [UserName As String], [Password As String]	Binds to and opens the item specified by the URL.
OpenObject	Source As Object, InterfaceName As String	Binds to and opens data from the specified object.
Save	None	Saves data into the currently bound object.
SaveTo	SourceURL As String, [ActiveConnection As Object], [Mode As ConnectionModeEnum], [CreateOptions As RecordCreateOptionsEnum], [Options As RecordOpenOptionsEnum], [UserName As String], [Password As String]	Binds to and saves data into the item with the specified URL.
SaveToContainer	ContainerURL As String, [ActiveConnection As Object], [Mode As ConnectionModeEnum], [CreateOptions As RecordCreateOptionsEnum], [Options As RecordOpenOptionsEnum], [UserName As String], [Password As String]	Binds to and saves data into a new item in the folder or container specified by the URL. The name of the new item is a generated GUID. After successfully executing the method, in the **SourceURL** property you can get the full URL to the new item to which you are currently bound.
SaveToObject	Source As Object, InterfaceName As String	Binds to and saves data into the specified object.

The **IMailboxStore** methods are summarized in Table 16.9.

The IMailRecipient Interface

The **IMailRecipient** interface provides properties and methods to support e-mail to and from contacts. Table 16.10 summarizes the properties.

Table 16.8 Properties of the **IMailboxStore** Object

Property Name	Type	Values	Access Level	Description
DaysBeforeGarbageCollection	Long	The default value is 0.	Read/write	Specifies the number of days that deleted mail is retained before it is permanently deleted.
Delegates	Variant		Read/write	Contains a list of URLs of all users who have "Send On Behalf" right on the mailbox.
EnableStoreDefaults	Boolean	If set to True, only the default store values for storage limits are used. If set to False, the **HardLimit**, **OverQuotaLimit** and **StoreQuota** properties are used.	Read/write	Indicates whether the mailbox should use the quota limits set on the object or the default limits set on the database.
GarbageCollectOnlyAfterBackup	Boolean	If True, deleted messages can be permanently deleted only after the mailbox has been backed up. If False (the default value), deleted messages can be deleted permanently at any time.	Read/write	Specifies whether deleted messages can be permanently deleted only after the mailbox has been backed up.
HardLimit	Long	Maximum mailbox size in kilobytes (K).	Read/write	Specifies the maximum size of the mailbox, over which sending and receiving is restricted.
HomeMDB	String	A dn value, meaning a directory of the form **LDAP://server/cn=first tree item.**	Read-only	Specifies the directory URL of the database on which this recipient has a mailbox.
OverQuotaLimit	Long	Maximum mailbox size in kilobytes (K).	Read/write	Specifies the maximum size of a mailbox before sending messages is suspended.
OverrideStoreGarbage Collection	Boolean	If set to True, the store is prevented from permanently deleting messages. If set to False (the default value), the store can permanently delete messages.	Read/write	Defines whether the store will be prevented from deleting messages.

Continued on next page.

Table 16.8 Properties of the **IMailboxStore** Object *(continued)*

Property Name	Type	Values	Access Level	Description
RecipientLimit	Long	The default value is –1, meaning that there is no limit.	Read/write	Specifies the maximum number of recipients to which a message from this mailbox can be sent.
StoreQuota	Long	The recipient will get warning messages when this limit has been exceeded.	Read/write	Specifies the maximum size (in kilobytes) allowed for the mailbox.

Table 16.11 lists the **CDOEXMDeliverAndRedirect** values used in the **ForwardingStyle** property.

Table 16.12 lists the **CDOEXMRestrictedAddressType** values used in the **RestrictedAddresses** property.

The **IMailRecipient** interface has only two methods (see Table 16.13).

The MailboxStoreDB Interface

The **MailboxStoreDB** interface defines an object for managing a mailbox store of a single recipient. Its properties are summarized in Table 16.14.

Table 16.15 lists the **CDOEXMStoreDBStatus** values used in the **Status** property.

The methods of the **MailboxStoreDB** object are listed in Table 16.16.

Table 16.9 Methods of the **IMailboxStore** Object

Method Name	Arguments	Description
CreateMailbox	HomeMDBURL As String	Creates a mailbox at the specified URL. Configures the associated directory object to be mailbox enabled.
DeleteMailbox	None	Deletes a mailbox by configuring the associated directory object not to be mailbox enabled.
MoveMailbox	HomeMDBURL As String	Moves a mailbox to the specified URL.

Table 16.10 Properties of the **IMailRecipient** Object

Property Name	Type	Values	Access Level	Description
Alias	String	For example, for the e-mail address **gomeza@plural.com**, "gomeza" is the alias.	Read/write	Contains the e-mail alias of the recipient.
AutoGenerateE-mailAddresses	Boolean	If set to True, the Recipient Update Service automatically generates a default e-mail address for the recipient.	Read/write	Indicates whether the Recipient Update Service should perform updates to the recipient.
ForwardingStyle	CDOEXMDe-liverAndRedirect	See Table 16.11.	Read/write	Specifies whether the mail for the recipient is also forwarded to another address.
ForwardTo	String	"jamisons@plural.com," for example.	Read/write	Specifies the URL to which e-mail should be forwarded.
HideFromAd-dressBook	Boolean	If set to True, the address is not displayed in the address book. The default value is False, which means that the address is displayed in the address book.	Read/write	Indicates whether the recipient's address should be displayed in the address book.
IncomingLimit	Long	The default value is –1, which indicates no limit.	Read/write	Specifies the maximum size, in kilobytes (K), of a message that can be sent to the recipient.
OutgoingLimit	Long	The default value is –1, which indicates no limit.	Read/write	Specifies the maximum size, in kilobytes (K), of a message that can be sent from the recipient.
ProxyAddresses	Variant	smtp:proxy1@somewhere.plural.com SMTP:proxy2@somewhere.plural.com x400:c=us;a= ;p=Domain;o=First Organization;s=Surname;g=Name;	Read/write	Returns a variant array of proxy addresses for the recipient.

Continued on next page.

Table 16.10 Properties of the **IMailRecipient** Object *(continued)*

Property Name	Type	Values	Access Level	Description
RestrictedAddresses	CDOEXMRestrictedAddressType	See Table 16.12.	Read/write	Returns an object of type **RestrictedAddress** from which to accept or reject messages. Used in conjunction with the **RestrictedAddressList** property.
RestrictedAddressList	Variant		Read/write	Returns a variant array of addresses from which to accept or reject messages. Used in conjunction with the **RestrictedAddresses** property.
SMTPEmail	String	"gomeza@plural.com," for example.	Read/write	Contains the primary SMTP address used for the recipient.
TargetAddress	String	Set and cleared using the **MailEnable** and **MailDisable** methods.	Read-only	Specifies the address to which mail sent to the recipient should be delivered.

X400Email	String	c=us;
		a= ;
		p=First Organization;
		o=Exchange;
		s=Administrator;
			Read/write	Specifies the X.400 address used for the recipient.

Table 16.11 **CDOEXMDeliverAndRedirect** Values

Name	Value	Description
cdoexmDeliverToBoth	1	Deliver mail to the recipient and the address specified in the **ForwardTo** property.
cdoexmRecipientOrForward	0	Deliver mail to the alternate e-mail address specified in the **ForwardTo** property only when mail cannot be delivered to the recipient.

Table 16.12 **CDOEXMRestrictedAddressType** Values

Name	Value	Description
cdoexmAccept	0	Accept mail only from the addresses listed in the **RestrictedAddresses** property.
cdoexmReject	1	Reject mail from the addresses listed in the **RestrictedAddresses** property.

Table 16.13 Methods of the **IMailRecipient** Object

Method Name	Arguments	Description
MailDisable	None	Disables mail for a user, folder, contact, or group. The method clears the **ProxyAddresses**, **SMTPEmail**, **X400Email**, and **TargetAddress** properties.
MailEnable	Optional TargetMailAddress As String	Enables mail for a user, folder, contact, or group. Sets the **ProxyAddresses**, **SMTPEmail**, and **X400Email** properties. **TargetAddress** is set if the object type is not a group.

Table 16.14 Properties of the **MailboxStoreDB** Object

Property Name	Type	Values	Access Level	Description
DataSource	IDataSource2	See the **IDataSource2** documentation earlier in the chapter.	Read-only	Returns the **IDataSource** interface on the object.
DaysBeforeDeletedMailbox-Cleanup	Long	The default value is –1, which means that there is no limit and deleted mailboxes are removed immediately.	Read/write	Gets or sets the number of days that deleted mailboxes are retained in the Exchange database.
DaysBeforeGarbageCollection	Long	The default value is –1, which means that there is no limit and deleted items are removed immediately.	Read/write	Gets or sets the number of days before deleted items are permanently deleted from the Exchange server.
DBPath	String		Read-only	Specifies the path to the Exchange database file.
Enabled	Boolean	If set to True, the store will be mounted at startup.	Read/write	Indicates whether the store should be mounted at startup.

Continued on next page.

Table 16.14 Properties of the **MailboxStoreDB** Object *(continued)*

Property Name	Type	Values	Access Level	Description
Fields	ADODB. Fields		Read-only	Returns the ADO **Fields** collection for the object.
GarbageCollectOn-lyAfterBackup	Boolean	If set to True, items in the store that have not been backed up cannot be permanently deleted.	Read/ write	Prevents permanent deletion of items from the store unless they have been backed up.
HardLimit	Long	Maximum mailbox size in kilobytes (K).	Read/ write	Specifies the maximum mailbox size, over which sending and receiving is restricted.
Name	String		Read/ write	Sets or gets the name of the mailbox.
OfflineAddressList	String		Read/ write	Contains the location of the offline address list for mailboxes on this database.
OverQuotaLimit	Long	Maximum mailbox size in kilobytes (K).	Read/ write	Specifies the maximum mailbox size before sending messages is suspended.
PublicStoreDB	String		Read/ write	Specifies the default public store path for mailboxes on this database.
SLVPath	String		Read/ write	Specifies the path to the Exchange streaming database file.
Status	CDOEXM-StoreDBStatus	See Table 16.15.	Read-only	Returns the status of the mailbox: online, offline, mounting, or dismounting.
StoreQuota	Long	The recipient will get warning messages when this limit has been exceeded. A value of 0 indicates that there is no limit.	Read/ write	Specifies the maximum size, in kilobytes, allowed for the mailbox.

Table 16.15 **CDOEXMStoreDBStatus** Values

Name	Value	Description
cdoexmDismounting	3	The database is being dismounted.
cdoexmMounting	2	The database is being mounted.
cdoexmOffline	1	The database is offline.
cdoexmOnline	0	The database is mounted and running.

The PublicStoreDB Interface

The **PublicStoreDB** interface gives you the ability to create, modify, and delete public stores. Table 16.17 summarizes its properties.

As you've seen, there is a considerable amount of overlap between the **MailboxStoreDB** and **PublicStoreDB** objects. It is not surprising, then, that the methods to the two are identical (see Table 16.16).

The StorageGroup Interface

The **StorageGroup** interface defines an object for managing groups of private or public stores. Table 16.18 lists its properties.

Table 16.19 lists the **StorageGroup** methods.

Table 16.16 Methods of the **MailboxStoreDB** and **PublicStoreDB** Objects

Method Name	Arguments	Description
Dismount	Optional Timeout As Long	Dismounts the mailbox store. The mailbox store can be dismounted even if the mailbox is enabled. The mailbox will automatically be mounted when the server is restarted.
GetInterface	Interface As String	Returns the specified interface. For details, see the section titled The GetInterface Method for CDOEXM earlier in the chapter.
Mount	Optional Timeout As Long	Mounts the mailbox store.
MoveDataFiles	DBPath As String, SLVPath As String	Allows you to change the path for the mailbox MDB and stream files. There is a third **Flags** parameter, which is reserved for future use. You must dismount the mailbox store before moving mailbox files.

Table 16.17 Properties of the **PublicStoreDB** Object

Property Name	Type	Values	Access Level	Description
DataSource	IDataSource2	See the **IDataSource2** documentation earlier in the chapter.	Read-only	Returns the **IDataSource** interface on the object.
DaysBeforeGarbage-Collection	Long	The default value is –1, which means that there is no limit and deleted items are removed immediately.	Read/write	Gets or sets the number of days before deleted items are permanently deleted from the Exchange server.
DaysBeforeItem-Expiration	Long	A value of 0 means that there is no expiration.	Read/write	Returns the age limit, in days, for folders in the store.
DBPath	String		Read-only	Specifies the path to the Exchange database file.
Enabled	Boolean	If set to True, the store will be mounted at startup.	Read/write	Indicates whether the store should be mounted at startup.
Fields	ADODB.Fields	See the ADO 2.5 documentation.	Read-only	Returns the ADO **Fields** collection for the object.
FolderTree	String		Read/write	Specifies the URL of the public folder tree associated with the database.
GarbageCollectOn-lyAfterBackup	Boolean	If set to True, items in the store that have not been backed up cannot be permanently deleted.	Read/write	Prevents permanent deletion of items from the store unless they have been backed up.
HardLimit	Long	Maximum mailbox size in kilobytes (K).	Read/write	Specifies the maximum mailbox size, over which sending and receiving is restricted.
ItemSizeLimit	Long	A value of 0 means that there is no limit.	Read/write	Specifies the maximum size of a message in kilobytes.
Name	String		Read/write	Sets or gets the name of the mailbox.

Table 16.17 Properties of the **PublicStoreDB** Object *(continued)*

Property Name	Type	Values	Access Level	Description
SLVPath	String		Read/ write	Specifies the path to the Exchange streaming database file.
Status	CDOEXM-StoreDBStatus	See Table 16.15.	Read-only	Returns the status of the mailbox: online, offline, mounting, or dismounting.
StoreQuota	Long	The recipient will get warning messages when this limit has been exceeded. A value of 0 indicates that there is no limit.	Read/ write	Specifies the maximum size, in kilobytes, allowed for the mailbox.

Table 16.18 Properties of the **StorageGroup** Object

Property Name	Type	Values	Access Level	Description
Circular-Logging	Boolean	If set to True, limits the size of the log file by overwriting the oldest logs once a limit has been reached.	Read/ write	Prevents log files from growing indefinitely.
DataSource	IDataSource2	See the **IDataSource2** documentation earlier in the chapter.	Read-only	Returns the **IDataSource** interface on the object.
Fields	ADODB.Fields	See the ADO 2.5 documentation.	Read-only	Returns the ADO **Fields** collection for the object.
LogFilePath	String		Read-only	Gets the transaction log path.
MailboxStore-DBs	Variant	Array of strings.	Read-only	Contains a list of mailbox store databases in the storage group.
Name	String		Read/ write	Gets or sets the name of the storage group.
PublicStore-DBs	String	Array of strings.	Read/ write	Contains a list of public store databases in the storage group.
SystemFile-Path	String		Read-only	Gets the system file path.
ZeroDatabase	Boolean		Read/ write	Indicates whether deleted database pages should be zeroed out.

Table 16.19 Methods of the **StorageGroup** Object

Method Name	Arguments	Description
GetInterface	Interface As String	Returns the specified interface. For details, see the section titled The GetInterface Method for CDOEXM earlier in the chapter.
MoveLogFiles	LogFilePath As String	Changes the log file path, which is just a directory in the file system. For new objects, the method sets the initial value of the **LogFilePath** property. For an existing object, the path can be changed only if you are on the local machine. Note that there is an optional second parameter (**Flags**), which has been reserved for future use.
MoveSystemFiles	SystemFilePath	Changes the system file path, which is just a directory in the file system. For new objects, the method sets the initial value of the **SystemFilePath** property. For an existing object, the path can be changed only if you are on the local machine. Note that there is an optional second parameter (**Flags**), which has been reserved for future use.

Summary

CDO for Exchange Management (CDOEXM) is a COM library that allows you to develop tools to manage your Exchange 2000 server and its related objects. In this chapter we discussed two main types of management tasks: server management and recipient management. Server management enables you to manage storage groups, databases, and other aspects of your server configuration. Recipient management enables you to create users, mailboxes, and other recipient types. CDOEXM enables Exchange administrators and developers alike to automate tasks and gather configuration information.

Part V

Additional Exchange 2000 Topics

Chapter 17

XML

Originally this chapter was going to be a long-winded explanation of XML and how to use it when building Exchange 2000 applications. Then we decided that there's already enough hype surrounding XML, as well as a plethora of books on the subject, so we cut the chapter down to a couple of short examples. The examples show how XML is used in Exchange 2000, how to use it as a parameter-passing scheme, and how to use XMLHTTP to send a WebDAV request from within Internet Explorer directly to Exchange 2000 and then have the browser display it natively.

Quick-and-Dirty XML Lesson

XML stands for eXtensible Markup Language, which is a standard for marking up data. XML is powerful because it is simple, interoperable, and open. It allows you to keep your data and presentation logic separate. Let's dive right in to an example.

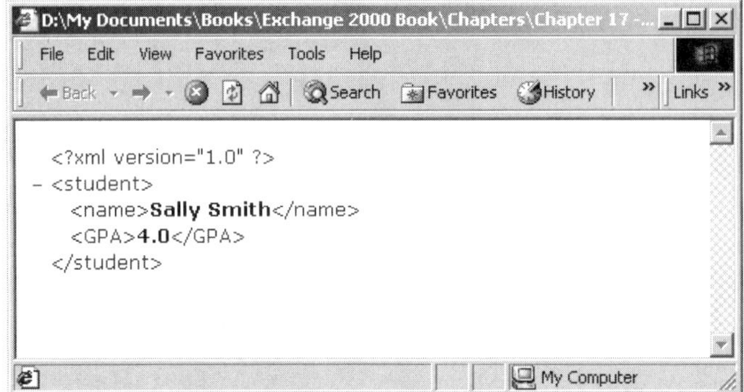

Figure 17.1 Internet Explorer 5 recognizes XML-formatted data and allows you to collapse and expand its layers

XML Example

Here's a simple XML example to get you started. We use the **<?XML ?>** tag to denote our version of XML. Next we define tag pairs (**<>** and **</>**) to denote **name/value** property pairs:

```
<?xml version="1.0"?>
<student>
    <name>Sally Smith</name>
    <GPA>4.0</GPA>
</student>
```

This example shows a student named Sally Smith and two properties associated with her (**name** and **GPA**). If we save this text with an extension of **.xml** and open it using Internet Explorer 5, the browser will recognize the format and render it appropriately (Figure 17.1). That's the basics. (We said we'd be brief!)

How XML Is Used in Exchange 2000

Internally, Exchange 2000 uses several formats for storing data. One of these formats is XML. Exchange 2000 uses XML for things like schema definitions, for certain properties of items in the Web Storage System, for returning information from WebDAV requests, in search and lock request details, and of course in any custom applications written by you, the developer. You can also use the Web Storage System to store XML documents, eXtensible Style Language (XSL) documents, and HTML files.

Exchange 2000 stores property information for contacts and calendar information in XML format. Here's some sample contact information:

```
<D:prop xmlns:D="DAV"
        xmlns:C="urn:schemas:contacts:">
    <D:href>http://mysrv/exchange/jamisons/
        Contacts/jamisons.eml</D:href>
    <C:fileas>Jamison, Scott</C:fileas>
    <C:email1>jamisons@plural.com</C:email1>
    <C:title>Managing Associate</C:title>
    <C:department>Development</C:department>
    <C:l>Boston</C:l>
</D:prop>
```

Calendar information is stored in this way as well:

```
<D:prop xmlns:D="DAV"
        xmlns:C="urn:schemas:calendar:"
        xmlns:H="urn:schemas:httpmail:">
    <D:uri>http://mysrv/exchange/jamisons/
     Calendar/appt.eml</D:uri>
    <H:subject>Team Meeting</H:subject>
    <C:dtstart>20011010T0400</C:dtstart>
    <C:dtend>20011010T0500</C:dtend>
    <C:busystatus>BUSY</C:busystatus>
</D:prop>
```

Now that we've seen some ways in which Exchange 2000 uses XML, let's request it using Internet Explorer 5 and WebDAV. The next section shows us how.

Using a Rich Browser Such as Internet Explorer 5

Internet Explorer 5 (IE5) and later versions enable you to use XML and browser development tools against Exchange 2000 Server. Because IE5 renders XML data natively, you can stream information directly to the client for formatting.

As we saw in Chapter 4, you can use the **XMLHTTPRequest** object to access data in the Web Storage System using the HTTP/WebDAV protocol. In this chapter we'll make those requests directly from a Web page in Internet Explorer.

Retrieving XML with XMLHTTP

The following example shows how you can construct the body of an HTTP/WebDAV **PROPFIND** request against a direct Exchange URL:

```
<html>
<head>
<title>Get Contents of Folder</title>
</head>
<script language=vbscript>
Dim xmlDoc
Sub cmdGo_OnClick()
    Dim strURL, strPropReq
    ' strURL should be something like "http://jamisondc/public/
    '                                        documents/"
    strURL = txtURL.value

    ' Build the string indicating which properties to return
    strPropReq = "<?xml version='1.0'?>"
    strPropReq = strPropReq & "<d:propfind xmlns:d='DAV:'>"
    strPropReq = strPropReq & "<d:prop>"
    strPropReq = strPropReq & "<d:displayname/>"
    strPropReq = strPropReq & "<d:creationdate/>"
    strPropReq = strPropReq & "</d:prop>"
    strPropReq = strPropReq & "</d:propfind>"

    With CreateObject("microsoft.xmlhttp")
        .Open "PROPFIND", strURL, True
        .setRequestHeader "Content-type:", "text/xml"

        ' Return only the contents of a folder
        .setRequestHeader "Depth", "1,noroot"

        ' Send the XML body string
        .send (strPropReq)

        ' Write out the response
        responsehere.innerText = .responseText
    End With
End Sub
</script>

<body>

<h2>Get Contents of Folder Using XMLHTTP</h2>
<BR>
<p>Enter a URL, something like http://jamisondc/public/documents/</p>
```

```
<p><input type="text" width=100 name="txtURL"></p>
<p><input type="button" value="Go" name="cmdGo"></p>
<p/>
<div id=responsehere/>
</body>
</html>
```

Using XML to Pass Recordset Data

While we're on the topic of XML, there's one more thing we want to recommend. When you create COM interfaces for your business components, one way to format and return data is through XML. For example, a function signature might look like this:

```
GetFolderContents(FolderURL as String, Depth as Long) as String
```

In this way you pass back a string, which is actually an XML stream. As a result, marshaling is easy and platform neutral. You can even take it one step further by formatting your input parameters as XML:

```
GetFolderContents(InputXML as String) as String
```

As you'll see in the "gradebook 2001" example introduced in Chapter 21, we used this XML technique to return data to our business components and to our ASP pages.

Summary

This chapter provided a brief introduction to XML and introduced places where XML can be used in Exchange 2000 applications. We make use of XML in our sample application (gradebook 2001), so refer to Chapter 21 for more uses and explanations of XML.

Chapter 18

Accessing the Web Storage System Using the Installable File System

There's more than one way to access the Web Storage System. This versatility is due to the fact that the Web Storage System plays many roles. It is a database technology introduced with the Windows 2000 operating system that you can use to store, share, and manage many types of data. For example, you can store e-mail messages, Web content, multimedia files, and Office documents all together in the Web Storage System. It is organized as a hierarchy of folders much like a traditional file system in which each folder can contain any number of items, including other folders. It combines the features and functionality of the file system, the Web, and a collaboration server all in a single repository for storing, accessing, and managing information, as well as building and running applications.

A developer can access items and item properties in the Web Storage System through the Exchange OLE DB provider, which enables the use of Microsoft ActiveX Data Objects (ADO) 2.5 (see Chapters 7 and 8) and Collaboration Data Objects (CDO) for Exchange 2000 (see Chapters 10 through 16) in server-side applications, including Active Server Pages (ASP), COM+ components, and Web Storage System event sinks (see Chapter 9). A developer can access items and item properties in the Web Storage System using the HyperText Transfer Protocol (HTTP) enhanced through the WebDAV specification (see Chapter 4) using eXtensible Markup Language (XML; see Chapter 17).

A developer can also access items using the Microsoft Win32 file APIs because all Exchange 2000 private and public stores are now available through the operating system's native file system. This chapter explores the technology that makes this accessibility possible and gives examples of how to use the Win32 APIs to access items.

■ The M: Drive

With Exchange 5.5 and earlier releases, all Exchange data were squirreled away in a proprietary database that a user could manipulate really only from within Exchange itself, through an Exchange client (such as Microsoft Outlook), or programmatically through the Collaboration Data Objects (CDO) 1.21 API or MAPI. With Exchange 2000, all Exchange data is now stored in either the Web Storage System or the Active Directory. The Windows 2000 Active Directory contains information about users, groups, organizations, and services in an enterprise, including which users have Exchange mailboxes on the system and what their e-mail addresses are. Exchange 2000 uses the Web Storage System to store the items that users place in their private or public Exchange stores.

As Figure 18.1 shows, Exchange 2000 data saved in the Web Storage System appears in your standard Windows Explorer just like anything else saved on your

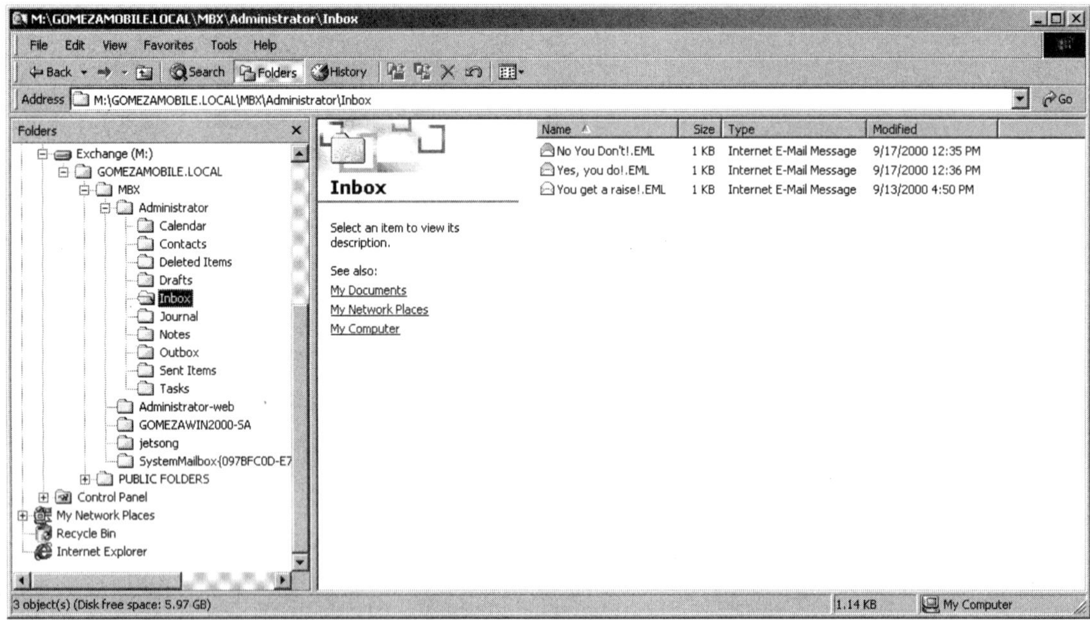

Figure 18.1 Exchange 2000 e-mail messages in the Web Storage System

file system (assuming you are using the Exchange server machine directly). In this figure we are actually using a regular Windows 2000 Explorer to view the Administrator's inbox, represented as **M:\GOMEZAMOBILE.LOCAL\MBX\Administrator\Inbox** in the file system. We can see three messages in the inbox, each with a **.EML** extension. This extension denotes an Internet E-Mail Message file type as specified by the RFC 822 document. The Web Storage System assumes that any item with a **.EML** extension contains a message. Whenever an item with this extension is saved in the Web Storage System, the Web Storage System parses the message content stream and sets the various messaging-related fields in the schema (e.g., **urn:schemas:httpmail:subject**). The message stream is then always synchronized with the messaging fields.

Contrast the Windows Explorer view of the inbox items with the view from within Outlook 2000, shown in Figure 18.2. You should see the same items navigating through the folders in Outlook as you do navigating in Windows Explorer.

Now then, what exactly is the M: drive? Well, first of all it is a virtual drive. If you were to shut down the Microsoft Exchange Information Store service, you would find that the M: drive and all of its files and folders would no longer be accessible. We'll discuss why in the next section.

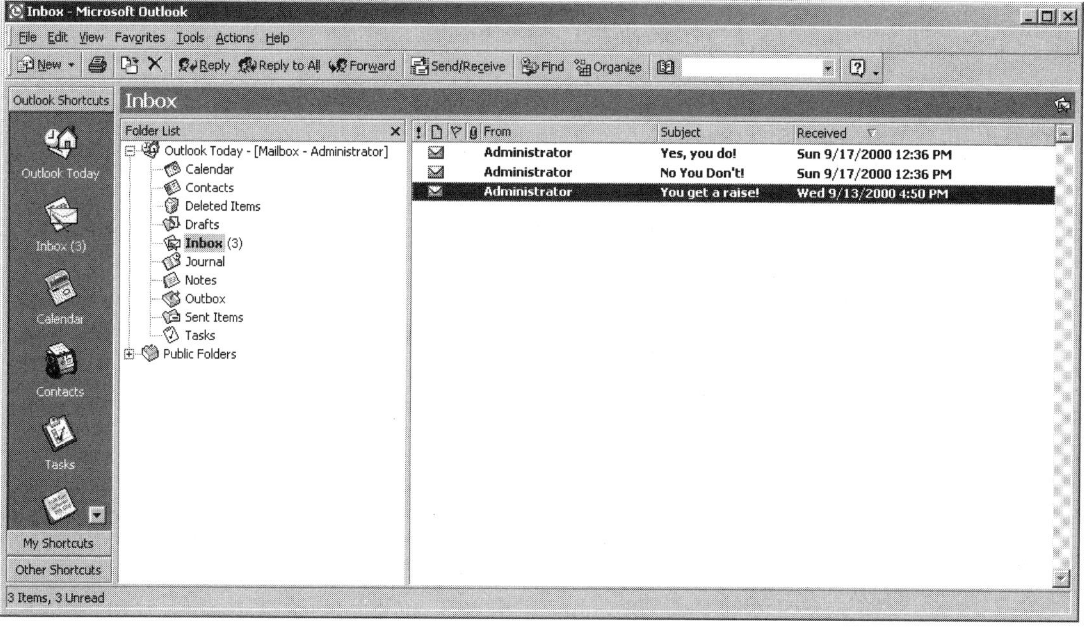

Figure 18.2 Exchange 2000 e-mail messages displayed in Outlook 2000

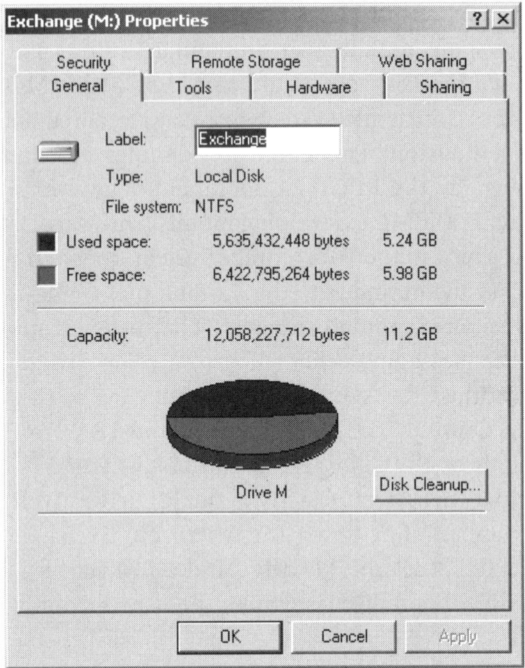

Figure 18.3 Sample Exchange 2000 M: drive properties

Another giveaway that the M: drive is a virtual drive is the similarity between what you get when you right-click on it in Windows Explorer and select **Properties** (see Figure 18.3) and what you get when you right-click on the drive where you have Exchange 2000 installed and select **Properties** (see Figure 18.4).

Note that values in the **Used space**, **Free space**, and **Capacity** fields are identical between the drives. The reason is that they are the same physical drive. Exchange 2000 is displaying the Exchange items physically stored in the C: drive as a logical folder hierarchy made up of mailboxes and public folders called the M: drive.

Note: The Exchange Installable File System virtual drive does not have to be the M: drive. In fact, it can be any unused drive letter on the server. If the letter M is already used, Exchange will use the next available letter in the alphabet, so avoid hard-coding M as the drive letter in any production code.

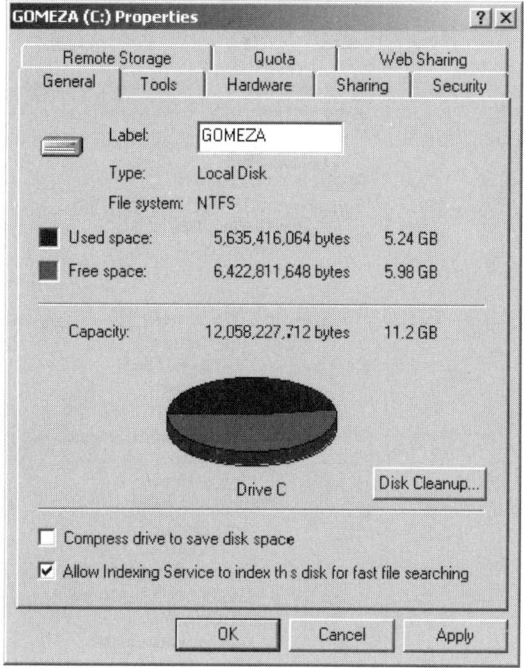

Figure 18.4 Sample C: drive properties (the same drive where Exchange 2000 is installed)

To inspect Exchange items on the M: drive, you must be logged into the Exchange Server as the user whose mailbox you are inspecting *or* as an Exchange "super user." Figure 18.1 was captured while we were logged on as the Administrator account. Note that we can see only the private mailbox folders, including the **Inbox**, under the Administrator. In Figure 18.5, however, we were logged in as an Exchange "super user." Note that now we can see everyone's private mailbox folders. Of course, since this right provides access to everyone's items, it should not be granted to everyone!

Note: For information on how to set up this "super user," see Chapter 9.

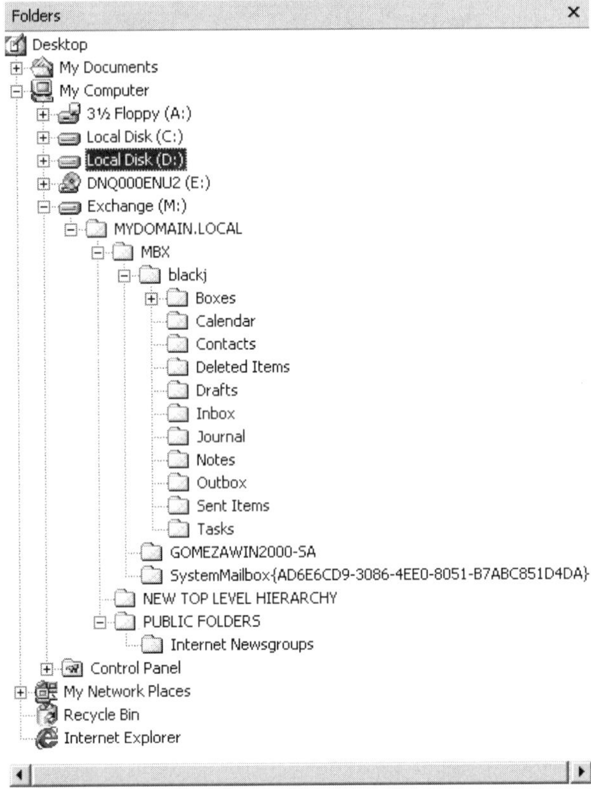

Figure 18.5 What the Exchange "super user" can see in the Web Storage System

■ The Exchange Installable File System

The Exchange Installable File System (ExIFS) is the Exchange 2000 component responsible for mapping the virtual M: drive and allowing access to the Exchange Information Store through the file system. ExIFS provides access to the Exchange Information Store through Windows Explorer, command prompt access, and even Win32 file system API access.

Each Web store (since there can be several on a single host) exists as a file folder mounted under the M: drive of the local computer. These stores can be shared out to other machines just like standard file system folders (we will say more about M: drive sharing later in this chapter). The M: drive itself is automatically mapped to **BackOfficeStorage**. So you can access ExIFS remotely by mapping a drive to **\\<servername>\BackOfficeStorage**, where "<servername>" is the name of the server with the Web store. The ExIFS hierarchy starts with two folders: **MBX** and **Public Folders**.

Public Folders represents the standard public folders, which can be seen through Outlook 2000. **MBX** is the root for all mailboxes in Exchange 2000. Items in **Public Folders** can be enumerated with the standard **DIR** command and manipulated through other file system operations, such as **COPY** and **DELETE**. The same holds true for items under **MBX**, provided you have access permissions as either the Exchange "super user" or the owner of the mailbox.

All standard message items end with **.EML** extensions, and the message stream can be seen through the **TYPE** command. In the command prompt session that follows, we navigated to the **NewFolder** folder under **Public Folders** using a simple **CD** command. We were then able to see the contents of the folder through a **DIR** command. We then picked one of the messages and executed the **TYPE** command to see it:

```
M:\GOMEZAMOBILE.LOCAL\Public Folders\NewFolder>dir
   Volume in drive M is Exchange
   Volume Serial Number is 00A9-8AC7

   Directory of M:\GOMEZAMOBILE.LOCAL\Public Folders\NewFolder

09/18/2000 06:21p   <DIR>      .
09/18/2000 06:21p   <DIR>      ..
06/22/2000 11:58a          31,301 Welcome to Microsoft Outlook 2000!.EML
06/22/2000 01:12p          642 MyMessage.EML
06/22/2000 01:21p          810 OurEmail.EML
        3 File(s)     32,753 bytes
        2 Dir(s)     6,413,411,328 bytes free

M:\GOMEZAMOBILE.LOCAL\Public Folders\NewFolder>type OurEmail.EML
Received: by gomezawin2000.GomezaMobile.local
   id <01BFDC6E.30F33D70@gomezawin2000.GomezaMobile.local>; Thu, 22 Jun 200
0 13:20:41 -0400
content-class: urn:content-classes:message
Subject: OurEmail
Date: Thu, 22 Jun 2000 13:20:36 -0400
Message-ID:
<CB6D3FF647626141A11321A3E557EDEB33D3@gomezawin2000.GomezaMobile.local>
X-MS-Has-Attach:
MIME-Version: 1.0
Content-Type: text/html;
   charset="iso-8859-1"
Content-Transfer-Encoding: binary
X-MS-TNEF-Correlator:
Thread-Topic: OurEmail
```

```
Thread-Index: Ab/cbi2jCvaquuxlTuKwC9M94sR4sw==
From: "Administrator" <Administrator@GomezaMobile.local>
X-MimeOLE: Produced By Microsoft Exchange V6.0.4417.0
To: "Administrator" <Administrator@GomezaMobile.local>,
    "George Jetson" <jetsong@GomezaMobile.local>

<!DOCTYPE HTML PUBLIC "-//W3C//DTD HTML 3.2//EN">
<HTML>
<HEAD>
<META HTTP-EQUIV="Content-Type" CONTENT="text/html; charset=iso-8859-1">
<META NAME="Generator" CONTENT="MS Exchange Server version 6.0.4417.0">
<TITLE>OurEmail</TITLE>
</HEAD>
<BODY>
<!-- Converted from text/rtf format -->

<P><FONT SIZE=2 FACE="Arial">This says nothing!</FONT>
</P>

<P><B><FONT SIZE=2 FACE="Tahoma">Alex Gomez, MSCS, MCSD</FONT></B>

<BR><FONT SIZE=2 FACE="Tahoma">e:gomeza@plural.com</FONT>

<BR><FONT SIZE=2 FACE="Tahoma">w:www.plural.com</FONT>

<BR><FONT SIZE=2 FACE="Tahoma">t: 617-951-2522 Ext: 241</FONT>

<BR><FONT SIZE=2 FACE="Tahoma">f: 617-737-9888</FONT>

<BR><FONT COLOR="#FF0000" SIZE=2 FACE="Arial">plural</FONT>
</P>
<BR>

</BODY>
</HTML>
M:\GOMEZAMOBILE.LOCAL\Public Folders\NewFolder>
```

As we have seen in many code examples throughout the book, every item is accessible through a URL. For example, the URL to the item of the preceding example is

```
file://./backofficestorage/GomezaMobile.local/Public Folders/
NewFolder/OurEmail.EML
```

while the URL to an item in the Administrator's **Contacts** folder is

```
file://./backofficestorage/GomezaMobile.local/MBX/Administrator/
Contacts/JoeBlack.EML
```

Note: For more information on the syntax for creating file URLs and plenty of other examples, see Chapter 7.

So what controls ExIFS? The Microsoft Exchange Information Store service uses the **eifs.sys** and **exifsmsg.dll** files typically found in the **C:\WINNT\system32\drivers** directory to display the relevant Exchange data in the M: drive.

As we mentioned earlier, the Exchange IFS drive does not necessarily have to be the M: drive. In fact, the drive that ExIFS uses is stored in the following registry key:

```
HKEY_LOCAL_MACHINE\SYSTEM\CurrentControlSet\Services\EXIFS\
Parameters\DriveLetter
```

You can technically change the drive that ExIFS uses by changing the key value. However, editing the registry is always risky business, so back it up before you do anything and be careful.

Note: For more information on changing the ExIFS drive, see article Q239747 in the Microsoft Knowledge Base (**http://support.microsoft.com/support/kb/articles/q239/7/47.asp**).

When to Use ExIFS

Essentially, you should use ExIFS when your application needs access to an item's contents and not its properties because the Microsoft Win32 APIs can access only an item's stream. Also do not fall into the trap of thinking that all Exchange administrative tasks can be accomplished through the file system. Remember, this is still a virtual drive. ExIFS is busy translating items from the Exchange store into a form that can be recognized by Windows Explorer with only a tiny subset of the properties of Exchange 2000 available through the file system. So, for example, backing up files on the M: drive does *not* constitute successfully backing up your Exchange server.

You may also run into problems if your application combines ExIFS and other data access technologies such as ExOLEDB and CDO. For example, if your application uses ExOLEDB to open and write to an item using the ADO **Stream** object and then subsequently reads the same item using a Win32 API and ExIFS, you may notice that data appear to be missing. The reason is that ExOLEDB uses an asynchronous model to update data streams, and the changes may not be committed by the time you read the file using ExIFS. However, if you use ExOLEDB to read the stream, you will see the changes.

Microsoft Win32 File System APIs

Because ExIFS provides a view of the Exchange public and private folder hierarchy as a file system, it is possible to use ordinary Win32 file system APIs to access Exchange folders and files. The limitation, of course, is that you do not have access to DAV or custom properties using the Win32 API. Instead, you have access to only basic file system properties, such as name, size, creation date, and file attribute bits.

Sample: The ExIFSWin32Lib Component

The ExIFSWin32Lib component is an in-process COM component implemented in C++ through Visual C++ 6.0 and the ActiveX Template Library (ATL). It exposes methods that perform various file system operations, such as adding a folder; moving, copying, and deleting items; and getting file system properties of an item. (An item can be a file or a folder.) Note that you can pass these methods via any path to which you have access on your local system. Because ExIFS is a file system abstraction of Exchange data, this component will operate on your local C: drive files exactly as it does on the ExIFS M: drive.

Sample: The ExIFSFileSystem Component

The ExIFSFileSystem component is also an in-process COM component, but it is implemented through Visual Basic 6.0, which references the file system object. It implements exactly the same interface as ExIFSWin32Lib. You can also use this component to perform file system operations on the local IFS drive, or any other local or network drive.

Given that both of these samples accomplish exactly the same thing, which should you use? That depends on whether you're a VB programmer or a C++ programmer. Since the FileSystemObject component is really a COM wrapper for the subset of the Win32 API that deals with file systems, the C++ version will execute a millisecond or two faster. Compared to the VB version, however, the C++ version requires more code, a longer development cycle, and a different developer skill set. The slight gain in performance may not be worth the extra effort.

Known Issues with ExIFSWin32Lib and ExIFSFileSystem

If your application does not really care about DAV properties or custom properties and does not use ExOLEDB to access Exchange data, the ExIFSWin32Lib and ExIFSFileSystem components will do the job. However, if you combine the use of ExOLEDB and ExIFS to perform file system operations such as moving and copying files, you may find the results unpredictable. The reason is that ExOLEDB is an asynchronous data access method. If you need ExOLEDB because you are using custom properties or DAV properties, you should also use ExOLEDB to do file system operations.

Another limitation is that ExIFS gives you a view of only the Exchange enterprise data that is located on the local server. For example, if your organization has 26 Exchange servers, ExIFS can provide a view of only the files and folders that are housed on the local machine. If you need to view files and folders on another server, you'll need to create a network share of the M: drive on the other server. (More on this later in the chapter.)

Setting File Permissions Using the Access Control List

One great benefit of Exchange 2000 security in general is the fact that it uses standard Windows 2000 security primitives such as file access control lists (ACLs). Thus you can take advantage of the great security subsystem that's built into the Windows 2000 operating system.

Windows 2000 File System Security in a Nutshell

To understand the following code sample that sets an ACL using the Win32 API, it is important first to have a bit of background in how security works in Windows 2000.

When a user logs onto a Windows 2000 domain, the user's security identifier (SID) is mapped to a token that gives that user access to any of various operating system objects, such as files and folders. When an attempt is made to access a specific file or folder, the operating system checks the token against the ACL of the object. The ACL contains access control entries (ACEs) that enumerate the users and/or groups and the specific access level that is desired. The users and groups are known as *trustees*. Examples of access levels are "granting read-only access" or "denying all access." In addition, an ACE can grant (or deny) a specific user access to a single folder only, a folder and all subfolders, or a folder and all its contents, including files. A file or folder ACE can also allow an access level to be *inherited* from its parent folder.

Sample: The ACLAPILib Component

The sample ACLAPILib component is an in-process COM component implemented in C++ through Visual C++ 6.0 and the ActiveX Template Library (ATL). The component exposes three public methods via its interface: **ModifySecurity**, **ResetSecurity**, and **TakeOwnership**.

The **ModifySecurity** method adds an explicit ACE to an ACL. The resulting ACL contains all the ACEs that were present before the call (both *explicit* ACEs specifically set on the object and those inherited from the parent), plus one ACE that applies the desired access level specified by the parameters. You can use this method to grant a user access to an Exchange folder without changing anyone else's permissions.

The **ResetSecurity** method does the same thing that **ModifySecurity** does, except that it creates a new ACL with one ACE that applies the desired access level. In other words, it removes all other explicit ACEs in the ACL and adds one new ACE. You can use this method to grant a user access to an Exchange folder while removing everyone else's permissions.

The **TakeOwnership** method is used to take ownership of a file or folder. To call either **ResetSecurity** or **ModifySecurity** to modify permissions, you must either have write permissions to the object or be the object's owner. **TakeOwnership** allows you to take ownership of a file or folder before trying to modify permissions.

To use the ACLAPILib component effectively, refer to Tables 18.1 and 18.2 for the parameters that need to be passed for each method call. Because these parameters are passed directly to the actual Win32 functions in the component, you can

Table 18.1 Parameters of the **ModifySecurity** and **ResetSecurity** Methods of the ACLAPILib Component

Parameter Name	Type	Value
Inheritance	Long	The Win32 **AceFlags** member of the **ACE_HEADER** structure.
ObjectName	BSTR	The full path of the Exchange file or folder (e.g., "M:\<domain name>\Public Folders\").
ObjectType	Long	The Win32 **SE_OBJECT_TYPE** enumeration: 1 for files and folders; 5 for a network share.
Option	Long	The Win32 **ACCESS_MODE** enumeration: 1 for granting access; 2 for setting access (removes all other existing access for the trustee); 3 for denying access.
Permission	Long	The Win32 **ACCESS_MASK DWORD**. Key values are 2032127 for full access (0x001F01FF), 1179817 for read-only access (0x001200A9), 1048855 for write-only access (0x00100117), and 1245631 for read/write access (0x001301BF).
Trustee	BSTR	The existing Windows 2000 user or group for which you are giving permissions.

Table 18.2 Parameters of the **TakeOwnership** Method of the ACLAPILib Component

Parameter Name	Type	Value
AccountName	BSTR	The Windows 2000 user name or group name of the new owner.
ObjectName	BSTR	The full path of the Exchange file or folder (e.g., "M:\<domain name>\Public Folders\").
ObjectType	Long	The Win32 **SE_OBJECT_TYPE** enumeration: 1 for files and folders; 5 for a network share.
SystemName	Long	The Windows 2000 domain name.

consult the MSDN help files for more information on some of the reference structures and enumerations. This is a very generic component, so you can use it to set permissions on any files and folders on the hard drive (or any other objects such as services, network shares, or Active Directory objects, for that matter). Listed in Tables 18.1 and 18.2 are the values you'll most likely use for ExIFS.

Included is a test harness, ACLAPILibVBTest, written in Visual Basic, that you can use to exercise the component and set various permissions in ExIFS.

Known Issues with ACLAPILib

At the time of this writing, there is a known issue with using Win32 APIs to set ACLs on an ExIFS folder and accessing custom item properties using ADO and ExOLEDB. If you use ExOLEDB to set custom properties on files and folders and you then use ACLAPILib to set access permissions on the parent folder, some of the custom properties that you previously set will disappear. If you are using ExOLEDB and custom properties in your application, you're probably better off using the custom MAPI properties and XML to set access permissions, as described in Chapter 8. This is an example of how combining data access technologies such as ExOLEDB (which is an asynchronous data access method) and ExIFS can lead to problems.

Remotely Accessing ExIFS Using a Network Share

Given that local Exchange 2000 public and private Web stores may be accessed as an ordinary drive letter via ExIFS, you may find it desirable to access these stores remotely via a network share. As is the case with any other local drive, sharing may be accomplished through either Windows Explorer or the command prompt.

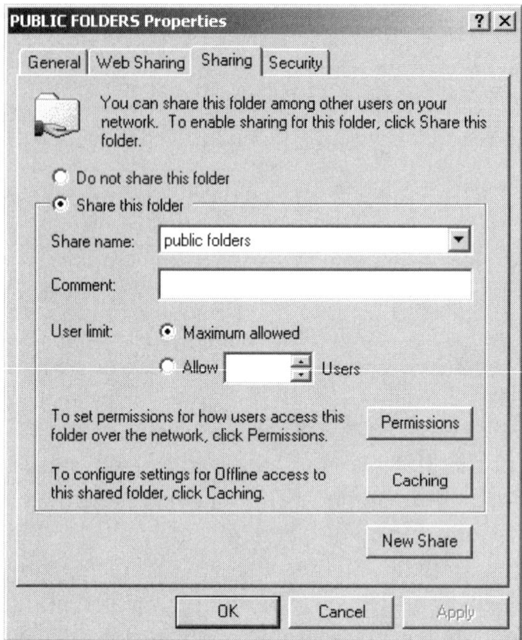

Figure 18.6 Sharing **M:\<my domain>\public folders** using Windows Explorer

Figure 18.6 shows an example of sharing the root public folder of the local M: drive using a share name of **public folders**. Alternatively, for people who prefer to use the command prompt, the following **net share** command may be used:

```
C:\>net share "public folders"="m:\<domain>\public folders"
```

Using either of these methods, you can access any public folder in the Exchange 2000 public Web store via a network share. However, if you've ever tried to do this and you've needed to either restart the Microsoft Exchange Information Store service or reboot the server machine entirely, you will have noticed that the folder you shared was no longer shared. The reason is that Windows 2000 processes all network shares at startup *before* the Microsoft Exchange Information Store starts. (The Information Store service creates the IFS drive.) There are two (maybe more) possible solutions to this problem:

1. Put a note on your server that says, "Don't forget to share the M: drive."
2. Write a simple NT service that shares the desired folder(s) of the M: drive.

Solution 1 requires manual intervention, but you may find it sufficient. However, if you would like to automate the process and have one or more folders be shared as soon as the Exchange IFS becomes available, then solution 2 is for you. Although creating and installing a Windows 2000 service may seem like a daunting task, the following sections explain in detail how to do it quickly.

Windows 2000 Services in a Nutshell

Before attempting to implement your own service, it's important to have a little background into what a Windows 2000 service is and what is possible to implement with a Windows 2000 service.

Windows 2000 services are executable programs that run in the background on a Windows 2000 server. They are essentially identical to NT services that run on prior versions of Windows NT. (For those familiar with UNIX, a service is roughly the equivalent of a *daemon*.) Services typically perform a particular function at a periodic interval or in response to a certain message or event. Usually they perform background tasks such as system monitoring, resource pooling, or other tasks that don't require any client interaction. In fact, Microsoft BackOffice applications such as SQL Server and Exchange are implemented as services.

Windows 2000 (and Windows NT) services are controlled by a subsystem of the operating system known as the Service Control Manager, or SCM (pronounced "scum"). The SCM is responsible for installing, launching, and maintaining the lifetimes of all services installed on the server machine.

Services can be configured to start automatically at system startup time by the SCM, or they can be started manually via either the **Services** administrative tool or a command prompt. The SCM maintains a static database of services installed on the server via the system registry. It also maintains a dynamic database of the status of services currently executing.

Services can be configured to run under a specific security context or under the default privileged "system" account that has special access to local resources. Finally, services can be configured to have startup dependencies. This last configuration allows the administrator to configure a service to start only after one or more other services have successfully started.

Historically, Windows 2000 (and NT) services have been implemented in C or C++ because services typically have multiple threads, with one or more threads receiving messages from the SCM, and one or more threads doing the work of the application. In addition, Win32 API calls are required to communicate with the SCM. Both of these reasons favor C or C++ development over Visual Basic. However, Visual C++ 6.0 offers an ATL project template that creates the service framework; all you need to do is supply your specific application logic.

Sample: The ExIFS Share Service

Now that you know the basics of Windows 2000 services, it's time to create a simple service that makes sure that your IFS drive is shared whenever your server is rebooted. The key elements of this service are as follows:

1. The service will be capable of being installed and uninstalled.
2. The service will be started automatically at system startup by the SCM.
3. The service will *depend* on the Microsoft Exchange Information Store service.

The third element is the key to our share service. Because this service will depend on the Exchange Information Store service, the service will not be allowed to start until the Exchange Information Store service has been started by the SCM. Since one of the tasks of the Exchange Information Store is to create the IFS drive, the drive will already exist and be ready to be shared by the time the share service starts.

The ExIFS share service sample project was created with Visual C++ version 6.0 using the ATL COM AppWizard. (You'll also need to install the Windows 2000 SDK to get the latest Win32 code libraries.) You can use the wizard as shown in Figures 18.7 and 18.8 to create the framework of a simple "do-nothing" service and then make the minor changes described below to turn it into the ExIFS share service.

Once you have run the wizard, you have successfully created a boilerplate service that is capable of being installed, uninstalled, started, and stopped by the SCM. If you name your project **ExIFS Share Service**, a majority of the C+ code will be located in **ExIFS Share Service.cpp.** First you'll need to modify the **CServiceModule::Install** module as shown here:

```
inline BOOL CServiceModule::Install()
{
    if (IsInstalled())
        return TRUE;

    SC_HANDLE hSCM = ::OpenSCManager(NULL, NULL, SC_MANAGER_ALL_ACCESS);
    if (hSCM == NULL)
    {
        MessageBox(NULL, _T("Couldn't open service manager"),
            m_szServiceName, MB_OK);
    return FALSE;
}
```

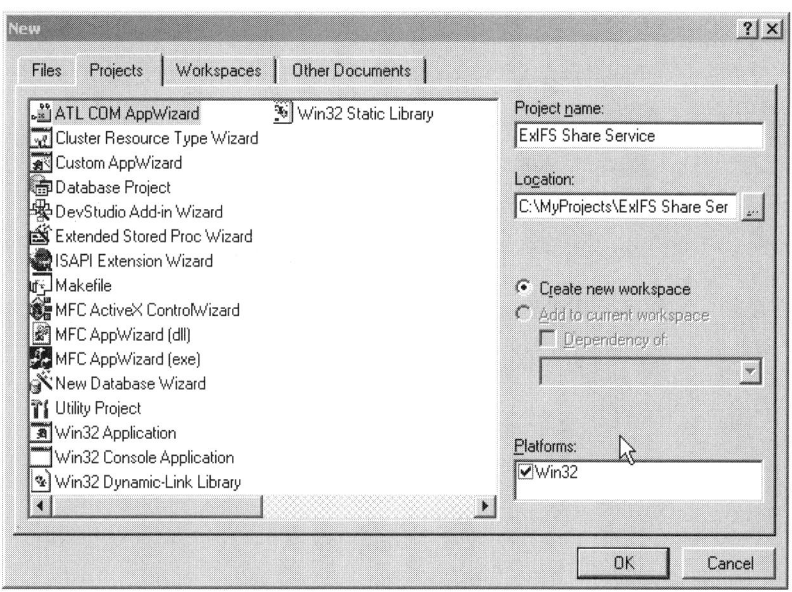

Figure 18.7 Using the ATL COM AppWizard to create a service: Step 1

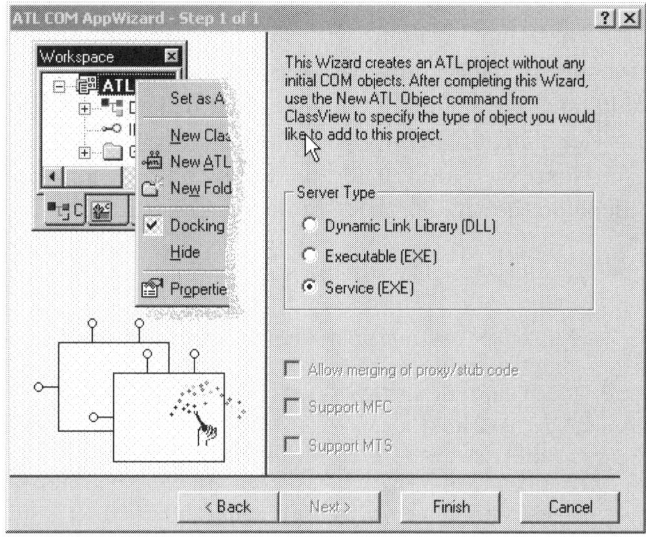

Figure 18.8 Using the ATL COM AppWizard to create a service: Step 2

```
// Get the executable file path
TCHAR szFilePath[_MAX_PATH];
::GetModuleFileName(NULL, szFilePath, _MAX_PATH);

SC_HANDLE hService = ::CreateService(
   hSCM, m_szServiceName, m_szServiceName,
   SERVICE_ALL_ACCESS, SERVICE_WIN32_OWN_PROCESS,
   SERVICE_AUTO_START, SERVICE_ERROR_NORMAL,
   szFilePath, NULL, NULL, _T("RPCSS\0MSExchangeIS\0"), NULL, NULL);

      SERVICE_DESCRIPTION sd;
      sd.lpDescription = _T("Sample ExIFS Share Service");
      ::ChangeServiceConfig2(hService, SERVICE_CONFIG_DESCRIPTION, &sd);

   if (hService == NULL)
   {
      ::CloseServiceHandle(hSCM);
      MessageBox(NULL, _T("Couldn't create service"),
         m_szServiceName, MB_OK);
   return FALSE;
}

::CloseServiceHandle(hService);
::CloseServiceHandle(hSCM);
return TRUE;
}
```

These modifications will cause the service to be installed with a dependency for the Exchange Information Store service, which in turn creates the ExIFS. In addition, we've added a comment that will appear when you view properties of the service using the **Services** administrative tool.

Next you'll need to add the following code to the **CServiceModule::Run** module to do the actual sharing of the desired path:

```
void CServiceModule::Run()
{
   _Module.dwThreadID = GetCurrentThreadId();

   HRESULT hr = CoInitialize(NULL);
// If you are running on NT 4.0 or higher, you can use the following
// call instead to make the EXE free threaded.
// This means that calls come in on a random RPC thread
// HRESULT hr = CoInitializeEx(NULL, COINIT_MULTITHREADED);

_ASSERTE(SUCCEEDED(hr));
```

```
// This provides a NULL DACL, which will allow access to everyone.
CSecurityDescriptor sd;
sd.InitializeFromThreadToken();
hr = CoInitializeSecurity(sd, -1, NULL, NULL,
   RPC_C_AUTHN_LEVEL_PKT, RPC_C_IMP_LEVEL_IMPERSONATE, NULL, EOAC_NONE,
      NULL);
_ASSERTE(SUCCEEDED(hr));

hr = _Module.RegisterClassObjects(CLSCTX_LOCAL_SERVER |
     CLSCTX_REMOTE_SERVER, REGCLS_MULTIPLEUSE);
_ASSERTE(SUCCEEDED(hr));

LogEvent(_T("Service started"));
if (m_bService)
   SetServiceStatus(SERVICE_RUNNING);

      NET_API_STATUS res;
      SHARE_INFO_2 p;
      DWORD parm_err = 0;

      // Fill in the SHARE_INFO_2 structure ...
      p.shi2_netname = _T("Public Folders");
      p.shi2_type = STYPE_DISKTREE; // disk drive
      p.shi2_remark = _T("Shared by the ExIFS Share Service");
      p.shi2_permissions = 0;
      p.shi2_max_uses = -1;
      p.shi2_current_uses = 0;

      // Get the domain name for use in the M: drive path ...
      WCHAR szDomainName[255];
      DWORD dwSize = 255;
      GetComputerNameEx(ComputerNameDnsDomain, szDomainName, &dwSize);
      WCHAR szPath[255];
      wsprintf(szPath, L"M:\\%s\\Public Folders", szDomainName);
      p.shi2_path = szPath;
      p.shi2_passwd = NULL; // no password

      // Share the drive ...
      res = NetShareAdd(NULL, 2, (LPBYTE) &p, &parm_err);

   MSG msg;
   while (GetMessage(&msg, 0, 0, 0))
      DispatchMessage(&msg);

   _Module.RevokeClassObjects();

   CoUninitialize();
}
```

Basically, those are all the *code* modifications you'll need to make to implement the ExIFS share service. However, you'll need to make a few minor project modifications to compile, link, and build the project.

First you'll need to edit **StdAfx.h**. Change

```
#define _WIN32_WINNT 0x0400
```

to

```
#define _WIN32_WINNT 0x0500
```

to indicate that you're compiling against Windows 2000 libraries instead of NT 4.0.

You'll also need to add

```
#include <lm.h>
```

immediately following the other **#include** statement in order for the code we added to compile.

Finally, you'll need to set the active configuration to **Win32 Unicode Release MinDependency** using the **Build | Set Active Configuration** menu option, and link to **kernel32.lib** and **netapi32.lib** using the **Project | Settings** menu option (see Figure 18.9).

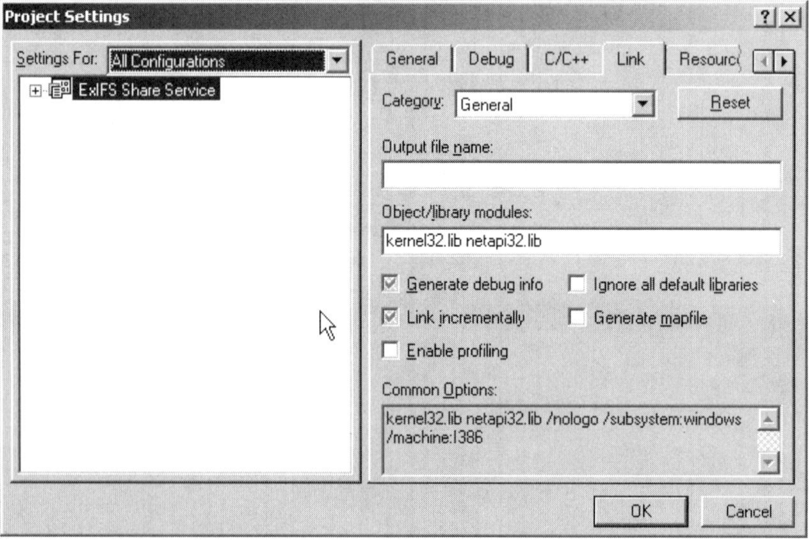

Figure 18.9 Adding required object/library modules using the **Project Settings** dialog box

You should now be able to successfully build the ExIFS share service executable by pressing **F7**.

Installing and Uninstalling the ExIFS Share Service

If you examine the **_tWinMain** function, you'll notice that the service uses three command-line switches: **–Service**, **–UnregServer**, and **–RegServer**.

The **–Service** switch is used to install the executable as a service. Thus the **"ExIFS Share Service" –Service** command issued at a command prompt (in the directory that contains our service, of course) will install the service. You can check that the service is installed correctly by opening the **Services** administrative tool and verifying that **ExIFS Share Service** is included in the list of installed services (see Figure 18.10).

> **Note:** Using the command window to run an application or service whose name contains spaces will not work without quotation marks delineating the name. For example, the command **ExIFS Share Service –Service** would not work properly.

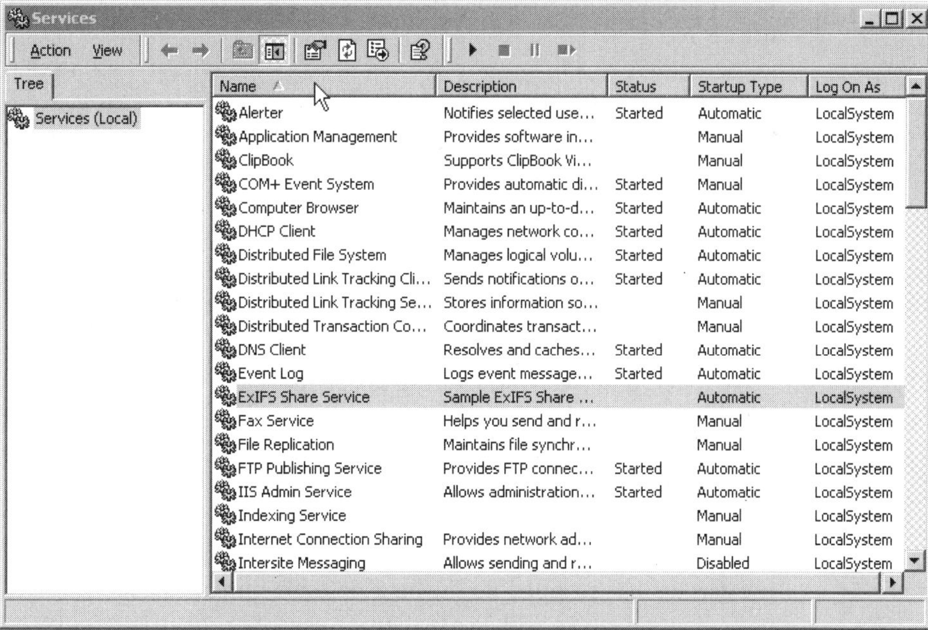

Figure 18.10 Using the Windows 2000 **Services** administrative tool to check whether the share service has been installed correctly

The **–UnregServer** is used to unregister the service. "**ExIFS Share Service**" **–UnregServer** issued at a command prompt will unregister the service and remove it from the list of services displayed by the **Services** administrative tool.

The **–RegServer** switch is used to register the service not as an actual Windows 2000 service, but instead as a COM out-of-process executable. This feature is useful in debugging your server application.

Starting and Stopping the ExIFS Share Service

The ExIFS share service can be started (and stopped) in one of two ways. If you're a command-line fan, you can use the **net start** command as follows:

```
C:\>net start "ExIFS Share Service"
```

Conversely, the service can be stopped with the **net stop** command:

```
C:\>net stop "ExIFS Share Service"
```

The command-line method is preferable if you are creating a **setup.exe** or batch file to install your service. However, you can also use the **Services** administrative tool to stop, start, and restart (stop, then start) your service as shown in Figure 18.10.

Possible Future Enhancements to the ExIFS Share Service

You probably noticed that the M: drive was hard-coded into the logic of the service. We hope this alarmed you, since earlier in the chapter we mentioned that there's no guarantee that the ExIFS will be mounted as the M: drive in your system, depending on its configuration. Therefore, a great enhancement would be to make this user (or system) configurable. Some options include scanning all drive letters for a volume label of "Exchange," using your own registry key to store the drive letter, or, better yet, reading the registry key that ExIFS itself reads to mount the drive.

You might also have noticed that this service does nothing but attempt to create a share at system startup. We are simply relying on the service dependency mechanism to share the drive *after* Exchange has mounted it. When the service is stopped, the share does *not* go away. The ability to make the share disappear after the service has stopped might be a possible enhancement. You could also poll at periodic intervals to make sure that the share (or the drive itself!) is still there.

We leave these and all other possible enhancements to you as exercises.

Summary

The Exchange Installable File System (ExIFS) can be a viable alternative for Exchange data access if you are interested not in DAV or custom properties, but rather only in the actual contents of files. ExIFS uses the file system metaphor to view Exchange public and private store data as if they were on a local disk. However, take care when mixing this data access technology with other technologies, such as ExOLEDB and CDO, because the results will be unpredictable.

Chapter 19

Weighing Your Development Options

This chapter attempts to address the difficult task of recommending the appropriate development library for accessing the Web Storage System (WSS), given a set of business and infrastructure requirements. We recap the wide range of choices with regard to APIs and object libraries, providing the pros and cons of each. We also provide some scenarios that illustrate why a given API or library can or cannot, or should or should not, be used in that scenario. Since this is not a language comparison, we'll use Visual Basic as the language for all of the examples.

Reviewing the Exchange 2000 Development Choices

In this first section we'll recap the development choices. We'll focus on eight ways to access, store, and use information from the WSS:

1. ADO 2.5 over ExOLEDB
2. WebDAV over HTTP
3. ADO 2.5 using MSDAIPP over HTTP
4. CDO for Exchange over ExOLEDB
5. CDO for Exchange over MSDAIPP
6. FileSystemObject over ExIFS
7. Outlook 2000 object model over MAPI
8. CDO 1.21 over MAPI

We will present the various techniques in two sections. The first section (Feature Comparison) will review the pros and cons of using each library. The second section (Selecting the Best Solution: Scenarios) will present several fictitious scenarios to help you wade through the choices in real-world settings. At the end of the chapter we will summarize the eight techniques in an easy-to-read table.

> **Note:** Be careful when using multiple access methods against the WSS in the same application. Since each of the various option libraries have their own caching mechanisms, using more that one at a time may cause unwanted behavior.

Feature Comparison

This section covers the features that are supported by each of the various access methods, as well as the pros and cons of each object library.

ADO 2.5 over ExOLEDB

Discussed in Chapters 7 and 8, using ADO over the ExOLEDB provider is perhaps the most common and recommended way to access the WSS. If you write Web pages that access data in an Exchange 2000 server, you will most likely want to use ADO with ExOLEDB. ExOLEDB is a native OLE DB provider for the Exchange 2000 Web Storage System. The provider supports direct URLs and a limited range of SQL **SELECT** queries.

When to Use

You would use ADO and the ExOLEDB provider for general access to the WSS database. ADO 2.5 can also be used for updating the store. Typical applications include same-server COM+ components, same-server ASP pages, and same-server Exchange event sinks.

Pros

The benefits of using ADO and ExOLEDB include the familiar programming interface (ADO 2.5), which allows developers who are not familiar with MAPI to program against Exchange. The provider also performs well, keeping up with (and in many cases surpassing) traditional Exchange access methods.

In addition, the ExOLEDB provider enables access to all property types, including WebDAV, Exchange, and MAPI properties, to name a few.

Cons

One of the drawbacks of the ExOLEDB provider is that it supports only a subset of the potential OLE DB functionality. For example, it does not support dynamic logon (using a user name and password), nor does it support asynchronous updates.

Another drawback is that you cannot "remote" ExOLEDB. That is, you cannot use it from clients; rather you can use ADO 2.5 and the Exchange OLE DB provider only on the same server on which you are running your process. See Chapter 8 for one possible way around this serious limitation.

WebDAV over HTTP

Discussed in Chapter 4, the WebDAV protocol is supported for accessing and updating information in the WSS. WebDAV enables you to read and write information over HTTP. WebDAV also allows you to use XML to define property sets. You can send raw WebDAV verbs to read and update the Web Storage System

When to Use

You would typically use WebDAV as a client-side or server-side access solution. You can either deploy your own Windows-based client application or ensure that the user has a rich Web client such as Internet Explorer 5.0 or higher installed. Your choices for client-side direct WSS access are essentially MAPI and WebDAV. On the server, you would typically make remote server requests from within components or web pages.

Pros

A huge benefit of support for WebDAV is that you can access remote Exchange 2000 servers over HTTP. This ability eliminates any dependence on proprietary access methods such as the Outlook 2000 object model or CDO 1.21.

Another benefit of WebDAV is that you have raw access to data formatted in XML. Thus you can manipulate the data yourself or format the data for display using XSL.

Now that version 3 of the XMLHTTP component is out (which is technically part of MSXML), you can make scalable server-to-server WebDAV requests. This is your best option for requests that originate from your Web server and call your back-end Exchange 2000 server.

Cons

You get no built-in collaboration functionality with WebDAV alone. CDO for Exchange is not supported over a WebDAV connection (it is supported only over ExOLEDB).

ADO 2.5 Using MSDAIPP over HTTP

Our next option, using ADO 2.5 with the Microsoft OLE DB Provider for Internet Publishing (MSDAIPP) is really just the WebDAV option with an ADO wrapper. We run into pretty much the same pros and cons; we simply get a different object model to deal with.

When to Use

You would typically use MSDAIPP as a client-side access solution. You would use this to deploy your own Windows-based client application (you lose the option to feed XML directly into Internet Explorer 5.0).

Pros

Again, the huge benefit is that you can access remote Exchange 2000 servers over HTTP. This ability eliminates any dependence on proprietary access methods such as the Outlook 2000 object model or CDO 1.21.

The other major benefit of this option is that you can use standard ADO 2.5 code rather than having to format your own XML and DAV verbs.

Cons

MSDAIPP is not officially supported by Microsoft for requesting information from an Exchange 2000 or Web Storage System server. MSDAIPP works in many situations, but it is not the recommended way to access remote Exchange 2000 data.

CDO for Exchange over ExOLEDB

Using CDO for Exchange 2000 requires you to use the ExOLEDB provider, so this option is really the same as ADO over ExOLEDB, except that you get collaboration features. Discussed in Chapters 12 through 16, using CDO for Exchange 2000 over the ExOLEDB provider is perhaps the most common and recommended way to access the WSS. If you write any code that requires collaboration functionality, you'll want to use CDO for Exchange 2000.

When to Use

You would use CDO and the ExOLEDB provider for collaboration functionality on the Exchange 2000 server. Typical applications include same-server COM+ components, same-server ASP pages, and same-server Exchange event sinks.

Pros

The principal benefit of using CDO for Exchange 2000 is that it provides a significant amount of Exchange 2000 functionality so that you can automate your applications.

Cons

Because CDO for Exchange uses ExOLEDB, you cannot "remote" CDO for Exchange. That is, you cannot use it from clients; rather you can use CDO for Exchange 2000 only on the same server on which you are running your process. See Chapter 8 for one possible way around this serious limitation.

CDO for Exchange over MSDAIPP

You simply can't do this. Period.

FileSystemObject over ExIFS

Discussed in Chapter 18, the Exchange 2000 Installable File System (ExIFS) provides a way to access the WSS by using a drive mapping. Your code can use the FileSystemObject, the Win32 API functions, or something as simple as the Windows File Explorer. By default, Exchange maps the M: drive to the entire logical Exchange Information Store on the server. Some sample paths include **M:\domain.com\MBX\useralias\Inbox** (for someone's **Inbox** folder) and **M:\domain.com\public folders\stuff** (for the **stuff** public folder).

When to Use

You would use ExIFS for browsing the contents of an Exchange 2000 database, saving files to the Web Storage System using common dialogs, or any other place where you don't need Exchange properties.

Pros

ExIFS is a very interesting concept because it allows you to store documents and other files directly in the store. It provides an easy way to access the WSS via the FileSystemObject. In addition, it can be shared like any other drive for remote access.

We did some testing against ExIFS, and it is really fast. It fared just as well as ExOLEDB and better than MAPI.

Cons

ExIFS is *not* for backing up your Exchange database. Be sure to use a standard backup utility so that the logs can be committed and flushed properly.

The biggest drawback to ExIFS is that you have no access to Exchange or custom properties (only file system properties). You have access only to an item's stream.

Note: Be very careful when using the M: drive. ExIFS actually destroys both standard and custom properties when certain Win32 functions are used on it. This is an issue that has been confirmed by Microsoft.

Outlook 2000 Object Model over MAPI

Outlook 2000, still an acceptable way of accessing an Exchange 2000 server, provides a significant amount of functionality in its own right. Discussed in Chapter 6, Outlook 2000 has a rich object model, and it has been the primary development platform for collaboration.

When to Use

The Outlook 2000 object model is ideal for client-side, collaborative applications. You can use the object model for extending Outlook itself, or you can use it as a pure object library for creating your own applications.

Pros

The Outlook 2000 object model, which uses MAPI as its underlying communication scheme, is rich in features and backward compatible with pre-Exchange 2000 servers. Outlook 2000 is also still the best bet for accessing Outlook contacts and tasks. In addition, you can control the Outlook user interface (Explorer/Inspector) only by using its object model.

Cons

Outlook 2000 is for client-side use only. Although it has some interesting features for manipulating tasks that CDO for Exchange 2000 lacks, resist the urge to install it on the server.

CDO 1.21 over MAPI

CDO 1.21, which also uses MAPI, provides similar functionality to that of Outlook. As discussed in Chapter 11, CDO 1.21 is still a supported access mechanism for Exchange 2000. In fact, it is the most universally supported technique because it can be used on both the client and the server, it can be used to access remote servers, and it is backward compatible.

When to Use

CDO 1.21 is most useful for creating applications that are backward compatible with Exchange 5.5. CDO 1.21 is also useful on the client side, combined with the Outlook object model.

Pros

The CDO 1.21 object model, which uses MAPI as its underlying communication scheme, is fast and backward compatible with pre-Exchange 2000 servers. CDO 1.21 is thread-safe and may be used on both a client and a server. In many cases, CDO 1.21 can be up to 20 times faster than the Outlook object model.

Cons

CDO 1.21 lacks access to Outlook properties and WebDAV properties. It is basically limited to MAPI properties.

Selecting the Best Solution: Scenarios

In this section we provide some brief case studies, or scenarios, each of which illustrates a potential customer request. These scenarios should help you select the appropriate object library for your own projects.

Case Study 1: A Mixed Exchange 5.5 and 2000 Environment

This case study illustrates a common scenario: a mixed Exchange 5.5 and Exchange 2000 environment.

Scenario

Suppose that a customer has both Exchange 5.5 and Exchange 2000 servers. The customer wants the ability to move information from another database quickly, as well as a Visual Basic application that will run on a Windows client. The application should be able to update lots of data quickly. How would you develop this application?

Solution

First you will need access to both Exchange 5.5 and Exchange 2000. Your best bet would be to use either CDO 1.21 or Outlook 2000 because they are each compatible with both 5.5 and 2000. Since CDO 1.21 is up to 20 times faster than the Outlook object model, you'll probably want to lean toward using CDO 1.21. As long as support for all Outlook data types is not required, CDO 1.21 is the better choice.

Case Study 2: Levels of Web Support in Exchange 2000 over Exchange 5.5

This case study illustrates the various levels of Web support in Exchange 2000 over Exchange 5.5.

Scenario

The customer is running in an Exchange environment and wants a Web-based planning calendar for the team.

Solution

Since the version of Exchange server was not specified, let's look at both possibilities. If the customer is using Exchange 5.5, the only choice is to use CDO 1.21 because the Exchange OLE DB provider is Exchange 2000 only, and Outlook should not be run on the Web server. If the customer is using Exchange 2000, the best choice is to use ADO 2.5 and CDO for Exchange 2000 over ExOLEDB because they are designed for Web applications.

Case Study 3: Using Exchange in a Workgroup Environment

This scenario illustrates the use of Exchange 2000 in a workgroup environment.

Scenario

The customer is rolling out Windows 2000 and wants to create a group-level, Web-based document storage and retrieval application.

Solution

The customer would benefit most from Exchange 2000 Server. After installing Exchange 2000, write an ASP application using ADO 2.5 against the local Exchange 2000 Web Storage System database.

Case Study 4: Accessing Remote Exchange 2000 Information from a Web Server

This scenario illustrates the options for accessing remote Exchange 2000 information from a Web server.

Scenario

The customer wants a Web application to run on a Windows 2000 server. The Web application should access information on a remote Exchange 2000 server via the Web application.

Solution

The ideal solution here would be to write ADO code that accesses the remote store over ExOLEDB. However, this option is *not* supported. Do not use ADO over MSDAIPP because this option is not supported against the Web Storage System.

The alternatives, then, are to use CDO 1.21, which can be used in ASP against remote stores. You can also use WebDAV over XMLHTTP (version 3 or above). Finally, you can use ADO 2.5 and ExOLEDB wrapped in a custom component that is accessed via COM+ (DCOM) from server to server. Chapter 8 discusses how to do this.

Summary

We have covered several ways to access the Exchange 2000 Web Storage System. Each technique has a distinct set of advantages and disadvantages, so consider each business scenario carefully. Table 19.1 summarizes the choices and their implications. Note that development choices are always evolving, so you should check the latest versions of your client and server technologies for updates to the information in this table.

Table 19.1 Feature Comparison of Exchange 2000 Access Methods

Method	Speed	Property Access	Remote Access?	Server-Side	Client-Side	Collaboration Features?
ADO 2.5 over ExOLEDB	Fast	Yes	No	Yes	No	No
WebDAV over HTTP	Fast	Yes	Yes	Yes (version 3)	Yes	No
ADO 2.5 using MSDAIPP over HTTP (not officially supported)	Fast	Yes	Yes	No	Yes	No
CDO for Exchange over ExOLEDB	Fast	Yes	No	Yes	No	Yes
CDO for Exchange over MSDAIPP	N/A	N/A	N/A	N/A	N/A	N/A
FileSystemObject over ExIFS	Fast	No	Yes, over a share	Yes	Yes	No
Outlook 2000 object model over MAPI	Slow	Yes, but only MAPI properties	Yes	Yes	No	Yes
CDO 1.21 over MAPI	Medium	Yes, but only MAPI properties	Yes	Yes	Yes	Some

Part VI

Sample Applications

Chapter 20

Exchange 2000 Web Storage System Property Viewer Applications

This chapter demonstrates how to create useful tools for property inspection. We present two applications that provide views into Exchange 2000 Web Storage System data. Both applications use ADO 2.5 and the ExOLEDB provider. The first is a simple Web-based property viewer; the second is a Windows-based tool.

Tool 1: Web-Based Property Viewer

This section presents a sample ASP application that uses both the ADO 2.5 **Record** and **Recordset** objects. The application lists the contents of a folder and allows us to inspect the properties of an item or folder.

The HTML Page

The first page of the tool is a standard HTML form that allows users to select what they want to see (Figure 20.1). The following is the complete code listing for the page:

```
<html>
<head>
<title>Exchange 2000 Server Property Viewer</title>
</head>
<body>
<p>
```

```
<font size="5"><img border="0" src="view.jpg" width="108"
   height="69"></font>
<font size="6">Exchange 2000 Server/ADO 2.5 Property Viewer</font>
</p>

<form action="viewprops.asp" method="post">

<p>Folder name:  public folders/<input type="text"
      name="txtFolderPath" size="42"></p>
   <p><input type="radio" value="Folder" checked name="Radio1">Get
      Folder Properties</p>
   <p><input type="radio" value="FolderContents" name="Radio1">Get
      Contents of this folder</p>
   <p><input type="radio" value="Item" name="Radio1">Get Item
      Properties for this item:
   <input type="text" name="txtItemName" size="42"></p>

   <p>Retrieve the following properties:</p>
   <p><input type="radio" value="All" checked name="Radio2">All
      Properties</p>
   <p><input type="radio" value="DAV" name="Radio2">DAV Properties
      Only</p>
   <p><input type="radio" value="Exchange" name="Radio2">Exchange
      Properties Only</p>
   <p><input type="radio" value="Office" name="Radio2">Office
      Properties Only</p>
   <p><input type="radio" value="Custom" name="Radio2">Properties From
      a Custom Namespace: <input type="text" name="txtNamespace"
      size="42"></p>
   <p><input type="submit" value="Submit" name="B1"></p>

</form>
</body>
</html>
```

The ASP Page

The second page (the one that does the real work) is an Active Server Page that executes ADO code based on the user's preferences. The code does one of the following:

- Retrieves a single **Record** object using a folder URL and displays the properties of the folder
- Retrieves a single **Record** object using an item URL and displays the properties of the item

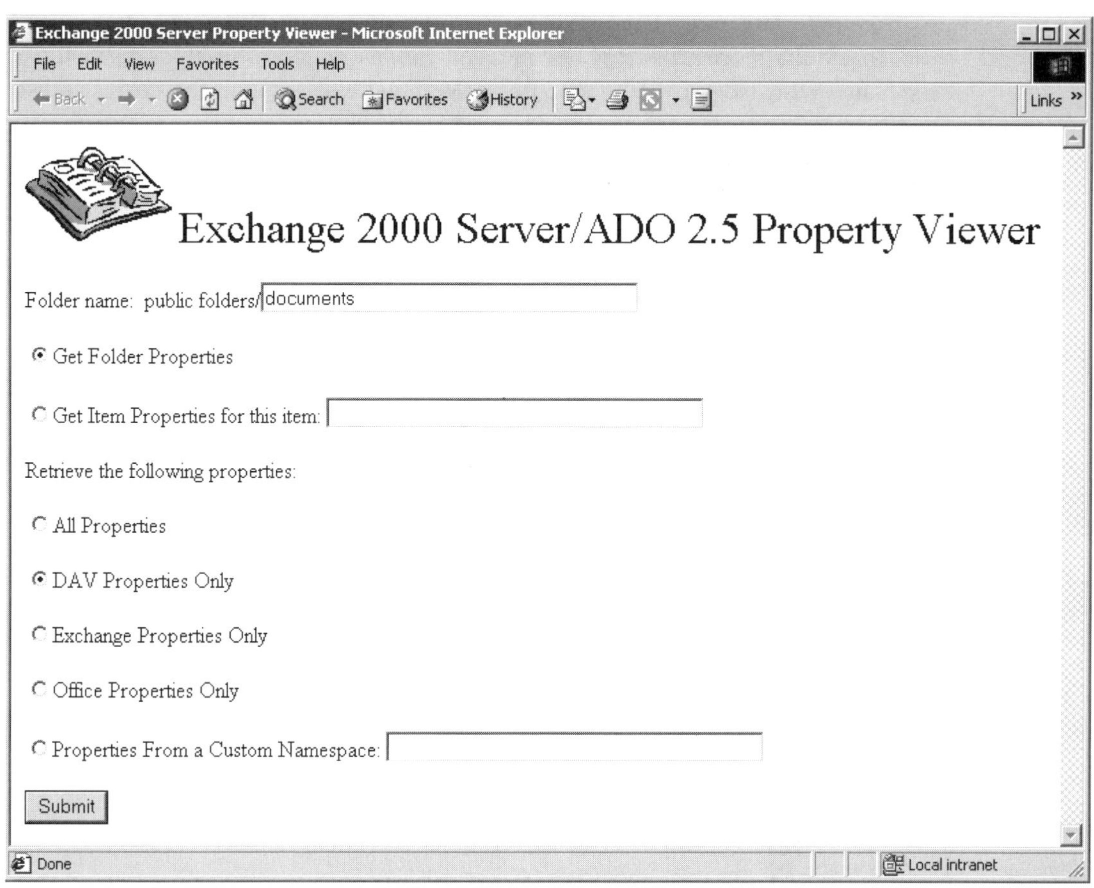

Figure 20.1 The first page of the sample Web application allows the user to select options

- Retrieves a single **Record** object using a folder URL, and then retrieves a **Recordset** object by using the **GetChildren** method of the **Record** object and displays the contents of the folder

> **Note:** The **GetChildren** method can be an expensive operation because it is similar to doing a **SELECT *** query without a filter. See Chapter 7 for more information on using ADO and how to optimize your operations by using **WHERE** clauses. As you'll see in the second application of this chapter (ADO Explorer), we use a **SELECT** query with a **WHERE** clause to limit our scope and speed up the operation.

An important part of the code is building the correct URL. We must include the "backofficestorage" string as part of the name because this is what the Exchange OLE DB provider recognizes. We must also include the correct server name; in this case "Exchdom.local" is hard-coded, but you can change this to your Exchange server. If the user wants to see an item, we must append the item's name to the end of the URL:

```
' Build the correct URL
if strRadio1 = "Item" then
    strURL = _
    "file://./backofficestorage/" & _
    "Exchdom.local/" & _
    "public folders/" & _
    strFolderPath & "/" & _
    strItemName
Else
    strURL = _
    "file://./backofficestorage/" & _
    "Exchdom.local/" & _
    "public folders/" & _
    strFolderPath
End If
```

To access the **Record** object for the item we want, we simply execute the **Open** method:

```
Set objRec = _
    Server.CreateObject("ADODB.Record")
objRec.Open strURL
```

The ASP, when executed, accesses a resource directly; there's no need to recursively iterate through folders and items. We get a result that allows us to easily explore properties on any public folder or item stored there by looping through the **Fields** collection (Figure 20.2).

To get the contents of a folder, we use the **GetChildren** method:

```
Set objRS = objRec.GetChildren
```

We also allow users to enter a filter for the type of property they want to see. To accomplish this, we simply check the namespace of the property as we're looping through the **Fields** collection (admittedly, this is a poor man's filter; we should really do a **SELECT** statement with a **WHERE** clause). As we saw in Chapter 3, a namespace is simply a way to distinguish attributes (e.g., is this an Office attribute,

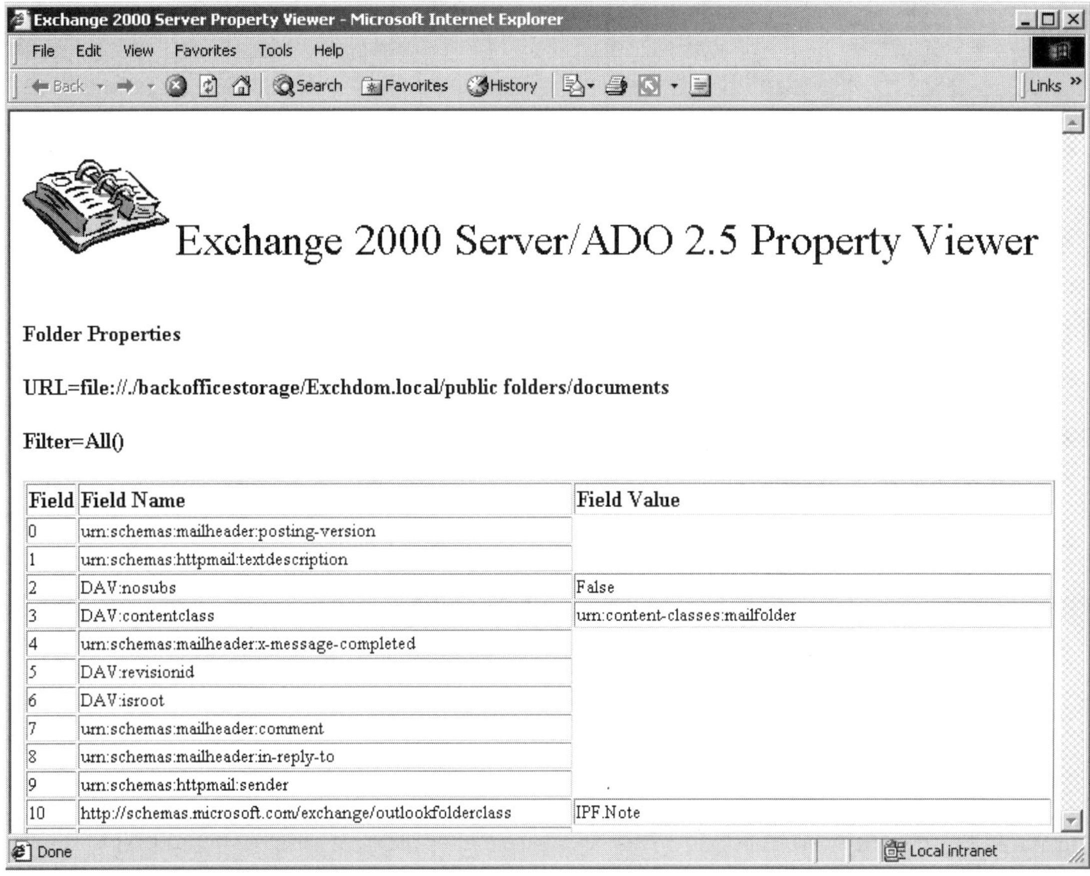

Figure 20.2 The sample Web application displays folder properties

an Exchange attribute, or a DAV attribute?). Figure 20.2 shows what the user would see if a folder were selected and no filter were applied. Figure 20.3 lists the contents of a folder; items were received by iterating the records of the **Recordset** object.

The following listing provides the complete code for this form:

```
<%@ Language=VBScript %>
<HTML>
<head>
<title>Exchange 2000 Server Property Viewer</title>
</head>
<body>
<p>
```

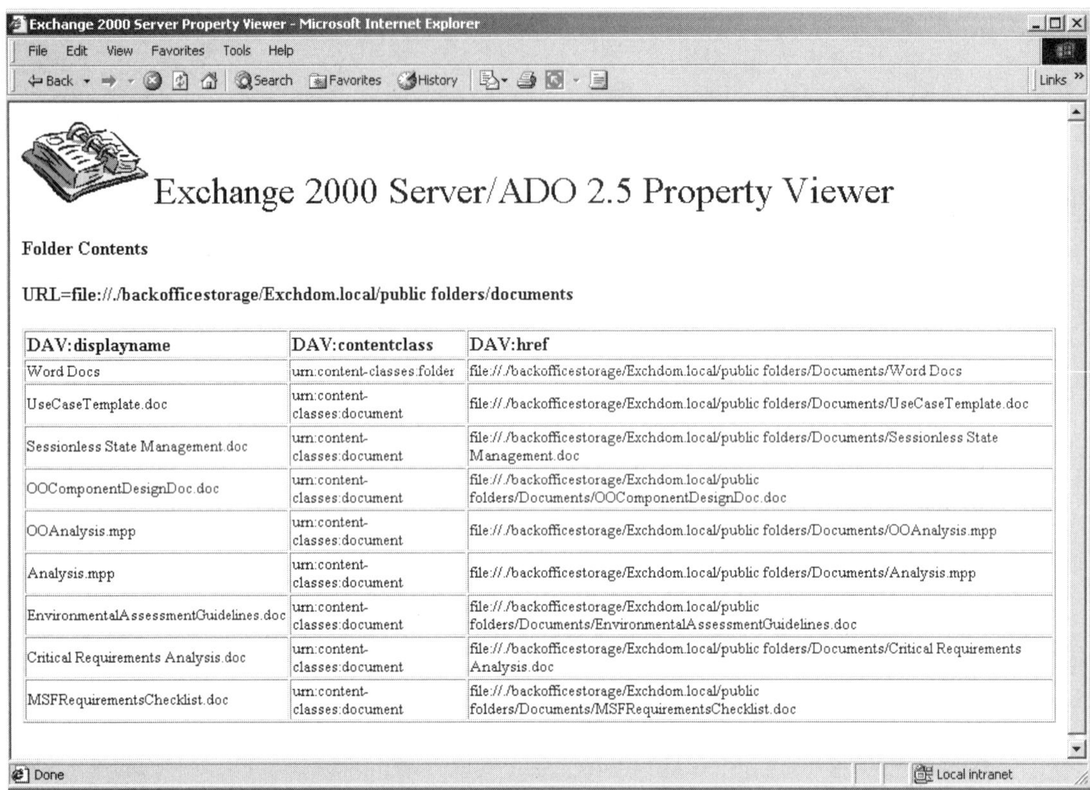

Figure 20.3 The sample Web application can also display folder contents and item properties

```
<font size="5">
<img border="0" src="view.jpg" width="108" height="69"></font>
<font size="6">Exchange 2000 Server/ADO 2.5 Property Viewer</font>
</p>
<%
    Dim i
    Dim objRec
    Dim strURL
    Dim strRadio1
    Dim strRadio2
    Dim strFolderPath
    Dim strItemName
    Dim strNamespace
    Dim iNamespaceLen

    ' Get data from previous form
    strRadio1 = Request.Form("Radio1")
```

```
    strRadio2 = Request.Form("Radio2")
    strFolderPath = _
        Request.Form("txtFolderPath")
    strItemName = _
        Request.Form("txtItemName")

    ' Build the correct URL
    if strRadio1 = "Item" then
        strURL = _
        "file://./backofficestorage/" & _
        "Exchdom.local/" & _
        "public folders/" & _
        strFolderPath & "/" & _
        strItemName
    else
    strURL = _
        "file://./backofficestorage/" & _
        "Exchdom.local/" & _
        "public folders/" & _
        strFolderPath
    end if

Select case strRadio2
    case "All"
        strNamespace = ""
        iNamespaceLen = 0
    case "DAV"
        strNamespace = "DAV:"
        iNamespaceLen = 4
    case "Exchange"
        strNamespace = "http://schemas.microsoft.com/exchange"
        iNamespaceLen = 37
    case "Office"
        strNamespace = "urn:schemas-microsoft-com:office"
        iNamespaceLen = 32
    case "Custom"
        strNamespace = _
        Request.Form("txtNamespace")
        iNamespaceLen = Len(strNamespace)
End Select

    ' Open our Record object
Set objRec = _
Server.CreateObject("ADODB.Record")
objRec.Open strURL

If strRadio1 = "FolderContents" then
    %>
```

```
<Strong>Folder Contents</Strong><p>
<Strong>URL=<%=strURL%></Strong><p>
<TABLE WIDTH=100% border=1 CELLSPACING=1 CELLPADDING=1>
<TH align=left>DAV:displayname</TH>
<TH align=left>DAV:contentclass</TH>
<TH align=left>DAV:href</TH>

<%
    ' Create our Recordset
    Set objRS = objRec.GetChildren
    ' Loop through
    Do Until objRS.EOF
    ' Write it out
Response.Write "<TR>"
Response.Write "<TD><FONT size=2>" & objRS.Fields("dav:displayname") & _
    "</TD></FONT>"
Response.Write "<TD><FONT size=2>" & objRS.Fields("dav:contentclass") & _
    "</TD></FONT>"
Response.Write "<TD><FONT size=2>" & objRS.Fields("dav:href")
    & "</TD></FONT>"
Response.Write "</TR>"
objRS.MoveNext
    Loop
objRS.Close
%>
</Table>
<BR>
<%
    Else
%>
<BR>

<Strong><%=strRadio1%> Properties</Strong><p>
<Strong>URL=<%=strURL%></Strong><p>
<Strong>Filter=<%=strRadio2%>(<%=strNamespace%>)</Strong><p>
<TABLE WIDTH=100% border=1 CELLSPACING=1 CELLPADDING=1>
<TH align=left>Field</TH>
<TH align=left>Field Name</TH>
<TH align=left>Field Value</TH>

<%
    For i=0 to objRec.Fields.Count-1
        on error resume next

    ' Filter out fields
    If (iNamespaceLen > 0) and (Left(objRec.Fields(i). _
        Name,iNamespaceLen) <> strNamespace) then
    ' Skip this field
    Else
```

```
        ' Write it out
        Response.Write "<TR>"
            Response.Write "<TD><FONT size=2>" & i & "</TD> </FONT>"
             Response.Write "<TD><FONT size=2>" & objRec.Fields(i).Name & _
                "</TD></FONT>"
             Response.Write "<TD><FONT size=2>" & objRec.Fields(i).Value & _
                "</TD></FONT>"
        Response.Write "</TR>"
        End If
 Next  %>
</Table>
<BR>
<%
End if
' Clean up objects
objRec.close
Set objRec = Nothing
Set objRS = Nothing
%>
</TABLE>
</P>
</BODY>
</HTML>
```

In the next section we discuss a Windows-based tool (available free on the book's Web site, at **http://www.plural.com/outlookexchange.asp**) that provides richer exploration of Web Storage System folders, files, and properties.

Tool 2: ADO Explorer

The second application we present in this chapter, ADO Explorer, displays a folder list in a tree view, similar to the one in Outlook. In addition, ADO Explorer shows all items in the folder along with their properties. The application shows both regular and hidden messages, as well as the properties of the selected folder or item. Figure 20.4 shows the ADO Explorer application in action.

Using the ADO Explorer Application to Display Property Values

For certain properties, such as the text of a message, the list view does not show carriage returns and line feeds. The ADO Explorer application provides a way to simply click on the property name in the list view pane and reveal a message box that will show the entire property correctly. Figure 20.5 shows a sample result of clicking on the text property of a message.

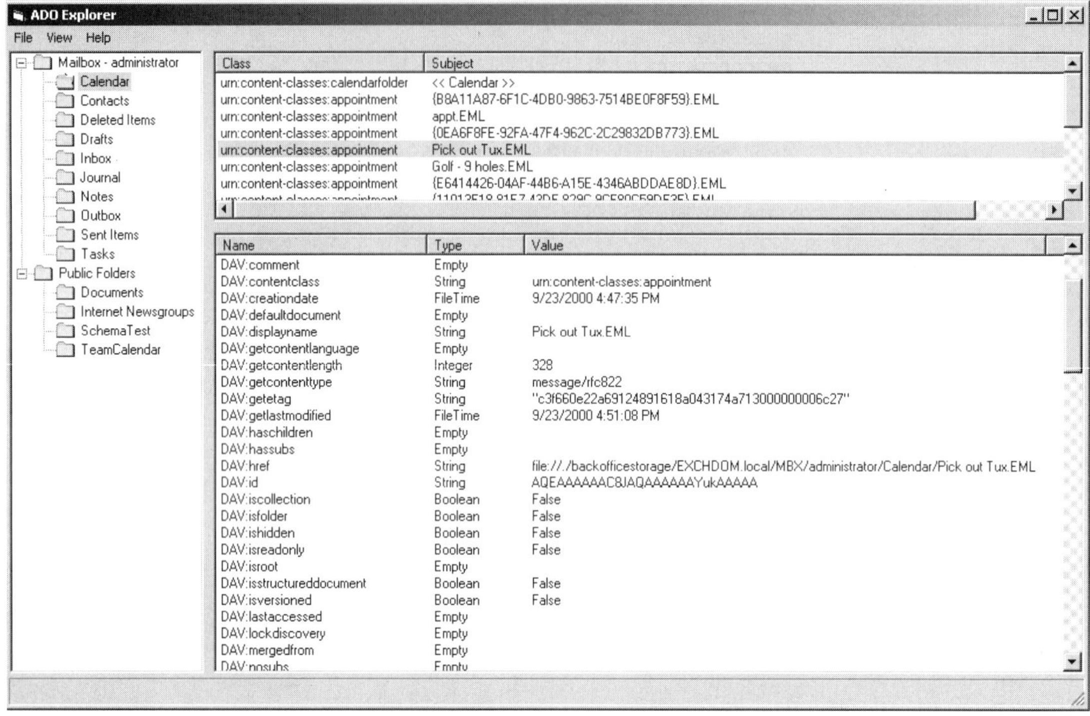

Figure 20.4 The ADO Explorer application shows a folder list and item properties

Another feature is the **Refresh** menu command. The ADO Explorer application provides a way to refresh the property values in the list view pane when an item has changed (see Figure 20.6).

The Main Form

The ADO Explorer application has a primary form with three Visual Basic common controls: the tree view, the list view, and the image list. The design-time version of the form is shown in Figure 20.7. The next section will describe what each section is used for.

The Tree View

To provide a hierarchical folder list, the application uses the tree view control. As you will see, the code uses a recursive routine to traverse the folder structure and build a folder list, just like the one in Outlook.

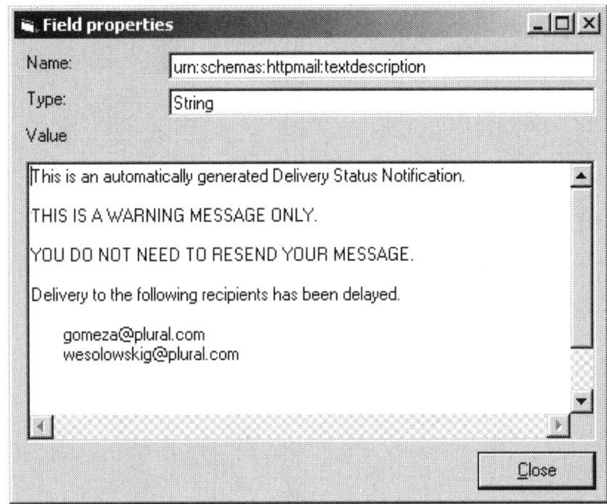

Figure 20.5 Clicking on a property name shows its value, including carriage returns and line feeds

The List View

To provide a list of folder and item properties, the application uses the list view control. When the user selects a message or folder from the tree view, the application identifies the type of item, retrieves its properties, and displays the results in the list view.

The Image List

To provide icons in the hierarchical folder list, the application uses the image list control.

A Look at the Code

For access to Outlook and Exchange data, the application uses the ADO 2.5 object model and the ExOLEDB provider to traverse folders and display properties. The

Figure 20.6 The ADO Explorer application includes a **Refresh** command, which reloads the property values for the selected item

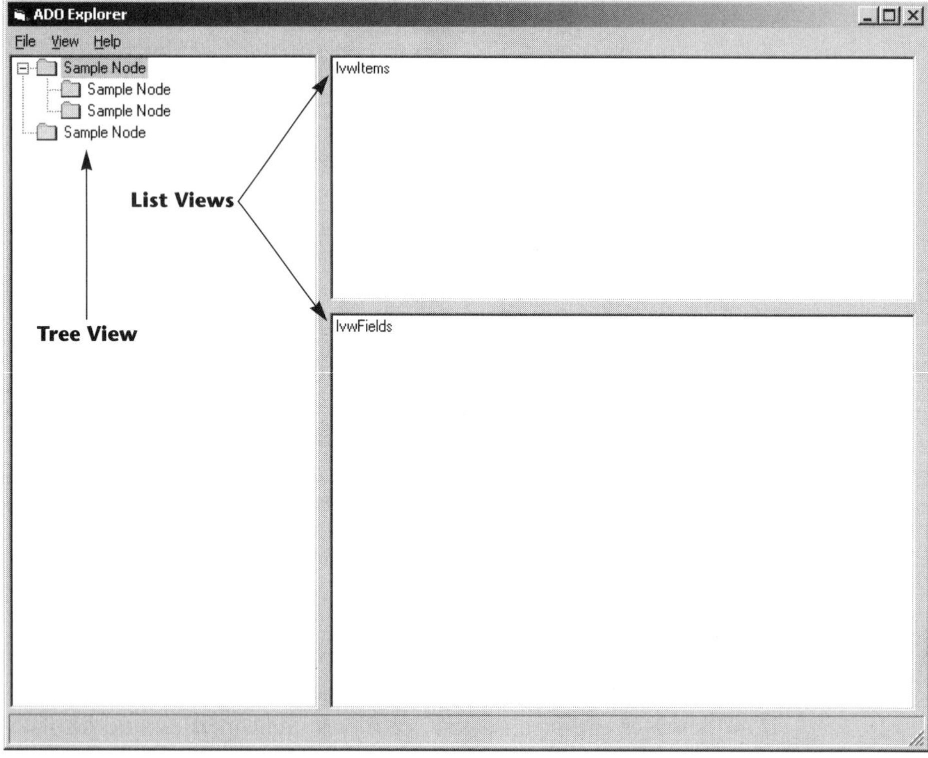

Figure 20.7 The application's main form uses the tree view, list view, and image list (not visible here) controls

application is written in Visual Basic 6.0. For access to the Web Storage System, the application uses the **New** keyword to create an instance of ADO **Connection**, **Record**, and **Recordset** objects. Typically, connections are opened with a "file://" URL like this:

```
Dim conn As New ADODB.Connection
strURL = "file://./backofficestorage/" & sDNSdomain & "/MBX/" & _
        sUsername
conn.Provider = "ExOLEDB.Datasource"  ' Use Exchange OLE DB provider
conn.Open strURL
```

Building the Folder Tree

The first thing the application does is initialize the view. It calls a subroutine that builds the folder tree for the current user's mailbox and the standard public folders hierarchy. The **FillFolders** routine creates the root folders—one for each of the two information stores. The rest of the folder hierarchy items (the subfolders) are created when the user requests them:

```
'******************************************************************************
'* Fill the folders hierarchy
'******************************************************************************
Sub FillFolders()
    Dim conn As New ADODB.Connection
    Dim rs As New ADODB.Recordset
    Dim rs2 As ADODB.Recordset
    Dim rec As New ADODB.Record
    Dim objNode As Node
    Dim strURL As String
    Dim strSQL As String

        On Error GoTo ErrHandler
        strURL = "file://./backofficestorage/"
        ' Use Exchange OLE DB provider
        & Environ("userdnsdomain") & "/MBX/" & Environ("username")
        conn.Provider = "ExOLEDB.Datasource"
        conn.Open strURL
            ' First get the mailbox
        strSQL = "SELECT ""DAV:href"", ""DAV:displayname"",
        ""DAV:parentname""" _
            & " FROM scope('""" & strURL & """')" _
                & " WHERE ""DAV:iscollection"" = True" _
                & " ORDER BY ""DAV:displayname"""

        rs.Open strSQL, conn
        rs.MoveFirst
            ' First clear current hierarchy
        tvwFolders.Nodes.Clear
        rec.Open strURL, conn
        Set objNode = tvwFolders.Nodes.Add(, , CStr(rec.
Fields("DAV:href")), "Mailbox - " & Environ("username"), 1, 2)
        ' Get the contents of the folder
        FillFolder objNode, rs
        rs.Close
        rec.Close
        conn.Close

        ' Now get the public folders
        strURL = "file://./backofficestorage/"
            & Environ("userdnsdomain") & "/Public Folders/"
        'strURL = "http:" & Environ("logonserver") & "/Public"
        strSQL = "SELECT ""DAV:href"", ""DAV:displayname"",
            ""DAV:parentname""" _
```

```
            & " FROM scope('shallow traversal of """ & strURL & """')" _
                & " WHERE ""DAV:iscollection"" = True" _
                & " ORDER BY ""DAV:displayname"""
        conn.Open strURL
        rs.Open strSQL, conn
        rs.MoveFirst
        rec.Open strURL
        Set objNode = tvwFolders.Nodes.Add(, , CStr(rec.
Fields("DAV:href")), "Public Folders", 1, 2)
        FillFolderWithGetChildren objNode, rs
        rs.Close
        rec.Close
        conn.Close
            ' Select first node
        tvwFolders.Nodes(1).Selected = True
        tvwFolders.Nodes(1).Expanded = True
            ' Emulate selection of first entry
        tvwFolders_NodeClick tvwFolders.Nodes(1)

        Exit Sub

    ErrHandler:
        If Err.Number < 0 Then
        MsgBox "&H" & Hex(Err.Number) & " --- " & Err.Description
    Else
        MsgBox Err.Number & " --- " & Err.Description
    End If
End Sub
```

Listing Property Values

The **FillFields** routine fills the list view with the object's **Fields** collection:

```
'**********************************************************************
'* Fill the fields list view with the given collection.
'**********************************************************************
Public Sub FillFields(strURL As String)
Dim rec As New ADODB.Record
Dim objField As ADODB.Field
Dim objItem As ListItem
Dim strName As String
Dim strType As String
Dim strValue As String

    On Error Resume Next

    rec.Open strURL

    lvwFields.ListItems.Clear
```

```
        For Each objField In rec.Fields
            Set objItem = lvwFields.ListItems.Add(, , objField.Name)
            GetFieldDetails objField, strType, strValue
            objItem.SubItems(1) = strType
            objItem.SubItems(2) = strValue
        Next

        rec.Close
    End Sub
```

Using the ADO Explorer Application

Since the ADO Explorer application shows properties for all types of Outlook and Exchange items, you can use the application to view values quickly when writing applications. Rather than opening up each item in an Outlook form or trying to get hundreds of fields in a table view, you can view the properties with a mouse click. You can download the source code for the ADO Explorer application from the book's Web site (**http://www.plural.com/outlookexchange.asp**).

> **Note:** Special thanks to Martin Tirion, who developed and contributed this handy application.

Summary

This chapter introduced the Web Explorer (an ASP-based property viewer) and the Windows-based ADO Explorer application, a Visual Basic program that is designed to help inspect folder and item values when writing Outlook and Exchange applications. You can use the techniques and code in this application when developing your own applications.

Chapter 21

Sample Application: gradebook 2001

This chapter introduces a sample application that was written on Exchange 2000 Server. The application was written to be simple to understand, yet rich enough to take advantage of various Exchange 2000 features. The complete application, as well as the complete step-by-step walk-through, is available on the book's Web site, at **http://www.plural.com/outlookexchange.asp.** All source code was written with ASP, VB, and COM+.

We originally considered explaining the application in excruciating detail in this chapter. Then we realized that it would be better to continually update the application with new features, putting the new code and its relevant explanation up on the Web. Therefore, this chapter simply explains a bit about the application; most of the code samples can be found on the book's Web site.

About the Sample Application

The application uses Exchange 2000 as a semistructured database for students, schedules, student assignments, and transcripts. It also uses a SQL Server 2000 database for storing relational information, such as the relationship between students and classes. The application shows how to update students (stored in the active directory), schedules (each student has a private calendar), and transcript archives (stored in the transcripts folder) on the server using ADO 2.5 and CDO 3.0. We'll discuss the features of the application and how its design is mapped into an Exchange 2000 Server solution.

Features

The goal of the application is to provide a self-service Web site for teachers and students alike. Some of the features include schedule tracking, grade reporting, and paper submissions. The application is designed to use the Windows 2000 Active Directory for storing students, teachers, and staff members. We then take advantage of the Web Storage System's ability to store documents and other semistructured data by storing exams and archived transcripts in XML format, as well as original papers as document streams. Let's take a look at a sampling of the application's features.

Query Screens

The first example, a screen that shows a list of student names, is generated from a SQL request to either the SQL 2000 database or the Active Directory, depending on user preference. Figure 21.1 shows a sample page that returns the list of students for a given class.

Schedules: Exchange Calendars

For student schedules we take advantage of Exchange 2000's calendaring functionality. Since every student and teacher has an Active Directory account, we can assign each one an Exchange private mailbox. This arrangement allows us to populate each user's calendar with his or her unique schedule. Links within each appointment provide ways to hyperlink to associated class, student, and teacher information. Figure 21.2 shows a day in the life of a student.

Archiving Transcripts

We store transcript information for each student in an XML data island for archival and data transmission purposes. This example shows a student transcript for a single semester:

```
<?xml version="1.0"?>
<transcript
    xmlns:student="http://beantownhigh.org/transcript/student"
    xmlns:course="http://beantownhigh.org/transcript/course"
>
    <student>
        <name>Sally Smith</name>
        <description>Transcript for 1/5/2001 to 6/25/2001</description>

            <semester term="Spring 2001">
                <course>
                <course:name>English 101</course:name>
```

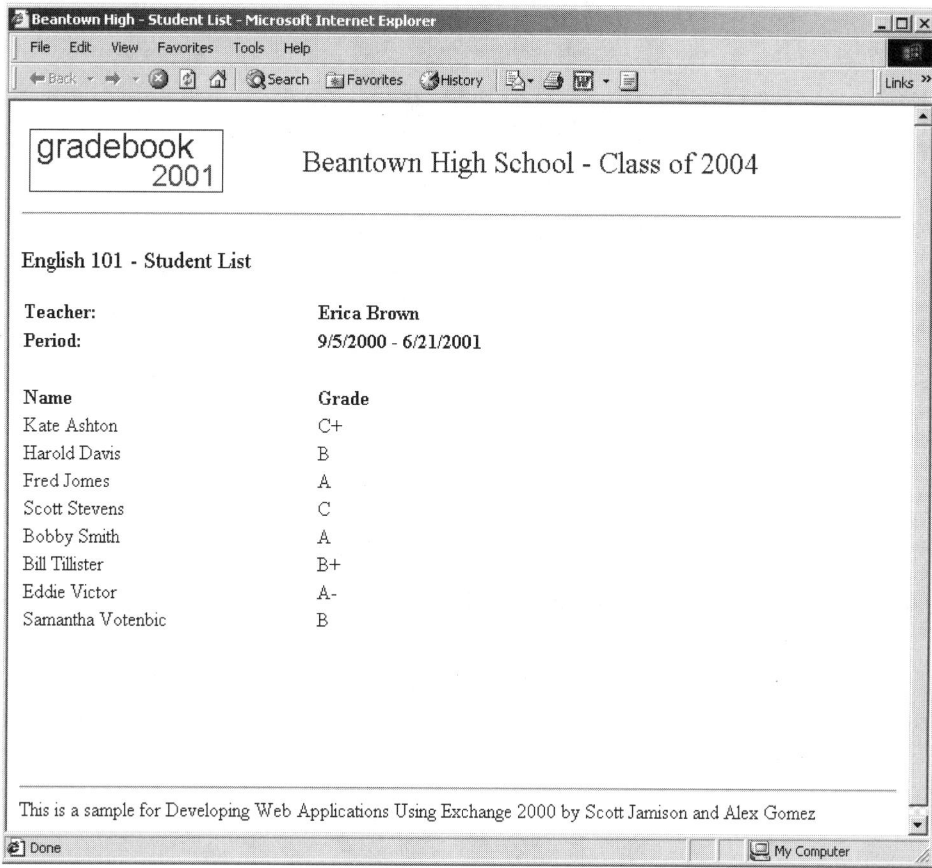

Figure 21.1 The "gradebook 2001" application features a way to query a student list, using both the SQL database and the Active Directory

```
<course:grade>A</course:grade>
</course>
<course>
<course:name>Math 101</course:name>
<course:grade>A</course:grade>
</course>
<course>
<course:name>Spanish 101</course:name>
<course:grade>B</course:grade>
</course>
<course>
<course:name>History 101</course:name>
<course:grade>C+</course:grade>
```

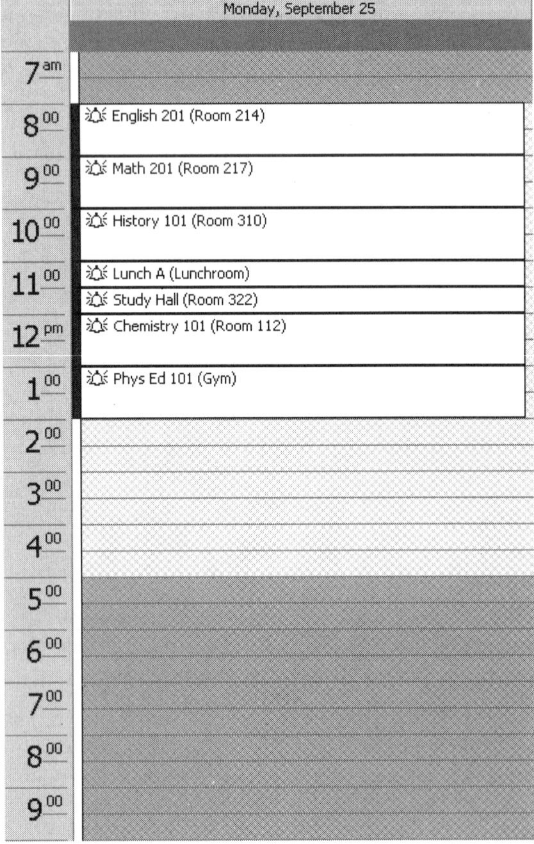

Figure 21.2 With Exchange 2000's built-in calendaring functionality, students can track their schedules using Outlook or Outlook Web Access

```
                </course>
                <course>
                <course:name>Science 101</course:name>
                <course:grade>A-</course:grade>
                </course>
            </semester>
        </student>
    </transcript>
```

There are advantages to using the XML format, such as the ability to use XSL in rich browsers (see Figure 21.3), and the ability to transmit the schedule information via a stream at any time without the need for a real-time query.

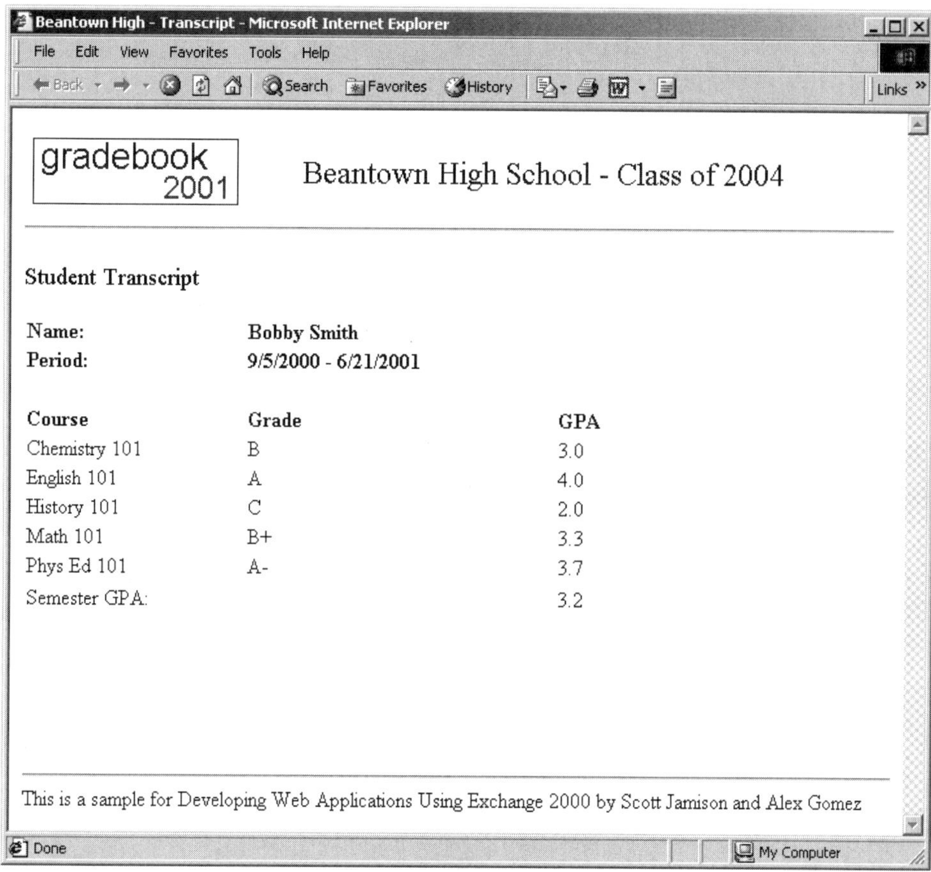

Figure 21.3 The "gradebook 2001" application provides features such as the transcript viewer, which uses XML and XSL for rich clients like Internet Explorer 5

Summary

We hope this chapter piqued your interest in the sample application we wrote using Exchange 2000 Server. We used the Windows 2000 Active Directory, an Exchange 2000 private store, an Exchange 2000 application public store, and several varieties of CDO for Exchange 2000. The application and a complete explanation of the code are available on the book's Web site, at **http://www.plural.com/outlookexchange.asp**, complete with source code. Enjoy, and feel free to make your own suggestions and enhancements!

Index

E

Q

R

X

Also Available from Addison-Wesley

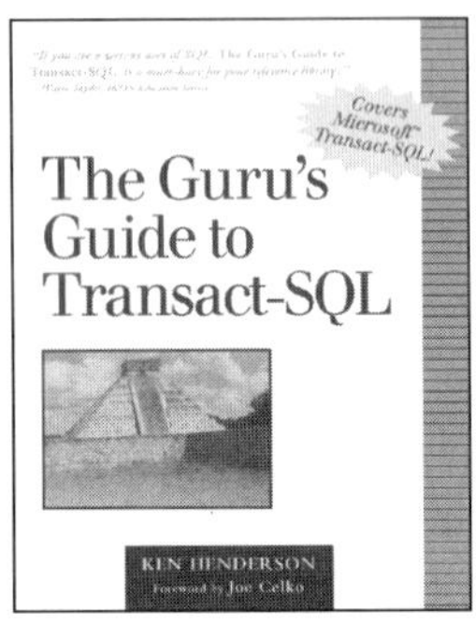

The Guru's Guide to Transact-SQL

Ken Henderson

Since its introduction more than a decade ago, the Microsoft SQL Server query language, Transact-SQL, has become increasingly popular and more powerful. The current version sports advanced features such as OLE Automation support, cross-platform querying facilities, and full-text search management. This book is the consummate guide to Microsoft Transact-SQL. From data type nuances to complex statistical computations to the bevy of undocumented features in the language, *The Guru's Guide to Transact-SQL* imparts the knowledge you need to become a virtuoso of the language as quickly as possible. This book contains the information, explanations, and advice needed to master Transact-SQL and develop the best possible Transact-SQL code. Some 600 code examples not only illustrate important concepts and best practices, but also provide working Transact-SQL code that can be incorporated into your own real-world DBMS applications.

0-201-61576-2 • Paperback • 592 pages w/CD-ROM • ©2000

OLE DB Consumer Templates

A Programmer's Guide

Pierre Nallet

A comprehensive and practical guide, *OLE DB Consumer Templates* is an essential resource for all database programmers working with Microsoft technologies. The book is filled with examples that show you how to harness the power of OLE DB using consumer templates to create efficient, scalable, and manageable database applications. *OLE DB Consumer Templates* presents an overview of DNA, COM, universal data access, and how OLE DB fits in with Microsoft's component and data access strategies—it explains the differences between OLE DB and ADO architectures. The author provides detailed and practical information on using OLE DB consumer templates to develop all the major elements and functions of database applications, including: OLE DB wizard, OLE DB errors, OLE DB properties, and data sources and sessions.

0-201-65792-9 • Paperback • 448 pages • ©2001

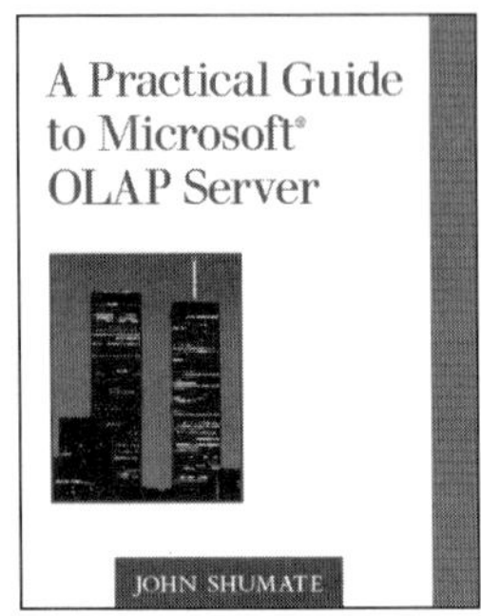

A Practical Guide to Microsoft® OLAP Server

John Shumate

With the introduction of Microsoft's OLAP Services, Online Analytical Processing (OLAP) technology has become a major force in today's marketplace. OLAP, which enables multidimensional databases for sophisticated decision support, is a technology that IT and database professionals simply need to know. *A Practical Guide to Microsoft® OLAP Server* introduces you to OLAP technology and leads you step-by-step through the process of deploying an OLAP server, focusing particularly on Microsoft's OLAP Services. This book explains the basic concepts underlying OLAP, compares various OLAP products, and describes Microsoft's OLAP Services architecture. In addition, it enumerates the development lifecycle of an OLAP Services application from planning and design through installation and administration, discussing the goals and approaches for each phase and task.

0-201-48557-5 • Paperback • 432 pages • ©2000

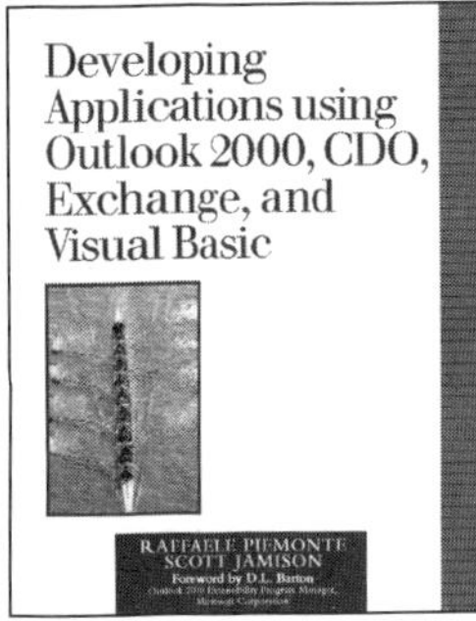

Developing Applications Using Outlook 2000, CDO, Exchange, and Visual Basic
Raffaele Piemonte and Scott Jamison

Written for IT developers who build collaborative and workflow applications, this book provides a comprehensive reference to working with Microsoft's powerful collaborative development environment, including Outlook 2000, Exchange Server, Visual Basic, and the Collaboration Data Objects (CDO) Library. It demonstrates ways in which these technologies can be tied together into effective business solutions—from small-scale groupware to large-scale enterprisewide systems. *Developing Applications Using Outlook 2000, CDO, Exchange, and Visual Basic* offers an overview of the Microsoft collaborative landscape, and then examines each element of that environment in detail. Numerous examples showcase the applications made possible with these technologies.

0-201-61575-4 • Paperback • 592 pages • ©2000

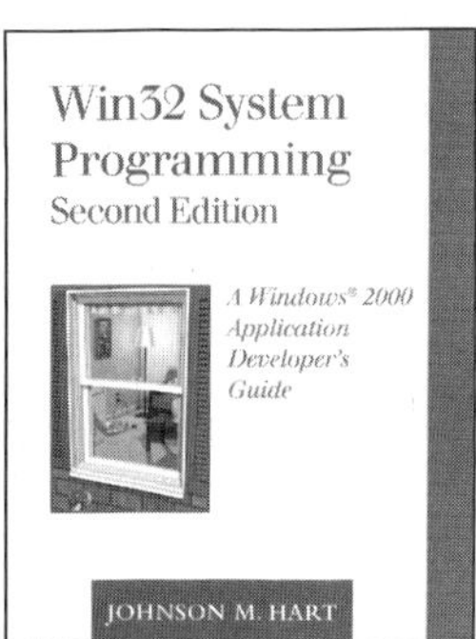

Win32 System Programming, Second Edition
A Windows® 2000 Application Developer's Guide
Johnson M. Hart

A practical guide to the central features and functions of the Win32 API, *Win32 System Programming, Second Edition,* will get you up and running with Windows NT and Windows 2000. Unlike most Windows programming resources, this book focuses exclusively on the core system services—file system, memory, processes, communication, and security—rather than on the more commonly featured graphical user interface functions. Especially geared for those already familiar with UNIX or other high-end operating systems, *Win32 System Programming, Second Edition,* helps you to build on your knowledge base to learn Win32 features quickly and easily. This new edition has been updated and enhanced with new coverage of network programming, servers, NT services, thread performance, and synchronization. It also offers a preview of Win64, the new 64-bit API for Windows 2000.

0-201-70310-6 • Hardcover • 544 pages w/CD-ROM • ©2001

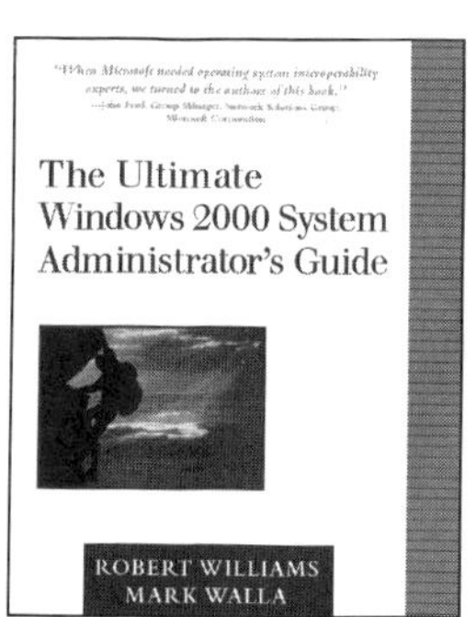

The Ultimate Windows 2000 System Administrator's Guide
Robert Williams and Mark Walla

The Ultimate Windows 2000 System Administrator's Guide is an essential resource for planning, deploying, and administering a Windows 2000 enterprise system. The authors draw on years of experience designing and administering Windows NT and UNIX systems in order to guide you through the varied tasks involved in real-world system administration. The book provides an overview of the entire Windows 2000 server family, including Advanced Server, DataCenter, and Professional. There are detailed discussions of key Windows 2000 administrative functions and descriptions of many advanced tools and optional components. In addition, the authors have included a comprehensive and convenient Windows 2000 command reference.

0-201-61580-0 • Paperback • 928 pages • ©2000

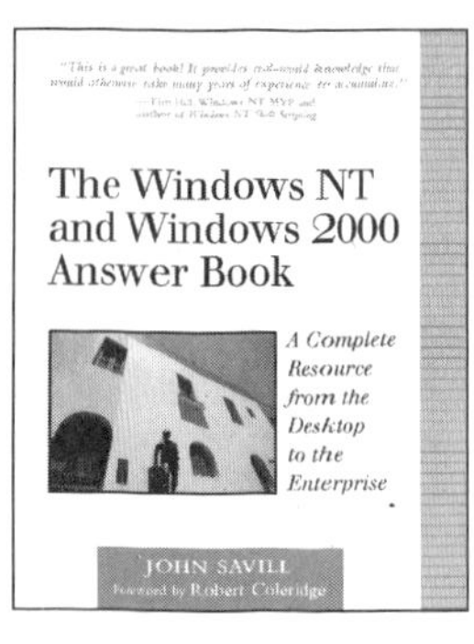

The Windows NT and Windows 2000 Answer Book

A Complete Resource from the Desktop to the Enterprise

John Savill

Using *The Windows NT and Windows 2000 Answer Book,* administrators, developers, and users will be able to quickly and effectively find answers, solve problems, and get the best performance possible from Windows NT. John Savill offers answers to more than eight hundred common Windows NT and Windows 2000 questions, all carefully organized in an accessible format for quick reference. *The Windows NT and Windows 2000 Answer Book* is a significantly expanded and more detailed version of the author's highly regarded *Windows NT FAQ (www.ntfaq.com),* cited by Microsoft's Online Developer Network (MSDN) as the most comprehensive and current Web-based Windows NT resource of its kind. This book addresses a broad range of topics, from the simple to the complex: installation, system and desktop configuration, the Registry, recovery and backups, network issues, Internet topics, e-mail, file systems, administration, security, hardware, and much more.

0-201-60636-4 • Paperback • 864 pages • ©1999

The Windows CE Technology Tutorial

Windows Powered Solutions for the Developer

Chris Muench

This practical guide is designed to get programmers up and running with Windows CE, Microsoft's emerging operating system for handheld PCs and other alternative computing devices. This book helps you learn Windows CE programming by building on your experience with Windows 98 and NT. Although other resources may take a more theoretical approach to Windows CE, *The Windows CE Technology Tutorial* focuses on the essential topics and practical programming techniques you will need to create real-world Windows CE applications. By using a sample application that is explored throughout the book, Muench walks you step-by-step through all of Windows CE's major technologies, functions, and capabilities—from the most basic skills through advanced techniques.

0-201-61642-4 • Paperback • 624 pages w/CD-ROM • ©2000